Accounting for Business

B *contemporary*
H **BUSINESS SERIES**

Series Editor: Professor Andrew Lock
Manchester Metropolitan University

The Contemporary Business Series is designed with the needs of business studies undergraduates and MBA students in mind, and each title is written in a straightforward, student friendly style. Though all of the books in the series reflect the individuality of their authors, you will find that you can count on certain key features in each text which maintain high standards of structure and approach:

- excellent coverage of core and option subject
- UK/international examples or case studies throughout
- full references and further reading suggestions
- written in direct, easily accessible style, for ease of use by full, part-time and self-study students

Books in the series include:

Accounting for Business
Peter Atrill, David Harvey and Edward McLaney

Information Resources Management
John R. Beaumont and Ewan Sutherland

International Business Strategy
Werner Ketelhõhn

Management Accounting for Financial Decisions
Keith Ward, Sri Srikanthan and Richard Neal

The Management and Marketing of Services
Peter Mudie and Angela Cottam

Organizational Behaviour in International Management
Terence Jackson

Quantitative Approaches to Management
Robert Ball

Accounting for Business

Second edition

Peter Atrill,
David Harvey
and
Edward McLaney

Butterworth-Heinemann Ltd
Linacre House, Jordan Hill, Oxford OX2 8DP

A member of the Reed Elsevier plc group

OXFORD LONDON BOSTON
MUNICH NEW DELHI SINGAPORE SYDNEY
TOKYO TORONTO WELLINGTON

First published 1991
Reprinted 1992, 1993, 1994
Second edition 1994
Reprinted 1995

British Library Cataloguing in Publication Data
Atrill, Peter
    Accounting for Business. – 2Rev.ed. –
    (Contemporary Business Series)
    I. Title II. Series
    657

ISBN 0 7506 1948 1

Composition by Scribe Design, Gillingham, Kent
Printed in Great Britain by Martins The Printers
Berwick upon Tweed

Contents

Preface

This book has been written for the business studies student who wishes to study accounting but may not necessarily wish to specialize in this subject. Although the student may ultimately decide to specialize in another area, it is almost certain that he or she will need to understand the role of accounting within a business and will need to use accounting information in order to make informed economic decisions. This book aims to satisfy this need. Given this perspective, it seemed inappropriate when writing this book to provide a detailed explanation of the way in which we record financial transactions and the nature of accounting systems. Although we have included an appendix on the recording of financial transactions in practice, this is designed to provide the reader with an overview rather than a comprehensive picture of the recording process. While a detailed understanding of the recording process may be important for the specialist, who may need to prepare financial statements, it is far less important for those who simply wish to use accounting as a tool for decision-making. However, users of accounting still require a basic understanding of its underlying principles, and should be aware of the impact of most business transactions on the accounting statements prepared. This book aims to satisfy both needs.

In order to achieve this the book is divided into four sections. The first section provides an introduction to the role and nature of accounting. The second provides a detailed explanation of the underlying principles of the major accounting statements and the problems and limitations which beset them. This is followed by a section dealing with companies and the regulatory framework within which companies operate. An understanding of this framework is necessary if accounting statements are to be properly interpreted. This section also includes an introduction to the accounts of groups of companies, since most large businesses take the form of groups. The final section concentrates on the analysis and interpretation of accounts, and explains the way in which financial statements can be used for decision-making purposes, including their use as a tool for planning the future direction of the business. The use of spreadsheets and financial modelling is illustrated. In the final chapter we return to the problems of financial statements and also consider some of the ways in which we might improve the quality of financial information provided.

For the second edition we have tried to respond to the comments of readers of the first edition, and to follow our own instincts, to make the book more 'streamlined'. In doing this we have reduced the amount of detailed recording of transactions and have concentrated more on what the resulting accounting information means. We have also brought the book up to date in terms of recent changes, particularly to reporting regulations for companies.

The book has been aimed primarily at those studying for a BA or HND in Business Studies or for an MBA degree, but it could be used on a variety of other courses. It has been designed in such a way that it can be used to support a lecture\tutorial programme or can be used for more independent forms of learning. Within each chapter there are worked examples. There are also activities, at a variety of levels and self-assessment questions, which help readers test their understanding of the principles being dealt with. Answers to each of the activities and self-assessment questions are supplied at the end of the book. In addition, there are further exercises at the end of each chapter. We are grateful to the Chartered Association of Certified Accountants for allowing us to use past examination questions from the Certified Diploma in Finance and Accounting.

We believe that this book should provide a firm foundation for those wishing to understand accounting information.

Peter Atrill
David Harvey
Edward McLaney

Part One

Introduction to Accounting

This part, which consists of one chapter, aims to provide you with an introduction to the role of accounting and to the type of accounting information typically provided for a variety of users. It aims to provide you with a broad framework within which your subsequent studies can be set.

1

Introduction to accounting

1.1 Introduction

This chapter is concerned with introducing the role and nature of accounting, the users of accounting information and their information needs. The chapter also provides an introduction to the major accounting reports.

1.2 Objectives

On completion of this chapter you should be able:

- to discuss the nature and purpose of accounting;
- to identify the main users of accounting information and their needs;
- to outline the nature and purpose of each of the major financial statements;
- to identify and to discuss the desirable features of accounting information.

1.3 Activities and self-assessment questions

There are activities interspersed throughout this and succeeding chapters. The aim of these activities is to help you find out if you have grasped the points which have been raised and to get you to think about issues which relate to the subjects being discussed. Suggested answers to these questions are provided immediately below each activity. You will also find one or more self-assessment questions within each chapter. These questions are usually more demanding than the activities. They may cover a number of the topics or may try to extend your understanding of particular areas. Answers to the self-assessment questions are given at the end of the book. You should make a serious attempt at each activity and self-assessment question before referring to the answers provided.

1.4 The role of accounting

Accounting is concerned with the provision of economic information which will be useful to those directly (and to some extent indirectly) connected with an organization. The information provided should be useful both in assessing the performance of those who manage the organization and in assessing the performance and position of the organization itself. Once these assessments have been made by the interested parties, they will be in a position to make more informed economic decisions concerning the organization.

This view of accounting as an aid to economic decision-making has achieved increasing acceptance in recent years. The American Accounting Association adopted this perspective when it defined accounting as '*the process of identifying, measuring and communicating economic information to permit informed judgements and decisions by the users of the information*'. Though this is only one of very many published definitions of accounting, it is widely quoted in accounting texts because it emphasizes the primary purpose of accounting as providing information which will help users make decisions.

This decision-making emphasis is one which you should constantly bear in mind. There seems to be a feeling held by many people, including many who work in accounting, that accounting is concerned with getting accounting statements prepared each month or each year as if that were an end in itself. While this may describe what some accountings *do*, it does not describe the *purpose* of accounting. Unfortunately, some textbooks on accounting do not really emphasize that accounting is not, or should not be, carried on for its own sake. Never lose sight of the decision-making objective of accounting information.

1.5   Users of financial information

Having established that accounting exists in order to provide information for interested parties to make decisions, it is logical to ask: '*Who are these interested parties?*' and '*For what kind of decisions is accounting information required?*' Figure 1.1 shows the major groups of people who have an interest in an organization. The figure, as constructed, relates to a private sector business but minor alterations in the titles of the participants would make it equally relevant to any organization – for example, a government, a local government unit, a charity, a nationalized industry, a school or college.

Staying with the example of a private enterprise business, it is possible to identify the types of decision that each of the participants might need to make with respect to the organization and the information required. These are as follows:

Owners

Owners are concerned with making two types of decisions. These are:

- investment decisions; and
- stewardship decisions.

Figure 1.1 *Typical participants in the private-sector organization*

Investment decisions are primarily concerned with increasing the wealth of the owners. Those who own businesses normally do so with the intention of increasing their wealth. Owners will, therefore, wish to assess the extent to which the business has generated financial benefits (profits etc.) and the likely future prospects of the business. They will also wish to assess the degree of risk associated with their investment in the business. Information relating to associated risks and returns will be useful when deciding whether to hold or sell their ownership interest in the business.

In larger businesses, the owners tend not to exercise day-to-day control over the activities of the business. Instead, managers will often run the business on behalf of the owners. Although managers are expected to operate the business in the interests of the owners, they do have discretion over the way in which the resources of the business are used and there is, therefore, the potential for conflict between managers and owners. This potential conflict creates a need amongst owners to receive accounting information from the managers which reveals how the resources of the business have been used. The provision of information by managers to owners for this purpose is referred to as *stewardship accounting*. This information may be used by owners, amongst other things, as a basis for rewarding or dismissing managers.

Government

A government may require information from a business for a variety of reasons. These include:

Taxation

Businesses are taxed on the basis of their accounting profits (subject to certain adjustments); government (in the form of the Inland Revenue) needs information on each business in order to decide how much tax to charge.

Regulation

A government may also need information relating to a business for regulatory purposes. For example, information relating to costs and profits may be required in order to decide whether policies promoting greater competition are being adhered to or are necessary.

Economic management

Governments may also use accounting information relating to businesses to help in the general management of the economy. For example, accounting information may be useful in deciding whether to give support to businesses in a particular industry.

Government contracts

The government may award contracts on a 'cost plus' basis (i.e. the cost of supplying the goods or service plus an additional profit element) and therefore will be interested in the costs of goods or services supplied by the contractor. This approach is often used when awarding defence contracts. The government will also be interested to see if businesses are making excessive profits as a result of their dealings with the government.

Management

The management of the business is the user group who need most accounting information. Managers are charged with *planning* the activities of the business. They, therefore, require forecast information in order to assess the likely outcome of implementing particular policies in order to decide whether such policies are feasible. Forecast information is also useful in identifying future problems and opportunities for the business, i.e. they may try to ensure that the actual results of the business coincide with the earlier planned results. They therefore require information concerning actual performance and the extent of any deviation from earlier planned performance.

Because managers must plan and control every aspect of the business, detailed information on a wide range of matters is required by them.

Activity 1

Can you think of four types of decisions that a manager of a business might make and which would require accounting information?

Types of management decisions requiring accounting information include:

- the pricing of goods and services
- the quantity of goods to produce
- the most appropriate mix of goods to produce
- the investment in new equipment, etc.
- the raising of finance to maintain or expand the business
- the level of payments to make to the owners
- the purchase of stock

This is not an exhaustive list. You may have thought of others.

Of course, managers will also be interested in accounting information which measures financial performance of a business as it may be of direct interest to their future prosperity. For example, good performance may result in a bonus being payable whereas poor performance may result in dismissal.

Customers

These users need information to enable them to answer questions such as 'Will the supplying business be able to remain in business and thus give continuity of supply?' This point may not be important to the domestic consumer buying a tin of peas, but it may well be very important to the supermarket buying the peas from the canner. This is because the supermarket will typically invest quite a lot of time and effort in negotiating a detailed contract with the canner, including visits to the cannery to assess the quality control, etc. If the canner's business fails, this would mean that a different canner would need to be identified and assessed – perhaps a costly business for the supermarket. Accounting information can be useful in trying to assess the ability of a business to survive and to continue to supply its products.

Suppliers of goods and services

As with customers, suppliers will need to satisfy themselves that their customer businesses will be able to honour contracts, etc. Another reason arises from the fact that most commercial sales are made on credit (the goods are delivered or the service is rendered some weeks before cash is paid), so suppliers will be keen to assess the likely ability of customer businesses to meet their obligations.

Lenders

Typically, businesses obtain part of the finance needed to set up and run the business by borrowing from banks, etc. (The other part is supplied by the owners.) Lenders to the business will seek to assess the likely ability of the borrowing business to be able to repay the principal borrowed at the end of the period of the loan (perhaps many years into the future), as well as its ability to pay the interest when it falls due. Lenders may also need to assess the value of any security offered in respect of the loan.

Employees

These are suppliers of a service to the business and their position is much the same as suppliers of goods and other services mentioned above. Employees are typically in a much more profound and longstanding relationship with their employer business than are other suppliers, if only because the employer business may represent the individual employee's only 'customer' at the time and even the only feasible one in the locality. Employees (or their representatives) will therefore have a very direct interest in the ability of the business to survive and to provide employment. They will also be interested in assessing financial performance and position in order to help bargain for improvements in wages and conditions of employment. In some cases, payments to employees may be directly related to the financial performance of the business, e.g. profit-sharing schemes.

Competitors

Competitors have an interest in the accounting information of a business for two reasons:

- they may wish to use the information as a benchmark for measuring their own performance and efficiency. For example, they may wish to see if they are more or less profitable than the business.
- they may wish to assess the financial strength of the business, as a basis for making decisions concerning future policies. For example, competitors may wish to know if the business could withstand a takeover bid or engage in a price-cutting campaign.

These are just a few examples of the types of decision which the different users need to make; in reality, there may be many more.

It is important to recognize that the users identified above represent the major users of accounting information rather than an exhaustive list. There may be others who use the accounting information produced by businesses for particular purposes. For example, *community representatives* may require information to see whether or not the business is a 'good citizen' and is investing in the community in which it is based. *Environmental protection bodies* may require information to see whether the business has the resources to make compensation payments for environmental damage it has inflicted. *Academic researchers* may require information about various aspects of the business to develop or test particular theories, etc.

Activity 2
Are all of the users of equal importance when it comes to the provision of financial information? Do you think that a particular user group should be regarded as more important than the others?

There is no single correct answer to this activity. Some may argue that, in a capitalist system, businesses are created by the owners and operate primarily for their benefit. The owners bear the major risks associated with the business, they also incur the costs of producing the financial information. As a result, the owners' information needs (and those of their appointed agents, the managers) should be considered of primary importance. However, others may argue that many of the users identified have a stake in the business. They contribute towards the success of the business and bear risks by being associated with the business. Thus, it would not be appropriate to single out the owners (or any other group) as the most important group.

1.6   Conflict between the user groups

It is possible for there to be a conflict of interest between the different user groups. Potential conflict is likely to concern the way in which the wealth of the business is either generated or distributed. For this reason, users may require accounting information to monitor the way in which other users have benefited from the business.

Activity 3
Can you think of an example where accounting information would be useful in dealing with areas of potential conflict between:

*   owners and managers?
*   lenders and owners?

> - government and owners?
>
> (We have already identified some examples in our earlier discussions.)

We can think of the following examples:

Owners and managers

Where managers' pay is linked to performance, the owners may wish to check that the basis for making payments to managers has been properly adhered to and that managers have not been overpaid. This is part of the stewardship role of accounting referred to earlier.

Lenders and owners

Lenders may wish to check that the amounts borrowed by the business have been used for their intended purpose and have not been used to make distributions to owners.

Government and owners

The government may wish to check to see whether government contractors are not making excessive profits from contracts awarded or that price increases charged to customers by a utility company, such as a gas, electricity or water company, do not exceed the amount stipulated by the government, thereby increasing the owners' wealth.

You may have thought of other valid examples.

1.7 The usefulness of accounting information

You should be clear that accounting information does not provide answers to all the information needs of users; in fact it probably does not provide perfect answers to any of them. However, you should also be clear that accounting as it is practised has grown to its present state because accounting information is perceived as being useful. This is for two reasons:

- it helps to reduce any uncertainty in users' minds concerning the financial health of the business. Accounting information can give answers to questions such as 'Does the business have the money to repay the loan outstanding?' 'Has the business made enough profit to pay the owners a return on their investment?'

- other sources of information available may not be as directly relevant, or as reliable, as that produced by the accounting system.

Activity 4

Accounting information does not represent the only source of financial information concerning a business. Can you think of other sources which may be of value when assessing the financial health of a business?

In answering this activity you may have thought of the following:

- announcement by the business concerning new funds being raised, new contracts won, new products being launched, etc.
- newspaper and journal articles reporting on aspects of the business, such as the degree of competition being faced, any reorganization occurring, internal conflict between senior managers, etc.
- industry-wide reports on matters such as consumer demand for the products, new government legislation relating to the industry, the impact of new technology, etc.
- economy-wide reports on matters such as movements in inflation, levels of consumer confidence, likely changes in taxation or economic policies, etc.

It should be emphasized that a thorough examination of the financial health of a business should use all of the sources of information available and should not rely on a single source. Even though other sources may be less useful than the accounting information produced, each source may help contribute towards the development of a complete picture.

1.8 Accounting and human behaviour

The usefulness of accounting reports can be viewed from the perspective of its effect on behaviour. We have seen that accounting exists to provide users with information. The generally accepted definition of information is that it is something which leads to changes in expectations about the outcome of future events, sufficiently large to affect behaviour. Thus accounting reports and statements which do not, and perhaps cannot, affect behaviour are not information, have no practical benefit and are a waste of money.

It is often difficult to judge the usefulness of the accounting information produced by a business. However, there is one area where some assessment can be made of the ability of accounting information to affect behaviour, because the effects can be observed and measured. This is the reaction of investors to the annual accounting profits announced by companies whose shares (portions of the ownership) are traded on the Stock Exchange. There is strong research evidence to suggest that the prices, at which the shares are traded, change and that the amount of shares that are bought and sold increases when new accounting information is released by companies. This suggests that investors alter their expectations as to the value of the company (hence changes in share price) and that they take action to buy and sell shares (hence increases in trading volume) as a result of an item of accounting information. What, of course, we do not know is whether the cost of producing the annual accounting report is justified by the benefits it bestows on shareholders, in terms of their ability to put a fairer value on their shares.

1.9   The costs of accounting information

Accounting information can be an expensive commodity. In a business of any size, a large amount of scarce resources can be utilized in paying wages of accounting staff, purchasing computers for the preparation of accounting reports, etc. However, the costs of providing accounting information go beyond the out-of-pocket expenditure incurred. For example, there is also the time spent by managers in evaluating the accounting information received. In addition, the information produced may be employed by users to the disadvantage (cost) of the business and its owners.

Activity 5
How might accounting information produced by the business be employed by certain user groups to its disadvantage?

Some examples are as follows:

Competitors may use the information in a way which reduces the competitiveness of a business. For example, a competitor may engage in a price-cutting war in order to improve market share because it knows, from the accounting reports available, that the business is in a weak position to respond to such action.
Employees may respond to high reported profits by insisting on high wage increases, thereby reducing the future competitiveness and profits of the business.
Government may respond to high reported profits by restricting future price increases to customers of the business (where it has the power to do so, such as in the case of a utility) or may levy an excess profits tax.
Suppliers and lenders may respond to the reporting of a weak financial position by refusing or withdrawing credit or loan capital.
Customers may respond to a weak financial position by going elsewhere for their goods and services to ensure continuity of supplies.

We have seen earlier that the benefits of producing accounting information are difficult to judge. However, many of the costs of providing accounting information identified above will also be difficult to judge. Nevertheless, when making decisions about the amount and type of accounting information to provide to users, some weighing of costs and benefits should take place.

1.10   Access to accounting information

Without making any judgements about the relative importance of the typical users and their information needs identified in section 1.5 above, it is by the nature of things that managers will have access to as much information as exists or can be compiled within the organization, whereas the other interested groups may be more reliant on what managers are prepared to provide. However, what the 'outsiders' are provided with is not entirely determined by managers, since many organizations, public and private, must, as a result of regulations emanating from government, the accountancy profession, or the Stock Exchange, provide prescribed minimum amounts of information. This does not necessarily mean, however, that managers will restrict the amount of information to outsiders to the minimum requirements prescribed by accounting regulations. In some cases managers may be prepared to go beyond these minimum requirements. A business with 'good news' to announce or simply 'nothing to hide' may feel that it is in its best interests to provide additional accounting information to outside users which reveals this. The benefits to the business may take the form of being able to raise future funds more easily and/or at lower cost than might otherwise be the case.

In addition, certain interested groups such as government and lenders (in particular circumstances, such as loan negotiations) may be in a position to demand the information they require. Nevertheless, the outsiders, which include the shareholders in private sector companies, will not normally have free access to the accounting records of the business or be in a position to *demand* information beyond what the various accounting regulations require.

1.11   Financial and management accounting

It was seen above that managers of a business will normally have a need for more comprehensive and detailed accounting information than the other users identified. As a result accounting has developed in two major directions – management and financial accounting.

Management accounting

Management accounting is concerned with the provision of information to the managers of the business. The major features of this form of accounting are:

- *Detailed information.* The information provided, as stated earlier, is often very detailed in nature, e.g. information concerning the costs relating to a particular product, the profit made by a particular division of the business, the feasibility of acquiring a particular machine, etc. However, managers will also require accounting reports which provide a general overview at regular intervals to help them retain a proper perspective on the business.
- *Forward looking.* The accounting information provided may incorporate plans as well as information based on actual costs, profits, etc.
- *Frequent reporting intervals.* Feedback of information to managers is provided on a frequent and regularly recurring basis in order to help managers monitor the performance of the business closely. Thus, in a business of any size, some accounting reports are likely to be provided to managers on a monthly basis.
- *Flexibility.* The accounting reports provided to managers can be produced in a form which best suits their needs. There are no regulations governing what accounting information should be produced or in what form it should be provided.

Financial accounting

Financial accounting is concerned with the provision of information to the other interested groups identified above. The major features of this form of accounting are:

- *Summarized form.* The information is usually in the form of a summary of the performance of the business for the preceding period and a statement of the financial position at the end of the period. Data is often aggregated and so detail may be missing. The information provided is intended to give an overview of the financial health of the business.
- *Backward-looking.* The information is based on actual results and it would be unusual for a business to disclose planned results to outsiders.
- *Infrequent reporting.* Financial accounting reports are usually produced on a regular basis, but not so frequently as is the case with management accounting reports. The majority of businesses produce financial accounting reports on an annual basis, with a few large businesses producing accounting reports more frequently (usually half-yearly but occasionally quarterly).
- *Standardized format.* The financial reports produced by many businesses are subject to accounting regulations from the sources identified earlier. This means that the financial statements are produced in a particular format, will disclose certain minimum information and will adopt certain accounting policies. This requirement for uniformity in financial reporting enables meaningful comparisons to be made between different businesses.

Activity 6

It has been stated earlier that accounting is concerned with decision-making and it can be argued that decision-making is concerned with the future rather than the past. As a result, would it not be a good idea to provide outsiders with information on planned performance? Why do you think that managers are often reluctant to provide information on planned performance to outsiders?

Some believe that, as the move towards meeting the needs of users gathers momentum, there will be eventual acceptance of the need to produce information on planned performance for outsiders. As managers find this kind of information useful, it is difficult to argue that other users will not. In certain exceptional situations, such as when a company is seeking to raise new capital or is fighting off a hostile takeover, information on planned performance may already be provided to outsiders. However, this is not the norm. Managers are usually reluctant to provide such information to outsiders even though they produce it for their own purposes. There are two important reasons for this:

- managers are often concerned that disclosure of plans will damage the competitive position of the business. It may provide competitors with a forewarning of future strategies and policies.
- managers are concerned that the information concerning planned performance will be misinterpreted by some users who may not fully appreciate the risk of error in producing such information.

It should be mentioned that, for large companies listed on the Stock Exchange, forecasts of future profits are produced by outside investment analysts and made available to investors. Although the evidence is mixed, some studies have shown that profit forecasts produced by investment analysts are as close to the actual profit achieved as the profit plans produced by managers of the relevant companies. If this is the case, it can be argued that there is no need for these companies to produce information on profit plans as profit forecasts provided by other sources are equally useful to investors.

In this book, our primary concern is with financial accounting. We shall examine the major financial statements prepared for outsiders and show how they can be analysed and interpreted. However, it must be emphasized that the division between management accounting and financial accounting is not clear-cut. The financial statements and the techniques of financial analysis which will be discussed are also used by managers to help assess the position and performance of the business.

1.12   Accounting in the private sector – profitability and viability

It was seen above that the different users of accounting information each have different needs. However, when assessing the performance of a business there are two aspects which are likely to be of concern to each group identified. The first aspect is *profitability*. A private-sector business must generate wealth (profits) in order to satisfy the needs of the owners and to ensure that there are sufficient funds to maintain or expand operations. This does not mean, however, that a business must be profitable in every period. It is possible for a business to incur losses, from time to time, provided it is profitable in the long term. The second aspect is *viability*. Profitability and viability are inter-related concepts. In order to survive it is necessary, but not sufficient, for a business to be profitable. A business must also possess a constant capacity to meet its maturing obligations when they fall due. This means that the business must retain sufficient cash (liquidity) in the business. Cash has been described as the life blood of a business. Unless there is sufficient cash available to pay suppliers and lenders when required, the business can be forced to cease trading even though it may be profitable. Viability may also depend on other characteristics such as the way in which the business conducts its operations within the community in which it is based, the degree of risk associated with its operations, etc.

Users of financial reports are likely to share a common interest in these aspects of business performance; however, it is likely that the emphasis placed on each aspect will vary between the different user groups.

Activity 7

Which would each of the following groups be primarily interested in – profitability or viability?

- Owners
- Lenders
- Suppliers
- Employees

We think the primary concern of each group is likely to be:

- Owners – profitability
- Lenders – viability
- Suppliers – viability
- Employees – viability

1.13 General-purpose or specific-purpose reports?

As each user group has different objectives it is possible to argue that each group should receive financial reports which are specifically designed to meet these needs. However, this approach is likely to be extremely costly to a business in relation to the expected benefits. It has been suggested above that, despite the differing objectives of users, it is possible to identify certain aspects of financial performance in which all users are likely to have an interest. Hence, it can be argued that businesses could satisfy the major needs of all users by producing financial reports which deal with the profitability and viability of the enterprise. In practice, businesses produce what are described as *general-purpose reports*, which reveal this information. This approach appears to be broadly acceptable to users.

Although general-purpose reports are capable of covering areas of interest for different user groups it is, nevertheless, a fact that some users of financial information have a more sophisticated understanding of financial matters than others. There may still be a need therefore to provide different types of reports which are aimed at different levels of understanding. In recent years, there has been a growing recognition of this issue by preparers of financial reports. Many large businesses now produce financial reports for employees which are usually a simplified version of the general-purpose financial reports available to outsiders (including employees). In addition, it is now possible for private individuals who own shares (portions of ownership) in a company, but do not have a good understanding of accounting, to receive simplified reports based on the general-purpose reports which are currently being produced.

Activity 8
Do you think it is a good thing to produce simplified reports to help less sophisticated users? What is the argument against producing such reports?

The idea of preparing simplified financial reports for those with a limited understanding of financial reports has intuitive appeal, particularly as the extent of accounting regulation has increased considerably in recent years, and this has made accounting reports much more complex documents. However, there are potential dangers in providing simplified reports. Businesses can be extremely complex economic organizations and to try and reduce the level of financial complexity of such organizations in order for less sophisticated users to understand may not be possible without seriously distorting the picture which is finally produced. Some argue that it is not the accountant's role to provide potentially misleading information. They believe that if a user cannot understand the financial reports, he or she should seek financial advice from an expert (or study accounting!).

1.14   Types of business enterprise

A business enterprise will usually take one of three forms. A *sole proprietor-ship* (or sole trader) is a type of business in which there is a single owner. This type of business tends to be fairly small in size and many small shops, hotels, service contractors (e.g. plumbers, TV repairs, etc.) and farms are of this type. In order to start up and then carry on such a business there are no specific legal requirements to comply with, thus, providing the business keeps within the general law of the land, the owner has considerable flexibility in the way in which the business is carried out. In law the business is not regarded as a separate legal entity and, therefore, the business will cease on the retirement or death of the owner. However, for accounting purposes the business is regarded as being separate from the owner. This is an important point, as will be shown later. A sole proprietorship does not even have to keep financial records or prepare accounts except in so far as they are required for taxation purposes. Although there are no formal legal requirements to keep accounts it would, however, be extremely unwise for a sole proprietor not to keep some form of accounts. It is difficult to see how the owner would be able to make sensible economic decisions in the absence of appropriate information.

A *partnership* exists where two or more persons carry on a business with a view to making profits. The maximum number of owners is normally 20. Once again, partnership businesses tend to be fairly small in size; the amount of capital the partners are able to raise is usually an important limiting factor to growth. There are no special legal formalities to comply with in order to start up a partnership. The formation of the partnership can take place simply through a verbal agreement or through the actions of the owners. However, it would be unwise not to have some clear written agreement between the parties on how the business should be conducted, the division of profits, the contribution of capital, etc. A partnership does not have to keep financial records or prepare accounts except in so far as they are required for taxation purposes. However, as there is more than one owner, it is probably even more important for a partnership to keep proper accounts than for a sole proprietor. The partnership can carry out its business in any way it sees fit provided the business complies with general legal requirements. Although there is a Partnership Act, this is only designed to cover disputes which arise between partners where they have failed to come to a clear agreement on a particular matter. The law does not recognize a partnership as a separate legal entity and, therefore, a partner-ship cannot enter into contracts in its own name but must do so through the individuals who make up the partnership. However, for accounting purposes the partnership is treated as a separate entity.

A *limited company* is regarded as a separate legal entity, which means that it can enter into contracts in its own name and is given a perpetual existence which is unaffected by changes in the membership of the company. Limited companies can be very large indeed as there can be no upper limit to the number of people permitted to subscribe capital to the business. This type of business enterprise has limited liability which means that the members of the company are only liable for the debts of the company up to the amount which they have agreed to contribute. This is in contrast to the position of sole proprietors or partners where they will be liable for the debts of the business up to and including the extent of their own personal wealth. In order to start a limited company, documents of incorporation must be prepared which set out the name of the company, the objectives of the business and the way in which its affairs will be conducted. The company will be subject to the accounting regulations set out in the Companies Acts, the accounting standards developed by the accountancy profession and, if it is listed on the Stock Exchange, the requirements of the Stock Exchange. A limited company must keep proper financial records and prepare accounts on an annual basis. Moreover, the accounts prepared must be subject to an independent audit. This means that an independent firm of accountants must examine the accounts and the underlying records and form an opinion as to whether the accounts give a true and fair view of the company's financial performance and position and comply with the Companies Acts' requirements and relevant accounting rules.

Activity 9
When setting up a new business, what factors might you consider in deciding upon the particular form of business enterprise to adopt?

We can think of the following factors:

- *Finance*. A business may require a large amount of funding from the owners, which is beyond the capacity of a single individual. In this situation, a partnership or a limited company may be appropriate.
- *Degree of risk*. The more risky the venture, the more attractive limited liability status may appear to the owners.
- *Administration costs*. We have seen that a limited liability company must conform to various legal requirements. This can be both time-consuming and costly and may not appear to the owners to be worth the benefits which flow.
- *Sharing the burden*. The responsibilities of ownership may be lightened where there is more than one owner. However, this must be weighed against any loss of control over decision-making which will arise from having multiple ownership.
- *Flexibility*. Sole traders and partnerships can be formed, dissolved and restructured in line with the owners' wishes and without having to consider any legal regulations. This is not the case for limited companies.

In this book the main focus will be on accounting for limited liability companies as this form of business enterprise is, in economic terms, the most significant. Limited companies dominate the economies of most western industrialized nations. However, it is probably not a good idea to introduce the accounts of limited liability companies at this early stage. Instead, we shall begin by looking at the accounts of a sole-proprietorship-type of business as this is the simplest form of business organization and provides a useful means of introducing the basic principles of accounting. Having examined these principles, which are identical for all three forms of business enterprise, we will then move on to examine the accounts of limited companies.

1.15   The major financial reports

Having discussed the nature and purpose of accounting, we can now introduce the main financial reports which are usually prepared. These reports are designed to give users an insight to the financial position and performance of the business. We will start by considering the problem of simply measuring changes in the cash position of the business as a means of providing users with a picture of the financial health of a business.

What is wrong with reporting cash movements alone?

At first sight, since wealth generation is important to users of accounting and wealth is usually measured in monetary terms, it might be thought that a statement of the amount of cash generated, perhaps augmented by some information on how it was generated, would be sufficient for users. However, this would not be the case. To begin with, the amount of cash generated may not be the same as the amount of wealth generated during a period. In order to see why this is, it may be useful to consider a simple example.

Example

Jim, who has been unemployed, decided to start a business selling boxes of matches on a street corner. On Monday he went to the local cash and carry wholesaler and used £20 he had saved to buy £20 worth of boxes of matches. These he sold quite easily during the day for £40. How much wealth (profit) did he generate?

The answer is simply the difference between the amount that he paid for the stock (£20), and what he sold it for (£40), i.e. £20. This is, of course, the difference between the cash he started the day with and that with which he finished the day. So, in this case, the amount of cash generated *is* the same as the wealth generated. However, let us continue with our example.

On Tuesday Jim decided that since the trip to the cash and carry was time-consuming, it would be useful to buy two days' supply. With this in mind, he bought £40 worth of matches. During Tuesday Jim sold exactly half of the matches for £40. When he came to assess how well the day had gone Jim (a simple soul) was alarmed to realize that he had no more cash at the end of the day than he had at the start. He deduced from this that he had generated no wealth (profit) and that he had therefore wasted his time. Was he correct?

Clearly, he was incorrect since he had actually increased his wealth from the £40 in cash with which he started the day, to £40 in cash plus £20 worth of matches by the end of the day, i.e. a £20 increase in wealth.

This example shows that cash increases and decreases are inadequate as a measure of wealth generation (profit) since wealth can be, and usually to a great extent is, held in other things of value instead of cash. Thus, in order to assess wealth generation, we need to look more widely than just at cash.

The circumstances arising on Tuesday are much more like the typical business where much of any wealth generated will find its way into such things as stock-in-trade, new buildings, new machinery, etc. This should not lead us to the conclusion that where cash comes from, where it goes to and how much is left is not important to businesses. Cash is the life blood of the business and managers need to monitor it, but as a measure of success and achievement, cash is inadequate.

In much of the public sector, where economic wealth generation is not necessarily the objective, the emphasis is often rather less on this and more on other factors. However, even here considerable interest is found in increasing the wealth of society in general, and the measurement of surpluses and assessment of efficiency remain important factors.

The need for more than one financial statement

If Jim, the matchseller in the above example, were to be asked what he needed to know about his business at the end of each day (or perhaps less frequently) his answer would probably be along the following lines:

(a)   A statement of how well he had done as far as trading was concerned, i.e. how much wealth he had generated during the day in question. This statement is referred to as the *profit and loss account* or *income statement*. It will take his sales figure and deduct from it the costs incurred relative to those sales. The resulting figure would not necessarily be his net increase in cash, as we have seen, because payment for the stock does not necessarily occur on the day on which it is sold.

For Tuesday (from the above example) such a statement would be something like the following:

Profit and loss account (income statement) for Tuesday

		£
Sales of matches		40
Purchases of matches	40	
Less: closing stock of matches	20	
Cost of matches sold		20
Net profit (increase in wealth)		20

(b)   A statement of where cash had come from and gone to during the day. This is known as a *cash flow statement*. As we have seen, though cash is not the only form that wealth can take, it is very important, if only because generally it is the only form of wealth which can readily be converted into other forms (i.e. spent).

For Tuesday, such a statement would show the cash received from sales and the cash paid out in buying stocks. The difference between these can then be added to (or subtracted from) the opening cash balance in order to establish the closing cash balance.

Cash flow statement for Tuesday

	£
Receipts from sales	40
Less: payment for stock	40
Net increase in cash	Zero
Opening balance	40
Closing balance	40

From this Jim can see why, though he made a profit, he is not better off in cash terms.

(c)   A statement of where his business wealth lay at the end of the day. This statement is referred to as the *balance sheet* or *position statement*. For Tuesday such a statement would be as follows:

Balance sheet (position statement) as at end of Tuesday

	£
Stock of unsold matches	20
Cash (closing balance on Tuesday)	40
	60
Therefore:	
Jim's business wealth is	60

Obviously, in the very simple circumstances of Jim's business activities on Tuesday, the information contained in the statements could be deduced without any formal written statements. However, it does not take much imagination to see that, if we were dealing with a business any larger than that of Jim, or even Jim's business over a longer period than a day or two, this would not be possible.

These three statements are what is produced periodically by most private-sector, and by many public-sector, organizations. Between them they can give interested parties valuable insights concerning what has taken place within the organization. When used as the framework for projections, they can also give very valuable information on the probable future direction of the business, in financial terms.

The early part of this book is concerned with the preparation of these statements, particularly Chapters 2, 3 and 4. However, as the book progresses, much more emphasis will be placed on the use of these statements, and their analysis and interpretation.

Activity 10

On Wednesday Jim started the day with £20 worth of matches. For some reason or other, trade was bad on that day and Jim had great difficulty in selling matches. In fact, he had to resort to selling them at less than his usual price to sell them at all. Even then, he was left with matches which had cost him £5. His takings for the day totalled £25.

Show the three main accounting statements for Jim's business for Wednesday.

Jim – Profit and loss account for Wednesday

		£
Sales of matches		25
Opening stock of matches	20	
Less: closing stock of matches	5	
Cost of sales		15
Net profit for the day		10

Jim – Cash flow statement for Wednesday

	£
Receipts from sales	25
Less: payment for stock	Zero
Net increase in cash	25
Opening balance (Tuesday's closing balance)	40
Closing balance	65

Jim – Balance sheet as at end of Wednesday

	£
Stock of matches	5
Cash (closing balance on Wednesday)	65
	70
Jim's business wealth	70

(Note that Jim's business wealth has increased from £60 on Tuesday to £70 on Wednesday, the amount of Wednesday's profit.)

This answer assumes that Jim, for the time being, regards the cash generated by the business as part of his business wealth. In practice, of course, he may well withdraw cash to live on.

Self-assessment question 1.1

Russell was following a business studies course at his local university. As the summer was approaching, he decided to try and earn some extra money to help finance a holiday in France. As he lived in a seaside town, he decided to try and sell ice cream on the beach. He had £100 to invest and was able to buy 10 boxes of ice cream from a local manufacturer at a cost of £10 per box. He expected to sell the ice creams in each box for a total of £15. On the first day, he sold 8 boxes and stored the unsold boxes in his parent's freezer overnight. The next day he bought a further 10 boxes and managed to sell 11 boxes at £15 per box. On the third day he bought another 10 boxes, but only managed to sell 4 boxes as the weather had turned cold. As the long-term forecast was not good, Russell decided to abandon this venture and sold the remaining boxes at £8 per box.

Required:

(a) Prepare a profit and loss account and cash flow statement for each of the four days of trading.

(b) Prepare a balance sheet at the end of each day's trading.

(c) What do you deduce from an examination of the statements you have prepared?

(The answer to this question is given at the end of the book.)

1.16 Desirable qualities of accounting information

It was mentioned above that accounting information should be useful as a basis for decision-making. In order to determine what sort of accounting information will be useful for this purpose, it is possible to identify certain desirable attributes or qualities which accounting information should possess. It can be argued that *relevance* and *reliability* are the two primary attributes which financial information must have in order to be useful.

Relevance means that the information produced should be capable of influencing the decision to be made. In order to be relevant to decision-makers, accounting information should have

- *predictive value* and/or
- *confirmatory (feedback) value*

Predictive value means that the information should be capable of helping the decision-maker to predict likely future outcomes. This does not necessarily imply that the information should take the form of a prediction. It can mean that the information would be useful in helping to form a prediction. For example, an oil company may announce that its oilfields in a foreign country have been expropriated by the foreign government without compensation. Such information is not a prediction but rather a statement of what has already happened. It may, nevertheless, be extremely useful in helping to predict future profits of the oil company.

Confirmatory value means that the information should help in confirming or correcting expectations about past events. This is extremely important for decision-makers. Information relating to past performance or events can be used to compare actual performance with earlier planned performance which can be used to identify past problems or difficulties. It can also help in confirming or revising predictions about the future.

Activity 11

Can you think of an example where a particular piece of accounting information can help in both predicting the future and confirming the past?

Information concerning the amount of sales made during a period may be of value in forming a prediction about likely sales in the following period. It can also confirm earlier predictions concerning the likely sales for the period.

You may have thought of another example where a piece of financial information could serve this dual purpose.

Reliability is concerned with portraying what is supposed to be portrayed. In order to be reliable, the accounting information provided must possess a number of characteristics. These are shown in Figure 1.2.

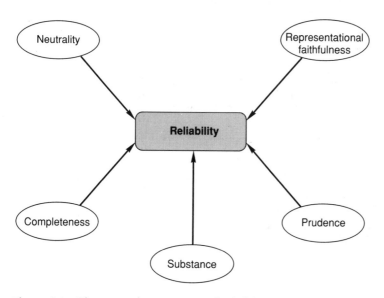

Figure 1.2 *The main characteristics of reliability*

To be reliable, accounting information must also be *neutral*. This means that the methods of measurement used and those who measure should be free from any bias. Neutrality is important in giving accounting reports credibility in the eyes of users. If users suspect that the information they receive is biased, it will undermine the perceived value of the reports. Accounting information should also possess *representational faithfulness* in order to be reliable. This means that the information provided should be a valid description of what it purports to represent and should be free from error. Users must be satisfied that the accounting numbers and any descriptions used faithfully reflect the underlying economic conditions which they are attempting to represent.

Accounting information should also be *complete* in order to be reliable. A significant omission from the information may create a false impression and may mislead users. This, of course, would render the information unreliable. Many believe that accounting information should also be *prudent* and any estimates or judgements made should be done with a degree of caution. It would certainly be misleading to paint a rosier picture of the position and performance of the business than is actually the case. However, in exercising prudence we must be careful not to paint a gloomier picture than is warranted by the facts.

Accounting information should also portray the *substance* of the transaction rather than its legal form. If, for example, a business does not own a particular resource but nevertheless has control over it, then for all intents and purposes, it belongs to the business and this fact should be portrayed in the financial statements. Suppose a business decides to lease a machine for the whole of the machine's working life. This transaction will give the business effective control over the machine and it will become a resource of the business. The fact that the legal ownership still rests elsewhere should not prevent us from recognizing that the machine is part of the economic resource base of the business and so should be included as such in the financial statements. This portrayal of underlying economic reality is more important than excluding the machine from the total resources shown simply because the legal title is not held by the business.

Although, in an ideal world, accounting information should be both relevant and reliable, we must recognize that, at times, a conflict may occur between the two.

Activity 12

A business owns a piece of land which was purchased earlier in the year. When the land was purchased it cost £100 000 but the owners believe it has a current market value of £120 000. How can these two different values create a conflict between relevance and reliability when producing accounting information?

It may be argued that the current value of the land is likely to be more relevant than the original cost for many types of decisions, e.g. when considering an offer to sell the land. However, the current market value may be difficult to establish with a high degree of reliability. The more unique the item being valued, the more subjective any valuation is likely to be and the greater the likelihood of error. The original cost, on the other hand, can usually be verified and this figure will normally have a high degree of reliability. However, this information may be of limited value for decision-making purposes.

In practice, it may be necessary to trade off one quality against another. Which quality is to be traded off is often a matter of judgement; however, the overriding aim should always be to meet the decision-making needs of users.

Timeliness is closely related to the qualities of relevance and reliability discussed above. This refers to the time lag in reporting accounting information and it can influence both the relevance and reliability of accounting information.

Activity 13
Timely reporting is considered to be essential in providing relevant information. Why is this, do you think? Can the timely reporting of accounting information undermine the quality of reliability?

Although the production of timely reports does not, of itself, ensure relevance, the absence of timeliness can destroy the potential relevance of accounting information. If the time lag in reporting is too long, then the usefulness of the information can diminish or perhaps disappear. For example, if a manager wished to make a decision in November on the results of the business in October, eventual production of the financial reports in December would mean that the information could not be used. However, timely reporting may impair the reliability of the reports. Timely reporting can increase the risk that errors will be made and may increase the need for estimates to be made as all information concerning a particular item may not be known at the time of reporting.

In addition to the primary characteristics of relevance and reliability, accounting information should also possess two secondary characteristics to be useful. These are *understandability* and *comparability*. Understandability means that accounting information should be presented in a form which is readily understandable. However, this raises the question, understandable by whom? We saw earlier that there are compelling reasons for not attempting to simplify complex economic reality in order to satisfy the needs of unsophisticated users as there is a real danger that the message will be distorted. This has led some to argue that we should only seek to address the needs of sophisticated users (e.g. bankers, accountants, investment analysts, etc). However, many prefer to take a less extreme position than this and believe we should meet the needs of users who have a *reasonable knowledge of accounting* and are prepared to study the financial information with *reasonable diligence*. What is meant by the term reasonable in this context, however, is open to debate.

Comparability has two dimensions. The first concerns the adoption of accounting policies and procedures by a business in a consistent manner between periods. This characteristic is important as users must be able to make comparisons from one period to another in order to assess changes in performance and position. Unless the business adopts the same methods of accounting over time, any such comparisons would be hindered. The second dimension concerns the consistency of accounting policies in relation to other businesses. This can be important when making comparisons between businesses.

In order for users to assess the degree of comparability which exists, it is important for a business to reveal its accounting policies and to indicate when any changes have been made.

1.17   Summary

In this chapter we have seen that the purpose of accounting is to help interested parties make economic decisions about an organization. Economic decisions require economic information and it is the role of accounting to provide the economic information required. The use of accounting information should help ensure that users employ the limited resources available to them in the most efficient and profitable manner. A number of groups of users of accounting information can be identified and each group has different objectives to pursue. However, it is possible to argue that each group will have a concern for the profitability and viability of the business enterprise. For those users who have limited access to financial information concerning a business, general-purpose financial reports may be prepared which help reveal the profitability and viability of the business.

We have seen that accounting information produced for users must have certain qualities if it is to be useful for decision-making purposes. These are relevance, reliability, understandability and comparability. In practice, it is not always possible to provide information which supplies all of these qualities to a high degree and it may be necessary on occasions to trade off one quality against another.

Exercises

1   You are the owner of Hope Springs and you have been approached by the management of Goodtime Clocks with a view to your firm supplying clock springs on credit.

What information about Goodtime Clocks would be useful to you in assessing the contract?

2   What formal evidence is there that accounting information actually can affect the behaviour of some individuals?

3   Helen, a student, has decided to try and earn some extra income in order to purchase a new car. She has been appointed an agent for her region for a business which manufactures a new type of squash racket. She has agreed to buy from the manufacturer at £24 per racket and intends to sell at £36 per racket. In the first month of trading Helen purchased 30 rackets and managed to sell 25 of these. In the second month she purchased 40 rackets and sold 22. In the third month Helen decided that the new venture was taking up too much of her time and therefore decided to cease trading. She purchased no further rackets during the month and sold off her remaining stock at £20 per racket.

(a) Prepare a profit and loss account and cash flow statement for each month of trading.
(b) Prepare a balance sheet at the end of each month.

Part Two

Accounting Statements:
Nature and Preparation

This part comprises three chapters. It aims to provide you with an introduction to the nature and purpose of the balance sheet and profit and loss account. The underlying rules, known as conventions, relating to the preparation of financial statements, are identified and their limitations discussed. Some of the important problems associated with measuring profit are also dealt with.

Chapters 2, 3 and 4 aim to provide you with a framework which can be used to prepare financial statements from a limited number of transactions. Given the aim of this text, this framework should be sufficient, in that it should enable you to understand the basic principles of the accounting process, which can then be applied to more complex issues.

2

The balance sheet

2.1 Introduction

This chapter aims to set out the nature, form and content of the balance sheet. This is the first of the major financial statements to be studied in detail.

2.2 Objectives

On completion of this chapter you should be able:

- to explain the nature and purpose of a balance sheet;
- to define the terms asset, liability and capital;
- to identify the typical form and content of a balance sheet;
- to explain the major conventions which underpin the balance sheet;
- to explain why a balance sheet on its own does not provide an adequate record of events.

2.3 The nature and purpose of a balance sheet

A balance sheet is *a statement of the assets of, and claims against, a business at a particular point in time*. It may therefore be viewed as a statement of financial position. An asset is, in simple terms, something which provides a benefit to the business, while a claim is a financial obligation of the business to a person, group of people, or an organization. However, in practice, rather more precise criteria exist with regard to the inclusion of an item in a balance sheet as either an asset or a claim.

An *asset* may be more formally defined for accounting purposes as probable future economic benefits obtained and controlled by a particular business. This benefit is typically the result of some current or past transaction or event affecting that business. In order to be recorded in a business balance sheet, an asset should normally have the following characteristics:

- The benefits to be obtained must relate to the future. So, if no future benefits remained from an asset at the date of a balance sheet, it would stop being included in the balance sheet.

- Access to the benefits is controllable by the business. A car hired by a business for a week would not be included as an asset of that business, since access is controlled by the hire company.
- The benefits must have been acquired as the result of a past transaction or event. Typically, this will have involved the business in some kind of money sacrifice, or led to it incurring some future liability. This provides the basis for quantifying or measuring the asset.

Activity 1

Which of the following would be defined as an asset for accounting purposes?

- A chief executive who has succeeded in increasing profits by £1m per annum since her appointment.
- Goodwill from customers which has been built up by the business over the years as a result of the quality of its products.
- The M4 motorway which is used daily by a parcel delivery business in order to deliver on time.
- A piece of equipment owned by the company which is obsolete and has no scrap value.
- A new machine purchased by a business for £2,000 and which should lead to cost savings but has not yet been paid for.

Your answer to this activity should be along the following lines:

- The chief executive would not be regarded as an accounting asset as the business does not control access to its employees.
- The goodwill would not be an asset as it did not arise as a result of a past transaction.
- The M4 motorway would not be an asset of the business because it cannot control the access of others to the motorway.
- An obsolete piece of equipment would not be an asset as it can provide no future benefits.
- The new equipment would meet the criteria for an asset. The fact that payment for the asset has not yet been made does not affect the situation.

This activity illustrates that not all resources which are of value to the business may be defined as an asset for accounting purposes.

As with the definition of an asset, so the definition of a claim as an obligation of the business requires further clarification. A more formal definition is that a *claim* is an existing obligation to provide goods (including money) or services to an individual or organization outside of the business, at some time in the future. To be recorded in a business balance sheet, a claim should normally exhibit the following characteristics:

- The claim exists at the time of the balance sheet. In other words, the transaction or event causing the obligation must already have occurred.
- There is a reasonable expectation that the claim will have to be met.

It is important to note that *potential* future claims, frequently associated with such things as legal cases and the possibility of some future award for damages, are not recorded in a balance sheet. Such claims are known as *contingent liabilities*. While not recorded in the balance sheet, knowledge of such claims is clearly important, since they represent potential problem areas. Contingent liabilities tend to be shown as a separate note to the financial statements.

Claims fall into two distinct types, with further subdivision into categories being found within these two broad types.

- External claims, i.e. liabilities to parties outside of the business.
- Claims by the owners or investors in a business, also known as *capital* or *equity*.

In order to explain the idea of capital or equity it is necessary to introduce the convention of the *business entity*. In essence, the business entity convention says that, for accounting purposes, a distinction needs to be drawn between the owners of a business and the business itself. The financial statements, which include the balance sheet, are prepared *for the business*, and the owners' entitlement is shown as a claim on the business. The business entity convention may be viewed as being technically necessary, since without it, the balance sheet would not balance. It is important to recognize, however, the different nature of the owners' claim, as compared with other external claims.

Once the business entity convention has been introduced, it is possible to summarize the balance sheet as a statement in which:

Assets = claims (capital + external liabilities)

This sets out on one side of the equation the resources of the business which provide future benefits, and on the other side of the equation the claims on those resources.

The above equation is referred to as the balance sheet equation and it will always hold. If, for example, an owner introduced £5,000 cash into a new business, the effect would be to increase the assets (cash) of the business, and to increase the owner's claim (capital) of the business. The resulting balance sheet after this transaction would be:

Assets		*Claims*	
	£		£
Cash	+5,000	Capital	+5,000

This shows the assets equal to the claims. (In this case, the only claim is from the owner.)

If a friend of the owner loaned the business £2,000 cash, the effect would be to increase the assets (cash) and to increase the external liabilities (loans) of the business. The balance sheet after this transaction would be:

Assets			*Claims*		
		£			£
Cash		+5,000	Capital		+5,000
		+2,000	Loan		+2,000

We can see that, after these transactions, the balance sheet equation still holds (assets = claims).

We are now ready to look at a more detailed example concerning the balance sheet equation.

Example

This example shows how a balance sheet may be built up from a series of business transactions. You are given the following transactions and asked to prepare a balance sheet showing the resulting financial position.

(a) Jean Jones invests cash of £10,000 in a new business.
(b) The business buys goods which it plans to resell (known as stock or inventory) for £5,000 cash.
(c) It buys a further £1,000 worth of stock on credit (i.e. it undertakes to pay for them at a later date).
(d) It sells stock which had cost £1,000 for £1,500 cash.
(e) It acquires a new machine for £4,000 cash.

At this stage let us prepare a simple list of assets and claims and record the impact of each transaction on our list. The final position will be as set out below:

Workings

Assets				*Claims*			
			£				£
Cash	(a)	+10,000		Capital	(a)	+10,000	
	(b)	− 5,000			(d)	+ 500	
	(d)	+ 1,500					
	(e)	− 4,000					
Stock	(b)	+ 5,000		Creditors	(c)	+ 1,000	
	(c)	+ 1,000					
	(d)	− 1,000					
Machinery	(e)	+ 4,000					

Notes

Transaction

(a) Assets increase by £10,000 (cash)
     Claims increase by £10,000 (capital, due to the business entity convention)

(b) Assets do not change in total
     but cash goes down by £5,000
     while stock goes up by £5,000
     No change in claims

(c) Assets go up by £1,000 (stock)
     Claims go up by £1,000 (creditors, i.e. people to whom the business owes money)

(d) This transaction is a little more difficult than the earlier transactions. The effect on the assets side of the balance sheet will be as follows:
     Assets go up by a net amount of £500
     with stock going down by £1,000
     and cash going up by £1,500

     If assets go up by a net amount of £500 (i.e £1,500 – £1,000), then claims must also go up by £500, for the balance sheet to remain in balance. We therefore need to ask if there is any obvious claim which can be increased. The answer is provided by the business entity convention. The transaction in (d) has led to an increase in assets as a result of trading, namely a *profit*. The essence of most commercial enterprises is the search for profits, with a consequent risk of losses. If a profit or a loss results we need to ask who is the beneficiary (or loser)? The answer must be the *owner*. Hence, profitable transactions increase the owner's claim, while loss-making transactions reduce the owner's claim. In transaction (d) the remaining entry is therefore:

     Claims go up by £500, namely capital.

(e) Assets do not change in total
     but cash goes down by £4,000
     while machinery goes up by £4,000
     No change in liabilities

On completion of these five transactions the business balance sheet would therefore be:

Balance sheet as at (say) 31 December 19XX

Assets		£	Claims		£
Cash		2,500	Capital		10,500
Stock		5,000	Creditors		1,000
Machinery		4,000			
		11,500			11,500

It should be noted that a balance sheet prepared for a business at a particular date (and hence headed Balance Sheet as at 19XX) would normally only include the final figure for each type of asset or claim, and not the cumulative workings shown earlier. The workings shown above represent the effect of a series of transactions on the balance sheet and may therefore be seen as a series of balance sheets relating to the financial position after each transaction. For the purposes of this chapter, this method of working enables us to appreciate the impact of various transactions on the balance sheet. Indeed, for many small exercises (and some examination questions), such an approach is both quick and effective.

Activity 2

Using the layout given below, prepare a balance sheet to reflect the effect of the following transactions on the business.

(a) Helen Watkins invested £2,000 cash in a business.
(b) The business buys stock for £500 cash.
(c) The business buys stock for £100 on credit.
(d) Stock which cost £100 is sold for £150 on credit.
(e) New machinery costing £400 is purchased on credit.
(f) £50 is paid to creditors.
(g) £1,000 is borrowed from A. Wood.

Balance sheet

Assets	+	−	Net	Claims	+	−	Net
	£	£	£		£	£	£
Cash				Capital			
Stock				Creditors			
Debtors				Loan			
Machinery							

The effect on the balance sheet of the above transaction is as follows:

(a) Helen Watkins brings in cash to the business (an increase in cash) which increases her claim on the business (an increase in capital).
(b) The purchase of stock is reflected in the balance sheet as an increase in stock. The fact that it is paid for in cash is reflected in a reduction in cash.
(c) The purchase of stock on credit is reflected in an increase in stock and an increase in the amount owed, namely creditors.
(d) The sale of stock results in a reduction in the stock figure amounting to £100. It also results in an increase in the amount owed to the business (debtors) of £150. The resulting profit is reflected in an increase in capital.
(e) The purchase of machinery results in an increase in an asset (machinery). As this was not paid for, but purchased on credit, there will be a corresponding increase in a liability (creditors).
(f) Payment of an amount due to creditors will reduce both cash and creditors.
(g) Borrowing from A. Wood will result in an increase in cash and a corresponding increase in a liability.

The effect of these transactions can be seen below:

Assets	+	−	Net	Liabilities	+	−	Net
	£	£	£		£	£	£
Cash	2,000a	−500b	2,450	Capital	2,000a		2,050
	1,000g	− 50f			50d		
Stock	500b	−100d	500	Creditors	100c	−50f	450
	100c				400e		
Debtors	150d		150				
				Loan	1,000g		1,000
Machinery	400e		400				
			3,500				3,500

N.B.: The letters shown above relate to the transaction.

Activity 3
(a) Briefly outline the main purpose of a balance sheet. Can you suggest an alternative name?
(b) Why is it always necessary to include a date in the title of a balance sheet?

The main purpose of a balance sheet is to set out the assets and claims of a business at a particular point in time. As it aims to show the financial position of a business, the *financial position statement* is a possible alternative name.

The balance sheet is a statement of financial position *at a particular point of time*. The date at which the balance sheet is drawn up is therefore important.

Self-assessment question 2.1
Show the effect that each of the following transactions has on the balance sheet. The first answer has been entered as an example.

	Assets	*Liabilities*
(a) Purchased a vehicle for cash	+ vehicle – cash	
(b) Paid an amount owing to a supplier		
(c) Purchased a piece of equipment on credit		
(d) Received money owed by a customer		
(e) Borrowed money from E. Mac		
(f) Purchased stock for cash		
(g) Purchased stock on credit		
(h) The owner withdrew cash from the business		

Self-assessment question 2.2
Indicate whether the following items are assets or liabilities:

	Assets	*Liabilities*
(a) Office equipment		
(b) Fixtures and fittings		
(c) Creditors		
(d) Debtors		
(e) A loan from E. Mac		
(f) An unpaid bill for fuel		
(g) Bank balance		

2.4 Other important conventions

The business entity convention is just one of a number of rules, or conventions, which we apply in preparing the financial statements of a business. The earlier example and activity should help reinforce in your mind this particular convention. It is important to recognize its implications in terms of entries under capital or equity.

- Capital will be increased as a result of initial injections of cash or other assets, further injections by the owners, and profits.
- Capital will be reduced as a result of trading losses, and withdrawals of cash or other assets by the owners.

However, the earlier example and activity also illustrate other conventions. One important convention is that of *duality*. When working through the example and activity you may have noted that every transaction has two aspects. For example, an injection of cash by the owner will increase cash and will also increase the owner's capital; a purchase of a car by cash will decrease cash and will also increase the car asset, etc. By reflecting both aspects of each transaction in the balance sheet we ensure that the balance sheet will balance.

Another convention is that of *money measurement*, which holds that financial statements are concerned only with those items which can be measured in money terms. There are a great many factors which may be important to the well-being of a business which, none the less, cannot be objectively measured in money terms. These include such things as a good reputation, good staff morale, a skilled labour force, etc. Factors such as these, while undoubtedly important in any assessment of past success or future prospects, will not usually be found in a balance sheet. It can be argued that, for some businesses, the most valuable resources may be excluded from the balance sheet because of this convention. As a result the value of the balance sheet as a financial model of the business is undermined.

A further convention deserving attention is the *historic cost convention*. In essence, this convention states that assets should normally be shown at their historic cost, i.e. the amount at which they were acquired. Such an approach is based largely on arguments about objectivity, since the use of historic cost can be seen to be most in line with traditional ideas on objectivity. Alternative valuations for assets are typically seen as involving rather too much subjectivity (i.e personal opinion), and many argue that, wherever possible, financial statements should be based upon facts rather than opinions. In fact, changing price levels may well make financial statements, based upon the historic cost convention, less useful than those based upon alternative asset values. This problem, however, will be discussed in more detail in later chapters. At this stage, it is sufficient to note that historic cost is the normal valuation base.

Activity 4

(a) Which of the following could be found in a balance sheet? Give reasons for your answers.

- That the business has good staff morale
- That the business owes £10,000 to a creditor
- That the owner is very good at getting the best from the employees
- That the assets of the business could be used for a variety of other purposes
- That the business owns vehicles
- That increases in VAT are likely to result in lower sales volume in the future

(b) What is the common denominator of things appearing in the balance sheet?

The answers are:

(a) Good staff morale, while extremely important, will not be found in a balance sheet. It is difficult to measure its value in monetary terms, particularly with any degree of objectivity. It is unlikely that the benefits obtained from good staff morale can be attributed to any particular past transaction or event.

   Amounts owed to creditors will be included in a balance sheet. However, it will usually not show amounts owed to individual creditors. Only the total amount owed to creditors is usually shown.

   The fact that the owner is very good at getting the best from the employees will not appear in a balance sheet, for similar reasons given above relating to good staff morale.

   The fact that assets can be used for a variety of purposes cannot normally be gleaned from a balance sheet.

   If a business owns vehicles they will appear in the balance sheet, providing they can produce future benefits.

   Likely increases in VAT will not appear in the balance sheet. Such increases do not fit with the characteristics of assets or claims. They cannot be measured in monetary terms, nor are they the result of a past transaction or event relating to the business.

(b) The common denominator is the fact that the things included are capable of being measured in money terms (convention of money measurement).

In addition to the above conventions, two further conventions are implicit in preparing the balance sheet. The first of these is the assumption of *continuity*, frequently referred to as the *going concern* convention. Unless there is good evidence to the contrary, the balance sheet is prepared on the assumption that the business will continue to exist in future accounting periods. This assumption has the effect of weakening the objections to historic cost being the basis of asset values in the accounts, and provides a justification for depreciation, which is the spreading of the cost of assets with long lives over the period of those lives. (This will be dealt with in more detail later.) Without the assumption of continuity, liquidation (sales) values of assets would be a more sensible basis of asset valuation.

The second assumption is that traditional accounting statements are prepared on the basis of a *stable monetary unit*. In other words, no adjustments are made for inflation. In recent years, such an assumption has been somewhat unrealistic, and various proposals have been made to adjust financial statements for inflation. These proposals are dealt with in later chapters. At this stage, it is important to bear in mind this assumption, and its limitations, when analysing and interpreting financial statements which have not been adjusted for inflation.

Self-assessment question 2.3

(a) Why should a balance sheet always balance?

(b) Enter the missing amounts in each of the following:

Assets £15,000	Liabilities £5,000	Capital £
Assets £30,000	Liabilities £12,000	Capital £
Assets £30,000	Capital £15,000	Liabilities £
Assets £20,000	Capital £12,000	Liabilities £
Liabilities £5,000	Capital £15,000	Assets £
Capital £25,000	Liabilities £10,000	Assets £

(c) Jones has just bought a new car for £5,000. Indicate whether you would expect this to appear in the business balance sheet, giving reasons for your decision.

(d) You are asked by a business person to explain why capital in the business is shown as a claim.

2.5 A detailed example

This section illustrates how a balance sheet reflects the effect of the following transactions.

(a) C. Mille invests cash of £15,000 in a business known as Polyprint & Co.
(b) The business borrows £3,000 from the bank.
(c) It purchases plant for £10,000 cash, and a van for £3,000 cash.
(d) It purchases £7,500 of stock on credit.

(e) It purchases £2,000 of stock for cash.
(f) It sells stock which had cost £6,500 for £11,000 on credit.
(g) It receives £8,000 cash from debtors.
(h) It pays £5,000 cash to creditors.
(i) It pays £500 in wages.
(j) It pays £250 rent.
(k) C. Mille withdraws £500 for personal use.

The logic for recording each of these transactions is given below, and their cumulative effect is shown in the balance sheet list following.

		Assets		*Claims*	
(a)	Cash increases by £15,000	Cash	+15,000		
	Capital increases by £15,000			Capital	+15,000
(b)	Cash increases by £3,000	Cash	+3,000		
	Liabilities (a loan) increase by £3,000			Loan	+3,000
(c)	Plant increases by £10,000	Plant	+10,000		
	Vehicles increase by £3,000	Vehicles	3,000		
	Cash decreases by £13,000	Cash	−13,000		
(d)	Stock increases by £7,500	Stock	+7,500		
	Creditors increase by £7,500			Creditors	+7,500
(e)	Stock increases by £2,000	Stock	+2,000		
	Cash decreases by £2,000	Cash	−2,000		
(f)	Stock decreases by £6,500	Stock	−6,500		
	Debtors increase by £11,000	Debtors	+11,000		
	Capital increases by £4,500 (the profit)			Capital	4,500
(g)	Cash increases by £8,000	Cash	+8,000		
	Debtors reduce by £8,000	Debtors	−8,000		
(h)	Cash reduces by £5,000	Cash	−5,000		
	Creditors reduce by £5,000			Creditors	−5,000
(i)	Cash reduces by £500	Cash	−500		
	Capital reduces by £500			Capital	−500
(j)	Cash reduces by £250	Cash	−250		
	Capital reduces by £250			Capital	−250
(k)	Cash reduces by £500	Cash	−500		
	Capital reduces by £500			Capital	−500

Balance sheet as at——

Assets	+	–	Net	Claims	+	–	Net
	£	£	£		£	£	£
Cash	15,000a	13,000c	4,750	Capital	15,000a	500i	18,250
	3,000b	2,000e			4,500f	250j	
	8,000g	5,000h				500k	
		500i					
		250j					
		500k					
Plant and equipment	10,000c		10,000	Loan	3,000b		3,000
Vehicles	3,000c		3,000	Creditors	7,500d	5,000h	2,500
Stock	7,500d	6,500f	3,000				
	2,000e						
Debtors	11,000f	8,000g	3,000				
			23,750				23,750

The figures shown in the net columns reflect the balance sheet after the completion of all of the transactions.

2.6 Capital, revenue and expenses

At this stage, it is useful to consider in more detail the transactions which relate to capital, since these sometimes cause a certain amount of confusion; also to provide a more detailed introduction to the profit and loss account, and its relationship to the balance sheet.

In general terms, it may be said that most people invest in a business in the expectation of making a profit, but with the risk of loss. Such people may increase the amount of their capital by injecting further sums into the business. Similarly, they may reduce their claim by withdrawals of capital (drawings). Profits are added to the capital of the owner (his/her claim on the business), while losses are subtracted from it. The *effect of transactions on the capital account* may thus be summarized as follows:

Opening capital	x
+ Injections	x
+ Profits/ – Losses	x
	x
– Drawings	x
= Closing capital	x

The transactions included in the last example can now be reconsidered in the light of this summary. Transactions affecting capital are (a), (f), (i), (j) and (k).

- Transaction (a) reflects an initial injection of capital.
- Transaction (k) reflects a withdrawal of capital (drawings).
- Transactions (f), (i) and (j) together reflect the impact on capital of trading transactions, and will give the overall profit or loss resulting from trading, namely £3,750.

It is useful to keep these three types of transaction separate in practice, since their separation will lead to more useful information.

It is clear from Chapter 1 that a profit and loss account, or income statement, is generally seen as one of the most important financial statements. It is important to note at this stage that *the profit and loss account is nothing more than a summary of the effect of trading transactions on capital.* As such, it should be seen as being inextricably linked to the balance sheet. In fact, as will be shown in Chapter 3, it is effectively an appendix to the balance sheet.

Before considering this in more detail, two further terms need to be introduced, namely *revenues* and *expenses*. In broad terms (and subject to subsequent qualification and clarification in the next chapter), a revenue is an increase in capital (the owner's claim) which results from trading, while an expense is a decrease in capital which results from trading. *Revenues less expenses equals the profit or loss.*

It should be pointed out that expenses cover more than just the cost of any goods which are sold (the cost of sales). Transactions involving such things as rent, rates, heating and lighting, insurance, wages, etc. all reduce the owner's claim and should be seen as expenses.

When considering transactions relating to the sale of goods, the introduction of the idea of revenues and expenses enables such transactions to be broken down into two constituent parts. Consider (by way of example) transaction (f) above, the sale of stock which had cost £6,500, for £11,000 on credit. This transaction may be viewed as having two constituent parts:

- the sale, which brings in an asset (debtors) amounting to £11,000;
- the handing over of goods to the customer which had cost £6,500.

These two separate parts can be dealt with differently from the way set out earlier. The two parts are:

- The sale on credit may be seen as increasing debtors by £11,000 and increasing capital by £11,000, this latter increase being a revenue (sales), an increase in capital as a result of trading.
- The handing over of goods may be seen as reducing stock by £6,500 and reducing capital by £6,500, this latter decrease being an expense (cost of sales), a decrease in capital as a result of trading.

The capital will at this stage be showing a revenue (+£11,000) and an expense (–£6,500), which together give the correct profit figure of £4,500 on the transaction.

Transactions (i) and (j) reflect the incurring of other expenses, with a consequent reduction in capital.

Although the final result is the same, this approach enables all aspects of trading profits or losses to be separately identified. This is important, since most users of accounts will want to know not only *how much* profit has been made, but also *how* it has been made. A profit of £1,000 may be achieved by selling goods which had cost £3,000 for £4,000; by selling goods which had cost £100,000 for £101,000; or a variety of other combinations of revenues and expenses. Knowledge of the actual revenues and expenses will provide useful insights into past performance, and help in making decisions for the future. In the example shown above, revenues (sales) amount to £11,000, with expenses being (cost of sales) £6,500, (wages) £500, and (rent) £250, giving an overall profit of £3,750.

At this stage, all revenues are entered as additions to capital on the balance sheet, while expenses are entered as deductions from capital. In practice, revenues and expenses are collected separately in a profit and loss account (income statement), with only the net profit or loss being transferred to the capital section of the balance sheet. This will be dealt with in more detail in the next chapter. It is worth restating at this point that:

- Revenues are increases in capital as a result of trading
- Expenses are decreases in capital as a result of trading

with recordings being made to reflect this.

Activity 5

Show the effect of the following transactions on the balance sheet. Where transactions relate to capital indicate whether the entry is an injection, a drawing, a revenue or an expense.

(a) Stock is purchased on credit for £500.
(b) The owner withdraws £250.
(c) The owner brings her own car into the business, for use solely by the business. The car is currently valued at £3,000.
(d) Goods which cost £500 are sold for £600 cash.
(e) Rent of £200 is paid.
(f) Goods which cost £1,000 are sold for £1,250 on credit.
(g) Bank interest of £50 is paid.
(h) Receive £1,000 from debtors.
(i) Purchase equipment for £4,000 with a loan from the bank for the full amount.

The effect of the above transactions on the business balance sheet are shown below:

	Assets	*Claims*
(a)	Stock + £500	Creditors + £500
(b)	Cash – £250	Capital – £250 (drawings)
(c)	Vehicles + £3,000	Capital + £3,000

(d)   Earlier in the chapter you would probably have shown the effect of this transaction as:

	Stock – £500	Capital – £100 (the profit)
	Cash + £600	

In order to provide more detailed information about profit you should split this transaction into the following:

	Stock – £500	Capital – £500 (an expense)
	Cash + £600	Capital + £600 (a revenue)

(e)	Cash – £200	Capital – £200 (an expense)

(f)   As with (d) this transaction should be shown as:

	Stock – £1,000	Capital – £1,000 (an expense)
	Debtors + £1,250	Capital + £1,250 (a revenue)

(g)	Cash – £50	Capital – £50 (an expense)
(h)	Cash + £1,000	
	Debtors – £1,000	
(i)	Equipment + £4,000	Loan + £4,000

2.7   Types and classification of assets and liabilities

In order for users to analyse and interpret the balance sheet more easily, it is useful to classify assets and liabilities in a generally recognized manner. Standard classifications mean that less explanation is required from users concerning the nature of assets and liabilities shown in the balance sheet. *Assets* are normally classified under two main headings for balance sheet purposes:

- Fixed assets
- Current assets

Fixed assets are those assets which are held by the business to earn profit. They are not held primarily to resell, but are used to make the business more efficient in carrying out trading operations. Therefore, in a manufacturing business, plant and machinery will be a fixed asset while the goods manufactured by them are not.

Physical (or tangible) assets such as land, buildings, equipment, etc. are the more obvious fixed assets held by businesses. It should be remembered that only assets which cost the business something and which can be measured in money terms appear in the balance sheet. For example, the reputation that a business starting from scratch has built up over the years will not be shown in the balance sheet, even though it may be of considerable importance in assessing both past performance and future potential. However, if a good reputation is purchased, say in the form of a business name, rather than built up, it will be included in the balance sheet, provided that some benefits remain. Such purchased goodwill is an example of an *intangible asset* (one which cannot be physically touched). Other intangible assets which might appear on a balance sheet include such things as the acquisiton of patents, copyrights, licences, etc. which involve the business in a cost and provide benefits in the future.

Current assets are those assets which form the basis of business trading, in that they circulate and change in the short term. They include stock, short-term debtors and cash.

It should be borne in mind that an item could be classified as a fixed asset in one type of business, whereas in another business, exactly the same item could be classified as a current asset. The crucial factor determining the heading under which an asset will be shown is the *intention* with regard to the use to which the asset will be put. For instance, a motor van in a motor dealer's business would normally be a current asset, whilst in a grocery business it would be a fixed asset. The tendency is for fixed assets to remain in a business for some years, whereas the typical current asset has a much shorter life in the business. It is important to appreciate, however, that the length of life of the asset in the business is not a consideration when classifying assets as either fixed or current.

Claims are classified under three main headings for balance sheet purposes:

- Capital (or owner's equity)
- Long-term liabilities
- Current liabilities

Capital represents the owner's claim on the business and has already been dealt with in some detail. *Long-term liabilities* are those which have to be cleared at a future date more than 12 months from the balance sheet date. *Current liabilities* are those in respect of which settlement could be demanded by the claimant within the next 12 months.

Activity 6
Which of the following are fixed assets in a manufacturing business?

	Yes	*No*
(a) land and buildings		
(b) raw materials stocks		
(c) stocks of finished goods		
(d) debtors		
(e) plant and equipment		

(a) and (e) are fixed assets. The remainder are current assets.

Self-assessment question 2.4
Which of the following are current assets in a retailing business?

		Yes	No
(a)	stocks of goods for resale		
(b)	sales counters		
(c)	shop premises		
(d)	outstanding accounts due to the business (debtors)		
(e)	goodwill		
(f)	cash		
(g)	tills		
(h)	rent paid in advance		

2.8   Balance sheet formats

In order to help users find their way around the balance sheet, it is also useful to have the capital and the various classes of assets and liabilities arranged in some kind of logical order. An example of one format for a balance sheet is given below.

Balance sheet as at:

	£	£		£
Fixed assets			Capital	x
Premises		x		
Fixtures and fittings		x		
Plant and equipment		x		
Vehicles		x		
		x		
			Long-term liabilities	
			Loans	x
Current assets				
Stock	x		*Current liabilities*	
Debtors	x		Creditors	x
Cash	x			
		x		
	£	x		£ x

This form of presentation shows the assets on the left-hand side and reveals a progression from the most fixed to the most liquid, while on the claims side the progression is from long-term to short-term. This format is a particularly useful one to use initially, since it clearly reflects the balance sheet equation:

Assets = claims

Claims consist of capital and external liabilities, therefore we can extend the equation so that:

Assets = capital + liabilities

This format, however, is rarely used nowadays. In practice, the balance sheet is typically presented in a *narrative* or *vertical format*, rather than in the two-sided way shown above. An example of such a presentation is given below.

Balance sheet as at ——

Fixed assets		
Premises		x
Fixtures and fittings		x
Plant and equipment		x
Vehicles		x
		x
Current assets		
Stock	x	
Debtors	x	
Cash	x	
	x	
Less *Current liabilities*	x	
Working capital		x
		x
Less *Long-term liabilities*		x
Net assets		x
Financed by:		
Capital		x

It should be stressed that this format represents nothing more than a rearrangement of items in a two-sided balance sheet. Effectively it is saying:

Assets = capital + liabilities

Therefore:

Assets – liabilities = capital

Capital has been defined as the claim of the owner on a business. It should be clear that at any time this claim must be reflected by the sum of the assets less external liabilities.

In the narrative format, current assets minus current liabilities gives a figure known as *working capital* or *net current assets*. In practice, a business is likely to need to tie up funds in a variety of short-term, circulating assets, such as stock, debtors and cash, which are just as essential to the effective running of the business as fixed assets. Some of these can be funded by short-term liabilities, particularly creditors. The above layout makes clear the amount of working capital tied up in the business.

A two-sided format for the balance sheet will be used for the remainder of this chapter and the next, unless you are told anything to the contrary, since this will reinforce the underlying convention of duality. Thereafter, increased emphasis will be placed on presentational issues and so the narrative format will be used. However, even at this stage, the classification of assets and liabilities discussed earlier should be used.

2.9   Miscellaneous points on the balance sheet

It is often the case that, when a new business is created, a number of different assets and liabilities may be brought into the business.

For example, suppose that Ashok starts a business into which he brings equipment of his own, valued at £5,000, his own vehicle (for sole use by the business) valued at £3,000, and £2,000 cash. The opening balance sheet would thus be as follows:

Balance sheet as at ——

	£		£
Fixed assets		*Capital*	10,000
Equipment	5,000		
Vehicle	3,000		
	8,000		
Current assets			
Cash	2,000		
	£10,000		£10,000

The capital is calculated by adding together the assets brought in, and subtracting from this total the sum of any liabilities brought in (i.e. $C = A - L$).

The capital at any stage of a business may be calculated along similar lines.

In practice, most fixed assets will be used up over time. A piece of equipment which costs £5,000, and is expected to last for 5 years, may legitimately be recorded at cost when it is purchased, but after 5 years its future benefit is likely to be low and may even be zero. In reality, therefore, the cost of the asset, less any residual value expected, must be written off (i.e. treated as an expense) over the expected life of the asset. In other words, part of the asset's cost must become an expense – known as depreciation – as the asset is used up. This will result in a reduction in the figure shown under assets in the balance sheet, and a reduction in capital – an expense.

Self-assessment question 2.5

D. Wood owns and manages an agricultural engineering business, which was started three years ago. In discussions with the owner, you ascertain the following facts as at 31.12.19x7.

(a)   When the business was first started, premises were bought for £20,000.
(b)   Equipment is owned which cost him £8,000.
(c)   Stock of raw materials, work in progress, and finished goods are valued at £10,000.
(d)   A letter from the building society confirms that £12,000 is still owing on the mortgage taken out to buy the premises.
(e)   A schedule of amounts owing for credit sales totals £15,000.
(f)   Unpaid invoices for stock and expenses total £10,000.
(g)   The bank statement shows that £3,000 remains in the current account. £250 is held in cash on the premises.
(h)   D. Wood tells you that he originally put in £25,000 into the business.

Prepare a balance sheet for the business at 31 December 19x7.

Depreciation will be dealt with in more detail later in the book. It is mentioned at this stage to alert you to its existence. For many businesses depreciation is an important expense.

2.10   Summary

This chapter has provided an introduction to the nature and purpose of a balance sheet. It has also provided an introduction to the conventions underlying this basic financial statement. The rationale for these conventions, and their importance and limitations, should be carefully noted, since they are important when analysing and interpreting financial statements. The balance sheet contains much information which is useful, but its limitations need to be fully recognized by users of accounting information. This chapter has examined the effect of a variety of transactions on the balance sheet, and you should be familiar with these. In particular, it has considered the effect of transactions on the claim of the owner on the business, and it has distinguished between injections, drawings, revenues and expenses. A thorough understanding of these terms is necessary before moving on to the next chapter. At this stage you should be clear that revenues less expenses equals profit. The next chapter will provide an introduction to the profit and loss account, the second major financial statement, and will build on the ideas introduced in this chapter relating to revenues and expenses.

Exercises

1   Show the effect of each of the following transactions on the assets and liabilities (including capital) of a balance sheet.

(a) Purchased on credit, goods for resale amounting to £2,000.
(b) Paid creditors' accounts amounting to £200, by cheque.
(c) Received an invoice for repairs to buildings amounting to £250.
(d) Paid annual interest of £150, relating to a long-term loan.
(e) Purchased new machinery on credit for £1,500.
(f) Fire insurance of £100 is paid which relates to the buildings.
(g) Fuel for machinery is purchased for £500.
(h) Trade debts of £25 were written off (i.e. treated as an expense) as bad (i.e. unlikely to be paid).
(i) Machinery was depreciated by £500.
(j) The owner withdrew £150 for his own use.
(k) Stock which had cost £250 was sold for £350 cash.
(l) Leasehold property (on a 10-year lease) is purchased for £10,000.
(m) The owner used stock to the value of £75 in his own home.
(n) During the year the owner won £5,000 on a bet on a horse race, which he paid intact into the business bank account.
(o) Wages of £100 were paid in cash.

2   Write brief notes on the conventions and assumptions introduced in this chapter.

3   Record the following transactions on a list of assets and claims, showing each particular type separately. Show the balance sheet on completion of all the transactions.

(a) G. Mawgan started a business with £20,000 cash.
(b) The business borrowed £5,000 from the bank.
(c) Fixtures and fittings were purchased on credit for £1,500.
(d) Stock was purchased for £500 cash.
(e) Further stock was purchased for £3,500 on credit.
(f) A vehicle was purchased for £3,500, with a deposit of £1,000 being paid by cash.
(g) Faulty stock was returned to suppliers. The invoice value of this stock was £250.
(h) A small workshop unit was purchased for £15,000 cash.
(i) Mawgan won £1,500 on the football pools, and put this money immediately into the business.
(j) A creditor was paid £1,200.
(k) Stock which had cost £500 was sold for £700 on credit.
(l) £300 was received from debtors.
(m) Creditors were paid £2,000.

4 Record the following on a balance sheet list, and show the balance sheet as it appears on 31 January.

(a)	1 January	D. Harvey puts in £10,000 to start a new business of her own, calling it Wight Enterprises.
(b)	1 January	Borrows £5,000 from P. Perks.
(c)	1 January	Buys a small shop for £3,000 cash.
(d)	2 January	Buys stock for resale for £800 cash.
(e)	3 January	Buys further stock of £2,200 on credit.
(f)	4 January	Stock which cost £600 is sold for £600 cash.
(g)	5 January	Stock which cost £200 is sold for £200 on credit.
(h)	7 January	Cash of £800 is paid to creditor.
(i)	8 January	Cash of £200 is received from debtor.
(j)	11 January	Harvey withdraws £500 cash from the business for her private use.
(k)	11 January	Harvey pays the creditor £400 from her personal funds.
(l)	12 January	Goods which cost £600 are sold for £800 cash.
(m)	13 January	Goods which cost £100 are sold on credit for £90.
(n)	15 January	Stock to the value of £2,000 is bought on credit.
(o)	15 January	Rent of £30 is paid.
(p)	18 January	Stationery is bought for £100 cash.
(q)	20 January	Miscellaneous expenses of £50 are paid in cash.
(r)	28 January	Goods which cost £500 are sold for £750, £250 cash being received and £500 due at the end of February.

On 31 January it was discovered that only £80 of stationery was still in hand.

The profit and loss account

3.1 Introduction

The need for, and importance of, the profit and loss account have already been discussed in Chapters 1 and 2. This chapter aims to provide an understanding of the nature, form and content of the profit and loss account (also known as the income statement); the way in which profit is measured; and the way in which basic profit and loss accounts and balance sheets are prepared from a series of business transactions.

3.2 Objectives

On completion of this chapter you should be able to:

- explain the nature and purpose of the profit and loss account;
- set out the basic form of the profit and loss account and explain its relationship with the balance sheet;
- explain the major conventions underpinning the proft and loss account;
- prepare a profit and loss account and a balance sheet from basic transactions.

3.3 The nature and purpose of the profit and loss account

Chapter 2 made it clear that changes in capital (owner's claim), over time, may be attributable to:

- further injections of capital by the owners
- profits or losses from trading operations
- drawings by the owner

Injections of capital are likely to occur relatively infrequently. Drawings by owners, on the other hand, are likely to occur rather more frequently, often at regular intervals. Both may be of considerable importance to a business.

However, the essence of most commercial businesses is the search for profits, and the number of transactions arising from this search may be enormous. In practice, profits provide a very substantial part of the inflow of new finance to the business sector of the economy. The recording and measurement of profits or losses are, therefore, important parts of the accounting process.

We have already seen that profits or losses from trading operations are arrived at by deducting expenses from revenues. A revenue represents an *increase* in capital as a result of trading operations, while an expense is a *decrease* in capital as a result of trading operations. It should be clear from Chapter 2 that a balance sheet drawn up at a particular time will reflect any profits or losses made to date.

However, consideration of the examples and activities of Chapter 2 should also make it clear that the balance sheet alone will not show *how* profit has been made, or what has happened in terms of transactions carried out.

The balance sheet only shows the *end result* of the transactions. While such a statement is undeniably useful, it is not enough. Information about *how* a profit or loss has been made is also necessary, if a useful picture is to be built up. A separate statement covering this, the profit and loss account or income statement, is therefore usually prepared. Such a statement is necessary if users of accounts are to understand fully the impact of trading operations on the financial position of the business. It is also likely to provide a means of assessing the efficiency of past performance, and to provide indicators which may be useful in improving performance in the future.

The overall purpose of this profit and loss account or income statement is to set out the financial results of trading operations for a particular period.

At this stage is is worth emphasizing that a profit and loss account relates to a period, whereas a balance sheet relates to a particular point in time. This can be illustrated as follows:

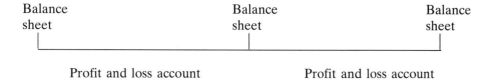

At the end of a financial period, users will usually be presented with both statements in order to help them assess financial performance and position. They will receive a profit and loss account for the period and a balance sheet as at the end of that period. The profit and loss account and balance sheet are together often referred to as the *final accounts*.

Activity 1

What piece of information do you think should be included in the title at the top of a particular profit and loss account?

The time period covered by the statement should be included. It would not be appropriate to head it as at a particular date, since it relates to a period. Hence, it should be headed *Profit and loss account for the year (or month etc.) ended 31 December* (or whatever date the period ended).

It is common to find profit and loss accounts prepared to cover periods such as one month, six months and a year, together with a balance sheet as at the end of the period covered. For example, financial statements for tax purposes are typically needed every year. Limited companies are required to prepare accounts annually. Companies listed on the Stock Exchange are required to prepare accounts on a half-yearly and an annual basis. More frequent accounts (e.g. monthly) are prepared by most larger businesses, for purposes of internal decision-making and control. In the final analysis, virtually every business has to produce financial statements on an annual basis at least, if only for tax purposes. Profit and loss accounts covering shorter periods are prepared as necessary, with usefulness and cost being important considerations.

The profit and loss account, being a statement of the increases and decreases in capital which result from trading, is in essence nothing more than a summary, in convenient form, of entries in the capital area of the balance sheet which relates to trading operations. These have already been outlined as:

*   Revenues, i.e. increases in capital attributable to trading operations, and
*   Expenses, i.e. decreases in capital attributable to trading operations.

Hence: Profit = revenue less expenses

To help analyse performance, it is useful if revenues and expenses can be identified in some detail. Thus, in the profit and loss account, we show each source of revenue generated and each type of expense incurred, providing that the amounts are significant.

Activity 2
Revenues generated by a business can come from various sources. Can you think of *four* different sources of revenue?

In answering this activity you may have thought of the following:

*   Sales revenue from goods or services
*   Rent receivable
*   Commission receivable
*   Fees receivable
*   Interest receivable

This is not an exhaustive list. You may have thought of others.

Activity 3

Expenses incurred by a business in carrying out trading operations can take various forms. Can you think of *six* different forms of expense?

You may have thought of some of the following expenses:

- Rent payable
- Rates payable
- Salaries and wages
- Interest payable
- Postage and telephone expenses
- Heat and light
- Printing and stationery
- Accountancy fees

There are many others which you may have identified.

3.4 Introduction to form and content of the profit and loss account

We have seen that, at any particular point in time:

Assets = capital + liabilities

We have further seen that after a period of trading:

The *assets* held at the end of a period
$=$
The *Capital* at the beginning of the period
+ *Injections* of new capital
+ *Net profit/ – net loss*
(i.e. revenues – expenses)
– *Drawings*
+ *Liabilities*

⎫
⎬
⎭
The net figure resulting from this represents the capital figure at the end of the period

---

Activity 4

Is it necessary to know all of the detailed revenues and expenses in order to complete the balance sheet?

Knowledge of all of the individual revenues and expenses is not necessary for completion of the balance sheet. Insertion of the *overall* figure of net profit or net loss into the balance sheet will be sufficient. However, it is useful if a separate summary of revenues and expenses can be made elsewhere (i.e. in the profit and loss account), from which the net profit or loss can be calculated. An outline framework for such an approach is shown below:

Balance sheet as at ——

	£	£		£
Fixed assets			*Capital*	
Premises		*x*	Opening capital	*x*
Fixtures and fittings		*x*	+ New injections	*x*
Plant and equipment		*x*	+ Net profit/ – net loss	*x**
Vehicles		*x*		*x*
			– Drawings	*x*
			= Closing capital	*x*
Current assets				
Stock	*x*		*Long-term liabilities*	*x*
Debtors	*x*			
Cash	*x*		*Current liabilities*	*x*
		x		
		x		*x*

Profit and loss account for the ....(period) ended on ....

	£		£
Expenses	*x*	*Revenues*	*x*
listed and totalled		listed and totalled	
Net profit*	*x*	(or net loss*)	*x*
	x		*x*

*The resulting net profit or loss is transferred to the balance sheet, thereby preserving its balance. You should remember that the profit and loss account is a supplement or appendix to the capital section of the balance sheet.

The following example should help reinforce some of the points made.

Example

Let us reconsider the detailed example shown in section 5 of Chapter 2, in which you were required to prepare a balance sheet resulting from the following transactions.

(a)   C. Mille invests cash of £15,000 in a business known as Polyprint & Co.
(b)   The business borrows £3,000 from the bank.
(c)   It purchases plant and equipment for £10,000 cash and a van for £3,000 cash.

(d) It purchases £7,500 worth of stock on credit.
(e) It purchases £2,000 worth of stock for cash.
(f) It sells stock which had cost £6,500 for £11,000, on credit.
(g) It receives £8,000 cash from debtors.
(h) It pays £5,000 cash to creditors.
(i) It pays £500 in wages.
(j) It pays £250 rent.
(k) C. Mille withdraws £500 for his own use.

Suppose now that you are asked to prepare final accounts for the business, i.e. both a profit and loss account covering the period in question, and a balance sheet as at the end of the period. In fact, the only changes needed to the treatment in Chapter 2 relate to revenues and expenses (i.e. transactions (f), (i), and (j)). All other transactions are treated exactly as before.

Transaction (f) will result in:

- a reduction in stock of £6,500, matched by a reduction in capital, an expense of £6,500;
- an increase in debtors of £11,000, matched by an increase in capital, a revenue of £11,000.

The revenue and expense will now be recorded initially in the profit and loss account, rather than in the capital account. The two sides of the balance sheet will still agree, provided that the profit and loss account figures are included.

Transactions (i) and (j), the incurring of expenses, will both result in decreases in cash and decreases in capital (expenses). These expenses will now also be recorded initially in the profit and loss account, rather than capital, but again with the understanding that they will be included in the calculation of the net profit figure.

The solution to this example should now look like that shown below:

Polyprint and Co
Balance sheet as at ——

	£	£	£		£	£	£
Fixed assets	+	–	Net	*Capital*	+	–	Net
Plant and	10,000c		10,000	Opening capital	15,000a		15,000
equipment				+ net profit			3,750*
Vehicles	3,000c		3,000				18,750
				– Drawings		500k	500
Current assets				= Closing capital			18,250
Stock	7,500d	6,500f	3,000				
	2,000e						

Debtors	11,000f	8,000g	3,000	Loan		3,000b		3,000
Cash	15,000a	13,000c	4,750					
	3,000b	2,000e		*Current liabilities*				
	8,000g	5,000h		Creditors		7,500d	5,000h	2,500
		500i						
		250j						
		500k						
			23,750					23,750

*Inserted from the profit and loss account

Profit and loss account for the period ended ——

	£	£	£		£	£	£
Expenses	+	–	Net	*Revenues*	+	–	Net
Cost of sales	6,500f		6,500	Sales	11,000f		11,000
Wages	500i		500				
Rent	250j		250				
			7,250				
Therefore net profit			3,750				
(i.e. revenues less expenses)							
			11,000				11,000

You are advised to check through this answer carefully to ensure that you fully understand it, then attempt the following self-assessment question.

Self-assessment question 3.1
Prepare a profit and loss account for January and a balance sheet as at 31 January from the following transactions.

(a) 1 January — D. Harvey puts in £10,000 to start a new business of her own, calling it Wight Enterprises.
(b) 1 January — Borrows £5,000 from P. Perks.
(c) 1 January — Buys a small shop for £3,000 cash.
(d) 2 January — Buys stock for resale for £800 cash.
(e) 3 January — Buys further stock of £2,200 on credit.
(f) 4 January — Stock which cost £600 is sold for £600 cash.
(g) 5 January — Stock which cost £200 is sold for £200 on credit.
(h) 7 January — Cash of £800 is paid to creditors.
(i) 8 January — Cash of £200 is received from debtors.
(j) 10 January — Harvey withdrew £500 cash from the business for her private use.
(k) 11 January — Harvey pays the creditor £400 from her personal funds.
(l) 12 January — Goods which cost £600 are sold for £800 cash.
(m) 13 January — Goods which cost £100 are sold on credit for £90.

(n) 15 January   Stock to the value of £2,000 is bought on credit.
(o) 15 January   Rent of £30 is paid.
(p) 18 January   Stationery is bought for £100 cash.
(q) 20 January   Miscellaneous expenses of £50 are paid in cash.
(r) 28 January   Goods which cost £500 are sold for £750, £250 cash
                    being received and £500 due at the end of February.

On 31 January it was discovered that only £80 of stationery was still in hand.

   These transactions formed the basis of one of the exercises in Chapter 2, so their treatment should not pose particular problems. The emphasis of this question is on the preparation of a separate profit and loss account.

3.5 The measurement of profit

Measurement of revenues

Revenues were defined earlier as an increase in capital resulting from trading activities. This seems straightforward enough at first sight, but closer investigation shows that there is still doubt about exactly *when* revenue is recognized. If a business sells goods it could logically recognize revenue at one of several points of time, e.g.

• when the goods in which it deals are purchased
• when an order is received from a customer
• when goods are delivered to the customer
• when payment is received from the customer

Obviously, it would be useful if there was general agreement on when revenue should be recognized. The *realization convention* provides a basis for the recognition of revenue. This convention states that revenue should be recognized when:

• it is capable of objective measurement (i.e. the selling price is established), and
• the asset value receivable from the customer is reasonably certain.

A variation to this states that revenue should be recognized when the legal title to the goods passes to the customer.

   For most practical purposes, this means that when goods or services are sold, the revenue is normally recognized when they are delivered to, and accepted by, the customer. At these stages, the revenue (the price charged) will normally have been agreed, and, assuming that the customer is creditworthy, the asset value receivable (the amount included in debtors) can also be looked upon as reasonably certain. In most cases, legal title will pass with delivery.

For *example*, suppose that a business received an order for goods in December. Suppose further that the goods in question were handed over in January, and paid for by the customer in February. If *monthly* profit and loss accounts were prepared it would be necessary to decide whether the revenue would be recognized in December, January or February. Using the criteria outlined above, the revenue would be recognized in January.

Clearly some records relating to the order should be maintained by the business, but it is generally considered inappropriate to record the sale until the goods or service pass to the customer. Thus nothing will be included in the accounts which anticipates any revenue or profit.

The transactions will be first recorded in the accounts in January, on delivery of the goods to the customer as follows:

- reduce stock by the cost of the good sold
- increase cost of sales by the cost of the good sold
- increase debtors by the sale proceeds
- increase sales by the sale proceeds

On receipt of the cash from the customer in February, the following recordings will be made:

- decrease debtors
- increase cash

Activity 5
When would revenue have been recognized if the goods had been handed over in December?
    How would the transactions be reflected in the accounts?

If, in the above example, goods had been handed over in December, revenue would have been recognized in December. Whenever the goods are handed over the transaction would then be recorded as follows:

- increase debtors by the amount of the sale
- increase revenues (sales) by the amount of the sale (effectively an increase in capital)
- reduce stock by the cost of sales
- increase expenses (cost of sales) by the cost of sales (effectively a reduction in capital)

That is the same transaction as had the sale been recognized in January, but a month earlier.

In fact, the possible options for revenue recognition can become quite complex. For example, suppose that an order is received in December, along with the necessary cash from the customer to pay for the goods ordered. Assume that sufficient goods are not on hand, and have to be ordered. The order for these goods is made in January. They are received, and then delivered to the customer, in February. Payment for them is made to the creditor in March. If profit and loss accounts were prepared monthly, the question must be asked as to the appropriate month in which to recognize revenues? Following the rules of the realization convention, revenue would normally be recognized in February, on delivery of the goods to the customer. It might be argued that the two criteria – objective measurement and reasonably certain asset value – would be satisfied in December, when the order was received with cash. However, at this stage, the obligation of the business to the customer has not been satisfied, and, in practice, the second criterion is not deemed to have been met until the obligation has been satisfied.

From the above it can be seen that the recognition of revenue is not necessarily linked with the receipt of cash. In practice, revenue can be recognized:

- before the receipt of cash
- at the same time as cash is received
- after the receipt of cash

This area of accounting is one of the more difficult, mainly because of the problem of deciding what constitutes *objective measurement*, and what *reasonably certain* means. In certain types of business, the adoption of the realization convention can be a problem.

Activity 6
What problems might be found in applying the realization convention to the following:

(a) a business selling goods on hire purchase?
(b) a civil engineering business involved in a large number of long-term contracts?

(a) In businesses which sell goods on hire purchase, which typically is associated with a high proportion of bad debts, application of that part of the realization concept relating to relative certainty of receipt frequently results in revenue being recognized piecemeal, as the cash is received, rather than at the time of delivery.

(b) A civil engineering business would have problems with obtaining an objective measure of revenues for partially completed contracts, as well as some degree of uncertainty regarding payment. Typically, revenue is recognized on the basis of a proportion of certified work completed.

Self-assessment question 3.2

(a)   A business sells goods on credit to a customer in December 19X6, amounting to £1,500. Cash is received in January 19X7. How much would be shown as a revenue under the heading 'sales' in a profit and loss account prepared for the year ended 31 December 19X6? What figure, if any, relating to this transaction, would be shown in the balance sheet as at 31 December 19X6? What heading would it be shown under?

(b)   A business rents out part of its property at an annual rental of £6,000 per annum, commencing 1 January 19X7. During the year to 31 December 19X7 cash received amounts to £5,000. How much would be shown as a revenue under the heading 'rent receivable' in a profit and loss account prepared for the year ended 31 December 19X7? What figure, if any, relating to this transaction, would be shown in the balance sheet as at 31 December 19X7? What heading would it be shown under?

(c)   Assume the same information as in (b) except that during the year to 31 December 19X7 cash received amounted to £7,500.

The matching convention

The identification of revenues for a particular period is an important stage in the process of measuring profit for that period. However, it still remains necessary to identify the expenses for the period. In order to do this, we apply the *matching convention*. This convention states that *all the expenses connected with a particular revenue are to be recognized in the same period as that revenue.* This convention enables the calculation of a logical profit figure in respect of the revenues generated. Application of the matching convention means that if, for example, stock was purchased for £100 cash in December, and sold for £150 cash in January, the revenue of £150 would be recognized in January, and the expense of £100 would be matched with it in January. Thus both the £150 sale and the £100 expense would appear in January's profit and loss account.

With some types of expense, for example cost of sales (i.e. the cost of the goods which are the subject of the sale), it is fairly straightforward to match expenses to revenues in a direct way. This is because it is possible to match the *particular* expense to the *particular* revenue. Thus, it is quite straightforward, to establish the cost of a particular item of stock which has been sold. However, not all types of expense can be dealt with quite as precisely as the cost of sales expense. There are many other types of expense which either cannot be matched with a particular revenue, or where no effort is made to do so because of the cost of doing so outweighs any benefits derived. Under these circumstances, it is usual to *match on a time basis*, so that the revenues recognized in a particular period are matched with the expense incurred (but not necessarily paid for, in that period). If, for *example*, a business pays rent of £1,000 per month, which is impossible to trace to specific sales, it will normally be treated as an expense of the period to which it relates. Thus, if accounts were prepared on a monthly basis, the £1,000 rent due in (say) December would be charged as an expense against revenues earned in December, etc. Note it is the rent *incurred* rather than the actual rent *paid* which is the relevant expense item.

The accruals convention

Following the realization convention, revenues are normally recognized when the goods pass to, and are accepted by, the customer. It has also been shown, following the matching convention, that expenses should be matched with those revenues. The accruals convention complements these two by asserting that profit (or loss) for a period is the difference between the revenues recognized in that period and the expenses matched with those revenues. Profit (or loss) is *not* the difference between cash payments and cash receipts. As has already been shown, revenues can be recognized before any associated cash receipt, at the same time as any associated cash receipt, or after any associated cash receipt. The same possible relationships exist between expenses and any associated cash payment. In many cases, cash receipts *are* the same as revenues for a period, and cash payments the same as expenses. However, there are also many instances where this is not true, and the relationship between profit and cash changes is tenuous.

The measurement of expenses

It is important to remember that all transactions affect the balance sheet, whereas only certain transactions affect capital. For example, the purchase of an asset will affect the balance sheet, but will not necessarily affect capital. Such a purchase does not give rise to an expense immediately. In accounting, the name given to such an acquisition is an *expenditure* or a *cost*.

Assets are normally bought to generate wealth for a business over a period of time. Given a long enough period of time, most assets will be used up in the normal course of operations. When an asset has some part of its benefit to the business used up, that part becomes an expense. So the acquisition of an asset gives rise to an immediate cost but this will not immediately affect capital. However, as the benefit is used up, so capital will be reduced. Thus, an *expense* may be defined as an *expired cost*. An asset is an *unexpired cost*.

For *example*, suppose a business spent £2,000 on stationery in 19X6, and used a quarter of it in 19X6 and three-quarters in 19X7, there will be an expenditure of £2,000 in 19X6 and expenses of £500 and £1,500 in 19X6 and 19X7 respectively. If balance sheets were drawn up at 31 December 19X6 and 31 December 19X7 they would show £1,500 (£2,000 – £500) and nil respectively for the current asset of stationery.

The next important thing to be remembered is that, in calculating the effect on capital, it is not necessarily true that expenditure and expenses, or cash receipts and revenues, will have kept in step with each other. In other words, it is not necessarily true that the benefit of an asset will be used up in the same period as it is paid for.

For *example*, consider goods (stocks) which are acquired for the purpose of resale. When they are purchased they are an asset to the business. When they are sold they cease to be an asset and become an expense. It does not matter when they are paid for, they will cease to be an asset when they are handed over to the buyer. Stock for resale which has not been sold would be shown in the balance sheet as a current asset. The timing difference between cost (expenditure) and expenses can be more clearly seen when considering fixed assets, which usually have a life of several years. An expenditure will typically occur when the asset is first purchased. As its useful life shortens, the part of an asset which is deemed to have been consumed will be treated as an expense known as *depreciation*. The expenses associated with the earlier expenditure will thus be spread over a number of years, to match the expenses with the revenues generated.

There is often a tendency to think only of tangible items as being assets. However, services which are due to the business (i.e. which have been paid for) are also treated as assets until they are rendered. These are included in the balance sheet as *prepaid expenses*, or prepayments, as one of the items under current assets. Examples of prepaid expenses include rates paid in advance and insurance paid in advance. Once the service has been rendered, it will become an expense for the period and will cease to be shown as an asset because no further benefit can be obtained from them.

For *example*, consider a telephone rental of £75 paid quarterly in advance on 1 January 19X7. At the date this is paid there is three months' benefit remaining. At this stage, the rent paid is thus strictly an asset. However, if a balance sheet were to be drawn up at the end of January only £50 of the amount paid could reasonably be included as an asset, with the other £25 benefit having been used up in January, and hence having become an expense of January.

The above discussion relates to prepaid expenses, but in certain cases benefit can also be obtained from something before it has been paid for, as is illustrated by the following activity.

Activity 7

Suppose that on 1 December goods were purchased on credit for £1,000 and paid for on 1 January. These were subsequently sold for £1,500 cash on 15 December. If monthly profit and loss accounts were prepared would the £1,000 be treated as an expense in the December or January profit and loss account?

The answer is December, since the stock was used up in December, and could not be shown as an asset at the end of December. A moment's reflection should also make it clear that the sale of goods for £1,500 on credit would result in an increase in debtors of £1,500, and an increase in revenues (sales) of £1,500. The revenues relate to December and will be included in the December profit and loss account.

To calculate the profit, the corresponding expense should be matched with the revenue, in effect to include a net profit of £500 on the transaction. Inclusion of the expense in the January profit and loss account would lead to an understatement of expenses of £1,000 being shown in December and an overstatement of expenses of £1,000 in January. The result of this is that this particular transaction would appear to be causing profit to increase by £1,500 in December, and to decrease by £1,000 in January. Such a treatment is misleading, since the two aspects of the transaction are interrelated, and the profit and loss account should reflect this.

It can be seen from the above activity that the obligation to pay for something which has already been treated as an expense (benefit having already been used up) will be shown as a liability until payment is made. Such amounts are usually known as *accruals* or *accrued expenses*.

In summing up this section on expenses, it may be said that:

- a payment which relates to the period in which it is due will be treated as an expense, with a corresponding reduction in cash
- a payment which is made in advance will be treated as a current asset, labelled prepayments, with a corresponding reduction in cash
- an amount which is due but unpaid will be treated as an expense and as a current liability

---

Self-assessment question 3.3

(a) Stationery costing £500 was purchased on 1 January 19X6. At 31 December 19X6 £150-worth was left. How much would be shown as an expense under the heading 'stationery' in a profit and loss account prepared for the year ended 31 December 19X6? What figure would appear in a balance sheet prepared as at 31 December 19X6 relating to stationery? What heading would it be shown under?

(b) Electricity bills were paid during the year ended 31 December 19X6 amounting to £450. All of these bills relate to the year ending 31 December 19X6. One bill remains unpaid, covering the period 1 November 19X6 to 31 January 19X7, amounting to £150. How much would appear as an expense under the heading 'heating and lighting' in a profit and loss account prepared for the year ended 31 December 19X6? What figure would appear in a balance sheet prepared as at 31 December 19X6 relating to electricity? What heading would it be shown under?

(c) Rates of £200 were paid on 1 January 19X7. They relate to the period 1 October 19X6 to 31 March 19X7. How much would be included as an expense under the heading 'rates' in a profit and loss account prepared for the year ended 31 December 19X6? What figure would appear in a balance sheet prepared as at 31 December 19X6 relating to rates? What heading would it be shown under?

Assume that the level of rates is constant over the years concerned.

Self-assessment question 3.4
The following items appear in the balance sheet of Patel and Co. at 31 December 19X6:

Under current assets		*Under current liabilities*	
Debtors and prepayments		Creditors and accruals	
Rates	200	Rent	500
		Electricity	100
		Deferred revenue	
		Interest receivable	200

During the year to 31 December 19X7 the following cash receipts and payments were recorded:

Receipts
Interest – covering the 6 months from 1 April to 30 September £400

Payments

Rent – covering the quarter ending	31 December 19X6	£500
	31 March 19X7	£500
	30 June 19X7	£500
	30 September 19X7	£500
	31 December 19X7	£500
	31 March 19X8	£500
Electricity – covering the quarter ending	31 January 19X7	£150
	30 April 19X7	£120
	31 July 19X7	£ 70
	31 October 19X7	£120
Rates – covering the 6 months ending	30 September 19X7	£450
	31 March 19X8	£450

Show the revenues and expenses which would appear in the profit and loss account prepared for the year ended 31 December 19X7, and the extracts from the balance sheet as at 31 December 19X7 which relate to the above transactions.

3.6   Practical implications of accruals accounting for the preparation of final accounts

Section 3.4 sets out the basic form of final accounts, together with associated examples. The accruals convention and its associated measurement implications complicate the preparation of accounts somewhat. For example, the payment of cash for, say, rates may result in both an expense and a prepayment.

Stationery purchased may be used, in which case its cost becomes an expense, or remain on hand, in which case it is an asset. Expenses may not all be paid for when due, with the result that accruals may need to be introduced into the balance sheet. Such complications make it rather less obvious, when cash flows in and out of a business, whether these flows relate to revenues, expenses, assets or liabilities. In practice, it is usual to record transactions under an appropriate heading, and then, *at the end of the period* for which accounts are being drawn up, to allocate the total amount between assets, liabilities, revenues and expenses.

Example

The following is the balance sheet of Shah & Co as at 31.12.19X6:

Balance sheet as at 31.12.19X6

	£	£		£
Fixed assets			*Capital*	20,000
Buildings		8,000		
Equipment		5,000		
Vehicles		3,000	*Loan*	5,000
		16,000		
Current assets			*Current liabilities*	
Stock	5,000		Creditors	3,500
Debtors	3,000			
Cash	4,500			
		12,500		
		28.500		28.500

Given below is a summary of the transactions which took place during the year to 31 December 19X7. (N.B. This list does not reflect the order in which transactions took place.)

(a) Stock purchased on credit £42,000.
(b) Sales for cash £10,000 (original cost of goods £6,000).
(c) Sales on credit £40,000 (original cost of goods £24,000).
(d) Cash received from debtors £36,000.
(e) Cash paid to creditors £35,000.
(f) Cash paid for wages (all relating to the year) £5,000.
(g) Cash paid for other expenses £3,000.
(h) Rent paid amounts to £1,500, covering the period 1 January 19X7 to 31 March 19X8.
(i) Rates paid amount to £750, covering the period 1 January 19X7 to 30 September 19X7.
(j) The owner withdrew £2,500 in cash.

At the end of the year you note the following:

(a) A rates demand has been received, relating to the period 1 October 19X7 to 31 March 19X8, amounting to £500;
(b) Depreciation of equipment is to be taken, amounting to £1,000, together with depreciation of vehicles, amounting to £600.

The first stage is to record all of the transactions in the way described earlier, other than the two adjustments set out above. The result, before totalling, should appear as follows:

Balance sheet as at 31 December 19X7

	+	−	Net		+	−	Net
	£	£	£		£	£	£
Fixed assets				*Capital*			
Buildings	8,000			Opening balance	20,000		
Equipment	5,000			+ Net profit			
Vehicles	3,000			− Drawings		2,500	
Current assets							
Stock	5,000	6,000b		*Loan*	5,000		
	42,000a	24,000b					
Debtors	3,000	36,000d		*Current liabilities*			
	40,000c			Creditors	3,500	35,000e	
					42,000a		
Cash	4,500	35,000e					
	10,000b	5,000f					
	36,000d	3,000g					
		1,500h					
		750i					
		2,500j					

Profit and loss account for the year ended 31 December 19X7

Expenses	+	−	Net	*Revenues*	+	−	Net
	£	£	£		£	£	£
Cost of sales	6,000b			Sales − cash	10,000b		
	24,000c			− credit	40,000c		
Wages	5,000f						
Other expenses	3,000g						
Rent	1,500h						
Rates	750i						
Net profit							

At this stage note needs to be taken of any adjustments needed. As well as the two identified above, it is important to note that the amount paid for rent was recorded initially as an expense, even though part of this amount relates to the following year. A further adjustment is thus needed for this, giving three adjustments to be made overall:

(a) *Rent*. Of the £1,500 paid it may reasonably be inferred that £300 relates to the period 1 January to 31 March 19X8. The adjustment needed is thus:

- reduce the expense rent by £300
- increase an asset (prepayments) by £300

(b) *Rates*. Since the period of profit calculation is 1 January to 31 December 19X7, the rates due for this period should be included as an expense. Only 9 months have so far been included, so an additional £250 should be added to the expense (relating to the period 1 October to 31 December), with the appropriate amount outstanding being shown as an accrual. The adjustment needed is thus:

- increase the expense rates by £250
- increase a liability (accruals) by £250

(c) *Depreciation*. Since the asset is being used up and becoming an expense the adjustments needed are:

Equipment:
- increase an expense (depreciation of equipment) by £1,000
- reduce the asset equipment by £1,000

Vehicles:
- increase an expense (depreciation of vehicles) by £600
- reduce the asset vehicles by £600

These adjustments, and the resulting final accounts, are shown below.

Balance sheet as at 31 December 19X7

	+	–	Net		+	–	Net
	£	£	£		£	£	£
Fixed assets				*Capital*			
Buildings	8,000		8,000	Opening balance	20,000		20,000
Equipment	5,000	1,000adj	4,000	+ Net profit	8,200		8,200
Vehicles	3,000	600adj	2,400				28,200
			14,400	–Drawings		2,500	–2,500
							25,700
Current assets							
Stock	5,000	6,000b	17,000	*Loan*	5,000		5,000
	42,000a	24,000b					
Prepayments	300adj		300				

Debtors	3,000	36,000d	7,000	*Current liabilities*			
	40,000c			Creditors	3,500	35,000e	10,500
					42,000a		
Cash	4,500	35,000e	2,750				
	10,000b	5,000f		Accruals	250adj		250
	36,000d	3,000g					
		1,500h					
		750i					
		2,500j					
			41,450				41,450

Profit and loss account for the year ended 31 December 19X7

Expenses	+	–	Net	*Revenues*	+	–	Net
	£	£	£		£	£	£
Cost of sales	6,000b		30,000	Sales – cash	10,000b		10,000
	24,000c			– credit	40,000c		40,000
Wages	5,000f		5,000				
Other expenses	3,000g		3,000				
Rent	1,500h	300adj	1,200				
Rates	750i		1,000				
	250adj						
Depreciation							
equipment	1,000adj		1,000				
vehicles	600adj		600				
			41,800				
Net profit			8,200				
			50,000				50,000

Adjustments between the various headings are commonly found to be needed for the following:

(a) prepayments and accruals
(b) prepayments to a business and deferred revenues
(c) depreciation
(d) debtors (to cover any bad debts)
(e) stock (depending upon the approach used, see below)

The adjustments for prepayments and accruals have been seen above. A similar process is needed for adjustments related to prepayments to a business and deferred revenues, albeit on opposite sides. The adjustments needed for depreciation have also been seen above, although a more informative treatment will be discussed in Chapter 4. The adjustment for debtors relates to bad debts and effectively results in part of the asset debtors becoming an expense.

Self-assessment question 3.5

Milly commenced business on 1 January 19X7. The following information has been collected concerning the business transactions over the first two months of trading.

January 1   Paid £60,000 cash into the business.
            Borrowed £20,000 from her parents (interest-free).
        2   Purchased a property for £55,000 cash.
        3   Purchased a delivery van for £3,000 cash.
            Paid road tax and insurance for the van for 1 year, ending 31 December 19X7. Total amount £360.
        4   Purchased new till for £500.
        5   Paid £2,000 cash for shop fittings.
            Arranged with bank that overdraft facilities up to £5,000 would be available as required.
        6   Acquired stock costing £2,000 on credit.

On 7 January the shop was opened for business and the following is a summary of the transactions up to the end of February:

(a) Further stock purchased on credit £4,200.
(b) Cash sales £5,000 (cost of sales £2,900).
(c) Credit sales £2,000 (cost of sales £1,250).
(d) Shop assistants' wages £500.
(e) Vehicle expenses £150.
(f) Goods returned to suppliers at cost £150.
(g) Paid to suppliers for goods supplied £3,500, in satisfaction of debts of £3,600, the difference being discount.
(h) Received from debtors £1,800.
(i) Paid rates on the shop for the period 2 January to 31 March, amounting to £300.
(j) Paid an electricity bill for January, amounting to £75.
(k) Milly withdrew £1,000 for her personal use.

You have been asked to prepare a profit and loss account for the period 1 January to 28 February and a balance sheet as at 28 February. By the time you do this, a telephone bill covering the 10 weeks to mid-March has been received, amounting to £60. Depreciation of vehicles is to be calculated at the equivalent of 20% per annum on cost.

3.7 Form and content of profit and loss accounts

The guidance given so far on the form of the profit and loss account has been somewhat limited, effectively saying that it consisted of revenues on the one hand and expenses on the other. In practice, rather more thought is given to grouping revenues and expenses under appropriate headings, and the profit and loss account is typically split into various sections, according to the type of activity in which the business is engaged. This section is particularly concerned with trading businesses.

When a business is engaged in buying and selling, it is common to split the profit and loss account into two sections:

- one which matches cost of sales with sales, to show a figure known as *gross profit*;
- a second one which deducts any remaining expenses from the gross profit.

The first section is referred to as the *trading account*. The second section is typically referred to as the *profit and loss account*. The trading account is in fact nothing more than a subdivision of the profit and loss account or income statement. An overall heading of '*Trading and profit and loss account for the year ended ...*' is frequently used. Many users of accounts feel that highlighting the gross profit figure is useful, hence the existence of the trading account.

In previous examples we have used a two-sided format for the profit and loss account. Whilst this is quite useful for illustrating the way in which the profit and loss account is built up, it is usual to present profit and loss accounts in a narrative or vertical format. An example of this format is as follows:

Trading and profit and loss account for the year ended ——

	£	£	£
Sales			x
Less cost of sales			x
Gross profit			x
Add Other revenues			
Rent		x	
Interest		x	
			x
			x
Less Other expenses			
Administration*		x	
Finance*		x	
Selling and distribution*		x	
			x
Net profit			x

*These headings are suggestions only. Each business should choose headings which are appropriate to the information needs of its accounts' users. Further subdivisions into individual expense headings are also dependent upon the needs of the business.

This format will be used in subsequent chapters and so it is important to be familiar with it.

Self-assessment question 3.6
On 1 January, Janet has the following balances in her accounts:

Premises	£25,000	Equipment	£6,000	Loan (interest	
Vehicles	£3,500	Stock	£3,000	at 10%)	£10,000
Cash	£2,000	Accrued wages	£300	Debtors	£4,500
Prepaid rent	£200	Creditors	£2,000	Accrued rates	£500
				Capital	£31,400

During the year the following transactions took place:

(a) Purchased stock for £30,000 on credit.
(b) Sales (all on credit) amounted to £59,700 (original cost of stock sold £27,500).
(c) Carriage paid on sales £300.
(d) Rent paid £3,000.
(e) Wages paid amounting to £8,000.
(f) Janet withdraws £5,000 cash and £1,500 of stock for her own use.
(g) Rates of £2,000 are paid.
(h) Stationery amounting to £250 is purchased.
(i) General expenses amounting to £2,500 are paid.
(j) Cash of £59,000 is received from debtors.
(k) Cash paid to creditors £28,000.
(l) Fuel and electricity bills are paid amounting to £1,000.
(m) Motor expenses of £1,250 are paid.

At the year end the following information is available:

(i) Stationery on hand is valued at £150.
(ii) An unpaid electricity bill amounting to £150 exists, covering the last quarter.
(iii) £100 of the motor expenses relates to tax for the following year.
(iv) General expenses of £250 are outstanding.
(v) Depreciation on equipment of £800, and on vehicles of £1,000 is to be provided for.

Prepare a trading and profit and loss account for the year and a balance sheet as at the year end.

Where a business provides a service, rather than goods, the profit and loss account will simply deduct expenses from revenues, without the use of a trading account. In manufacturing businesses, goods will typically be produced, rather than bought in. Manufacturing brings with it its own associated costs, and these are generally shown separately in a manufacturing account. This account accumulates the various costs of manufacture and the total cost is then transferred to the trading account. This amount replaces purchases (of bought-in goods) in the trading account.

3.8   Summary

This chapter has provided you with an appreciation of the nature and purpose of a profit and loss account, and its likely format. In particular, it has emphasized that the profit and loss account is effectively an appendix to the capital section of the balance sheet, presented in a form which is rather more useful to users of accounting information. The profit (or loss) for a period is calculated by deducting expenses from revenues. The realization convention was explained, and applied to the definition of revenues. Expenses were then matched against appropriate revenues to calculate profit. Particular attention was paid to this aspect of profit measurement, and to the explanation of the accruals convention. Profit is the difference between revenues and expenses, not the difference between cash receipts and cash payments. Differences between cash payments and expenses will be reflected in prepayments or accruals in the balance sheet, while differences between cash receipts and revenues will be reflected in the balance sheet as debtors or deferred revenues. You should now be able to prepare a profit and loss account and balance sheet, in good style, from a set of basic transactions.

Exercises

1   The following cash payments are made relating to electricity for a business:

Payment date	Period covered	Amount
15 April 19X1	1 January to 28 February 19X1	£200
1 July 19X1	1 March to 31 May 19X1	£350
30 September 19X1	1 June to 31 August 19X1	£200
20 December 19X1	1 September to 30 November 19X1	£350
10 April 19X2	1 December 19X1 to 28 February 19X2	£300
5 July 19X2	1 March to 31 May 19X2	£300
1 October 19X2	1 June to 31 August 19X2	£200
1 January 19X3	1 September to 30 November	£350
1 April 19X3	1 December to 28 February 19X3	£450

Assuming that the business has a financial year from 1 January to 31 December, show:

(a) the expense for electricity which will be included in the profit and loss accounts for the years ended 31 December 19X1 and 19X2.

(b) any amounts relating to electricity which will be included in the balance sheets as at 31 December 19X1 and 19X2.

2 (a) One business lends £10,000 to another business on 1 January 19X1, at an annual rate of interest of 15%. Its financial year is from 1 October to 30 September. Cash received relating to interest on the loan is as follows:

30 June 19X1	£750
1 January 19X2	£750
30 June 19X2	£750
31 December 19X2	£750

Show how the revenue (rent receivable) would appear in the profit and loss account for the years ending 30 September 19X1 and 19X2, and any related entries in the balance sheets as at 30 September 19X1 and 19X2.

(b) A business rents a property to a tenant from 1 January 19X7 at an agreed rental of £10,000 per annum. Its financial year runs from 1 January to 31 December.

Cash relating to the rental is received as follows:

1 January 19X6	£5,000
30 June 19X6	£5,000
31 December 19X6	£5,000
1 July 19X7	£5,000
1 January 19X8	£5,000

The tenant was in financial difficulties from mid 19X8, and it is agreed that any arrears of rent will be paid in 19X9.

Show how the revenue (rent receivable) would appear in the profit and loss accounts for 19X6, 19X7 and 19X8, and any related entries in the balance sheets at the end of these years.

3 Complete the following table to show the relationship between expenditure, expenses, assets and liabilities by writing the appropriate figure, to replace each *x*.

	Balance sheet as at the beginning of a year		Expenditure during year	Expense for year	Balance sheet as at the end of the same year	
	Assets	Liabilities			Assets	Liabilities
	£	£	£	£	£	£
Stationery	25		125	x	20	
Fuel	50		220	200	x	
Equipment	1,000		1,000	x	x	
(depreciate @20% of balance at year end)						
Wages		10	900	x		20
Heating		30	300	x	30	
Rent	50		x	250		50
Rates	75		300	x	85	
Stock	1,250		x	7,750	1,000	
Lighting		15	x	65		25
Property	5,000		5,000		x	
(no depreciation)						

4 Complete the following table to show the relationship between expenditure, expenses, assets and liabilities by writing the appropriate figure, to replace each x.

	Balance sheet as at the beginning of a year		Expenditure during year	Revenue/ expense for year	Balance sheet as at the end of the same year	
	Assets	Liabilities			Assets	Liabilities
	£	£	£	£	£	£
Rent receivable	100		900	x	200	
Rent receivable	100		900	x	200	
Rent receivable		100	x	800	100	
Rent receivable		100	x	500		200
Sales/debtors	2,000		x	10,000	2,500	
Sales/debtors	2,000		10,000	x	3,000	
Sales/debtors	1,000		8,000	9,000	x	
Sales/debtors	x		9,000	8,000	3,000	

What is the name given to a liability which relates to a revenue?

5 A business has the following assets and liabilities at 31 December 19X6:

	£		£		£
Buildings	11,000	Motor vehicles	3,000	Prepaid rent	80
Plant	2,200	Stock	5,300	Debtors	3,700
Cash	2,200	Loan (12%)	3,000	Creditors	2,600
Accrued heat and light	90				

During 19X7 the following transactions took place:

(a) Purchased stock

- on credit for £27,000.
- for cash for £6,000.

(b) Paid creditors £23,000.
(c) Made sales

- cash £23,000 (stock originally cost £16,500).
- credit £27,000 (stock originally cost £17,800).

(d) Received cash from debtors amounting to £28,500.
(e) Expenses of packing/despatch, etc. were paid amounting to £750.
(f) Wages amounting to £9,800 were paid, £300 of which related to 19X8.
(g) Rent of £800 was paid, covering a period of 10 months.
(h) Heating and lighting of £780 were paid.
(i) Administration expenses of £2,100 were paid.
(j) General and miscellaneous expenses of £1,000 were paid.

At 31 December 19X7:

(a) £500 of debtors is believed unlikely to be received.
(b) The following expenses are found to be unpaid:

- Heat and light £100.
- Administration £200.

(c) Equipment and vehicles are to be depreciated at 25% p.a. on cost.

Prepare a profit and loss account for the year ended 31 December 19X7 and a balance sheet as at that date.

6 Pat Trill rents a property from which he runs a retailing business. The annual rental payable is £4,000. The property has three floors, and Pat decides to sublet one floor to a firm of solicitors who wish to open a small branch office in the town. The annual rent receivable is £1,500.

Pat's accounts are made up for the financial year ending 30 June.

The balance sheet prepared for Pat's business on 30 June 19X4 showed, among other things, the following:

Debtors and prepayments
Rent receivable   £375
Prepaid rent   £1,000

During the following years the following cash transactions are made relating to rent payable and rent receivable:

	Rent paid	Rent received
	£	£
Year to 30 June 19X5	4,000	1,875
Year to 30 June 19X6	3,000	1,125
Year to 30 June 19X7	3,000	2,250

Show:

(a) the amounts which will be included for the revenue 'rent receivable' and the expense 'rent payable', for each of the three financial years ended 30 June 19X5, 19X6 and 19X7;

(b) the relevant figures in the balance sheets prepared at the end of these three financial years.

7   The following is the balance sheet of a business at the beginning of its financial year (1 January 19X7):

	£		£
Fixed assets		*Capital*	8,000
Buildings	5,000		
Equipment	2,000		
	7,000		
Current assets		*Current liabilities*	
Stock	1,000	Creditors	2,000
Debtors	1,000		
Cash	1,000		
	10,000		10,000

The following is a summary of the transactions which took place during the next year:

1   Stock was purchased for £5,000 cash.
2   Stock was purchased for £8,000 on credit.
3   Cash sales were £20,000 (original cost £10,000).
4   Credit sales were £5,000 (original cost £2,500).
5   Wages paid were £2,000.
6   Rent of £500 was paid covering the 15 months to 31 March 19X8.
7   General expenses of £500 were paid.
8   Debtors paid cash amounting to £4,000.
9   Creditors were paid £7,000.
10 Further equipment was purchased for £2,000, financed by a loan (interest free).
11 The owner withdrew £1,000 in cash.

At the year end general expenses of £500 were owing.
   Prepare a profit and loss account for 19X7 and a balance sheet at 31.12.19X7.

4

The measurement of profit – further issues

4.1 Introduction

This chapter aims to give further consideration to the problems of measuring profit (income), particularly in the areas of depreciation, stock valuation and bad and doubtful debts. It also provides a review of the conventions dealt with so far.

4.2 Objectives

On completion of this chapter you should be able:

- to explain the concept of depreciation, and be able to apply this concept in a practical way with regard to final accounts;
- to justify and use the alternative valuation bases which may be used with regard to stock;
- to explain the nature of bad debts and bad debt provisions, and incorporate appropriate entries in a set of final accounts;
- to explain the need for, and role of accounting standards and conventions.

4.3 Problems of applying the matching convention

We have already seen that, in accounting, profit is measured following the matching convention.

Activity 1
Can you remember what the matching convention says?
  Jot your answer down on a piece of paper.

You should have answered something like this:

The matching convention says that, in measuring profit, we should match expenses to the revenues which they help to generate, in the same accounting period. In order to gain anything useful from the profit and loss account we need to be able to see the net effect of the revenues for the period. Unless we are careful to set the expenses incurred in earning the revenues against those revenues we shall get a distorted view of trading.

In examples which we have considered so far in this book, matching expenses to revenues has tended to be pretty straightforward. In practice, however, it is frequently problematical. This is because there are sometimes different views on what is the appropriate way to match. This leads to preparers of financial statements needing to make judgements on what is the most appropriate approach. In this chapter we are going to consider three areas where matching tends to raise problems. We shall see that, in practice, the profit figure which emerges from the profit and loss account is not, as you may previously have supposed, definite and unequivocal. The expenses set against the revenues for a period are the product of some factual information about transactions and some judgements about the application of the matching convention. As we shall see, the amounts involved can be very significant.

4.4   Measurement problems – depreciation

Depreciation theory

Assets have been broadly defined as expected future benefits, while expenses can be seen as benefits used up. When fixed assets are acquired they will be shown, in the balance sheet, as assets (at historic cost). However, the benefits inherent in fixed assets tend to be used up over time, with the result that after a period of time, the future benefit remaining will tend to be low, or even nil. Since the profit and loss account matches the expenses incurred in generating revenues to those revenues, some attempt needs to be made to calculate the amount of depreciation to be set against the revenues generated period by period.

Activity 2
Can you think of any fixed assets which do not depreciate?
  Jot your answer down on a piece of paper.

The obvious one which occurred to us is freehold land. Land is an asset which tends not to depreciate as a result either of usage or the mere passage of time. This is because land tends to hold its value. You may well have thought of some other answer which is equally correct.

It is clear that the amount of benefit which has actually been used up can only be ascertained at the end of a fixed asset's life. It is impossible to tell with complete accuracy how much benefit has been used up in each accounting period. All that can be done is to make an *estimate* of the amount of benefit used up in each year, on some *systematic and rational basis*. When a fixed asset is disposed of, the total *actual* depreciation over its life can be ascertained. This can be compared with the estimated depreciation, which has been treated as an expense over the life of the asset. If there is a difference between these two figures, the necessary adjustment can be made.

It is important to note that depreciation is not a process of valuation, but one of allocation. By way of example, suppose that a retail business paid £800 for a sign to be put up in front of one of its shops, with the name of the business on the sign. This is a fixed asset because it has likely future economic benefit and it is not bought for resale. Suppose also that the business has a policy of changing its signs for more up-to-date ones every four years. It seems pretty likely that the sign will have zero second-hand value, even when it is brand new. No other person or business would be likely to want to buy it. If the annual depreciation expense were the fall in market value, the annual depreciation charges would be £800 in the year of purchase of the sign and zero for each of the next three years of the life of the sign. Since this asset has been purchased in the expectation that it will be kept for four years and that it will perform to the same level of efficiency for each of the four years of its life, with negligible charges for repairs and maintenance, the amount of the benefit expected to be obtained from the asset would be much the same for each year, and annual charges based upon the above figures would not appear appropriate. A more rational and systematic approach would be to charge depreciation evenly over the asset's life, namely £200 for each year.

Such an approach has the result that fixed assets will not be shown in balance sheets at their current value, but at cost less depreciation, the resulting figure being known as *net book value* or *written-down value*. Given the going concern convention (see Chapter 2) it is not necessary to show current values of fixed assets, since it is assumed that the business will not be sold. In interpreting accounts, however, it is important to recognize that potentially significant differences may exist between book and current market values.

The second approach suggested above (namely £200 depreciation each year) is the result of *allocating* depreciation over the estimated life of the asset, in line with the benefits used up. It is based upon an assumption that the total expense of having the asset for the four years is £800, and this has been allocated equally to each year in line with the estimated benefit used up.

Depreciation can therefore be defined as a systematic and rational method of allocating that part of the cost of an asset, the benefit of which has been used up during an accounting period. It is important to remember that, in considering depreciation, the charge for each period will be dependent on factors, not all of which are known at the time that the charge is made. Depreciation is thus not a precise measurement process.

There are four main factors which need to be considered in arriving at an appropriate depreciation figure:

(a) The cost of the asset
(b) The disposal or salvage value of the asset

These two are necessary to be able to ascertain the estimated total depreciation which is to be allocated, namely the difference between the two items.

(c)   The useful life of the asset in the business

Obviously some idea of the period over which the total is to be allocated is
necessary.

(d)   A method of depreciation which is both systematic and rational

Each of these four factors will now be considered in detail.
   The *cost of an asset* will include all costs incurred in acquiring an asset, in
installing it, and generally making it ready for use. For example, part of the cost
of a shop sign will be the cost of installing it in front of the shop. Similarly, in
the purchase of an asset such as a building, legal costs would be treated as part
of the cost. Since buildings cannot normally be bought without incurring legal
expenses these must be seen as an integral part of their cost. Installation costs
of machinery are frequently necessary. They are as necessary to the ability of
the machine to carry out its purpose as are the costs of obtaining the machine,
because without them the machine will lie idle. Costs such as installation and
legal costs cannot reasonably be matched against the revenues of just the period
during which they are incurred. In the balance sheet they are therefore added
to the cost of obtaining the machine.
   The *useful life of an asset* depends on two factors, deterioration and obsolescence. Most fixed assets suffer a deterioration in their physical condition, either
due to usage or to the passage of time or perhaps both. In time they will deteri-
orate to such a condition that no further benefit can be obtained from them.
The time that it takes to get to this condition represents their useful physical
life. Given a guarantee of reasonable care it is usually fairly easy for a technical expert to make an estimate of the physical useful life of an asset. However,
there is another factor to be taken into account in estimating the useful life of
an asset to the business. This is the factor known as *obsolescence*, which relates
to the fact that an asset may become out of date, and cease to be able to
compete effectively with newer assets. The period of expected useful life with
regard to competing effectively is known as the *economic life* of an asset.
   It is quite possible that an asset may be purchased with a physical life well
in excess of its economic life. For example, suppose that a business buys equipment which has a virtually guaranteed physical life of 10 years, but that this
business then finds that after three years new equipment is invented which does
the same job as the old, at half the cost. Under such circumstances it is highly
likely that use of the old equipment would cease after three years. This would
mean that the amounts charged for depreciation during the three years of useful
life would not cover the actual depreciation over that period. This in turn means
that the amount of depreciation matched against the revenues of those three
years will be very much less than it should have been. This will result in an
overstatement of profit for each of the three years. Clearly, therefore, a realistic

attempt should be made to estimate the likely economic life of an asset, and not just its physical life, since the economic life may be the more important factor. Depreciation should be based upon the shorter of the two lives. Useful economic life may be influenced by such factors as technological progress, changes in consumer demand, and changes in supply due to greater competition. Such factors are difficult for the individual business to anticipate or control, but some attempt should be made if a sensible depreciation policy is to be achieved. As much objective evidence as is obtainable should be considered in arriving at the estimate.

Activity 3

Which types of fixed asset would tend to have economic lives shorter than their physical lives?

For which types of fixed asset would the two lives tend to be the same?

Jot your answer down on a piece of paper.

Generally it is assets in areas where innovation and changing technology are important which tend to have economic lives which are shorter than the economic ones. Thus computers tend to have economic lives shorter than their physical lives. Many old computers still work as well as ever they did. Their economic life may well be over, however, because more recently developed hardware may be able to perform a much better job, perhaps at no great cost.

Generally assets in traditional, low-technology areas tend to have economic value for as long as they continue to do the job. An example is a hammer used by a carpenter.

The *disposal* or *salvage value*, which needs to be estimated in order to calculate the total expense to be allocated over the useful life of the asset, poses similar problems, and can often be little more than an informed guess. If the useful life is expected to be the physical life then it is likely that a technical expert could make a reasonable estimate of salvage value. Where the useful life is the economic life, any estimate made is unlikely to be very accurate. It is very difficult to estimate whether a change in economic factors will make an asset completely obsolete, or whether it will simply make it obsolete for one particular business (i.e. some other business may still be able to use it profitably). It is, therefore, difficult to tell whether the disposal value will be a fairly high second-hand value, or a very low scrap value. Any such judgement will be highly subjective. The convention of prudence (dealt with immediately below) means that a pessimistic view of disposal value is usually taken.

Prudence (or conservatism)

Depreciation provides us with our first real meeting with the prudence convention. This convention says that in preparing financial statements, we should err on the cautious side. Hence profits are usually only recognized when they have been realized (see realization convention), while losses are usually taken fully into account as soon as their likelihood is seen. Accounting has a number of areas, of which depreciation is just one, where more than one approach may be taken. This convention maintains that the more prudent approach should always be taken.

In the context of depreciation, the prudence convention encourages preparers of accounting statements to underestimate both the useful lives of assets and their likely disposal values, rather than to overestimate them.

In practice, deducing the depreciation expense for a period is somewhat unsatisfactory, in that objectivity can rarely be achieved, while prudence tends to encourage the use of pessimistic figures. Clearly the information necessary to calculate depreciation charges for a period is extremely difficult to estimate. Depreciation should be based on information which is as objective as possible. Nevertheless a high degree of subjectivity exists.

Activity 4

Can you define depreciation, and outline the four main factors which are needed to ensure an appropriate depreciation charge in the profit and loss account?

See if you can remember the answers without looking back. Jot your answer down on a sheet of paper.

We saw above that depreciation can be defined as a systematic and rational method of allocating that part of the cost of an asset, the benefit of which has been used up during an accounting period.

The four main factors which need to be considered in arriving at an appropriate depreciation figure are:

(a)   The cost of the asset,
(b)   The disposal or salvage value of the asset,
(c)   The useful life of the asset in the business, and
(d)   A method of depreciation which is both systematic and rational.

Methods of depreciation

This section deals with possible methods of allocating depreciation to each accounting period on a systematic and rational basis. Once the cost of the asset has been identified and the disposal proceeds (residual value) estimated, the estimated expense of owning the asset, over its useful life, is identifiable (i.e. cost less residual value). This total expense can be allocated in any way considered appropriate, and a number of variations can be found in practice. Nevertheless, most businesses appear to have adopted one of two methods, namely:

(a) straight-line depreciation, and
(b) reducing-balance depreciation.

Straight-line depreciation

The basis of this method is that the amount of benefit lost during the useful life of an asset is spread evenly over the whole of that life. This can be summarized in the following:

$$\textbf{Annual depreciation} = \frac{\textbf{original cost} - \textbf{disposal value}}{\textbf{useful life}}$$

For example, consider an asset which costs £550, which has an estimated useful life of five years and scrap value of £50. The total cost which has to be allocated over the five years is £500, being the original cost less the scrap value. Using the straight-line method the assumption is made that benefit is obtained equally in each of the five years. The annual depreciation charge would therefore be £100, being the total cost to be allocated divided by the time over which it is to be allocated. This method is by far the most popular of those used in practice in the UK.

The reason that this method of depreciation is called straight-line depreciation is because, if the net book value (cost less depreciation) is graphed against time, the result is a straight line. Such a graph for the above example is shown in Figure 4.1.

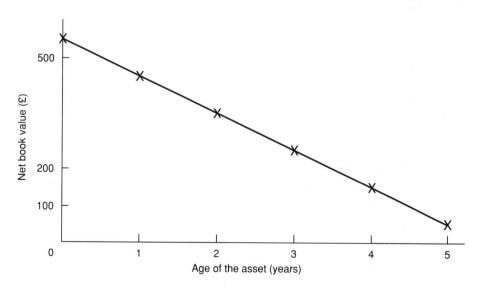

Figure 4.1 *Graph of net book value against age, using the straight-line depreciation method*

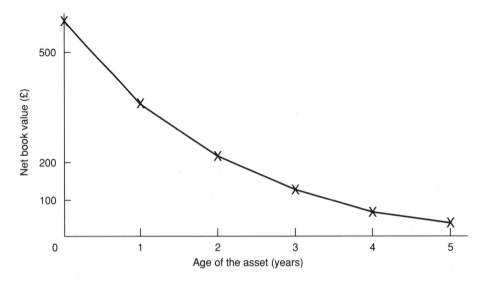

Figure 4.2 *Graph of net book value against age, using the reducing-balance depreciation method*

Reducing-balance depreciation

This method leads to a relatively large annual depreciation expense in the first year of ownership of the asset, reducing year by year as the life of the asset increases. Figure 4.2 uses the same data as in Figure 4.1, except that the reducing-balance method of depreciation has been used.

There are two main justifications for taking this approach:

- prudence
- matching

By treating relatively large parts of the cost of assets as a depreciation expense in the early years, a prudent view is taken. This is justified by the difficult judgements which often need to be made in assessing the two unknown factors (economic life and residual value) which are not known when annual depreciation expenses are being assessed.

This approach also recognizes that with certain assets, it is necessary to pay an increasing sum for repairs and maintenance in order to preserve the same operating efficiency from year to year. The cost of the asset and the cost of repairs and maintenance are thus *both* integral parts of the preservation of efficiency, and therefore a system should be devised which equates the total charge for the year. This will include both depreciation and repairs and maintenance charges. Since in the early years of an asset's life repairs and maintenance costs are likely to be low while in later years they rise, the amount of depreciation charged each year must decrease if the total charge for each accounting period is to be approximately the same. Where the asset concerned is helping to generate a fairly steady level of revenues over its life, it is appropriate that a fairly steady expense of operating the asset is matched against each year's revenues.

Activity 5

Consider an asset which cost £550, which is expected to have a residual value of £50 after a life of 5 years. Suppose now that the costs of repairs and maintenance are expected to be as shown in the table below.

Complete the table assuming straight-line depreciation.

Year	Depreciation	Repairs and maintenance	Total
	£	£	£
1	....	nil	....
2	....	50	....
3	....	100	....
4	....	150	....
5	....	200	....

Your answer should look like this:

Year	Depreciation	Repairs and maintenance	Total
	£	£	£
1	100	nil	100
2	100	50	150
3	100	100	200
4	100	150	250
5	100	200	300

In respect of the above activity, let us assume that the repairs and maintenance costs have been incurred to preserve the same operating efficiency of the asset from year to year. Under this assumption it seems inappropriate to allocate depreciation on the straight-line basis, and thus to charge an increasing total amount from year to year. What is required is a system which allocates depreciation in such a way that a decrease in depreciation from year to year approximately equals the expected increase in repairs and maintenance over the same period, thus equating the total cost.

The usual method of reducing the depreciation charge each year is to take a fixed percentage of the written-down value at the beginning of the period. In other words, depreciation is charged as a percentage of a reducing balance. A formula exists which enables a percentage rate to be calculated which will spread the total depreciation expense over the expected life.

Activity 6

Complete the following table for the asset referred to in Activity 5, using the reducing-balance method of depreciation, at a rate of 40%.

Year	Depreciation		Repairs and maintenance	Total
		£	£	£
1	Cost 550 × 40%	220	nil	220
2	Book value 330 × 40% =	......	50	....
3	Book value ...... × 40% =	......	100	....
4	Book value ...... × 40% =	......	150	....
5	Book value ...... × 40% =	......	200	....
	Residual value approximately			

Your table should look something like this:

Year	Depreciation	Repairs and maintenance	Total
	£	£	£
1	550 × 40% = 220	nil	220
2	330 × 40% = 132	50	182
3	198 × 40% = 80	100	180
4	118 × 40% = 48	150	198
5	70 × 40% = 28	200	228
	Residual value = £42		

It can be seen from Activity 6 that the annual total charge is more appropriate than the total charge in Activity 5, given the assumptions made. The reducing-balance method would also be appropriate for assets where the benefits are expected to be greater in earlier years, so a greater portion needs to be matched to revenues in earlier years.

For assets where time is the chief factor, as far as using up assets is concerned, the straight-line method is more likely to be used. Where assets become less efficient with age and increases in repairs and maintenance result, the reducing-balance method is the more appropriate.

Activity 7

Can you think of any assets where the passage of time, rather than wear or obsolescence, is the only factor causing depreciation?

We believe that assets which involve the right to do something provide examples of such assets. A purchased lease, i.e. the right to occupy premises for some period of time, depreciates as the life of the lease moves towards its end. Provided that the premises are not physically deteriorating, or becoming obsolete in some way, passage of time is likely to be the only reason for the depreciation.

A variation on the reducing-balance method is the *sum of the digits method*. This method is so called because the number of years (the digits) of the asset's life are summed, and the depreciation allocated each year is expressed as a fraction of this figure. To make this clearer, consider an example.

Suppose an asset is expected to last for three years. The sum of the digits is one plus two plus three, the years of its life, giving a total of six. The depreciation allocated each year is then arrived at by expressing the digits as fractions of the total, six, putting them in descending order, to make the depreciation expense higher in the earlier years. In other words, in Year 1 the depreciation allocated would be 3/6, in Year 2 it would be 2/6 and in Year 3, 1/6. This again gives us a reducing amount of depreciation from year to year. This method has the not inconsiderable advantage of being easy to understand and to apply.

Activity 8

Using the same figures as in Activities 5 and 6, namely an asset which costs £550, with a disposal value of £50, and repairs and maintenance costs as shown, complete the table below, assuming depreciation has been calculated using the sum of the digits method.

Year	Depreciation	Repairs and maintenance	Total
	£	£	£
1	....	nil	....
2	....	50	....
3	....	100	....
4	....	150	....
5	....	200	....

Is this method more or less suitable than that of Activity 6, given the assumptions made?

Your table should look something like this:

Year	Depreciation	Repairs and maintenance	Total
	£	£	£
1	5/15 × 500 = 167	nil	167
2	4/15 × 500 = 133	50	183
3	3/15 × 500 = 100	100	200
4	2/15 × 500 = 67	150	217
5	1/15 × 500 = 33	200	233

The resulting figures suggest that this method is less suitable than the reducing-balance method used in Activity 6, given the assumptions made, since the total charge is less steady over the 5 years.

Accounting entries

Once the figure for annual depreciation has been calculated, appropriate entries must be made in the profit and loss account and balance sheet. You will recall that, when an expense is recognized, we:

- increase expenses (in effect, reduce capital)
- reduce an asset or increase a claim

by the amount of the expense.
    As an example of dealing with the depreciation expense, let us consider the figures from Activity 8 (an asset which cost £550, has a disposal value of £50, which is expected to last 5 years) the entries would be as follows, assuming straight-line depreciation:

Year 1
- include depreciation expense in profit and loss account
- reduce the asset

by £100 (the depreciation expense for the year).
The asset will thus be shown in the balance sheet at £550 – £100 = £450 written-down (or book) value.

Year 2
- include depreciation expense in profit and loss account
- reduce the asset

by £100 (the depreciation expense for the year).
    The asset will thus be shown in the balance sheet at £550 – £200 = £350 written-down (or book) value.

Year 3
- include depreciation expense in profit and loss account
- reduce the asset

by £100 (the depreciation expense for the year).

The asset will thus be shown in the balance sheet at £550 – £300 = £250 written-down (or book) value.

Year 4
- include the depreciation expense in profit and loss account
- reduce the asset

by £100 (the depreciation expense for the year).

The asset will thus be shown in the balance sheet at £550 – £400 = £150 written-down (or book) value.

Year 5
- include depreciation expense in profit and loss account
- reduce the asset

by £100 (the depreciation expense for the year).

The asset will thus be shown in the balance sheet at £550 – £500 = £50 written-down (or book) value, which is also (by design) the estimated disposal value.

This procedure results in an appropriate charge to the profit and loss account each year, and ensures that the asset in the balance sheet will be shown at its written-down value, namely cost less the *total* depreciation to date. For example, in Year 3 the written-down value of £250 reflects the cost figure, less the £300 total depreciation taken to that time.

This will be followed until the disposal of the asset. If the asset is kept in use for a period of time *after* Year 5, no further depreciation will be charged, since the total expense relating to the cost of the asset will already have been charged to profit and loss over the first 5 years.

If the asset is disposed of for £50, its estimated disposal value, the entries will be simply:

- increase cash by £50
- reduce asset by £50 (effectively eliminating it from the accounts)

If the asset is disposed of for a higher amount, say £75, the entries will be:

- increase cash by £75
- reduce asset by £50 (eliminating it)
- increase revenues (profit on disposal) by £25

If the asset is disposed of for a lower amount, say £25, the entries will be:

- increase cash by £25
- reduce asset by £50 (eliminating it)
- increase expenses (loss on disposal) by £25

Profits or losses on disposal are included in the profit and loss account for the year of disposal. They should be seen as an adjustment to bring depreciation taken to date (based on estimates) into line with *actual* depreciation. In fact, unless the magnitude of the profits or losses on disposals is large, the amounts are usually added to or subtracted from the normal depreciation expense for the accounting period, shown in the profit and loss account.

Irrespective of when the asset disposal takes place, the profit or loss on disposal is calculated by taking the difference between the sale proceeds and the written-down value of the asset at the time of disposal.

Activity 9

A vehicle costs £5,000. It is expected to be kept for 5 years, and then sold for £500. Depreciation is to be calculated using the sum of the digits method. In fact, the vehicle is sold at the end of Year 3, for £1,500.

Have a try at showing the accounting entries for each of the 3 years, clearly identifying the expense included in the profit and loss account each year, also the written-down value at the end of each year.

You should have come up with something like this:

Total amount to be depreciated = cost less disposal value = £5,000 – £500 = £4,500. This is to be spread over 5 years using sum of the digits (i.e. 5+4+3+2+1=15).

Depreciation would, therefore, be expected to be charged as follows:

Year 1	5/15 × 4,500 =	£1,500
Year 2	4/15 × 4,500 =	£1,200
Year 3	3/15 × 4,500 =	£900
Year 4	2/15 × 4,500 =	£600
Year 5	1/15 × 4,500 =	£300

Entries in the accounts:
Year 1
- increase expense (depreciation) in the profit and loss account by £1,500
- reduce asset (vehicle) by £1,500

Therefore written-down value = £5,000 – £1,500 = £3,500.

Year 2
- increase expense (depreciation) in the profit and loss account by £1,200
- reduce asset (vehicle) by £1,200

Therefore written-down value = £3,500 – £1,200 = £2,300.

Year 3
Sale of asset with written-down value of £2,300, for £1,500, gives a loss of £800. The accounting entries are:

- increase cash by £1,500
- increase an expense (loss on disposal) by £800
- reduce asset (vehicle) by £2,300.

Note that in Year 3, depreciation has not been taken in the usual way. This is because the asset is disposed of in the period (albeit at the end). The Year 3 depreciation expense must be the difference between the book value of the asset at the end of Year 2 and its disposal proceeds. It can be argued that depreciation should be calculated on a pro-rata basis for the period of use in the year of disposal. Depreciation in Year 3 would thus be taken at £900 (3/15 $\times$ £4,500), reducing the written-down value of the asset to £1,400. Disposal of the asset for £1,500 would then result in a profit on disposal of £100. The entries for Year 3 would be as follows:

- increase expenses (depreciation) by £900
- reduce asset (vehicles) by £900
- increase cash by £1,500
- reduce asset (vehicles) by £1,400
- increase revenue (profit on disposal) by £100.

The result of this more complex approach is effectively the same as that reached earlier, in that the total effective expense for Year 3 is £800. In the first treatment this was shown as a loss on disposal. In the second treatment this is reflected in depreciation of £900 and a profit on disposal of £100. Clearly calculating depreciation in the year of disposal is not necessary to arrive at the correct total charge for the year. Remember that so-called profits or losses on disposal are really final year adjustments to depreciation, to bring estimated depreciation in line with actual depreciation.

In the treatment to date, the asset being depreciated is shown at its written-down value on the balance sheet. It is considered more informative to show the asset at cost, and deduct from it the related total depreciation taken to date. The end result, the written-down value, is the same, but the additional information provides useful insights into the business in terms of the expectations with regard to asset holding and asset replacement. The entries are slightly more complex, since inevitably the asset must remain in the accounts at cost. In fact what happens is that the reductions in the asset are shown under a separate heading, known as depreciation provision or aggregate depreciation, and that this is combined with the asset (at cost) in the balance sheet. A record of the depreciation provision is kept for each type of asset being depreciated.

Using the same example which we met earlier (namely an asset which costs £550, is expected to last 5 years, with an expected disposal value of £50, being depreciated using straight-line depreciation), this revised procedure would result in the following entries.

Year 1
- include depreciation expense in the profit and loss account – £100
- increase depreciation provision (aggregate depreciation)   – £100

The balance sheet would thus show:

Asset – cost	£550
Less depreciation	£100
	£450

Year 2
- include depreciation expense in the profit and loss account – £100
- increase depreciation provision (aggregate depreciation)   – £100

The balance sheet would thus show:

Asset – cost	£550
Less depreciation	£200
	£350

The remaining years will follow the same principles. In the year of disposal the sale proceeds will be compared with the written-down value as before, with the asset and its associated depreciation being eliminated. For example, assume that the asset was sold at the end of Year 3, for £300. The entries would be:

- increase cash   £300
- reduce asset   £550 (eliminating it) ⎤ the written-
- reduce depreciation provision   £200 (eliminating it) ⎦ down value
- increase expense (loss on disposal)   £50

Where assets are acquired part-way through a year it is common to calculate depreciation on a strict time basis. Sometimes, however, a less precise approach is adopted and depreciation is taken on the balance held at the year end, irrespective of the date of acquisition.

Self-assessment question 4.1
F.O. Leo and company purchased a lorry on 1 July 19X5 for £20,000. It was estimated that the lorry would last for 5 years, after which it was likely

to be sold for £4,000. Leo's accounting year is from 1 January to 31 December.

(a) Assuming straight-line depreciation, show the entries relating to vehicles and depreciation for 19X5 and 19X6, clearly identifying the expense for depreciation for each year, and the balance sheet figures for vehicles. Assets are to be shown at cost and associated depreciation provisions.

(b) On 31 December 19X7 the lorry was sold for £11,000. Show the 19X7 entries.

(c) What other methods of depreciation could be used? Are they appropriate in this case?

A suggested solution to this question appears at the end of the book.

4.5 Measurement problems – stock valuation

Background

We saw in Chapters 2 and 3 that cost of sales is an important expense, which is matched against sales revenue in the trading account, to arrive at a figure for gross profit. According to the historic cost convention, assets should be shown at cost, so the question as to the value to be attached to stock sold, and matched with the sales revenue generated, would appear to be simple; stock is valued at cost. This cost should include all costs incurred in bringing the stock to its present location and condition, such as transport costs, if the buyer bears this cost. However, arriving at the appropriate cost of stock is not quite as simple as it appears to be, certainly in times of inflation or changing prices.

For example, a garden centre has in stock 100 bags of peat which had cost £1.50 each, when they were bought a few weeks ago. A further 500 bags of peat were bought for £1.60 each. What is the cost (which should be matched against the sales revenue) of the next bag of peat sold?

Various approaches are possible, but (as with depreciation) a small number appear to be the most widely used, and three of these are given below.

Stock valuation methods

First in, first out (FIFO)

The stock is valued *as if* the first item held in stock is the first item issued. On this assumption the next bag of peat sold would be costed out (i.e. treated as an expense) at £1.50. This method seems logical, in that the oldest stocks would normally be sold first, but it does mean that the price at which goods are costed out will probably be insufficient to replace those goods in times of inflation. The result of this is that it may be argued that the cost of sales does not really represent the value leaving the business as a result of the sale. If we are to match an expense to the revenue, it seems illogical to match an old cost (£1.50) to a current revenue.

Activity 10

The garden centre, in the above example, decided to stock a new line of bags of fertilizer. Purchases and sales during the first few weeks of stocking the product were, chronological order, as follows:

Bought	60 bags	@	£1.00 each
Sold	40 bags		
Bought	60 bags	@	£1.10 each
Sold	70 bags		

Try to work out the cost of sales figure for the period and the value of the stock at the various points during the period, assuming that stock usages are priced on a FIFO basis.

Your answer should be something like this:

	Cost of sales	Value of remaining stock
	£	£
Bought 60 bags @ £1.00 each		60.00
Sold 40 bags	40.00 (i.e. 40 @ £1.00)	40.00
		20.00
Bought 60 bags @ £1.10 each		66.00
Sold 70 bags	75.00 (i.e. 20 @ £1.00	86.00
	plus 50 @ £1.10)	75.00
		11.00

Last in, first out (LIFO)

In answer to the criticism made about FIFO, it may be seen as being preferable to value stock issues on the basis of last in, first out (LIFO). Note that this relates only to the process of valuation. Where possible oldest stocks should normally be issued first, though in the case of non-perishable goods like peat, this may not be too important. Using LIFO, issues are simply valued at the most recent value of stock in hand. It is argued that this results in something much nearer to replacement cost being included in cost of sales figure in the trading account. It also means that the current cost is being matched to a current revenue.

Using LIFO, the transfer to cost of sales for the next bag of peat sold would be £1.60.

Activity 11

Can you say what will be the general effect on the value of the remaining stock of using LIFO, to value stock issues, during a period of changing prices?

The answer is that it will reflect old costs of buying the stock.

Unfortunately, under LIFO it is possible for the balance sheet values of stock to become significantly out of line with the current cost of the stock in hand (because the value placed on the stock in hand would be as if it is old stock). LIFO is not currently permitted to be used for tax purposes in the UK, a fact which has tended to reduce its practical importance. Also the use of current cost accounting (discussed in a later chapter) has meant that the advantages of LIFO, in terms of measuring profit, can be obtained without its balance sheet disadvantages.

Activity 12

Using exactly the same data as in Activity 10, try to work out the cost of sales figure for the period and the value of the stock at the various points during the period, assuming that stock usages are priced on a LIFO basis.

Your answer should be something like this:

		Cost of sales	Value of remaining stock
		£	£
Bought	60 bags @ £1.00 each		60.00
Sold	40 bags	40.00 (i.e. 40 @ £1.00)	40.00
			20.00
Bought	60 bags @ £1.10 each		66.00
			86.00
Sold	70 bags	76.00 (i.e. 60 @ £1.10 plus 10 @ £1.00)	76.00
			10.00

The weighted average cost (AVCO)

Using this method the value of any existing stock is added to the value of new stock, and a weighted average is calculated. All subsequent stock issues are at this average cost, until such time as new receipts of goods require a further calculation. Using the above example the AVCO per bag of peat would be arrived at as follows:

$$((100 \times 1.50) + (500 \times 1.60))/600 = £1.583$$

The next bag issued would thus be costed at £1.583.

Activity 13
Using exactly the same data as in Activity 10, try to work out the cost of sales figure for the period and the value of the stock at the various points during the period, assuming that stock usages are priced on a AVCO basis.

Your answer should be something like this:

			Cost of sales	Value of remaining stock
			£	£
Bought	60 bags @	£1.00 each		60.00
Sold	40 bags		40.00 (i.e. 40 @ £1.00)	40.00
				20.00
Bought	60 bags @	£1.10 each		66.00
				86.00
Sold	70 bags		75.25 (i.e. 70 @ £86/80)	75.25
				10.75

Activity 14
A business is very careful about always using the oldest stock first.
    Which method of stock valuation would be most appropriate?

This is a bit of a trick question. The method of stock valuation used has absolutely nothing to do with the way in which the stock is handled. The choice between FIFO, LIFO and AVCO would depend on the attitudes of the managers of the business to how most logically to match expenses against revenues. Obviously you do not know what their attitude would be.

Self-assessment question 4.2
(a) Explain why the statement 'you value stock at historic cost' is not as simple as it appears.

(b) The Polybike Company started trading on 1 January 19X5, to sell bicycles to students. During the first 3 years of business the FIFO method of stock valuation is used in the preparation of its annual accounts.

The following information relates to the first 3 years of business.

	19X5	19X6	19X7
Sales	200 @ £80	250 @ £100	300 @ £120
Purchases	300 @ £50	300 @ £60	250 @ £80
Overheads (paid and incurred)	£4,000	£5,000	£6,000

All purchases may be assumed to have taken place on 1 January of the relevant year, before any sales for the year have occurred.

Using the layout given below show:

- the figure for closing stock at the end of each year, using FIFO, LIFO and AVCO
- the figure for cost of sales for each of the three years, using FIFO, LIFO and AVCO
- the profit figure for each of the three years under each of the three methods.

FIFO method

Trading and profit and loss account

	19X5	19X6	19X7
Sales			
Cost of sales			
Gross profit			
Overheads			
Net profit			

Stock account	Qty price £	Qty Price £	Qty Price £
Opening balance			
Purchases			
Issues (cost of sales)			
Therefore closing stock			

LIFO method

Trading and profit and loss account

	19X5	19X6	19X7
Sales			
Cost of sales			

Gross profit
Overheads
Net profit

Stock account	Qty Price £	Qty Price £	Qty Price £
Opening balance			
Purchases			
Issues (cost of sales)			
Therefore closing stock			

AVCO method

Trading and profit and loss account

	19Xt	19X6	19X7
Sales			
Cost of sales			
Gross profit			
Overheads			
Net profit			

Stock account	Qty Price £	Qty Price £	Qty Price £
Opening balance			
Purchases			
Therefore weighted average cost			
Issues (cost of sales)			
Therefore closing stock			

Clearly the calculation of an appropriate cost of sales figure, and the associated balance sheet figure for stock, is not quite as straightforward as it seems. The impact of the different approaches on the measurement of profit, and the statement of financial position (the balance sheet), must be clearly recognized.

In a time of cost inflation, the use of FIFO will result in the highest profit of the three methods, but the most current valuation figure for stock remaining in hand. The use of LIFO will result in the lowest figure for profit. Its use will also give the most out-of-date stock figure in the balance sheet. The use of AVCO gives a compromise solution to the two. Which is the most appropriate or useful figure for profit is a subject which will be returned to in later chapters, particularly in Chapter 12 which includes a more general discussion of the problems of accounting during periods of inflation. It is worth repeating the point that the method used (FIFO, LIFO or AVCO) has nothing to do with the actual order in which stock is used.

The 'lower of cost or net realizable value' rule

Certain exceptions arise to the rule that stock is valued at historic cost (however calculated). It should be remembered that an asset has been defined as expected future benefit. As long as there is an expectation that stock can be sold at a future date, at a price in excess of cost, there is no reason to show it at other than historic cost. In the event, however, of the expectations changing, so that future sale value is expected to be lower than cost, it would not be reasonable to include the asset in the balance sheet at cost, since this expected future benefit is less than the cost. Under such circumstances stock should be valued at the expected net realizable value. Net realizable value is arrived at by deducting any costs of disposal from the *realizable value*. In most cases cost would be the basis used. This is because businesses would normally be in the position where the disposal value of their stock is higher than the cost of the stock. Where this is not normally the case it would mean that the business would be constantly sustaining trading losses.

The choice of the lower of cost and net realizable value means that a more cautious view is taken of the value of stock remaining in hand. This is obviously another example of the prudence convention at work.

Stock valuation of manufactured goods

When a business is engaged in the manufacture of goods, the problems of stock valuation become greater, since stocks will include a variety of materials, work-in-progress, and finished goods. The identification of the cost of work-in-progress and finished goods is not always easy. Cost may be defined as the expenditure incurred in the normal course of business to bring a product to its current location and condition. For manufactured goods these normally include purchase costs, plus conversion costs. These latter costs include labour and expenses (e.g. subcontracted work) directly related to the stock concerned, an appropriate share of overheads incurred to get the stock into its present location and condition. Not surprisingly, stock valuation under such circumstances can be a somewhat imprecise process.

It is generally true of accounting for stock that judgements need to be made by the preparers of accounting statements. These judgements can, in certain types of business, have profound effects on the figures shown in the accounting statements. In turn this can greatly affect the perceptions of users of the accounting statements of the trading and position of the business.

4.6   Measurement problems – debtors and bad or doubtful debts

Assets are expected future benefits. The asset of debtors represents expected future cash inflows from goods and services which have been sold on credit, but for which the cash has yet to be forthcoming. In almost every business, however, there will be some debtors who will not pay their debts. This is despite the fact that most businesses take some care to try to ensure that all sales on credit result in a receipt of cash before too long.

We have already seen that, where an asset loses part or all of its expected future economic benefit, the following accounting entries are made:

- reduce the book value of the asset
- increase expenses

by the book value of the asset lost.

(Depreciation and cost of stock sold both provide examples of this.)

In the context of a debtor becoming a bad debt, the appropriate entries are, in principle:

- reduce the debtor's figure
- increase expenses (bad debts written off)

by the amount of the debt which has gone bad.

Under the matching convention, it is important that the expense of a particular bad debt written off is matched, in the same accounting period, to the original revenue which gave rise to that debt. This is because the bad debt is an expense directly caused by the revenue.

Where the debt is judged to have gone bad during the same period as that in which the relevant sale was made, the accounting entries are exactly as specified above.

Activity 15
Why do we not simply cancel the sale when a debt goes bad?

The answer is that the sale has taken place and, therefore, it is correct to record it as such. The fact that the cash is never received is a separate issue. The ratio of gross profit to sales is a useful, and much used one. This, and other, useful ratios would be distorted and give a wrong impression if all of the sales were not included.

A slight complication arises where a sale on credit in one accounting period results in a bad debt in a subsequent period. Even though there may be a reluctance to write off a debt until it has definitely gone bad, the preparers of the accounting statements often have a good idea that a particular debt is 'at risk'. This may be because there is information in circulation that the particular debtor is in financial difficulties, perhaps coupled with the fact that the debtor is being unusually slow to pay the particular debt under consideration. Usually the preparers will also have some data, based on past experience, on the proportion of debts which unexpectedly go bad.

Normally, at the end of each accounting period, a judgement will be made as to what extent the sales, which were made on credit during that period, seem likely to subsequently prove to be bad. This will usually be done by identifying specific 'at risk' debts. In addition a certain percentage of the total book value of the remaining debts will be treated as being 'at risk' as well. The total 'at risk' or doubtful debts will be treated as an expense for the accounting period, thus matched to the revenues which gave rise to them. Since the doubtful debts have not yet gone bad, and indeed may not ever go bad, the debtor's figure in the balance sheet is not directly reduced. Instead a 'provision for doubtful debts' is created and this is deducted from the debtor's figure in the balance sheet. This leads to the asset of debtors being shown in the balance sheet at a figure which reflects a prudent view of its value. When these debts actually go bad, they will be written off against the provision, not against the revenues of the period in which they go bad. If it subsequently transpires that a pessimistic view of the extent of doubtful debts has been taken, this expense can be reversed in the following accounting period, once the actual outcome is known.

The appropriate entries are:

In respect of debts which go bad during the same accounting period as the relevant sale was made:

- reduce the debtors figure
- increase expenses (bad debts written off)

by the amount of the debt which has gone bad.

At the end of each accounting period, make a judgement of the value of doubtful debts, then:

- create a provision (which will be set against the debtors figure)
- increase expenses (doubtful debt provision)

by the amount of the estimate of doubtful debts.

In respect of debts which go bad during the *subsequent* accounting period as the relevant sale was made:

- reduce the debtors figure
- reduce the doubtful debt provision

by the amount of the debt which has gone bad. Note that this has the effect of writing off the bad debt *without* causing an expense of the year in which the debt goes bad. This is because the provision was created by an expense of the previous year.

At the end of the second accounting period:

- write back any unused part of the provision
- increase revenues (doubtful debt provision written back)

If the judgement of the amount of the doubtful debts at the end of one accounting period is perfect, the provision will be completely extinguished by writing bad debts off against it, during the subsequent accounting period. Human error and the prudence convention will mean that provisions for doubtful debts will almost always be excessive.

Example

Wessex Enterprises had trade debtors on 31 December 19X5, the end of its accounting year, totalling £21,500. All of these debts arose from 19X5 sales.

On consideration of the debts outstanding it was found that debtors with debts totalling £100 were unlikely to pay their debts and it was decided to write them off. In addition it was decided to create a provision for doubtful debts of 5% of the remaining debts, based on past experience which indicated that typically about 5% of debtors would not pay.

The first stage is to deal with the bad debts which are to be written off to the 19X5 profit and loss account. The entries are:

* increase an expense (bad debts) by £100
* reduce debtors by £100

The second stage is to deal with the remaining suspected bad debts. The amount of provision required is £1,070 [(£21,500 – 100) × 5%]. The entries are:

* increase an expense (creation of doubtful debts provision) by £1,070
* increase doubtful debts provision by £1,070

The expense 'creation of doubtful debts provision' will be included in the profit and loss account. In the balance sheet debtors will appear as follows:

	£
debtors (21,500 – 100)	21,400
less bad debts provision	1,070
	20,330

The net amount of £20,330 represents the expected future benefit associated with debtors, taking a prudent view.

The next stage in the process occurs when (and if) any of the debts outstanding at 31 December 19X5 actually go bad. Let us now take the example a little further by saying that 19X5 debts totalling £850 actually went bad in 19X6; the remainder of the £21,400 debts were received in cash. The entries for the bad debts are:

* reduce debtors by £850
* reduce doubtful debts provision by £850

In practice the individual debts which total £850 would probably be written off to the provision as they were recognized as bad, in a piecemeal way, rather than in one lump sum as shown above.

Since all of the debts outstanding at 31 December 19X5 have now either been paid or have been written off as bad, the remainder of the provision is no longer needed and will be treated as a revenue for 19X6. The entries are:

- reduce doubtful debt provision by £220 (i.e. £1,070 – 850)
- increase revenues – doubtful debt provision no longer required – by £220.

Activity 16
Can you remember the reason why we create a doubtful debt provision?

The reason is to treat potential bad debts as expenses in the accounting period, during which the revenues with which they are associated are recognized. This is done in order to follow the matching convention. At the same time, the existence of the doubtful debt provision reduces the book value of the debtors. This is consistent with the prudence convention.

Self-assessment question 4.3
At 31 December 19X6, Wessex Enterprises had debts outstanding of £23,400. When these were considered in detail it was decided that none of them were definitely bad, but that two of them totalling £300 were very doubtful and should be provided for in full. In addition, a general doubtful debt provision of 5% of the remaining debts should be established.

During 19X7, the business sold goods on credit for a total of £147,800 and received cash from debtors totalling £143,700. Debts totalling £1,800 were written off during the year, £910 of which related to sales made during 19X6. By the end of 19X7, there were no remaining debts relating to 19X6 sales, either because the cash had been received or the debts had been written off. At 31 December 19X7, it was decided to create a provision equal to 5% of the debts outstanding at that date.

Show the balance sheet figures for debtors (including the provision) at 31 December 19X6 and 19X7.

Show the expenses and revenues relating to bad and doubtful debts for each of the 2 years ended 31 December 19X6 and 19X7.

Nothing that has been said so far should leave the impression that businesses lightly accept that an individual or organization which owes it money for goods or services bought on credit (or for any other reason) will not pay. In practice, businesses which sell on credit typically have quite sophisticated systems for dealing with credit control.

Activity 17
Do you know, or can you guess, the type of activities which a well-organized business would undertake in respect of making sales on credit?

The activities would include:

• Taking up references for new credit customers
• Making a judgement on how much credit to advance to new customers
• Reviewing the credit limits of existing customers
• Ensuring that no customer is allowed to exceed the established credit limit
• Ensuring that invoices, statements and reminders are sent to customers on a routine and prompt basis
• Taking steps to deal with customers who are exceeding the agreed credit period

Where payment cannot be obtained by normal methods the selling business may resort to the use of the law of contract to enforce payment. However, in some cases it will still prove impossible to collect the debts.

4.7   The conventions of accounting

So far in this book a number of conventions have been introduced. These will now be briefly reviewed. They are as follows:

Money measurement

Items in accounting statements are described in terms of money. Items or factors which are incapable of being described in this way must, therefore, be excluded from accounting statements.

Business entity

This convention simply says that, from an accounting point of view, the business is to be treated as a self-contained entity, separate from all who are connected with it.

Duality

This convention requires that each transaction affecting the business has two effects on the balance sheet.

Historic cost

This convention states that assets should be shown in accounts at their outlay cost to the business.

Stable monetary unit

This assumes that the measurement unit in accounting, the unit of currency, retains a stable value relative to other assets over time.

Going concern convention

This convention holds that, unless there is reason to take a different view, the business should be treated as if it will continue for the foreseeable future.

Realization

The convention of realization maintains that revenues should be recognized when they are capable of objective measurement and the asset value receivable is reasonably certain. This is typically taken to be when the goods or service pass to, and are accepted by, the customer.

Matching

This convention holds that expenses should be matched to the revenues which they helped to generate such that the revenue and its associated expenses are set against one another in deducing the income of a business for a particular accounting period.

Accruals

This convention maintains that profit (or loss) for a period is the difference between revenues earned during the period and their related expenses, *not* the difference between cash receipts and payments for the period.

Prudence (or conservatism)

In preparing financial statements accountants err on the cautious side. Hence profits are usually only recognized when they have been realized (see realization convention), while losses are usually taken fully into account as soon as their likelihood is seen. Accounting has a number of areas where more than one approach may be taken. This convention maintains that the more prudent approach should always be taken.

To these conventions must be added three more which have not expressly been discussed so far – consistency, materiality and objectivity.

Consistency

As has been seen, numerous ways frequently exist for dealing with certain matters associated with accounting (e.g. depreciation, stock and debtors valuation). Complete freedom with regard to accounting policies would make manipulation and 'window dressing' of financial data fairly easy. It would also make comparison of commercial effectiveness, etc. between one period and another very difficult. In order to prevent this, the convention of consistency requires a consistent application of a particular policy from one accounting period to the next. When a change of accounting policy is considered necessary, the change should be made on a semipermanent basis. Activity 18 illustrates the extent to which changes in accounting policies have the potential to mislead a user of the accounts.

Activity 18
The following final accounts relate to a business

Balance sheet as at 31 December

	19X6 £	19X7 £		19X6 £	19X7 £
Fixed assets			*Capital*		
Cost	20,000	20,000	Opening balance	25,000	30,000
Depreciation			Net profit	10,000	14,000
provision	–	4,000		35,000	44,000
	20,000	16,000	Less drawings	5,000	6,000
			Closing balance	30,000	38,000
Current assets					
Stock	8,000	12,000	*Current liabilities*		
Debtors	10,000	12,000	Creditors	10,000	8,000
Cash	2,000	6,000			
	40,000	46,000		40,000	46,000

Profit and loss account for the year ended 31 December 19X7

	£		£
Opening stock	8,000	Sales	70,000
Purchases	48,000		
	56,000		
Less closing stock	12,000		
Cost of sales	44,000		
Gross profit	26,000		
	70,000		70,000
Depreciation	4,000	Gross profit	26,000
Other expenses	8,000		
Net profit	14,000		
	26,000		26,000

Notes

1 Depreciation of fixed assets has been taken at 20% per annum straight-line.
2 Stock has been valued assuming FIFO.
3 No provision has been made for doubtful debts.

Recalculate the profit figure for 19X7 assuming:

1 Depreciation to be taken at 40% on a reducing-balance basis.
2 Stock to be valued on a LIFO basis. Assume that this will result in a closing stock figure of £8,000 (and thus a cost of sales figure of £48,000).
3 A doubtful debt provision is to be set up at 5% of debtors.

Revised accounts would be as follows:

Profit and loss account for the year ended 31 December 19X7

	£		£
Opening stock	8,000	Sales	70,000
Purchases	48,000		
	56,000		
less closing stock		8,000	
Cost of sales	48,000		
Gross profit	22,000		
	70,000		70,000
Depreciation	8,000	Gross profit	22,000
Other expenses	8,000		
Increase in DDP	600		
Net profit	5,400		
	22,000		22,000

Balance sheet as at 31 December 19X7

	£	£			£
Fixed assets			*Capital*		
Cost		20,000	Opening balance	30,000	
less depreciation					
provision		8,000	Net profit	5,400	
		12,000		35,400	
			less drawings	6,000	
			Closing balance	29,400	
Current assets					
Stock		8,000	*Current liabilities*		
Debtors	12,000		Creditors		8,000
less DDP	600	11,400			
Cash	6,000	25,400			
		37,400			37,400

Materiality

This convention recognizes that in preparing accounts the amount of detail given will need to be varied according to the size of the organization, and to the importance of particular items to the achievement of overall organizational goals. All important items must be shown in detail. Less important items may be included under more general headings, rather than be separately disclosed. (N.B. All items must be included: this convention is concerned with the number of detailed headings under which items are included.) The convention is also concerned with the extent to which it is necessary strictly to follow the other conventions. When the amounts involved are trivial it may be judged that the cost of strictly following a particular convention is not justified by the greater accuracy which may result. For example, where a particular type of expense is trivial and difficult to relate to a particular revenue, the matching convention may be disregarded and the expense set against the revenues of the period in which the cash, relating to the expense, was actually paid.

Objectivity

This convention basically says that, in preparing financial reports, the preparer should try to use data which is as objective and reliable as possible. Objective data is data which can be independently verified, which is not based upon the opinion of any person within the organization or involved in preparing the accounting statements. It is free from personal bias. In other words, the accounts should be concerned, as far as possible, with facts and as little as possible with opinions.

Each of these conventions will be critically discussed in some detail in Chapter 12.

4.8 Practical accounting

We have now completed our consideration of the basic elements of recording accounting data. In these first four chapters, we have concentrated on issues of principle, rather than on some of the more practical aspects of maintaining accounting records. The appendix to this book deals with some of these more detailed aspects of the practical ways in which accounting records are maintained, including a brief outline of how computers are used for this purpose. If you wish to go into these practicalities you should now work through the appendix. If not, continue into Chapter 5. There is nothing in the remainder of this book which demands that you have studied the appendix.

4.9 Summary

This chapter has provided you with an introduction to the problems of profit measurement in the areas of depreciation, stock valuation, and bad and doubtful debts. Possible methods of dealing with these problems have been identified, which try to match expenses with appropriate revenues. You should be aware of the likely impact of adjustments relating to depreciation, stock and bad and doubtful debts on the profit and loss account and balance sheet.

In considering the options set out in this chapter it should have become clear that the measurement of profit is rather less objective than might be expected. Different profit figures can be arrived at for individual accounting periods depending upon the methods chosen for dealing with the problems raised in this chapter. Over the entire life of a business the differences will even out. On a year by year basis this is not the case.

The chapter concludes with a brief consideration of the accounting conventions.

Exercises

1 The following is the balance sheet of a business at the beginning of 19X7 (i.e. 1 January)

		£	£		£	£
Fixed assets			*Capital*			54,000
Premises		30,000				
Fixtures and Fittings						
cost	12,000					
dep. prov'n	2,000	10,000				
Equipment						
cost	15,000					
dep. prov'n	5,000	10,000	*Loan* (10% interest)			10,000
		50,000				

Current assets			Current liabilities		
Stock	7,000		Creditors	8,000	
Prepaid insurance	100		Accrued wages	1,000	9,000
Debtors	10,000				
Cash	5,900				
		23,000			
		73,000			73,000

Note

The prepaid insurance relates to a premium which covers the 12 months to 31 March 19X7.

The accrued wages relate to overtime worked in December 19X6.

The following represents a *summary* of the transactions which took place during 19X7.

(a) Stock was purchased on credit for £70,000.

(b) Stock was purchased for cash for £15,000.

(c) Cash sales amounted to £40,000.

(d) Credit sales amounted to £100,000.

(e) Wages of £25,000 were paid.

(f) Rent of £1,250 was paid. This covered the 15 months to 31 March 19X8.

(g) General expenses of £5,000 were paid.

(h) Rates and insurance of £1,200 were paid. This included a £500 insurance premium covering the period 1 April 19X7 to 31 March 19X8.

(i) Additional equipment was purchased on 1 January, for £3,000. This was financed from a loan for the full amount, with interest payable at 20% per annum.

(j) Cash received from debtors amounted to £97,000.

(k) Cash paid to creditors amounted to £72,000.

(l) The owner withdrew £200 in stock and £6,000 in cash.

(m) Some of the fittings (cost £2,000, depreciation provision £1,000) were traded in in part exchange for new fittings. The total cost of the new fittings was £4,000, of which £1,500 was a part exchange allowance, and £2,500 was paid in cash.

(n) The owner won £5,000 on the football pools. This was paid into the business.

(o) A bill for holidays for the owner (total £500) was paid from the business bank account.

At the end of the year the following items of additional information are obtained:

(a) Bad debts amounting to £1,500 are to be written off.

(b) Depreciation is to be provided for as follows:

- premises – none
- equipment – 20% on cost
- fixtures and fittings – 10% on cost

Depreciation is to be taken on those assets still in use at the year end, not on those disposed of during the year.

(c) The two items of loan interest remain unpaid.
(d) Christmas overtime payments of £800 have not yet been paid.
(e) Closing stock is valued at £10,000.

Required

Prepare a trading and profit and loss account for the business for the year ended 31 December 19X7, and a balance sheet as at that date.

2   Compare the effect of using the reducing-balance method of depreciation, the sum of the digits method, and the straight-line method, by completing the following table in respect of an asset which cost £1,500, had a life of five years and a residual value of zero:

Year	Reducing balance using 40%		Sum of the digits		Straight-line	
	Book value at year end £	Depn for year £	Book value at year end £	Depn for year £	Book value at year end £	Depn for year £
0	1500	–	1500	–	1500	
1						
2						
3						
4						
5	0		0		0	

All calculations are to be made to the nearest whole number. Any balances remaining to be written off in the fifth year.

3   What is the nature of obsolescence in relation to plant and machinery? How can it be dealt with in the financial accounts of a business?

4   Assuming the data in Question 2, which method of depreciation would you recommend, if repairs and maintenance costs were steady? If these costs were rising as follows, which method would you use? Year 1 – £50, year 2 – £150, year 3 – £250, year 4 – £350, year 5 – £450.

5   A business with a year end at 31 December bought a van on 1 January 19X4, for £12,000. It bought a second van on 1 July 19X6 for £16,000. On 30 June 19X7 the first van was sold for £5,500. Depreciation is to be charged at

25% on a reducing balance basis.

Show the relevant extracts from the profit and loss account, and the balance sheet, as they relate to the financial years 19X4, 19X5, 19X6 and 19X7. You should assume that depreciation will be calculated on a pro-rata basis for equipment purchased part-way through a year, but that no calculation of depreciation is made in the year of disposal.

6   Discuss the extent to which depreciation will provide the necessary funds to replace an asset when it ceases to be productive.

7   Give three examples of methods of stock valuation, indicating the advantages and disadvantages of each.

8   The following information relates to your business:

Stock of goods on 1 January was 1000 units valued at £9.80 each
Purchases throughout the year:

1 January	1000 units at £10.20 each
1 March	1000 units at £10.60 each
1 May	1000 units at £10.90 each
1 July	1000 units at £11.40 each
1 September	1000 units at £11.60 each
1 November	1000 units at £11.90 each

Each month 500 units were sold.

Show clearly the cost of goods sold figure, and the closing stock valuation, assuming stock sold is valued at:

(a) Weighted-average price
(b) FIFO
(c) LIFO

Assuming that the selling price is £15 per unit, calculate the gross profit under each of these methods.

9   'Profit is an elusive concept'. Discuss this statement, illustrating the difficulties confronting accountants in their attempts to measure profit.

10   Comment on the suggestion that the measurement of financial accounting information of the type presently reported is as much based on subjective opinion as on objective evidence.

11   Discuss the importance of the following conventions:
(a) consistency
(b) prudence
(c) objectivity

Part Three

Accounting for Companies: The Regulatory Framework

This section comprises three chapters, and aims to introduce you to the important subject of the accounts of limited companies. Chapter 5 deals with the nature of limited companies and introduces company accounting.

Chapter 6 provides an introduction to the regulatory framework within which company accounting operates. This includes an introduction to company law, the Stock Exchange requirements and accounting standards. It is not intended that you should know the detailed provisions of the accounting regulations. Rather, it should provide you with sufficient understanding, when coupled with the knowledge derived from Chapter 5, to understand a set of company accounts.

Most published accounts relate to groups of companies and, as a result, include items not found in the accounts of individual companies. Chapter 7 aims to provide an understanding of groups, and the implications of group structures on published accounts.

An introduction to the accounts of limited companies

5.1 Introduction

This chapter aims to provide a broad introduction to the nature of limited companies, and the particular accounting aspects associated with them.

5.2 Objectives

On completion of this chapter you should be able:

- to identify the critical features of a company, notably its separate legal entity; the relationship between shareholders and directors; and limited liability;
- to explain how companies are typically financed;
- to identify the legal and practical restrictions which exist with regard to transferring funds to shareholders, including the payment of dividends;
- to prepare final accounts for a limited company and to identify the major differences between accounting for companies and for sole proprietors.

5.3 Limited companies – importance and environment – an overview

There are three basic types of legal form which a UK business tends to take:

(a) *Sole proprietorships (sometimes known as sole trading businesses).* This is where one person owns and manages the business, perhaps employing other people to help. The legal and financial obligations of the business are borne entirely by the owner of the business, with the law making little or no distinction between the obligations of the sole proprietor, as a business person, and as a private individual. Thus, for example, the law would not view differently a loan taken out by the sole proprietor to pay for a business asset and money borrowed by the sole proprietor to pay for a holiday. Many small businesses, like corner shops, public houses and plumbers, are sole proprietorships. So far in this book, we have looked at the accounts of sole proprietors.

(b) *Partnerships.* These are businesses owned and managed by a group of people, usually a small group. As is the case with sole proprietorships, the law does not draw a real distinction between the obligations of partners, as business people, and as private individuals. Partnerships are very like sole trading businesses, but with more than one participant. Many small businesses, of the type which are often sole trading businesses, are owned and managed by more than one person. Thus where, as is often the case, a corner shop is owned and managed by a married couple, it is a partnership business. Most partnerships are very small, both in terms of the number of partners and the scale of the business. Since the ethics of some professional bodies, like the Institute of Chartered Accountants, will not allow their members to practise except as sole proprietors and partners many professional partnerships are very large businesses, however.

(c) *Limited companies.* These are businesses owned by more than one person (shareholders) and managed by a committee (board of directors). Unlike sole proprietor and partnership businesses, the company is a distinct legal entity (separate legal person) separate from the owners and managers. As a result of the separateness of the company and its owners, the law *does* draw a real distinction between the obligations of the company and those of the owners. The private sector of the UK economy is dominated by limited companies.

The accounting peculiarities of limited companies arise directly from the particular legal status of the limited company. This chapter will, therefore, include a brief consideration of the *legal and administrative environment* in which limited companies operate. The aim here is not to provide a detailed legal examination of the limited company, but simply to outline its more significant aspects. More particularly the aim is to explain, in broad terms, those aspects which impinge on accounting.

In this context it is important to note that limited companies are regulated by a series of *Companies Acts* which were consolidated into the Companies Act 1985, and extended by the Companies Act of 1989. These acts lay down a large number of rules which must be followed by those who manage a limited company. These rules have the objective of ensuring, as far as it is reasonable to do so, that those who deal with a limited company are not misled by its managers.

5.4   The nature of a limited company

Legal entity

A limited company is an artificially created legal person. It is an entity which is legally separate from all other persons, including those who own and manage it. It is quite possible for a limited company to take legal action, say for breach of contract, against any other legal person, again including those who own and manage it. Actions between limited companies and their shareholders or managers do occur from time to time.

Obviously an artificial person can only function through the intervention of human beings. In the case of a limited company it is the owners who ultimately control the company.

The separate legal status which limited companies have should not be confused with the accounting convention of business entity. The business entity conversion applies to all businesses, whether or not they are limited companies.

Shares, shareholders and directors

A limited company must, by law, have at least two owners. Most limited companies have many more than two owners. Capital must, therefore, be subdivided in a way which will enable the relative proportions of ownership to be ascertained. Capital (the owners' claim) is thus divided into shares. The shareholders (or members, as they are sometimes known) are the owners of the company; profits and gains accrue to them; losses are borne by them up to a maximum of the amount of their agreed investment in the company.

For a variety of sound practical reasons the day to day management of the company is delegated, by the shareholders, to directors who may themselves own some shares in the company. Shareholders elect directors in much the same way as citizens elect Members of Parliament in a parliamentary democracy. They also fail to re-elect them if the directors' performance is judged by shareholders to be unsatisfactory. Usually one-third of the directors retire from office each year, frequently offering themselves for re-election. Typically, each share carries one vote, thus each shareholder has as many votes as shares. Where a company has a large number of shareholders, a particular individual holding a large number of shares, even though not a majority of them, can wield tremendous power. This is because most shareholders of large companies tend not to use their votes. The board of directors is the business's top level of management, so to control its composition is substantially to control the company.

As a separate legal entity, the company does not depend on the identity of its shareholders for its existence. *Transfer of shares* by buying and selling or by gift is therefore possible. Thus a part – even all – of the company's ownership or *equity* can change hands without it necessarily having any effect on the business activities of the company. It should be noted that the price at which shares change hands is of no *direct* concern to the company, and will not affect the accounts of the company at all. Nevertheless, a low price is likely to indicate a relatively poor market perception of the business. This may lead to pressure for changes in the board, difficulties in raising further funds from the financial markets, and then threat of a takeover by another business. A high price is likely to help the current board retain its position, and may assist in achieving effective takeovers of other businesses.

Since the company can continue irrespective of precisely who the shareholders happen to be at any given moment, the company can theoretically have a perpetual life span.

Limited liability

One of the results of the peculiar position of the company as having its own separate legal identity is that the *financial liability of the owners (shareholders) is limited* to the amount which they have paid (or have pledged to pay) for their shares. If the company becomes insolvent (financial obligations exceed value of assets) its liability is, like that of a human person, limited only by the amount of its assets. It can be forced to pay over all of its assets to meet or partially to meet its liabilities, but no more. Since the company and the owners are legally separate, owners cannot be compelled to introduce further finance. The position of a shareholder in this regard does not depend upon whether the shares were acquired by buying them from an existing shareholder or whether they were bought direct from the company.

This contrasts dramatically with the position of sole proprietors and partners. The owners of these *unincorporated* businesses cannot, in law, separate personal obligations and assets from those of the business. Thus, for example, a sole proprietor or partner, whose business debts exceed business assets, will be required to introduce personal assets to meet the unpaid business debts. It is not legally possible for sole proprietors and partners to protect what they might like to think of as non-business assets from being used to meet unsatisfied business obligations. Shareholders in a limited company are, however, able to 'ring fence' their financial obligations to the company and keep their personal assets safe from any of the company's claimants.

Activity 1
It was mentioned above that some professional bodies, like the Institute of Chartered Accountants, will not allow their members to practise in the form of a limited company.
   Can you think of the reason for this?

The reason for this is to stop professionals, who owe a duty of great care and expertise to their clients, avoiding the full implications of any action taken against those professionals for negligence, etc. as a result of trading through a limited company. The logic of this is that the professionals will tend to take their responsibilities more seriously, where they know that the effect of negligence, etc. could be that they lose everything, not just that part of their wealth which they think of as being involved in their professional business.

Activity 2
The tremendous growth in the economies of the western world over the last two centuries has often been attributed (at least in part) to the advent of limited companies.

Jot down a list of the features of limited companies which you consider likely to have been of most importance in the above phenomenon.

Most of the relevant points have been mentioned already in this chapter.

There are probably two main points here:

- The ability to split capital into shares, enabling more investors to own part of a single enterprise. Given the high cost of assets since the industrial revolution, it is unlikely that many enterprises could have grown as rapidly as they have without this widening of ownership. Without this growth, mass production and its benefits would probably not have been possible.
- The separate legal identity of limited companies and the consequent effect of this, in terms of limited liability, provided further impetus to the growth of industry, since the maximum loss for an individual investor is limited and clearly specified.

Types of company

Companies may be categorized into public companies and private companies. *Private limited companies* are companies with a limited number of shareholders, which generally have certain restrictions on the rights of owners to transfer their shares. Private companies tend to be smaller, family-held companies. Private companies use the word *Limited (Ltd)* after their name in all formal documentation.

Public limited companies are companies whose shares have been offered to the public at large, and which have no restrictions on transferability of shares. Typically public companies are larger companies with more widespread share ownership. Public companies use the words *public limited company (Plc)* after their name in all formal documentation.

The number of private companies is many times greater than the number of public companies. However, the public companies are far more important in terms of output, assets and contribution to gross national product.

Many public companies are *listed on the Stock Exchange*. This means that a market exists on the stock exchange for their shares. There is thus a facility to buy and sell shares in such a company easily and conveniently. Inevitably, therefore, shares in listed companies are likely to be seen by many investors as being more attractive than those of unlisted companies.

> **Activity 3**
> Can you think of any reason why the price at which shares are transferred from one person to another may be different to the amount originally invested in the company?
>
> (You may need to reconsider some of the basic accounting conventions referred to in earlier chapters in answering this question.)

A main reason is that, according to the historic cost convention, assets are shown in the books of a business at cost. The future earnings power of those assets will tend to determine the market value. Differences between book and market value of these assets is likely to make the ownership of shares in a company more or less attractive.

Retained profits are associated with increases in the net assets of a business, and thus with increases in the ownership equity. Other things being equal, the retention of profits should lead to increases in share price, provided that such retentions are put to good use.

Share prices reflect a variety of influences, some of which are worldwide (e.g. the 1987 crash), some are economy-wide, and some relate specifically to the prospects of an individual business (a prospective takeover, for example, may significantly affect the price of the shares of an individual company). In essence it is the supply/demand relationships for shares of a particular company which dictate price.

The share price is thus a reflection of a variety of factors, any of which may lead to share price being substantially different to the amount originally invested per share.

Formation of a limited company

Creating a new company is a very cheap and simple operation which can be carried out with little effort on the part of the promoters, for very little cost (less than £100 in total).

Formation basically requires the promoters to make an application to the Registrar of Companies (Department of Trade and Industry). The application must be accompanied by several documents, the most important of which is a proposed set of rules, or constitution, for the company defining how it will be administered. These rules are contained in two documents known as the *Memorandum of Association* and *Articles of Association*. Broadly speaking, the memorandum defines the company in relation to the outside world. It will thus include such things as:

* the name of the company, the area of the UK in which the registered office is situated;
* the objects for which the company was formed;

- a declaration that the liability of the members is to be limited;
- the amount of capital that the company takes power to acquire; and
- the shares into which it is to be divided.

A public limited company will also have a clause stating that it is a public limited company.

The articles of a company are its internal regulations, and are subordinate to, and controlled by, the memorandum. They will show how the company is to be administered and will give particular reference to matters relating to the raising of capital, directors' powers, dividends and reserves, and accounts and audit.

All of the documentation becomes public once the company has been formally registered. A file is opened at Companies House in Cardiff on which are placed the various documents. The file is constantly available for examination by any member of the public who wishes to see it. As we shall see later in the chapter, companies must also send the Registrar a copy of their annual accounts each year.

Activity 4

Can you guess why it is necessary for limited companies to include, either 'Plc' or 'Ltd' in their names?

These too are placed on the file and are, therefore, available for public scrutiny. The reason is to warn people and organizations who might deal with a company in some way that the liability is limited to the extent of the company's assets (i.e. the personal assets of the shareholders are not included in the fund available to creditors, in the event of the company having insufficient assets to meet its obligations). It also advises people that they can find out various bits of information about the company from Companies House.

5.5 Ownership of companies

As we have already seen, companies are owned by the shareholders, with an individual's portion of the ownership of the company defined by the number of shares owned. When a company is first formed, the entire owners' claim will be represented by share capital. Once the company starts to trade, it is likely that the amount of the owners' claim will increase. This is because profits and gains may not be drawn by the shareholders, but left in the company. The law requires that the balance sheet value of the share capital cannot be expanded to reflect the increase in the owners' claim; the shares must be left in the balance sheet at the value at which they were issued. The additional owners' claim is put, in the balance sheet, under the separate heading of *reserves*. The sum of the share capital and the reserves, at any particular time, represents the entire claim of the shareholders against the company.

5.6   Share capital

The share capital of a limited company may be subdivided into different categories. In practice, the two most important of these are:

- Ordinary share capital
- Preference share capital

Each of these types of share capital is made up of a number of shares, normally with an agreed nominal or par value. In other words, a company with ordinary share capital of, say, £1 million, may make up this capital in the form of 1 million shares of £1 each, 2 million shares of 50p each, or any other variation deemed appropriate.

Activity 5

Eight friends decide to form a company to start a business. They agree to supply £5,000 each to provide the original share capital. They are thinking of having a share capital of eight shares of £5,000 each. Their accountant has advised them to have 40,000 shares of £1 each.

  Can you think why the accountant gave this advice?

The reasons which we could think of are as follows:

- It will not be practical for the shareholders to sell part of their investment. They will either have to sell all of it or nothing. If there are £1 shares, the shareholders can sell virtually any portion of their total investment.
- A similar point is that, if the company wishes to raise additional share capital in the future, it will be saddled with having to raise it in very large amounts per investor. This may well make it impossible to raise additional share capital.

In fact, it is possible to subdivide existing shares into smaller denomination, but it is easier to establish smaller nominal share values from the outset.

  Shares may be issued in such a way that the agreed price can be payable in instalments. This would usually be where a company does not need the full amount of the cash immediately and it is felt that investors might find the issue more attractive if payment is by instalment. For reasons which were raised in respect of Activity 3, it is also quite common for shares to be issued at a price which is in excess of the nominal price.

  It might be useful to distinguish a number of terms with regard to capital.

  Authorized capital is the maximum amount of share capital which the company is empowered to issue under its memorandum of association. This figure can be increased, provided that certain procedures are followed, and approvals obtained, but this may take some time.

  Issued capital is the amount of capital which the company has specifically asked shareholders to subscribe.

Partly paid shares arise where shares are being issued on an instalment basis. Until such time as the total amount has been asked for by the company such shares will be *partly* paid. A shareholder holding a partly paid share is liable for payment of the unpaid part of the share on the agreed date, or, if no date is agreed, by a date to be fixed by the company. Failure to make such a payment could lead to the shares being forfeited. Once a share has become fully paid, the shareholders cannot be required to make any further payment to the company. Liability is limited to payment of the agreed amount.

Share premium is the difference between the agreed total price for a share and its nominal value. In the accounts of a limited company, share capital must be shown at the par value or, in the event of partly paid shares at the part called up, less any agreed portion for a share premium. Any premium paid to the company must be shown separately in the balance sheet.

The share premium account is an example of a reserve, i.e. part of the owners' claim over and above the nominal share capital. In many countries, the law does not require that a distinction be drawn between nominal share values and share premium; all of the proceeds of a share issue are treated as share capital. It is not clear why UK law makes the distinction, particularly when UK law requires that share premium is treated almost identically to share capital.

Example

A company with an authorized capital of 100,000 shares with a nominal value of £1 each issues 50,000 shares at their nominal value. The effect on the balance sheet would be as shown below.

Assets			Claims		
Cash	+	£50,000	Issued capital	+	£50,000
			(50,000 £1 shares fully paid)		

Activity 6

See if you can show the effect on the balance sheet of a company of the following transactions, by filling in the blank spaces below.

A company with an authorized capital of 100,000 shares with a nominal value of £1 each issues:

(a) 50,000 £1 shares payable 50p immediately, and the remaining 50p at some future date.

Assets		Claims	
Cash	....	Capital	....

(b) 50,000 shares payable in full, at a premium of 50p

Assets		Claims	
Cash	....	Capital	....
		Share premium	....

You should have come up with the following:

(a)	*Assets*	£	*Claims*	£
	Cash	+25,000	Share capital	+25,000

(b)	*Assets*		*Claims*	
	Cash	+75,000	Share capital	+50,000
			Share premium	+25,000

Where shares are issued on an instalment basis, and a premium is to be included in the price, it is usual for the premium to be taken as part of the first instalment. For example, if 50,000 £1 shares were issued at a premium of 50p, payable £1 immediately, and 50p a year from now, the effect on the balance sheet would be as follows:

Assets		*Claims*	
Cash	+£50,000	Share capital (partly paid)	£25,000
		Share premium	£25,000

Ordinary shares

These are issued by the company to investors who are prepared to expose themselves to risk in order also to expose themselves to the expectation of high investment returns, which both intuition and evidence tell us are associated with risk. Ordinary shareholders of successful companies usually receive cash dividends on an annual or more frequent basis. Dividends to shareholders are the equivalent of drawings by a sole proprietor. The fund available for payment of dividends is what remains after all expenses, including interest on long-term loans and any dividends on preference shares have been met. Dividends may be further restricted at the discretion of the directors. Dividends are therefore uncertain; prior claims may exhaust the available funds or the directors may decide to plough back profits at the expense of ordinary share dividends. The maximum amount of dividend which a company may pay at any particular time is restricted by law. Why this restriction exists, and how it is applied, will be discussed later in the chapter.

In principle, where funds are retained rather than distributed they remain the property of the ordinary shareholders who are the ultimate owners or equity holders. In that sense, retained profits are as much part of the ordinary shareholder's return as are the dividends, since profits retained should have a direct effect on the value of the shares. In fact, retained profits represent a major source of long-term finance for UK companies. Other things being equal, the retention of profits, and their subsequent reinvestment in profitable ventures, should lead to an expectation of increased earnings in the future, which is likely to lead to an increase in share price. In considering the adequacy of earnings for a company, it is thus important to bear in mind these two components, namely dividends and growth in share price.

Historically, in the UK, increases in the value of equities have tended to represent a larger element than have dividends in returns to shareholder, i.e. dividends have tended to be less important to shareholders than have capital gains.

Not surprisingly, given the above comments, there is no reason why shares, when traded between investors, should be priced according to the original issue price or their face value (nominal or par value). Perceptions of the value of a share in any particular company will change with varying economic circumstances, so that share prices will shift over time. It might be helpful to repeat that shareholders selling their shares in a particular company for some price has no direct effect on that company. The company will simply pay future dividends and give future voting rights to the new shareholder.

It is the ordinary shareholders who normally have the voting power within the company. It is thus the ordinary shareholders who effectively control the company. Each ordinary share confers equal rights on its owner in terms of dividend entitlement, voting power and a distribution of the company's assets, should the company be closed down (liquidated). Two shares carry exactly twice as much of these rights as does one share. The law forbids the directors from discriminating between the rights of different shareholders, other than on the basis of the number of shares owned (assuming that the shares owned are of the same class). Miss X owning 100 shares in Z Plc should have equal rights in respect of her shareholding as Mr Y who owns a similar number of shares in the same company. The Stock Exchange and other non-statutory agencies also seek to promote this equality.

Preference shares

These represent part of the risk-bearing ownership of the company, though they usually confer on their holders a right to receive the first slice of any dividend which is paid. There is an upper limit on the preference dividend per share, which is usually defined as a percentage of the nominal value of the share. Preference share dividends are usually paid in full, provided that sufficient profit (and cash) exists. Preference shares give more sure returns than equities (ordinary shares) do, though they by no means provide certain returns. Preference shares do not usually confer voting rights. They do not automatically give the same preference in repayment in a liquidation as they do in payment of dividends, though in some companies such preference does exist.

Preference shares of many public companies are traded in the capital market. As with equities, prices of preference shares will vary with investors' perceptions of future prospects. Generally preference share prices are less volatile than those of equities, as dividends tend to be fairly stable and usually have an upper limit.

In terms of the amount of funds raised, preference shares are not a very important source of funds.

Raising share capital

Share capital can be raised in a variety of ways, ranging from funds provided
by a small group of individuals (like a family), merchant bankers and other institutional backers, to funds raised directly from the public. A detailed examination of the advantages and disadvantages of the various sources of finance is
beyond the scope of this book.

Shares are not always issued for cash. Issuing shares in exchange for other
assets, including the shares of another company, is not uncommon. For
example, most takeovers are effected by the purchasing company issuing its own
shares to the shareholders of the target company, in exchange for the shares
held by those shareholders. In many cases, the takeover offer may also include
an element of cash and/or loan stocks. A bit more detail on how takeovers occur
is given in Chapter 7.

Shares issued at a premium

As we have seen, it is not uncommon for companies to issue shares at above
their nominal or face value.

For example, suppose that a business which has 100,000 shares of £1 each
continues in business successfully for several years, retaining some of its profits
(£100,000 in total) to help fund an expansion programme. This results in a
balance sheet which appears as follows (summary form only):

	£		£
Assets		*Claims*	
Net assets	200,000	Ordinary share capital	100,000
		(100,000 shares of £1	
		each fully paid)	
		Reserves (retained profit)	100,000
	200,000		200,000

If share prices reflected book values each share would be worth £2
(£200,000/100,000). If a further 100,000 £1 shares were issued at par (£1 each),
the resulting balance sheet would be:

	£		£
Assets		*Claims*	
Net assets	300,000	Ordinary share capital	200,000
		(200,000 shares of £1 each	
		fully paid)	
		Reserves	100,000
	300,000		300,000

If share prices continue to reflect book values, the above issue would result in
a share price of £1.50 (£300,000/100,000). Existing shareholders would effectively

lose part of their claim, to the advantage of the new shareholders. This is because all shareholders of a particular category have equal rights, irrespective of when such shares were issued.

Activity 7

In the above example, at what price would the new shares need to be issued to preserve the existing shareholders' effective wealth, assuming that book value reflects share price?

Show the revised balance sheet after the issue of new shares at this price.

You should have come up with the fact that the shares would need to be issued at £2, the current market price. The resulting balance sheet would appear something like as follows:

Assets	£	Claims	£
Net assets	400,000	Ordinary share capital	
		(200,000 shares of £1 each	
		fully paid)	200,000
		Reserves	100,000
		Share premium account	100,000
	400,000		400,000

This should leave the share price at £2 per share.

In practice, the share price is unlikely to be as closely related to book value as is implied above. However, the current market price per share is likely to provide a good guide to an appropriate issue price for any new shares, provided that expectations about the earnings associated with the new capital are similar to those associated with the existing business. In the final analysis, the price agreed will reflect a balance between the need for the new capital and the likely demand from investors for the new shares at various prices. Likely demand levels will in turn reflect expected future earnings.

Rights issues

Sometimes a new issue will be made to people, or organizations, which were not previously shareholders. It is more common, however, for new issues by existing companies to be offered, in the first instance, to existing shareholders. Such an issue is known as a rights issue. A rights issue is an offer to existing shareholders of a *right to acquire further shares in proportion to the shareholders' existing holdings*. When the rights are taken up *cash* is actually paid into the business by the shareholders. The price at which shares are offered in a rights issue is usually below the current share price. Rights to acquire shares at

Self-assessment question 5.1
A company, with the balance sheet given below, intends to issue 100,000
£1 ordinary shares at a price of £2.50 per share, which is the market price
of existing shares.

Assets	£000	Claims	£000
Net assets	200	Ordinary share capital (100,000 shares of £1 each fully paid)	100
		Reserves	100
	200		200

(a) What is the book value per share, before the new share issue?
(b) Show the balance sheet after the new issue
(c) What is the book value per share after the new issue?
(d) What reasons may exist for the book value per share to differ from
     market price per share?

A suggested solution to this question appears at the end of the book.

a preferential rate can be sold, so shareholders who do not wish to take up the
offer (or who cannot afford to) may sell their rights to others who might wish
to do so. Such an approach virtually guarantees the success of a rights issue.

Example

A company with 1 million shares of £1 each, with a market value of £5 each,
makes a rights issue on a one-for-five basis (all shareholders will be offered one
new share for every five which they already hold), at a price of £3 per share.
The value put on the company before the rights issue is thus £5m. Since the
rights issue will be 200,000 new shares at a price of £3, the proceeds will be
£600,000. *After* the issue, other things being equal, the market is likely to value
the company at £5.6m. Since there will now be 1.2m shares the market price
per share should settle at around £4.67 (i.e. 5.6m/1.2m). The new shares can be
obtained for £3 each, so it would be worth paying up to £1.67 to obtain a right.
  If the rights were traded at £1.67 each, the position of two shareholders taking
different approaches to the issue can be seen to be effectively identical. For a
shareholder owning five shares before the rights issue, the total value of the
investment will be £25 (5 × £5).
  A shareholder who takes up the right will pay a further £3, making the total
investment £28. After the issue this will be reflected in a holding of six shares,
each priced at £4.67.

A shareholder who does not take up the right, but sells it for £1.67, will thus own five shares at £4.67 per share (£23.33) and will have cash of £1.67, making a total of £25. Clearly, if the rights are traded at £1.67 there is no change in the relative wealth of shareholders who take up the rights and those who do not. In practice, of course, it is unlikely that prices will change with the precision implied above, but the general principles remain valid. If a rights issue is associated with expansion, or an improvement in prospects, the value of the shares after the rights issue may well be higher than would be suggested using the above approach.

The advantages of rights issues to a company are threefold:

- they are a relatively cheap form of finance, since there are no advertising costs and administrative costs are low;
- since rights are issued in proportion to existing shareholdings, control may be retained by existing shareholders; and
- the price at which the rights issue is set will not affect existing shareholders' wealth, provided that they either take up the rights or sell them. The example which precedes Activity 7 shows that this is not true with issues made to the general public.

5.7 Reserves

Amounts of shareholders' capital (owners' claim) over and above the share capital are known as reserves. Reserves are in essence retained profits and gains. They may arise in a number of ways, the most common of which are given below:

Revenue reserves

Profits should arise in the normal course of trading. From these dividends may be paid, along with any tax bills associated with the profits made (corporation tax). Any profits remaining are accumulated in various revenue reserve accounts. Typically, revenue reserves are shown under one or a combination of the following headings:

- revenue reserves
- profit and loss
- general reserve
- fixed asset replacement reserve

There is no legal difference between these, and the precise title used is a matter of preference. The reason for making the distinction between the various revenue reserves is normally to give some indication of the purpose of retaining the profit.

Capital reserves

Capital reserves are retained gains which have arisen from transactions *not related to trading* as such. The most common are:

(a) *Share premium.* The difference between the nominal or par value of a share (or the part called) and the agreed issue price, or that part of the nominal value which has been 'called'. We have discussed this reserve already.
(b) *Revaluation reserve.* This reflects the unrealized increase in value of an asset which has been revalued in the balance sheet. For example, suppose that a company which owned property shown in the books at £1 million wished to revalue it to £2 million. The property would be increased to £2 million in the fixed assets area of the balance sheet, and a corresponding increase in owners' claim would be needed. Since the share capital of a company must be shown at its nominal value, the increase in value will need to be shown elsewhere. It is, therefore, recorded in a revaluation reserve. It is important to note that the revaluation reserve reflects *unrealized profits*. This fact can have an important bearing on the payment of dividends, as will be seen later in this chapter.

Activity 8
Which accounting conventions are breached by reflecting market value of fixed assets in the balance sheet?

The breached conventions are:

• Historic cost.
• Realization.

These conventions are not infrequently breached by companies whose fixed assets have a market value greater than their cost. This departure from the accepted rule is tolerated by company law. Such deviations can be confusing to users of accounting information, however.

(c) *Capital redemption reserve.* This is a special reserve which is associated with the repayment of share capital, and will be dealt with in more detail shortly.

Companies are not legally required to distinguish between capital and revenue reserves in their balance sheets. Separate disclosure is required by law for certain capital reserves, namely the share premium and capital redemption reserve. Any other reserves should be classified under headings which are appropriate to a particular company's business.

5.8 Transferring funds to shareholders

Company law lays down strict rules surrounding the extent to which companies may transfer assets to their owners (i.e. their shareholders). This contrasts dramatically with the total absence of restriction surrounding the rights of sole proprietors and partners to take assets from their businesses.

Activity 9
Why do you think this contrast exists?

The contrast exists because of the separate legal status of companies and, springing from this, the limited liability of shareholders. If business assets are transferred to become personal assets of sole proprietors and partners, the accessibility of these assets to claimants against the business remains the same. Assets transferred by a company to its shareholders change their status in terms of their accessibility to claimants against the company.

As a result, company law restricts the right of companies to transfer assets to shareholders.

A buffer for creditors

The aim of company law, in this context, is to safeguard the interests of creditors and lenders. If capital could be paid out to shareholders, without restriction, it would be possible for unscrupulous shareholders to make large payments to themselves, leaving the creditors to salvage what they can. Company law seeks to establish that all existing and potential creditors or lenders know that the shareholders' interests in the company cannot be reduced below the amount of *effective fixed capital*, as a result of making payments to themselves out of the company's assets.

Example

Consider the balance sheet of Mario Ltd.

Fixed assets	£	*Claims*	£
Fixed assets	800	Ordinary share capital	2,000
Investments	1,200	(1,000 shares of £1 each	
Current assets		fully paid)	
Stock	500	Share premium	1,000
Debtors	500	Profit and loss account	400
Cash	1,200	Creditors	800
	4,200		4,200

Suppose that no rules about capital maintenance exist.

The company sold the investments and stock, at their balance sheet values, and collected the cash owing from the debtors in full. All of the owners' claims were then settled in cash.

The balance sheet after these transactions would appear as follows:

Fixed assets	£	*Claims*	£
Fixed assets	800	Ordinary share capital	—
Investments	—	(1,000 shares of £1 each	—
Current assets		fully paid)	
Stock	—	Share premium	—
Debtors	—	Profit and loss account	—
Cash	—	Creditors	800
	800		800

The creditors are in a very much less secure position after these transactions than they were before. Before the transactions, there were assets with book value totalling £4,200 available to meet the creditors' claim, including £1,200 in cash. As a result of the transactions it will mean that, unless the fixed assets realize at least their book value, the assets of the company will be unable to meet the claim of the creditors. Since the other assets are now in the hands of the shareholders, whose liability is limited, the creditors can do no more than hope that the fixed assets will realize at least £800 so that their claim can be met in full.

Clearly, people and organizations will be reluctant to work for, trade with or lend money to a company which can suddenly erode the security of external claimants in this way. This would make the limited company useless as a device for encouraging enterprise and commerce. As a result, company law has established that transfers of company assets to shareholders are restricted.

The purpose of the law is, therefore, to provide a buffer for the creditors and lenders. Creditors and lenders should be able to be confident that a certain part of the shareholders' equity cannot be taken out of the business. The law seeks to ensure that this buffer cannot be reduced below the amount of *effective fixed capital* (i.e. share capital + non-distributable reserves). The situation outlined in the above example could thus not arise. In fact, the effective capital could not normally be reduced below £3,000 as a result of payments being made to shareholders. Why it is this figure will be explained shortly.

It is worth noting that the conditions identified above do not ensure that effective fixed capital cannot be reduced under any circumstances. If the company were to sustain trading losses this could eat into the effective fixed capital.

It is also worth noting that company law does not set a minimum level of effective fixed capital. The law merely demands that whatever level of effective fixed capital has been set by the company cannot normally be reduced as a result of payments to shareholders.

Funds may be transferred from the company to shareholders as a result of three types of transaction:

(a) the payment of dividends
(b) the redemption of capital
(c) liquidation of the company

Very clear rules, set out in the 1985 Companies Act, exist in these areas.

Dividends

In essence dividends can only be paid out of realized profits. The total available will reflect the profits accumulated over the years, net of any losses. The total available will include trading profits and profits on disposal of fixed assets. Surpluses arising from revaluing fixed assets, however, cannot be distributed as a dividend.

Activity 10

Bubbly Ltd started trading in 19X6 when it made a loss for the year of £100,000. In 19X7 it made a profit of £80,000.

What do you think is the maximum dividend which the company could legally pay at the end of 19X7?

The answer is zero; there is still a cumulative net loss overall of £20,000.

Activity 11

Photo Ltd started trading in 19X6 when it made a profit of £100,000. In 19X7 it sustained a loss of £80,000.

What is the maximum dividend which the company could pay at the end of 19X7, assuming that no dividends were paid in 19X6?

The answer is £20,000, i.e. the cumulative net retained profit.

Activity 12

As well as the trading results given in Activity 11 you find that during 19X7 Photo Ltd sold a plot of land which had cost £100,000 for £150,000 and had revalued another similar plot which had also cost £100,000 to £150,000.

What is the maximum dividend which the company could pay at the end of 19X7?

Your answer should be £70,000 – the £50,000 profit on disposal plus the £20,000 from cumulative profits. The revaluation reserve of £50,000 could not be distributed as a dividend.

In paying dividends, it is important to note that preference shareholders will take priority over ordinary shareholders. An ordinary dividend cannot be paid until the due preference dividend has been paid. The directors are not obliged to declare dividends, either preference or ordinary, but in practice preference dividends are seldom missed.

In practice, the amount of dividend which is actually paid to ordinary shareholders usually falls well short of the legal maximum. Several reasons may be given for this.

(a)   It has already been noted that capital and reserves together must equal net assets (the balance sheet equation). However, there is no direct link between reserves and cash. A shortage of liquid funds is likely to lead to dividend payments which are a relatively small part of the distributable reserves. Legally, it is possible to borrow cash to pay dividends.

(b)   Retained profits, as has already been mentioned, represent the major source of funds for new investments by companies. Low dividends leave more funds for growth.

(c)   Differences in the basis of taxation may attract certain shareholders to companies associated with low dividends, high growth and thus increasing share price.

It is important to note that reserves are not cash balances, despite the fact that people talk about 'paying dividends out of reserves'. For example, consider the following balance sheet, relating to Andros Ltd, as at 31 December 19X7.

Assets	£	*Claims*	£
Net assets	173,000	Share capital (100,000 ordinary shares of £1 each)	100,000
		Revaluation reserve	20,000
		Profit and loss account	53,000
	173,000		173,000

(Note that in this example retained profits (revenue reserves) are shown simply under the heading 'profit and loss account'.)

If the directors of Andros Ltd decide to pay a dividend they will take part of the net assets (presumably cash, though dividends can, and very occasionally do, take other forms) and give it to the shareholders in accordance with the number of shares owned by each one. Suppose that a dividend of £25,000 is decided upon. This will have the effect of reducing the net assets to £148,000 (i.e. £173,000 – £25,000). The other aspect of this transaction is that the shareholders' claim against the company will be reduced by £25,000, thus reducing the profit and loss account balance from £53,000 to £28,000.

Reserves are part of the claim of the shareholders on the net assets of a business. The existence of reserves implies nothing about the availability of cash to pay out such reserves as dividends. It is perfectly possible to have substantial reserves and limited cash, indeed even an overdraft. Under such circumstances, while it may be legally possible to pay dividends, the liquidity position of the company may make this commercially imprudent. There is no legal reason why a company should not use borrowed funds to finance a dividend, provided that there are sufficient revenue reserves to cover the dividend. There may be good commercial reasons why such a policy should not be used. On the other hand, a company could quite feasibly have plenty of cash but no distributable reserves (see Activity 10), making a dividend illegal.

Redemption of shares and share repurchase

Subject to certain restrictions companies are allowed to reduce share capital, either by redeeming share capital or by buying some of their own shares, from the shareholders, and cancelling those shares. These are very similar activities, in terms of their overall effect on the company, so we shall refer to them both as share redemptions. Such redemptions occur relatively infrequently. One reason for redemptions is that sometimes companies find that they have more capital than they can effectively use. Another reason is that shares are sometimes issued on the understanding that they will be redeemed at some point.

We have already seen that, in the context of transferring funds to shareholders, the guiding principle is that the interests of creditors and lenders take priority over those of shareholders.

In order to preserve the relative position of the creditors and lenders, a redemption can only occur if certain rules are followed. In broad terms, a company may only redeem (repay) share capital where the total effective fixed capital is not reduced as a result of the redemption. Effective fixed capital means share capital plus non-distributable reserves.

Example

Suppose that the balance sheet of Crete Ltd is as follows:

Assets	£	*Claims*	£
Net assets	153,000	Ordinary share capital (100,000 shares of £1 each fully paid)	100,000
		Redeemable preference shares (20,000 shares of £1 each fully paid)	20,000
		Profit and loss account	33,000
	153,000		153,000

The company wishes to redeem the preference shares. In the above balance sheet the total effective fixed capital is £120,000 before redemption of the preference shares. This figure must be preserved *after* the redemption of the preference shares.

This can be effected in one (or a combination) of two ways:

(a) by issuing new shares to replace those redeemed;
(b) by converting an appropriate amount of distributable reserves into share capital (by the use of a bonus issue), or into a separate undistributable reserve which may be seen as being effectively the same as share capital.

It is worth noting that the overall effect of a share redemption is, in essence, much the same as the payment of a dividend. This is to say that the effective capital stays the same; distributable reserves go down by the same amount as the cash which is paid to the shareholders.

A bonus issue arises when a company converts part of its reserves into share capital. We shall consider bonus issues, and the reason for them, shortly.

If the redeemable preference shares were to be replaced by a new issue of 20,000 £1 ordinary shares at par the effect would be as follows:

Assets	£	Claims	£
Net assets	153,000	Ordinary share capital (120,000 shares of £1 each fully paid)	120,000
		Profit and loss account	33,000
	153,000		153,000

Since the total capital remains the same (£120,000) after the redemption of the preference shares, the legal provisions with regard to redemption have been satisfied.

Suppose now that the preference shares were to be redeemed at par, without a new issue of shares to replace them. The initial impact of redemption would be to change the balance sheet as follows:

Assets	£	Claims	£
Net assets	133,000	Ordinary share capital (100,000 shares of £1 each fully paid)	100,000
		Profit and loss account	33,000
	133,000		133,000

However, this balance sheet reflects a reduction in effective fixed capital, by £20,000. This is illegal. Under such circumstances, therefore, an amount equivalent to the effective reduction (i.e. the nominal value of the shares redeemed) must be transferred from distributable reserves to share capital or undistributable reserves, so as to maintain the effective fixed capital. This transfer may be done in two ways:

(a) by opening a new capital (i.e. undistributable) reserve known as the *capital redemption reserve*, and transferring the appropriate amount to it, from distributable reserves;
(b) by converting distributable reserves into share capital by a bonus issue;
(c) by a combination of (a) and (b) totalling £20,000.

If the first of these is done the balance sheet of Crete Ltd would appear as follows:

Assets	£	*Claims*	£
Net assets	133,000	Ordinary share capital (100,000 ordinary shares of £1 each)	100,000
		Capital redemption reserve	20,000
		Profit and loss account	13,000
	133,000		133,000

It should be noted that the capital redemption reserve is to be treated as if it is share capital, and thus may not be distributed as a dividend or reduced, other than by a court order. It may, however, be used to issue bonus shares, since this does not involve a reduction in effective fixed capital. In the balance sheet after the redemption the effective fixed capital is thus £120,000 (share capital plus the capital redemption reserve), thus maintaining it at the required level.

If a bonus issue on a one for five basis was made from distributable reserves the balance sheet would appear as follows:

Assets	£	*Claims*	£
Net assets	133,000	Ordinary share capital (100,000 shares of £1 each fully paid)	120,000
		Profit and loss account	13,000
	133,000		133,000

In this case the bonus issue *must* come from distributable reserves, to satisfy the legal conditions. As before, the capital *after* the redemption is £120,000, satisfying the legal requirements.

Activity 13

The balance sheets of Leonidas Ltd is as follows:

Assets	£	*Claims*	£
Net assets	200,000	Ordinary share capital (120,000 shares of £1 each fully paid)	120,000

		Redeemable preference share capital (30,000 shares of £1 each fully paid)	30,000
		Profit and loss account	50,000
	200,000		200,000

The directors decide to redeem all of the preference share capital at par. This is to be partially replaced by a new issue of 20,000 ordinary shares of £1 each, at par.

Show the balance sheet after the redemption and new issue.

The balance sheet should look something like this:

Assets	£	*Claims*	£
Net assets	190,000	Ordinary share capital (140,000 shares of £1 each fully paid)	140,000
		Capital redemption reserve	10,000
		Profit and loss account	40,000
	190,000		190,000

Activity 14

The balance sheet of Hopeful Ltd is as follows:

Assets	£	*Claims*	£
Net assets	170,000	Ordinary share capital (120,000 shares of £1 each fully paid)	120,000
		Redeemable preference share capital (30,000 shares of £1 each fully paid)	30,000
		Profit and loss account	20,000
	170,000		170,000

The directors decide to redeem all of the preference share capital at par. The directors do not intend to issue any new shares because the company has plenty of cash available for the redemption.

Show the balance sheet after the redemption and new issue.

This is a bit of a trick question. It would be illegal to redeem more than 20,000 of the preference shares because there are only distributable reserves available to that extent. The availability of cash is not the only important factor here.

Liquidation

A limited company, because it has separate existence from its shareholders, does not die when they do. The only way in which the company's demise can be brought about is by following the statutorily defined steps to liquidate the company. Liquidation involves appointing a liquidator to realize the company's assets, pay the claimants and formally to lay the company to rest.

The initiative to liquidate the company usually comes either from:

(a) the shareholders, perhaps because the purpose for which the company was formed has been served; or
(b) the company's creditors (including loan creditors), where the company is failing to pay its debts. In these circumstances the objective is to stop the company from trading and to ensure that non-cash assets are realized, the proceeds being used, along with any cash assets, to meet (perhaps only partially) the claims of the creditors. This type of liquidation is sometimes referred to colloquially as bankruptcy.

Order of paying claimants

Irrespective of which type of liquidation is involved, the liquidator, having realized all of the non-cash assets, must take great care as to the order in which the claimants are paid. Broadly speaking the order is:

(a) *Secured creditors*, where the security is on a specified asset or group of assets. The proceeds of disposal of the asset are to be applied to meeting the specific claim. If the proceeds are insufficient the creditor must stand with the unsecured creditors for the shortfall. If the proceeds exceed the amount of the claim, the excess goes into the fund available to unsecured creditors.
(b) *Unsecured creditors*. This would usually include most trade creditors. It would also include any unsecured loan creditors.

Only after the creditors have been paid in full will the balance of the funds be paid out to the shareholders. If the preference shares carry no right to priority of payment, each share (ordinary and preference) will be entitled to an equal portion of the residue of funds. Where preference shares bestow the right to payment before ordinary shareolders, each ordinary share will command an equal slice of the funds remaining after the creditors and preference share-holders have had their full entitlement.

The order of payment of creditors will be of little consequence except where there are insufficient funds to meet all claims. Where this is the case, each class of claim must be met in full before the next class may participate.

Activity 15

Failure Ltd has been trading unprofitably for several years and has recently experienced a cash shortage so severe that it has not been able to pay its debts. The creditors have successfully initiated a winding-up by the court. At the date of the winding-up order the balance sheet was as follows:

	£000	£000
Fixed assets (at cost less depreciation)		
Land and buildings	80	
Plant and machinery	10	
Motor vehicles	5	
	95	
Current assets		
Stock	10	
Trade debtors	12	
	22	
Creditors: amounts falling due within 1 year		
Bank overdraft	26	
Trade creditors	14	
	40	
	(18)	
Creditors: amounts due more than 1 year from now		
Loan stock (secured on land and buildings)	50	
		(68)
		27
Financed by:		
Share capital		60
Less *accumulated losses*		33
		27

When the liquidator realized the assets, the following amounts were received:

	£000
Land and buildings	70
Plant and machinery	2
Motor vehicles	3
Stock	9
Trade debtors	12

You are required to show how the available funds should be deployed by the liquidator.

Your answer should look something like this:

	£000
Proceeds from liquidation	96
Cost of assets disposed of	117
Therefore loss on disposal	21

The loss would be borne by the shareholders, thus reducing their claim to £6,000. The available funds would be distributed as follows:

		£000
1	Loan stock	50
2	Creditors and overdraft	40
3	Shareholders	6
		96

Note that the accumulated losses in the balance sheet of Failure Ltd are, in effect, a negative reserve.

It is clear that, after a liquidation, there will be a zero effective capital. This does not matter because the creditors will be entitled to receive all of their claim before shareholders are entitled to anything.

5.9   Bonus shares

A bonus share is a share which is given to shareholders 'free', with no cash being required by the company. It is not an increase in the shareholders' claim. It is not a transfer of company funds to the shareholders. This is why we are dealing with bonus issues in a separate section.

Bonus shares are issued in proportion to existing holdings of shares. Very little in life is really free, and bonus shares are no exception to this. If bonus shares are issued, and share capital is increased by the amount of the new shares issued, there must be a corresponding adjustment somewhere else in the balance sheet. Since no cash is received the adjustment cannot be to increase cash. In fact, all that happens with a bonus issue is that certain reserves are converted into paid-up share capital. The adjustment for a bonus issue is thus to increase share capital and to decrease reserves. A bonus issue does not therefore increase the owners' claims on the company (which is the sum of share capital and reserves), but simply shifts part of the claim from reserves to share capital. The directors may convert reserves into share capital by the use of bonus shares at any time. Any reserves, including capital redemption reserve and share premium, can legally be converted into bonus shares. The issue of bonus shares is also referred to as a *scrip or capitalization issue.*

Example

The balance sheet of Andros Ltd is as follows:

Assets	£	Claims	£
Net assets	173,000	Ordinary share capital (100,000 shares of £1 each fully paid)	100,000
		Revaluation reserve	20,000
		Profit and loss account	53,000
	173,000		173,000

The directors decide to convert the revaluation reserve, and £30,000 of the profit and loss account balance, into share capital, by making a one-for-two bonus issue to existing shareholders, i.e. giving each shareholder one additional new share in respect of every two shares already held.

The balance sheet immediately following the issue would be:

Assets	£	Claims	£
Net assets	173,000	Ordinary share capital (150,000 shares of £1 each fully paid)	150,000
		Profit and loss account	23,000
	173,000		173,000

Activity 16
(a) Do you think that the shareholders will be more wealthy after the bonus issue than they were before it?
(b) What do you believe to be the effect of the bonus issue on the reserves which are available for use as a dividend?

Your answers should have been along the following lines:

(a) The bonus issue should not make any difference to shareholder wealth, since the ownership claim remains at £173,000.
(b) Distributable reserves fall from £53,000 to £23,000.

It should be clear from this activity that bonus issues do not, of themselves, lead to increased shareholder wealth. They are certainly not free. Indeed, in the above example not only does the total claim of the shareholders remain the same, but the amount available for distribution as a dividend has fallen. Under such circumstances it is difficult to see much point in an issue of bonus shares. However, several reasons for their use may be given.

(a) In spite of the points made above many shareholders like receiving bonus issues, and may feel better off.

(b) For many well-established businesses the chance of a significant portion of reserves actually being distributed is minimal. Under such circumstances a movement from reserves into capital reflects the realities of the situation, that the reserves concerned are considered by the company to be part of the effective fixed capital.

(c) Where a company is seeking a loan, the potential lender may prefer that the ability of the company to make cash payments in the form of dividends to its shareholders be restricted. It may therefore set as a condition of any loan that revenue reserves are wholly or partly converted into shares.

(d) It is frequently anticipated that after the bonus issue the company will continue to pay the same dividend per share. Since each shareholder will then own more shares, the dividend paid will be higher. If shareholders prefer dividends this may be to their advantage.

(e) If the price per share becomes high it is sometimes the case that the shares become less easy to trade on the Stock Exchange, leading to a lessening of interest in the shares on the part of the investing public. Research studies have suggested that there are certain ranges of share price which are better than others, in terms of generating activity on the market. Under such circumstances a bonus issue, while leading to a fall in share price, may not result in as large a fall as might be expected, leaving shareholders slightly better off. This is because the increased marketability of the shares may have a beneficial effect on the share price.

Example

Kos Ltd has the following balance sheet:

Assets	£	Claims	£
Net assets	1,000,000	Ordinary share capital (100,000 shares of £1 each fully paid)	100,000
		Reserves	900,000
	1,000,000		1,000,000

The current share price on the Stock Exchange if £12. This means that the current market value of the company is £1.2m. Suppose now that a bonus issue on a five-for-one basis was made. The resulting balance sheet would be:

Assets	£	Claims	£
Net assets	1,000,000	Ordinary share capital (600,000 shares of £1 each fully paid)	600,000
		Reserves	400,000
	1,000,000		1,000,000

Only the capital structure of the business has changed. The net assets remain the same. It may reasonably be presumed that the future prospects of the business are unchanged by the bonus issue. Under such circumstances, the market value of the company should remain at £1.2m, which should in turn lead to a price of £2 per share. At this price shareholders are no better off, and no worse off. A holder of one share valued at £12 before the bonus issue now has six shares valued at £2 each. However, the implication of the argument put forward in (e) above is that there would be more interest from potential investors for shares with a price of £2 each than for shares with a price of £12. The result of an increase in investor interest may be that the new share price settles at a higher figure than £2 (say £2.10). In these circumstances, greater wealth may result from the bonus issue. The holder of one share, valued at £12, would now have six shares valued at £2.10, i.e. a total value of £12.60, giving an increase of 5% on the holding. Despite the possible reasons for bonus shares which are given here, it is still not clear why they exist. They occur, however, and their implications in terms of accounts need to be recognized.

Where a choice exists as to which reserves should be capitalized (i.e. converted into share capital), it is sensible to convert first those reserves which are not available for dividends, thus preserving maximum flexibility in the future with regard to cash dividends. Of course, where the bonus issue occurs for the reasons set out in (c) above this flexibility is precisely what a potential lender is trying to limit.

Activity 17

Spiros Ltd has the following balance sheet:

Assets	£	Claims	£
Net assets	850,000	Ordinary share capital (400,000 shares of £1 each fully paid)	400,000
		Share premium account	150,000
		Revaluation reserve	150,000
		Revenue reserves	150,000
	850,000		850,000

Have a try at showing the effect on the balance sheet of a bonus issue:

(a) on a one-for-four basis
(b) on a one-for-two basis
(c) on a one-for-one basis

Explain *why* you have done what you have done. You should assume that the company wishes to retain the maximum dividend payment potential.

Your balance sheets should look something like this:

(a)

Assets	£	Claims	£
Net assets	850,000	Ordinary share capital (500,000 shares of £1 each fully paid)	500,000
		Share premium account	50,000
		Revaluation reserve	150,000
		Revenue reserves	150,000
	850,000		850,000

(b)

	£		£
Net assets	850,000	Ordinary share capital (600,000 shares of £1 each fully paid)	600,000
		Revaluation reserve	100,000
		Revenue reserves	150,000
	850,000		850,000

(c)

	£		£
Net assets	850,000	Ordinary share capital (800,000 shares of £1 each fully paid)	800,000
		Revenue reserves	50,000
	850,000		850,000

In order to preserve flexibility with regard to the availability of reserves for distribution as cash dividends it would be prudent to convert reserves in the order:

(a) share premium – since this has very limited uses,
(b) revaluation reserve – not distributable unless the profit is actually realized,
(c) revenue reserves.

Self-assessment question 5.2
The balance sheet of Corfu Ltd is as follows:

Assets	£	Claims	£
Net assets	900,000	Ordinary share capital (400,000 shares of £1 each fully paid)	400,000
		Share premium account	100,000

		Revaluation reserve	200,000
		Revenue reserves	100,000
	900,000		900,000

The company decides to make a bonus issue on a one-for-four basis, followed by a rights issue on a one-for-five basis, at a premium of 50p.

Show the balance sheet after these issues.

Explain the movements in reserves fully.

A suggested solution to this questions appears at the back of the book.

5.10 Long-term loans

Most companies borrow funds on a long-term, occasionally on a perpetual, basis. Lenders enter into a contractual relationship, with the company with the rate of interest, its date of payment, the redemption date and amount all being terms of the contract. Many long-term lenders require rather more by way of security for their loan than the rights conferred on any lender under the law of contract. Typically they insist that the principal and sometimes the interest as well are secured on some specific asset of the borrowing company, frequently land. Such security might confer on lenders a right to seize the asset and sell it to satisfy their claims where repayment of principal or interest payment is overdue.

A particular form of long-term loan which is associated with companies is the *debenture*. This is essentially a loan evidenced by a deed. Debentures can be broken down into small parts, each for an agreed amount (say £10 for each unit). Holders of the debentures are then entitled to interest and repayment as set out in the overall loan agreement associated with the debenture issue. The debentures of many companies are traded on the Stock Exchange. It is thus possible for someone owed £100 by company X to sell this debt to another investor who, from the date of the sale, will become entitled to receive interest and repayment of the principal, in due course. Such payment amounts and dates are contractual obligations, so there is less doubt surrounding them than applies to returns from shares, more particularly where the loan is secured. For this reason, loan stocks tend not to fluctuate very much in their market value. To a lesser extent this is also true of preference shares.

In passing, it is worth noting that loan interest is regarded as a business expense, and is thus generally deducted from profits in assessing liability to tax.

Activity 18
Can you suggest reasons why companies typically raise some of their long-term finance from borrowing, instead of obtaining it from existing or new shareholders?

We came up with the following points:

- To fund expansion without any loss of control. Since lenders do not have any voting rights in a company, they cannot normally participate in management/decision-making.
- To fund expansion which could not otherwise take place, since the resources of the owners are limited.
- To obtain larger returns on projects by borrowing at a rate which is lower than the expected return on the project. The additional returns all accrue to the owners. This approach, and its associated risks, is dealt with more fully in later chapters.
- Interest on loans is a tax-deductible expense, making it quite a cheap form of finance.

5.11 Accounting for companies

Accountability of directors/published accounts

The law imposes a *duty on directors*:

- to keep accounting records sufficient to show and explain the company's transactions and sufficient to enable a balance sheet and a profit and loss account to be prepared, and
- to report annually both to the shareholders, and to some extent to the world at large, on the performance of the company's trading.

With regard to this latter duty directors are required to prepare annually (or to have prepared) a *report for the shareholders*. The minimum contents of the report are prescribed by law, though in practice this minimum is often exceeded. Principally the report consists of a profit and loss account, a balance sheet and a cash flow statement, though a directors' report is also required. These accounting statements, which are required to show a *true and fair view* of the trading results, financial position and cash flows of the company, are subject to audit by an independent firm of accountants.

A copy of the annual report must be sent to each shareholder and debenture holder. A copy must also be sent to the Registrar of Companies to be placed on the company's file, which is available for inspection by anyone wishing to do so. In practice, large companies also send copies of the report to financial analysts and journalists. Such companies will usually comply with a request from any private individual for a copy.

The annual report is a major, but not the only, source of information to interested parties, including existing and prospective shareholders, on the progress of the company. Companies whose shares are listed on the Stock Exchange are required by its rules to publish summarized accounting statements on a half-yearly basis. In practice, most large companies, from time to time, issue information over and above that which is contained in the annual and half-yearly reports.

The form and content of published accounts will be dealt with in more detail in the next chapter, on the regulatory framework of accounting.

It is worth emphasizing at this point that the accounting records kept by companies are basically the same as those of a sole proprietor, and follow the same principles as have been set out in earlier chapters. Similarly, the final accounts are much the same. It should be noted that at this stage the emphasis is on the broad principles of company financial reporting. A whole range of requirements exists with regard to the *publication* of accounting information relating to companies. These will be dealt with in Chapter 6, on the regulatory framework of accounting.

The profit and loss account

In essence, the various items included so far under revenues and expenses, in the trading and profit and loss accounts, are all likely to be found in the accounts of a limited company.

The profit and loss appropriation account

With a sole trading business it is clear that the net profit is the entitlement of the owner, and it is accordingly added to capital. Any drawings are deducted from capital. With a limited company there is a need for an appropriation account, in which the net profit is allocated. Part of the profit will almost certainly need to be set aside in order to pay corporation tax. (Corporation tax is, as its name implies, a tax levied on the profits and gains of companies.) The net profit after tax is all the entitlement of the shareholders, but some sharing out will be necessary if more than one category of shareholder exists. Dividends may be paid, while transfers may also be made to appropriate reserves (e.g. general reserve).

To deal with this need to share out, or appropriate, profits, an appropriation account is needed, in much the same way as was required for a partnership. The appropriation account would typically appear as follows:

Net profit for the year		*x*
Less: corporation tax		*x*
After-tax profit		*x*
Add profit and loss account balance		
brought forward		*x*
Total unappropriated profit		*x*
Less: Transfers to reserves	*x*	
Dividends	*x*	*x*
Profit and loss account balance		
carried forward		*x*

Activity 19

A company has a net profit of £50,000. It also has a balance of £10,000 on its profit and loss account from previous years. Corporation tax is expected to be £20,000. £5,000 is to be transferred to a general reserve. £16,000 is to be paid as an ordinary dividend, and £5,000 as a preference dividend.

Using the model shown above, draft the appropriation account.

Your appropriation account should look something like this:

	£000	£000	£000
Net profit for the year			50
Less Corporation tax			20
After tax profit			30
Add profit and loss account balance			
brought forward			10
Total unappropriated profit			40
Less Transfers to General reserve		5	
Dividends: Preference	5		
Ordinary	16	21	26
Profit and loss account balance			
carried forward			14

It should be noted that the appropriation account forms part of the accounting system, so the concept of duality applies to it. A corresponding entry is necessary for all the items in the appropriation account, with a resultant effect on the balance sheet. The corresponding entries are as follows:

- The net profit will be the figure entered in the profit and loss account.
- A claim for the estimated corporation tax (known as a corporation tax provision) will need to be set up.
- Dividends paid will typically result in a reduction in cash. Dividends proposed at the year end, but as yet unpaid, will need to be reflected in a current liability.
- Transfers to reserves will be added to any existing amounts in these reserve accounts, resulting in an increased total being shown.
- Any unappropriated profit will be carried forward as a balance on the profit and loss account. It will thus appear in the balance sheet at the end of the period, as a part of reserves, and will be carried forward as the opening balance on the appropriation account for the next period.

The balance sheet

The balance sheet of a company follows the same principles as the balance sheet of a sole proprietor, and the same general headings are used. The main differences arise in the area of capital and reserves, although a small number of differences elsewhere in the balance sheet may be noted.

Fixed assets

These must be disclosed at cost less aggregate depreciation provision, with totals for both cost and aggregate depreciation provisions being shown.

Current assets

No differences.

Current liabilities (i.e. liabilities payable within a year)

Additional items will be included to cover dividends unpaid and corporation tax.

Liabilities payable more than a year from the balance sheet date

These may include debentures and other loan stocks.

Capital and reserves

The share capital and reserves of a company are shown under separate headings.

Share capital

This will include the various categories of share capital which have been issued, at their nominal or par value.

Reserves

This section will include the various reserve accounts, normally with separate disclosure of the share premium, revaluation reserves, capital redemption reserves, and the distributable revenue reserves. The revenue reserves may be subdivided further, to include such things as general reserve, profit and loss account, etc.

Activity 20

A limited company has an authorized share capital of £1 million, divided into 250,000 preference shares (7%) of £1 each and 750,000 ordinary shares of £1 each.

All of the preference shares have been issued and fully paid, together with 500,000 ordinary shares, again fully paid. Both categories of share were issued at par.

At the beginning of the current financial year (1 January) the balance on general reserve was £150,000, while the profit and loss account balance was £15,000.

At the year end (31 December) the following claims and assets were found to exist:

- creditors £125,000
- fixed assets (at cost) £600,000
- fixed assets depreciation provision £120,000
- current assets £660,000

The net profit for the current year was £100,000. A corporation tax provision of £30,000 is to be set up, being the estimated liability on the profits, being payable in September of the following year. The directors also recommend that:

(a) the preference dividend is paid,
(b) £15,000 is transferred to general reserve, and
(c) a dividend of 10% of the nominal value of the shares is paid to ordinary shareholders.

Have a try at preparing a profit and loss appropriation account for the year and a balance sheet as at 31 December.

Your answer should look something like this:

Profit and loss appropriation account for the year ended 31 December

	£	£
Net profit for the year		100,000
Less: Corporation tax		30,000
Net profit after tax		70,000
Profit and loss account balance		
brought forward		15,000
Total available for appropriation		85,000
Less: Transfer to general reserve	15,000	
Preference dividends	17,500	
Ordinary dividends	50,000	
		82,500
Unappropriated profit carried forward		2,500

Balance sheet as at 31 December

	£	£	£
Fixed assets – cost			600,000
- depreciation provision			120,000
			480,000
Current assets		660,000	
Less: Creditors payable within a year			
Creditors	125,000		
Corporation tax	30,000		
Preference dividend	17,500		
Ordinary dividend	50,000		
		222,500	
			437,500
Net assets			917,500
Financed by:			
Capital			
Ordinary share capital			500,000
Preference share capital			250,000
			750,000
Reserves			
General reserve		165,000	
Profit and loss		2,500	
			167,500
			917,500

Self-assessment question 5.3

The following is a list of assets and expenses (left-hand column) and claims and revenues (right-hand column) of RAC Ltd as at 31 December 19X7. The figures represent the amounts concerned after all the transactions for the year had been recorded.

	Assets/ expenses £	Claims/ revenues £
Ordinary share capital		200,000
Preference share capital (10%)		50,000
Land and buildings	200,000	
Equipment – cost	50,000	
Equipment – depreciation provision		20,000
Fittings – cost	50,000	
Fittings – depreciation provision		25,000
Stock at 1 January 19X6	30,000	
Directors' remuneration	31,000	
Sales		530,000

Debtors	50,000	
Creditors		30,000
Purchases during the year	300,000	
Selling and distribution expenses	30,000	
Loan (10%)		40,000
Loan interest	2,000	
Administration expenses	40,000	
Profit and loss account balance brought forward		25,000
Wages and salaries	50,000	
Cash	100,000	
Bad debts written off	2,000	
General reserve		15,000
	935,000	935,000

You are given the following additional information relating to the year end, which is not incorporated into the figures above:

(a) Stock at 31 December 19X7 is valued at £35,000.
(b) Loan interest of £2,000 is due.
(c) £2,000 of administration expenses are outstanding.
(d) £1,000 of the selling and distribution expenses have been prepaid.
(e) Depreciation is to be taken in 19X7 on the basis of 10% on cost for equipment and fittings. No depreciation is to be calculated for land and buildings.
(f) The directors have recommended that the preference share dividend is to be paid, along with an ordinary dividend of 20% of the nominal value of the shares.
(g) £25,000 is to be transferred to general reserve.

Prepare trading, profit and loss and appropriation accounts for RAC Ltd for the year ended 31 December 19X7, and a balance sheet as at that date.

A suggested solution to this question appears at the end of the book.

5.12 Summary

This chapter has provided you with an introduction to the nature and accounts of limited companies. The various types of share capital were introduced, as were reserves (various types of retained profits). The rules which surround the transfer of funds to shareholders (dividends, redemptions and liquidations) were considered. The nature of loan stock was examined. The chapter concluded with an introduction to the final accounts of limited companies.

The next chapter considers the rules with which companies must comply in respect of their financial reporting to shareholders and to the world at large.

Exercises

1   Show the effect on the balance sheet of a company of the following transactions.

A company with an authorized capital of 100,000 ordinary shares of £1 each and 50,000 preference shares of £1 each issues:

(a)   50,000 ordinary shares of £1 each, at a premium of 25p, payable 75p immediately, and the remainder at some future date.

Assets		*Claims*	
Cash	£..................	....	£..................
		....	£..................
		....	£..................

(b)   100,000 ordinary shares of £1 each, at a premium of 50p, payable in full immediately, and 25,000 preference shares of £1 each, at par, also payable in full immediately.

Assets		*Claims*	
Cash	£..................	....	£..................
		....	£..................
		....	£..................

2   The balance sheet of XYZ Plc is presently as follows:

	£ millions	*£ millions*
Fixed assets at cost,		
less accumulated depreciation		210
Current assets		
Stock	158	
Debtors	68	
Cash	42	
	268	
Current liabilities		
Trade creditors	60	
		208
		418
Capital and reserves		
Ordinary shares of £1 each, fully paid		200
Profit and loss account (retained profit)		218
		418

The company's shares are traded on the Stock Exchange at a price which reflects the balance sheet value of the assets and claims.

The company wishes to make a one-for-two rights issue to ordinary shareholders at an issue price of £1.50 per share.

Required

(a) What is the current market price of the shares?
(b) How much will each ordinary share be worth after the rights issue?
(c) How much would a right to buy one new share be worth?
(d) Show the balance sheet immediately after the rights issue was completed, assuming that all of the shares are successfully issued.

3   The balance sheet of Abacus Ltd is currently as follows:

	£	£
Fixed assets at valuation and cost, less accumulated depreciation		350,000
Current assets		
Stock	75,000	
Debtors	43,000	
Cash	176,000	
	294,000	
Current liabilities		
Trade creditors	29,000	
		265,000
		615,000
Capital and reserves		
Ordinary shares of £1 each, fully paid		350,000
Preference shares of £1 each, fully paid		150,000
Revaluation reserve		50,000
Profit and loss account (retained profit)		65,000
		615,000

The directors wish to use most of the cash to redeem the whole of the preference shares at par. They are adamant that they do not wish to raise any new share capital. They have expressed a willingness to raise more cash by way of a debenture issue, if absolutely necessary.

Advise the directors of their best course of action in this.

4   The balance sheet of ABC Plc is as follows:

	£ millions	£ millions
Fixed assets at cost and valuation, less accumulated depreciation		34
Current assets		
Stock	26	
Debtors	23	
Cash	16	
	65	
Current liabilities		
Trade creditors	13	
		52
		86
Capital and reserves		
Ordinary shares of £1 each, fully paid		50
Share premium account		10
Capital redemption reserve		10
Revaluation reserve		9
Profit and loss account (retained profit)		7
		86

The directors wish to make a one-for-two bonus issue to ordinary share-holders.

Advise the directors of the most practical way to do this and show the 'capital and reserves' area of the balance sheet after the bonus issue, assuming that the directors take your advice.

5   The balance sheet of Aristo Ltd is as follows:

	£	£
Fixed assets at cost		425,000
less accumulated depreciation		227,000
		198,000
Current assets	87,000	
Stock	77,000	
Cash	12,000	
	176,000	

Current liabilities		
Trade creditors	69,000	
		107,000
		305,000

Capital and reserves		
Ordinary shares of £1 each, fully paid		150,000
Preference shares of £1 each, fully paid		
(redeemable at par)		100,000
Profit and loss account (retained profit)		55,000
		305,000

The directors of the company have made a few suggestions relating to the shares and reserves of the company and have asked the company's accountant to redraft the balance sheet as it would appear if the suggestions are acted upon. The accountant has checked that all of the suggestions are legally possible. The redrafted balance sheet is as follows:

	£	£
Fixed assets at cost and valuation		505,000
less accumulated depreciation		227,000
		278,000

Current assets		
Stock	87,000	
Debtors	77,000	
Cash	12,000	
	176,000	

Current liabilities		
Trade creditors	69,000	
		107,000
		385,000

Capital and reserves	£
Ordinary shares of £1 each, fully paid	200,000
Capital redemption reserve	50,000
Share premium	50,000
Revaluation reserve	80,000
Profit and loss account (retained profit)	5,000
	385,000

What do you think that the directors' proposals were? Explain your answer.
  How would the proposals, if implemented, affect the maximum legally permitted dividend?

6   As at 1 January 19X7 a company has a credit balance on its profit and loss account of £50,000. Net profit for the year ending 31 December 19X7 was £290,000. During the year a half-year's dividend was paid on the £500,000 (6%) preference shares, and the directors now propose that the balance available for distribution should be appropriated as follows:

(a) £100,000 to be provided for corporation tax.
(b) The second half of the preference dividend to be paid early in 19X8.
(c) An ordinary dividend of 10% on the 1,000,000 £1 ordinary shares to be paid early in 19X8.
(d) £20,000 to be transferred to the general reserve.

Show the appropriation account for the year.

7   X Ltd commenced business on 1 January 19X6, with an authorized share capital of 200,000 ordinary shares of £1 each, and 200,000 (5%) preference shares of £1 each. It issued all of the ordinary shares and 100,000 of the preference shares on 1 January 19X6, and the remaining preference shares on 1 January 19X7. All issues were fully paid and at par.
   In the year ending 31 December 19X6 the profit was £40,000, and in 19X7 was £60,000. Transfers to general reserve were to be £20,000 in each year, and dividends of 5% were declared on ordinary shares in 19X6, and of 10% in 19X7.
   Prepare appropriation accounts for each of the years ending 31 December 19X6 and 19X7.

8   The following balances remain in the records of the South Devon Engineering Company Ltd *after* the preparation of trading and profit and loss accounts for the year ending 31 December 19X7:

	£
180,000 £1 ordinary shares (fully paid)	180,000
9% Loan stock	100,000
Machinery (cost)	300,000
Motor vehicles (cost)	20,000
Furniture and fittings (cost)	25,000
General reserve	30,000
Profit and loss account balance brought forward	20,000
Net profit for year	50,000
Depreciation provisions: machinery	60,000

motor vehicles	5,000
furniture and fittings	5,000
Debtors	30,000
Creditors	15,000
Stocks	45,000
Cash	45,000

Prepare a profit and loss appropriation account for the year ended 31 December 19X7, and a balance sheet as at that date. The directors decide to recommend that £15,000 be transferred to general reserve, and that a dividend of 15% be paid on the ordinary shares.

9   The following is a list of the items which appeared in the accounting records of Caterers Ltd as at 31 December 19X7. These figures, which are classified as either assets and expenses or as claims and revenues, reflect all of the transactions for the year, except those which are specified towards the end of the question. The authorized capital was 500,000 ordinary shares of £1 each and 200,000 preference shares (6%) of £1 each.

	Assets/ expenses £	Claims/ revenues £
Ordinary share capital		500,000
Preference share capital		100,000
(100,000 fully paid)		
Properties at cost	400,000	
Motor vehicles at cost	80,000	
Motor vehicles depreciation provision		20,000
Investments (cost)	50,000	
Investment income		5,000
Profit and loss balance 1 January 19X7		40,000
Debtors	150,000	
Creditors		120,000
Directors' remuneration	50,000	
Sales		800,000
Purchases	500,000	
Wages and salaries	100,000	
Transport expenses	30,000	
Bad debts written off	5,000	
Bad debts provision		5,000
Administration expenses	40,000	
Advertising	20,000	
Stock	120,000	
Cash	45,000	
	1,590,000	1,590,000

Prepare trading, profit and loss and appropriation accounts for the year ending 31 December 19X7 and a balance sheet as at that date, incorporating the following adjustments:

(a) Depreciation on vehicles at the rate of 25% per annum on cost.
(b) £2,000 of the administration expenses have been prepaid at the year end.
(c) Wages of £3,000 are owing at the year end.
(d) The bad debts provision is to be maintained at 5% of debtors.
(e) Closing stock is valued at £150,000.
(f) £20,000 is to be transferred to the general reserve.
(g) A dividend of 12% on the ordinary shares is recommended.

6

The regulatory framework

6.1 Introduction

This chapter is concerned with the framework of regulations, legal and otherwise, which prescribe the way in which the accounts of limited companies are prepared and presented.

6.2 Objectives

On completion of this chapter you should be able to:

- discuss the influence of law in determining the form and content of corporate financial reports;
- discuss the influence of Stock Exchange requirements on the form and content of the accounts of listed companies.
- explain the need for accounting standards in financial reporting;
- discuss the advantages and disadvantages of setting accounting standards.

6.3 The regulatory framework

In the UK, it has long been accepted that limited liability companies require a framework of regulations to govern their financial accounting and reporting activities. At present, this regulatory framework consists of two main elements – statute law and non-statutorily determined accounting standards. Broadly, the law sets out the general framework and accounting standards are designed to support the legal requirements. Where companies are listed on the Stock Exchange, or have shares traded on the Unlisted Securities Market, there are certain Stock Exchange regulations to be adhered to. These represent a third element of financial reporting regulation.

6.4 The legislative framework

An important feature of limited liability companies is the separation of ownership from control. Shareholders appoint directors who then become responsible for the day-to-day running of the business. Such an arrangement, however, leads to a requirement for accountability. The directors, who act for and on behalf of the shareholders, have to account to the shareholders for their stewardship of the business. Since the mid 19th century, the law has been concerned with protecting the shareholder by trying to ensure appropriate accountability. The law has also been concerned with protecting creditors who lend to companies with limited liability status. Thus, to protect the interests of both investors and creditors it has been considered necessary to regulate, through statutory means, the form and content of company financial reports.

Activity 1
Can you think why the law concerns itself with protecting shareholders and creditors in this way?

We think that the answer is that it is generally considered to be beneficial to society to have a healthy private sector economy. This requires that businesses are able to raise capital from investors. In attracting investors, it helps if the business has limited liability. Unfortunately, limited liability tends to weaken the position of creditors. It is cumbersome to run a business without using credit. All of this tends to imply that the best interests of society are served by a legal environment in which the interests of both shareholders and creditors are protected. The provision of accounting information to shareholders, and to anyone else who wishes to see it, goes some part of the way to creating an environment in which people are prepared to invest in, or to trade with, limited companies.

The current law, which is set out in the Companies Acts 1985 and 1989, requires company directors to keep accounting records sufficient to show and explain the company's transactions and to enable a balance sheet and profit and loss account to be prepared. The directors must produce a profit and loss account on an annual basis with a balance sheet as at the last day of each accounting year. Both of these statements are required to show a true and fair view of that which they purport to indicate. The directors must also produce a 'directors' report' which provides further financial information. The published accounts must include these three statements together with an auditors' report which expresses the opinion of the independent auditors, concerning the statements. A copy of these accounts must be sent to each shareholder and debenture holder and must be laid before the annual general meeting of the company. (However, the shareholders of private companies may decide to dispense with this requirement if they feel such a formality is unnecessary, e.g. where the shareholders already have access to the company's financial reports.) A copy of the accounts must also be filed with the Registrar of Companies and this copy is made available for public scrutiny. In practice, large companies also send copies of their accounts to financial analysts and journalists. They will also usually comply with a request from any private individual for a copy of the accounts.

Over the years successive Companies Acts have sought to increase the extent of regulation concerning the preparation, form and content of company financial reports. Thus, statutory requirements now cover such areas as the accounting principles to be adopted, the financial items to be disclosed and the format of the financial statements. The requirements are now fairly comprehensive and try to ensure that, from a shareholders' perspective, the accounts provide a useful basis for investment decision-making in addition to fulfilling a stewardship role, i.e. the honest reporting by directors of what has been done with shareholder funds. It should be noted, however, that small and medium-sized companies are exempt from many of the disclosure requirements set out in the Companies Acts.

Activity 2

Is it really necessary for laws to be enacted to protect the interests of shareholders? Would it not be acceptable for shareholders to agree with the directors the kind of financial information they require?

Many would object to this idea. It may well be possible for shareholders to agree a suitable set of financial information with the directors. However, shareholders are not the only users of accounting information and therefore this could pose problems for other users. It could also lead to small shareholders being disadvantaged.

This approach to disclosure would almost certainly lead to significant variations in disclosure between companies. This, in turn, may create problems for potential investors.

Activity 3

Can you think of any reason why smaller companies are exempt from certain accounting provisions of the Companies Acts?

We could think of two reasons which are, to some extent, linked. These are:

- Compliance with accounting requirements costs money, at least in terms of accountants' time. In some cases, this cost will be much the same for all companies, irrespective of their size. This means that the burden of compliance falls proportionately more heavily on smaller companies.
- It is likely to be the case that users of the accounts of small companies have other means of obtaining information about the company. For example, in very many small companies the shareholders are fairly close to the directors; indeed all of the shareholders may be directors. In these circumstances, information about the company will probably be freely available to all of the shareholders. Creditors often do not rely on the accounts of small companies in making their credit decisions. Such decisions are more frequently made on the view of the creditors of the reliability of the direc-

tors. It is quite common for the directors of small companies personally to guarantee loans and credit given to the company. This has the effect of making a loan to a company much the same, in terms of limited liability, as a loan to a human individual.

The law tends to take the view that it is not necessary for smaller companies to bear the burden of full compliance.

The balance sheet and profit and loss account

Company law, in an effort to standardize the presentation of financial reports, prescribes that the published balance sheet and profit and loss account should adhere to certain formats. The law permits a choice of two formats for the balance sheet and a choice of four formats for the profit and loss account. These formats are shown in Appendix 1 to this chapter. With regard to the balance sheet formats, it appears that format 1 is the more widely used in the UK. You may have noticed that the vertical balance sheets used in previous chapters were based on this format. The formats for published profit and loss accounts indicate that a substantial amount of information must be disclosed. However, expenses are typically grouped under very broad headings and the published version of the profit and loss account is thus likely to be far less informative than that produced for internal management purposes.

As a substantial amount of information has to be disclosed it is not always possible to contain the information within the financial statements themselves, and recourse is often taken to the use of supporting notes. Thus, in looking at a set of published accounts, it is important to read the notes in conjunction with the main financial statements. A more detailed set of items which must be disclosed is included in Appendix 2 to this chapter. It is important to recognize that the law prescribes the minimum information to be disclosed. In practice, this minimum is often exceeded.

In addition to setting out the items to be disclosed and the format of the main financial statements, the law also states the accounting principles which must be adopted in preparing these statements. These principles are as follows:

(a) the company is presumed to be carrying on business as a going concern;
(b) accounting principles will be applied consistently between years;
(c) the amount of a particular item will be determined on a prudent (conservative) basis;
(d) the accruals concept will be applied in determining profits;
(e) each component of asset or liability will be separately determined in determining the aggregate figure to be shown in the accounts.

These principles have been widely applied in the preparation of accounts by companies for many years, but have only been incorporated into statute law in fairly recent times.

As we saw earlier, the profit and loss account and balance sheet must show a true and fair view of the trading results and financial position of the company. This is an overriding requirement, so much so that the Companies Acts permit the directors to depart from any of the other requirements concerning these financial statements, if they consider that this is necessary, to ensure that a true and fair view is shown. However, the directors must provide details of any departure along with the reasons for them.

The directors' report

In addition to the requirements concerning publication of a balance sheet and profit and loss account, there is also a legal requirement for a company to publish a directors' report. This report must set out, in respect of the financial year in question, a review of the development of the business of the company (and its subsidiaries) during the year and their position at the end of it. The report should contain details of the following:

- names of directors at any time in the period
- proposed dividends
- proposed transfers to reserves
- principal activities of the company (and its subsidiaries) and of any changes
- significant changes in fixed assets
- an indication of the difference between book and market values of land and buildings
- details of directors' shareholdings and debentures in the company at the start and close of the year.
- details of UK political and charitable donations where the average number of employees is over 250, details of employment and training of disabled people, health, safety and welfare at work of the company's employees and the involvement of employees in the affairs, policy and performance of the company
- important post-balance-sheet events
- the company's likely future developments
- the company's research and development activities
- the company's acquisition of its own shares.

The Companies Acts do not specify a particular format for the directors' report.

The auditors' report

Every company is required to appoint an independent firm of auditors. The auditors make a report to the shareholders which expresses their opinion as to whether:

(a) the balance sheet gives a true and fair view of the state of affairs at the balance sheet date:
(b) the profit and loss account gives a true and fair view of the profit or loss for the period;
(c) the accounts have been prepared in accordance with the Companies Act 1985.

To help them to form an opinion of the accounts, the auditors have the right of access to the company's underlying financial records at all times. They are also entitled to expect to be able to obtain information and explanations from the company's officers. If the auditors are not satisfied in any of the areas mentioned above they have a duty to qualify their report and set out the reason for this qualification. They must also qualify their report if they believe that the contents of the directors' report is inconsistent with the published accounts.

It is important to be clear that the auditors report their *opinion* on the truth and fairness of the accounts. They do not certify that the accounts are correct. The opinion is reached as a result of close examination of the balance sheet and the profit and loss account and by examining a sample of the documents and records on which those accounting statements are based.

Activity 4
Can you suggest why the law requires the audit of the published accounts of limited companies?

The answer really picks up the point made by Activity 1, namely that it is in the best interests of society for the position of creditors and shareholders to be protected. Part of this protection is in the form of information, supplied by the directors, on various aspects of the company's recent past activities and position. Clearly the directors have a vested interest in this information painting as rosy a picture of the company's fortunes as possible. In order that users of the information have a reasonable level of confidence in the accounting statements, they are subjected to audit. The auditors are required by law to be professionally qualified accountants. This should mean that the auditors will be skilled, experienced, independent and objective. The auditors have been seen as watchdogs of the shareholders, watching over the reporting activities of the directors.

6.5 Stock Exchange requirements

The requirements of the Stock Exchange are broadly concerned with the provision of more detailed information than is required by law. These requirements must be complied with by all companies listed on the Stock Exchange. (A company is said to be 'listed' if its shares are traded on the exchange.) The main requirements are as follows:

- the annual accounts must be published within six months of the relevant year-end;
- the annual accounts must include a geographical analysis of turnover, the principal country in which each subsidiary operates, details of borrowings falling within certain time categories, details of companies in which 20% or more of the equity is held, and the amount of interest capitalized by the company;
- the accounts must include explanations concerning any significant departures from accounting standards or any significant variation between actual trading results and published forecast results;
- publication of a half-yearly or interim report setting out details concerning turnover, profit, taxation and dividends.

Any company which fails to adhere to these regulations could be removed from the Stock Exchange list. This would mean the company's shares could not be traded on the market.

Activity 5

Why is removal from the Stock Exchange list of any importance to the company and its directors?

You may not have come across this point before, but you should be able to think through to the answer.

In general, potential investors will only be prepared to buy shares in a company where they know that the opportunity to sell these shares, in an orderly market, exists. Removal of a company's shares from the Stock Exchange list is likely to mean, therefore, that the company would find it extremely difficult to raise new money from a share issue. Perhaps more importantly, in the short term, existing shareholders are likely to become very unhappy about their inability to sell their shares. This could well have repercussions for the directors, whose right to be directors depends on being elected by the shareholders.

Activity 6

Obtain a copy of the published accounts of a limited company. Examine them so as to satisfy yourself that you are aware of their content.

Self-assessment question 6.1

The following information was extracted from the accounts of Marina Plc as at 31 December 19X7. These figures include all the transactions which took place during the year to 31 December 19X7, except those mentioned in Notes (a) to (g), below.

		£000
Preference share capital	£1 shares fully paid (10%)	500
Ordinary share capital	£0.50 shares fully paid	1,000
General reserve		200
Share premium		200
Profit and loss account balance as at 1 January		50
Sales		5,000
Purchases		3,000
Wages and salaries		
Production/warehousing		200
Administration		200
Selling and distribution		400
Motor expenses		
Administration		20
Distribution		80
General distribution expenses		350
General administration expenses		150
Debenture interest		28
Directors' remuneration		200
Bad debts written off		120
Debentures (redeemable in 1999) 7%		400
Loans repayable within 1 year		100
Bank overdraft		13
Debtors		600
Creditors		200
Stock		250
Premises (at cost)		1,800
Plant and machinery (at cost)		120
Vehicles (at cost)		200
Depreciation provision (plant and machinery)		30
Depreciation provision (vehicles)		50
Interim preference dividend paid		25

Notes – the following are not incorporated into the figures above:

(a)   Stock at 31 December was valued at £300,000.

(b)   Depreciation of vehicles is to be apportioned 20% administration 80% distribution.

(c) Depreciation of plant and machinery is to be regarded as an expense of distribution.

(d) Plant and machinery is to be depreciated at the rate of 20% on cost. Vehicles are to be depreciated at 25% on cost.

(e) Corporation tax on profits for the year is estimated to be £58,000, payable in nine months' time.

(f) £20,000 is to be transferred to the general reserve.

(g) The final preference dividend is to be paid, along with an ordinary dividend of 6%.

Required

(a) A trading and profit and loss account for the year ended 31 December 19X7, for internal use.

(b) A profit and loss account for the year ended 31 December, and a balance sheet as at 31 December, in a format suitable for publication (use Format 1 in both cases).

A suggested solution to this question appears at the end of the book.

6.6 Accounting standards

The need for standards

It has been made clear in previous chapters that accounting is not an exact science. There are several areas where subjective judgement is required in determining the appropriate accounting policy to be followed. In particular, judgement is required when allocating certain costs and revenues between accounting periods and when valuing assets. Depreciation, stock valuation and the treatment of doubtful debts (see Chapter 4) provide examples of the need for subjective judgement in cost allocation and asset valuation decisions. The problem of employing subjective judgement in preparing accounts is that different judgements concerning what is appropriate can lead to quite different views of financial position and performance.

In order to illustrate this point consider the following example:

Example

Dee Ltd and Gee Ltd operate in the same industry. Both companies commenced trading on 1 January. During the year to 31 December they have the following financial data:

	Dee Ltd	Gee Ltd
	£	£
Sales	180,000	180,000
Expenses (excluding depreciation)	15,000	15,000
Purchases	90,000	90,000
Land purchased, at cost	100,000	100,000
Plant and machinery purchased, at cost	40,000	40,000
Debtors	50,000	50,000
Cash	50,000	50,000
Share capital	160,000	160,000

Both companies believed that the plant and machinery would last for 5 years, with no residual value. Dee Ltd uses the sum-of-the-digits method to depreciate the assets, Gee Ltd uses the straight-line method. Dee Ltd uses the LIFO method of stock valuation, which values closing stock at £18,000, whereas Gee Ltd uses the FIFO method of stock valuation, which values closing stock at £25,000 (assume that both companies have identical stock levels).

The profit and loss account for the year ended 31 December and the balance sheet as at 31 December, for each company, would appear as follows:

Profit and loss accounts for the year ended 31 December

	Dee Ltd	Gee Ltd
	£	£
Sales	180,000	180,000
Less: Cost of sales		
(purchases, less closing stock)	(72,000)	(65,000)
Gross profit	108,000	115,000
Expenses	(15,000)	(15,000)
Depreciation*	(13,333)	(8,000)
Net profit	79,667	92,000

*Depreciation was calculated as follows:
Dee Ltd £40,000/5 = £8,000.
Gee Ltd (£40,000 × 5)/(5 + 4 + 3 + 2 + 1) = £13,333

Balance sheets as at 31 December

	Dee Ltd	Gee Ltd
Land	100,000	100,000
Plant and machinery, at cost	40,000	40,000
less: Depreciation	(13,333)	(8,000)
	126,667	132,000
Current assets		
Stock	18,000	25,000
Debtors	50,000	50,000
Cash	45,000	45,000
	239,667	252,000
Represented by:		
Share capital	160,000	160,000
Profit retained	79,667	92,000
	239,667	252,000

As we shall see in later chapters, a popular means of assessing the performance of a business is to compare the profit for a period with the investment of the owners (return on capital employed). The measures for these two companies are:

Dee Ltd   79,667/239,667 = 33%
Gee Ltd   92,000/252,000 = 37%

It should be particularly noted that the judgements made in preparing the accounts of these two companies were not at all unreasonable or extreme.

This example illustrates that, despite each company having the same basic financial data, different judgements concerning the most appropriate accounting policies to be followed lead to quite different results for the year. This means, of course, that the more the preparation of accounts can be influenced by the subjective judgement of the preparers, the more difficult it becomes to make proper comparisons between different companies.

Subjective judgement is an unavoidable and important part of preparing financial accounts. However, many users do not appear fully to appreciate the role, or extent, of subjectivity in accounting. For some users, it does not seem possible for there to be a number of acceptable ways of preparing accounts or that preparers can determine what is acceptable for a particular company.

In the late 1960s, a series of mergers between companies highlighted the problems of permitting discretion in preparing financial statements. In particular, the takeover of AEI Ltd by GEC Ltd aroused considerable concern amongst users at the time. Briefly, the facts were that, following an agreed takeover by GEC Ltd, the management of AEI Ltd published a profit forecast for the accounting year which was near to completion. The forecast profit was £10 m. However, after the takeover the actual results for AEI Ltd as reported by GEC Ltd, was a £4.5m loss. The difference of £14.5m between the forecast and actual result was attributed, in part, to matters of fact (£5m) but the remainder was attributed to matters of judgement (£9.5m), i.e. applying different accounting policies to the basic financial data.

Following this and other accounting 'scandals' resulting from merger activities, the financial press, through its letter columns and articles, criticized the accountancy profession for permitting too much discretion to preparers. It was argued that comparability of financial results between companies was being seriously undermined because of the excessive 'licence' given to preparers and that, as a result, users could be seriously misled.

Activity 7
Can you think of any arguments which justify preparers of accounting information retaining discretion over the way in which financial reports are prepared?

The arguments, which have been put forward by various people, include:

- Discretion might facilitate the reflection of a corporate personality, with risk-averse companies adopting very conservative accounting policies, and risk-seeking companies doing the opposite. This reflection might provide users of accounts with further information about the company.
- Use of discretion would permit a company to adopt accounting procedures considered to be most appropriate to its particular needs and circumstances. Since no two companies' needs and circumstances are identical, a 'horses for courses' approach to making accounting judgements, might be useful.
- Accounting standards may ossify accounting procedures, and inhibit development. Rule-makers tend often not to be great innovators.

The response of the accountancy profession

In December 1969, the public debate and criticism of the accounting profession led the Institute of Chartered Accountants in England and Wales (the largest of the UK professional accountancy bodies) to publish a *Statement of Intent on Accounting Standards in the 1970s*. In this document the Institute undertook to 'narrow the areas of difference and variety in accounting practice by publishing authoritative statements on best accounting practice which will, wherever possible, be definitive.'

The structure within which accounting standards have been created and enforced has developed over the years since 1969. The present institutional arrangements are now briefly described.

A body known as the Financial Reporting Council (FRC) is concerned with broad policy issues. It has 26 members who are drawn from various interest groups including accounting practices, local and central government, industry and banking. The aims of this body are:

- to establish the overall direction of standard-setting by providing the standard-setting body with guidance on its work programme
- to promote good financial reporting practice by preparing reports on financial reporting standards and exerting influence on government for legislative change where appropriate.

The FRC acts through two subsidiary bodies. One of these is the Accounting Standards Board (ASB). This board has 12 members (the Chairman and Technical Director are employed on a full-time basis), all of whom are qualified accountants. The ASB is charged with implementing the programme of standard-setting drawn up by the FRC.

The ASB has an offshoot which is known as the Urgent Issues Task Force. The purpose of the task force is to consider and deal with an emerging issue quickly. It is able to provide guidance on certain issues which require a rapid solution without the necessity of undertaking widespread consultation with various interest groups.

The other body through which the FRC acts is the Review Panel. The panel's role is to identify important departures from accounting standards, in the published accounts of companies, which could result in the accounts not showing a true and fair view of their financial position and/or performance. Where a particular departure is considered to be unacceptable, the directors of the company will be expected to amend the accounts. Failure to do so could result in the Review Panel (or the Secretary of State or the Stock Exchange) applying to the courts to require the directors of the company to comply with the legal requirement that the accounts show a true and fair view.

The standard-setting structure has an annual budget of more than £3 million. It is interesting to note that £1 million of the total budget is set aside to finance the ability of the Review Panel to initiate legal proceedings against companies which are unwilling to modify financial reporting procedures in line with agreed standards on a voluntary basis. The funding comes in roughly equal parts, from the accountancy profession, from the government and from the City, in the shape of the Stock Exchange and the Bank of England.

Activity 8
Should the setting of standards be the sole responsibility of accountants? Do you believe that non-accountants should be involved in the standard-setting process? Give reasons for your position.

Although accountants, as a profession, have considerable technical expertise, accounting reports are probably too important to leave to the profession alone. Accounting reports are for users, not accountants. Users and preparers can both bring different perspectives to the standard-setting process.

Setting accounting standards

In formulating an accounting standard on a particular topic the ASB undertakes considerable deliberation and consultation. The final outcome of these deliberations and consultations is a Financial Reporting Standard (FRS), often referred to as 'accounting standards'. This is a document which sets out rules prescribing the way in which accounting reports should be prepared and/or presented. Generally, FRSs are meant to be adhered to in respect of all financial reports designed to give a true and fair view of profits earned and of financial position. However, there are some standards which apply only to larger companies. FRSs used to be known as Statements of Standard Accounting Practice (SSAP).

The preparation of a standard involves various stages. The major stages are usually as follows:

1 identifying a suitable topic;
2 commissioning a research study on the topic;

3   preparing a draft FRS which is then published as an exposure draft (ED);
4   allowing an exposure period of usually six months to give interested parties
    the opportunity to comment;
5   summarizing and reviewing the comments received and producing a final
    draft of the FRS.

On the whole, the system of developing FRSs, based on the publication of
exposure drafts, has been successful. However, things do not always run
smoothly. Occasionally, an exposure draft will provoke such controversy that it
has to be withdrawn and a new exposure draft published or, in the extreme, the
ASB may feel that the comments received on the exposure draft indicate that
it is impossible to proceed with a standard. In some cases a published standard
has been revised or withdrawn following criticism of its operation in practice.
A list of accounting standards is given in Appendix 3 to this chapter.

Accounting standards are, in effect, legally binding on companies. This is
because accounting standards define what is meant by 'a true and fair view' in
particular contexts. Companies are required by law to produce accounts which
show such a view.

Activity 9
Accounting standards, in effect, have legal force. Can you think of any
good reason why they are not actually part of the statutes of company law?

We feel that the strongest argument is that there could well be a loss of flexibility if standards are placed on the statute book. At present it is possible to
withdraw, and perhaps amend, a particular standard if it is found that the
standard is flawed in some way. If, however, the standard were embedded in
law this would not be so easy to do. It would be necessary to ask parliament
to repeal the relevant law and this may take a considerable amount of time
and/or may be resisted by government. It would, for example, be difficult to
persuade Members of Parliament that they should devote time to what they
may consider to be a fairly obscure issue of financial reporting instead of using
that time to discuss, say, the plight of the homeless.

Where a company fails to comply with a particular standard the auditors have
a duty to qualify their audit report.

Types of standards

It has been said that accounting standards can be grouped into four main
categories. These are as follows:

1   *Description.* These standards require that principles and methods applied in
    preparing the accounts be described. An example of this type of standard is

SSAP 12 which is concerned with accounting for depreciation. This contains no detailed recommendations on the method of depreciation to be adopted but does require, among other things, the method of depreciation employed to be clearly described in the accounts.

2 *Presentation*. These standards prescribe how information should be presented in the accounts. An example of this type of standard is FRS 1. This aims to standardize the way in which various items are presented in the accounts.

3 *Disclosure*. These standards are concerned with how and what information should be disclosed. An example of this type of standard is FRS 1. This standard requires that, for all but the smallest companies, a cash flow statement (see Chapter 8) be included in the financial reports.

4 *Valuation and profit measurement*. These standards are concerned with setting out rules concerning the valuation of assets and the calculation of profit. An example of this type of standard is SSAP 9 which lays down principles concerning the valuation of stocks and work-in-progress.

Some of the standards produced could be assigned to more than one of the categories listed above. Nevertheless, the categories do provide an insight to the issues addressed by the ASB.

6.7 Summary

In this chapter the regulatory framework of accounting has been examined. It has been seen that there are two main sources of regulation – the law and accounting standards. Accounting standards are designed to complement the law and, in effect, have statutory backing. For companies which are listed on the Stock Exchange there are additional regulations emanating from this body. The amount of regulation relating to companies has increased significantly over the years and there is no sign that this trend towards greater regulation is likely to change.

Exercises

1 As a result of the development of the regulatory framework, companies are now required to disclose a great deal of information about their financial affairs. What do you think are the advantages and disadvantages of greater disclosure?

2 The following information has been extracted from the books of Simat Plc, after all of the normal transactions of the year ended 31 March 19X4 had been recorded:

	£
General distribution expenses	14,580
General administration expenses	17,350
Directors' remuneration	65,900
Debenture interest payable	11,200
Sales	748,850
Purchases	378,650
Wages and salaries	
Administrative	85,390
Distribution	67,400
Depreciation	
Plant and machinery	21,600
Motor vehicles	16,400
Interest receivable	4,200
Bad debts written off	6,380
Profit and loss account balance as at 1 April 19X3	87,740
Stock at 1 April 19X3	65,100
Auditors' remuneration	6,000

Notes
(a) Stock at 31 March 19X4 was valued at £68,000.
(b) Corporation tax on profits for the year is estimated at £19,800.
(c) Ordinary dividend proposed is £20,000.
(d) £21,000 is to be appropriated to fixed asset replacement reserve.
(e) Depreciation of plant and machinery should be apportioned two-thirds administration and one-third distribution. Depreciation of motor vehicles should be divided equally between administration and distribution.

Required
(a) A trading and profit and loss account for internal purposes.
(b) A trading and profit and loss account for publication, using format 1.

Companies Act 1985 formats for accounts

Balance sheet formats

Format 1

A Called-up share capital not paid
B Fixed assets
    I   Intangible assets
       (i)   Development costs
       (ii) Concessions, patents, licences, trade marks and similar rights and assets
       (iii) Goodwill
       (iv) Payments on account
    II Tangible assets
       (i)   Land and buildings
       (ii) Plant and machinery
       (iii) Fixtures, fittings, tools and equipment
       (iv) Payments on account and assets in course of construction
    III Investments
       (i)   Shares in group companies
       (ii) Loans to group companies
       (iii) Shares in related companies
       (iv) Loans to related companies
       (v) Other investments other than loans
       (vi) Other loans
       (vii) Own shares
C Current assets
    I   Stocks
       (i)   Raw materials and consumables
       (ii) Work-in-progress
       (iii) Finished goods and goods for resale
       (iv) Payments on account
    II Debtors
       (i)   Trade debtors
       (ii) Amounts owed by group companies
       (iii) Amounts owed by related companies

      (iv) Other debtors
      (v)   Called-up share capital not paid
      (vi) Prepayments and accrued income
  III Investments
      (i)   Shares in group companies
      (ii)   Own shares
      (iii) Other investments
  IV Cash at bank and in hand

D   Prepayments and accrued income

E   Creditors: amounts falling due within 1 year
      (i)   Debenture loans
      (ii)   Bank loans and overdrafts
      (iii)   Payments received on account
      (iv)   Trade creditors
      (v)   Bills of exchange payable
      (vi)   Amounts owed to group companies
      (vii) Amounts owed to related companies
      (viii) Other creditors including taxation and social security
      (ix)   Accruals and deferred income

F   Net current assets (liabilities)

G   Total assets less current liabilities

H   Creditors: amounts falling due after more than 1 year
      (i)   Debenture loans
      (ii)   Bank loans and overdrafts
      (iii)   Payments received on account
      (iv)   Trade creditors
      (v)   Bills of exchange payable
      (vi)   Amounts owed to group companies
      (vii) Amounts owed to related companies
      (viii) Other creditors, including taxation and social security
      (ix)   Accruals and deferred income

I   Provisions for liabilities and charges
      (i)   Pensions and similar obligations
      (ii)   Taxation, including deferred taxation
      (iii)   Other provisions

J   Accruals and deferred income

K   Capital and reserves
  I   Called-up share capital
  II   Share premium account
  III Revaluation reserve
  IV Other reserves
      (i)   Capital redemption reserve
      (ii)   Reserve for own shares
      (iii)   Reserves provided for by the articles of association
      (iv)   Other reserves
  V   Profit and loss account

Format 2

Assets

A   Called-up share capital not paid

B   Fixed assets
   I   Intangible assets
      (i)   Development costs
      (ii) Concessions, patents, licences, trade marks and similar rights and assets
      (iii) Goodwill
      (iv) Payments on account
   II   Tangible assets
      (i)   Land and buildings
      (ii) Plant and machinery
      (iii) Fixtures, fittings, tools and equipment
      (iv) Payments on account and assets in course of construction
   III   Investments
      (i)   Shares in group companies
      (ii) Loans to group companies
      (iii) Shares in related companies
      (iv) Loans to related companies
      (v) Other investments other than loans
      (vi) Other loans
      (vii) Own shares

C   Current assets
   I   Stocks
      (i)   Raw materials and consumables
      (ii) Work-in-progress
      (iii) Finished goods and goods for resale
      (iv) Payments on account
   II   Debtors
      (i)   Trade debtors
      (ii) Amounts owed by group companies
      (iii) Amounts owed by related companies
      (iv) Other debtors
      (v) Called-up share capital not paid
      (vi) Prepayments and accrued income
   III   Investments
      (i)   Shares in group companies
      (ii) Own shares
      (iii) Other investments
   IV   Cash at bank and in hand

D   Prepayments and accrued income

Liabilities

A   Capital and reserves
    I   Called-up share capital
    II   Share premium account
    III Revaluation reserve
    IV Other reserves
        (i)   Capital redemption reserve
        (ii)   Reserve for own shares
        (iii) Reserves provided for by the articles of association
        (iv) Other reserves
    V   Profit and loss account
B   Provisions for liabilities and charges
        (i)   Pensions and similar obligations
        (ii)   Taxation including deferred taxation
        (iii) Other provisions
C   Creditors
        (i)   Debenture loans
        (ii)   Bank loans and overdrafts
        (iii) Payments received on account
        (iv) Trade creditors
        (v)   Bills of exchange payable
        (vi) Amounts owed to group companies
        (vii) Amounts owed to related companies
        (viii) Other creditors including taxation and social security
        (ix) Accruals and deferred income
D   Accruals and deferred income

Profit and loss account formats

Format 1

1   Turnover
2   Cost of sales
3   Gross profit or loss
4   Distribution costs
5   Administrative expenses
6   Other operating income
7   Income from shares in group companies
8   Income from shares in related companies
9   Income from other fixed asset investments
10   Other interest receivable and similar income
11   Amounts written off investments
12   Interest payable and similar charges
13   Tax on profit or loss on ordinary activities

14   Profit or loss on ordinary activities after taxation
15   Extraordinary income
16   Extraordinary charges
17   Extraordinary profit or loss
18   Tax on extraordinary profit or loss
19   Other taxes not shown under the above items
20   Profit or loss for the financial year

Format 2

1   Turnover
2   Change in stocks of finished goods and in work-in-progress
3   Own work capitalized
4   Other operating income
5   (a) Raw materials and consumables
     (b) Other external charges
6   Staff costs
     (a) Wages and salaries
     (b) Social security costs
     (c) Other pension costs
7   (a) Depreciation and other amounts written off tangible and intangible
         fixed assets
     (b) Exceptional amounts written off current assets
8   Other operating charges
9   Income from shares in group companies
10   Income from shares in group companies
11   Income from other fixed-asset investments
12   Other interest receivable and similar income
13   Amounts written off investments
14   Interest payable and similar charges
15   Tax on profit or loss on ordinary activities
16   Profit or loss on ordinary activities after taxation
17   Extraordinary income
18   Extraordinary charges
19   Extraordinary profit or loss
20   Tax on extraordinary profit or loss
21   Other taxes not shown under the above items
22   Profit or loss for the financial year

Format 3

A   Charges
         (i)   Cost of sales
         (ii)   Distribution costs

(iii)   Administration expenses
(iv)   Amounts written off investments
(v)   Interest payable and similar charges
(vi)   Tax on profit or loss on ordinary activities
(vii)   Profit or loss on ordinary activities after taxation
(viii)   Extraordinary charges
(ix)   Tax on extraordinary profit or loss
(x)   Other taxes not shown under the above items
(xi)   Profit or loss for the financial year

B   Income
(i)   Turnover
(ii)   Other operating income
(iii)   Income from shares in group companies
(iv)   Income from shares in related companies
(v)   Income from other fixed-asset investments
(vi)   Other interest receivable and similar income
(vii)   Profit or loss on ordinary activities after taxation
(viii)   Extraordinary income
(ix)   Profit or loss for the financial year

Format 4

A   Charges
(i)   Reduction in stocks of finished goods and in work-in-progress
(ii)   (a)   Raw materials and consumables
(b)   Other external charges
(iii)   Staff costs
(a)   Wages and salaries
(b)   Social security costs
(c)   Other pension costs
(iv)   (a)   Depreciation and other amounts written off tangible and intangible fixed assets
(b)   Exceptional amounts written off current assets
(v)   Other operating charges
(vi)   Amounts written off investments
(vii)   Interest payable and similar charges
(viii)   Tax on profit or loss on ordinary activities
(ix)   Profit or loss on ordinary activities after taxation
(x)   Extraordinary charges
(xi)   Tax on extraordinary profit or loss
(xii)   Other taxes not shown under the above items
(xiii)   Profit or loss for the financial year

B   Income
(i)   Turnover
(ii)   Increase in stocks of finished goods and in work-in-progress

(iii)   Own work capitalized
(iv)   Other operating income
(v)   Income from shares in group companies
(vi)   Income from shares in related companies
(vii) Income from other fixed-asset investments
(viii) Other interest receivable and similar income
(ix)   Profit or loss on ordinary activities after taxation
(x)   Extraordinary income
(xi)   Profit or loss for the financial year

Appendix 2

Items which must be disclosed

The Companies Act 1985 includes a number of specific disclosure requirements. The more important of these are given below, but it must be recognized that this list is not intended to be exhaustive. Disclosure may be within the formats provided and/or by way of notes to the accounts.

General requirements

(a) *Accounting policies*
(b) *Corresponding figures* for the preceding year, for every item in the profit and loss account or balance sheet.

Disclosure requirements relating to the balance sheet

(a) *Share capital* and *debentures* – including the authorized capital, the number and aggregate value of shares of each class, information about redeemable preference shares, and details of any share or debenture issues.
(b) *Fixed assets* – showing associated depreciation provisions.
(c) *Investments* – broken down into listed and other, showing the aggregate market value if different to the amount stated.
(d) Movements in *reserves* and *provisions*.
(e) *Taxation*, including the basis on which the charge for UK corporation tax is computed.
(f) Details of *indebtedness* – divided into that which is due *within* 5 years and *beyond* 5 years. Terms of repayment and interest, details of any security given, and the amounts of any cumulative dividends in arrears must all be given.
(g) *Guarantees* and other *financial commitments*, including such items as details of contracts for capital expenditure and pension commitments.
(h) Aggregate *dividends*.

Disclosure requirements relating to the profit and loss account.

(a) the amount of the company's *profit and loss on ordinary activities* before taxation.

(b) *Certain kinds of income and expense* must be separately stated. These include interest on bank loans, interest on other loans, income from listed investments, rent from land, payments for the hire of plant and machinery and auditors' remuneration.

(c) *Prior-year adjustments.* These are amounts reported in the preceding financial statements as retained earnings which have been materially altered because of a change in accounting policies or the discovery of a fundamental error.

(d) *Extraordinary income or expenses.* These are amounts derived from transactions outside the ordinary activities of the company.

(e) The effect of any transactions that are *exceptional* by virtue of size or incidence, even though they fall within the ordinary activities of the company.

(f) Particulars of *turnover*, broken down by class of business and geographical markets.

(g) Particulars of *staff*, including the average number of persons employed in the year, the aggregate remuneration, social security costs and pension costs.

(h) The basis of any *foreign-currency* translation.

(i) *Transfers* to and from *reserves* and the aggregate amount of any *dividends* paid or proposed.

Other miscellaneous points

Schedule 5 of the Companies Act 1985 identifies a number of additional matters which must be disclosed in the annual accounts, either within the accounts or in a note to these accounts. Schedule 5 covers a number of areas, the most important of which relate to the following:

(a) the disclosure of particulars of the company's subsidiaries (i.e. companies which are partly or fully owned to such an extent that they can be effectively controlled) and of its other shareholdings;

(b) the disclosure of financial information relating to subsidiaries;

(c) the emoluments of directors (including emoluments waived), pensions of directors and past directors and compensation for loss of office to directors and past directors;

(d) the disclosure of the number of the company's employees who are remunerated at higher rates;

(e) particulars of loans and other transactions favouring directors and officers.

Appendix 3

UK accounting standards

		Issue date
SSAP 1	Accounting for associated companies	1982
SSAP 2	Disclosure of accounting policies	1971
SSAP 3	Earnings per share	1974
SSAP 4	Accounting for government grants	1990
SSAP 5	Accounting for value added tax	1974
SSAP 6	Extraordinary items and prior-year adjustments	1986
SSAP 8	The treatment of taxation under the imputation system in the accounts of companies	1977
SSAP 9	Stocks and long-term contracts	1988
SSAP 10	Statements of source and application of funds	1978
SSAP 12	Accounting for depreciation	1987
SSAP 13	Accounting for research and development	1989
SSAP 14	Group accounts	1978
SSAP 15	Accounting for deferred tax	1985
SSAP 17	Accounting for post-balance-sheet events	1980
SSAP 18	Accounting for contingencies	1980
SSAP 19	Accounting for investment properties	1981
SSAP 20	Foreign-currency translation	1983
SSAP 21	Accounting for leases and hire purchase contracts	1984
SSAP 22	Accounting for goodwill	1989
SSAP 23	Accounting for acquisitions and mergers	1985
SSAP 24	Accounting for pension costs	1988
SSAP 25	Segmental accounting	1990
FRS 1	Cash flow statements	1991
FRS 2	Reporting financial performance	1992
FRS 3	Accounting for subsidiary undertakings	1992
FRS 4	Capital instruments	1993
FRS 5	Reporting the substance of transactions	1994

The accounts of groups of companies

7.1 Introduction

The treatment of company accounts so far has dealt with single companies. In fact many companies form into groups, for a variety of reasons. Indeed, most large, well-known 'companies' are, in fact, groups. Accounting for groups of companies has its own particular aspects. This chapter aims to provide you with an appreciation of these aspects, so as to enable you to be able to understand a set of published accounts for a group of companies, and to apply the principles dealt with in subsequent chapters to groups as well as to individual companies.

7.2 Objectives

On completion of this chapter you should be able:

- to state the reasons why companies buy shares in the ownership of other companies;
- to explain the nature of a holding company/subsidiary relationship;
- to explain the rationale underlying the preparation of a set of group accounts;
- to prepare a simple set of group accounts.

7.3 Shareholdings in other companies

One company can become a shareholder of another company in a number of ways, and for a variety of reasons. The accounting treatment of such transactions will vary depending upon the size and nature of the investment, and can be divided into the following broad types.

(a) A company may have liquid resources in excess of those which it needs immediately to finance its normal commercial activities. Rather than placing cash in a bank deposit account or in some other fixed-interest-bearing deposit, the company's treasurer may decide to make an investment in the share of another company. This will probably expose the investor company to a higher level of risk than would an investment in a deposit account. It will also, however, expose the investor company to the possibility that the returns, in terms of dividends and capital gains, could be very much higher than those normally associated with fixed-interest deposits. In such circumstances, the investment would probably represent a *relatively small portion of the total ownership of the other company*. From an accounting point of view, such an investment is easily dealt with in the final accounts of the investor company. The investment will be shown as an asset, valued at cost. Any dividends from the investment would appear in the profit and loss account as income.

(b) A company may own a *substantial, but not a controlling, portion of another company*. Here the objective of the investor company might be to exert influence over the other company. In practice, to own 20% of a company's shares may easily be sufficient to be able to exercise considerable influence. This might be because the remainder of the shares are owned by a relatively large group of unconnected shareholders, possibly many of whom take little interest in the company, except as a fairly remote investment. The way in which the investor company deals with the investment, and with the income from that investment, when it holds a substantial but not a controlling interest in another company, will be considered later in the chapter under the heading Associated Companies.

(c) A company may own a *majority of the shares of another company and therefore be in a position to control that company*. This may have arisen from purchasing shares of an existing previously unconnected company or perhaps from forming a new company to undertake a new activity which the company is expanding into. This establishes a group. Most of the rest of this chapter will consider how the final accounting requirements of the investor company are affected by the group situation. Before considering group accounts, however, it may be useful briefly to consider the reasons for the existence of groups of companies.

7.4 Reasons for the existence of groups

Most businesses wish to expand or grow.

Activity 1
Can you think of reasons why businesses seek to expand? If you have never formally studied this you should be able to make some guesses using your common sense.

The reasons we came up with are:

- The elimination or at least reduction in competition.
- Safeguarding sources of supply or sales outlets.
- Access to the economies of scale available to larger businesses.
- Risk reduction through diversification.

Organic expansion by taking on more staff, developing new sources of supply, products, processes and markets can be a time-consuming way of achieving expansion. It may be easier, and more appropriate, to buy an existing business. In these circumstances three main possibilities exist:

1 Assets can be purchased from an existing business, with the purchase consideration being cash, debentures or shares. The selling business is then wound up. This process is typically referred to as *acquisition* or *absorption*. Since only one company remains after the acquisition, the final accounts of that company follow the normal pattern.
2 Assets of two or more businesses can be sold to a new company, and the existing businesses wound up. This process is typically referred to as *amalgamation*. Again, since only one company remains, the final accounts raise no new questions.
3 Shares may be purchased in another company. Clearly, if enough shares in another company are purchased, the activities of that company can be effectively controlled by the investor company. There is no winding up of either business. Where effective control is achieved, a parent/subsidiary relationship arises. This is usually known as a *takeover* or *merger*. In practice, probably the most popular means of acquiring an existing business is to buy enough shares to control it. The purchase consideration for the shares of the potential subsidiary may be cash, i.e. the shareholders of what will become the subsidiary company receive cash from the potential parent company for their shares. More common, however, is the exchange of shares or the issuing of potential parent company loan stock to satisfy at least part of the purchase consideration. Here the potential parent company issues new shares and/or loan stocks which are transferred to the shareholders of the subsidiary. Thus, those who were shareholders of the subsidiary become share and/or loan stockholders of the parent company and the parent company takes their place as shareholders of the subsidiary. Share exchanges tend to be quite popular with potential parent companies since they involve no cash payment. Quite frequently, however, the takeover involves some combination of shares and/or loan stocks and/or cash, in satisfaction of the purchase consideration.

Clearly a company which acquires sufficient shares in another company to control it, effectively can wind it up and use the assets as it wishes. However, there are advantages in not doing so.

Activity 2

Can you think of any reasons for keeping a subsidiary in existence as a separate company, even where it is wholly owned by the parent?

The reasons which occurred to us were:

- *Market identity.* The directors of the parent company may feel that customers may prefer to deal with what they see as being a small company rather than with a large group.
- *Administrative convenience.* It may be felt that the staff of the subsidiary will have a greater feeling of independence and autonomy if it retains its identity as much as possible. This might be seen as likely to lead to a better motivated staff.
- *Limited liability.* The directors of the parent company may prefer to retain the limited liability status of each company individually, rather than all parts of the group being one legal entity.

Expansion by takeover is not necessarily the only factor leading to the creation of a group. A company may decide that it wishes, for limited liability or other reasons, to have the various parts of the business established as separate companies, all under the umbrella of the original company, which now becomes the parent.

7.5 The definition of a group

A group consists of two or more companies between which there is a parent/subsidiary relationship. A parent company is also known as a *holding company*. The 1989 Companies Act sets out a number of criteria which need to be satisfied for a company to be classified as a holding company. These typically relate to some aspect of control, as exercised by one company over another. Probably the most obvious form of control, and the one which will be assumed for the remainder of this chapter, relates to control of the voting rights. A holding company can thus be defined as one which controls another by holding a majority of the voting rights of that company. For effective control to exist there must be a right to appoint or remove directors having a majority of voting rights at board meetings. A subsidiary is thus a company which is effectively controlled by another company.

For the remainder of this chapter it will be assumed that to own more than 50% of the ordinary shares gives control and a group, therefore, exists. In practice, this is the basis of most group relationships.

7.6 Types of group

Direct group

This arises where one holding company has control directly over one or more others, as follows:

Holding company $\qquad$ H Plc

Subsidiaries $\qquad$ S1 Ltd $\quad$ S2 Ltd $\quad$ S3 Ltd $\quad$ S4 Ltd

Here H Plc owns a majority of the ordinary shares of each of the four subsidiaries. The investment in the shares of each of the subsidiaries will appear as assets in the balance sheet of H Plc.

Vertical group

This arises where the holding company has a subsidiary with its own subsidiary, as follows:

Holding company $\qquad$ H Plc

Subsidiaries $\qquad$ S1 Ltd

$\qquad$ S2 Ltd

Here the investment in the shares of S1 Ltd will appear in the balance sheet of H Plc and the investment in the shares of S2 Ltd will appear in the balance sheet of S1 Ltd. Both S1 Ltd and S2 Ltd are subsidiaries of H Plc. This will still be true if H Plc owns only slightly over half of the ordinary shares of S1 Ltd which in turn owns just over half of the shares in S2 Ltd. In these circumstances H Plc would only own iust over a quarter of the shares of S2 Ltd. However, H Plc will control S1 Ltd, which in turn controls S2 Ltd. So the three companies form a group under the control of H Plc. A company like S2 Ltd in this context would usually be referred to as a sub-subsidiary.

Mixed group

This is where the holding company has two or more subsidiaries and at least one sub-subsidiary.

Holding company $\qquad$ H Plc

Subsidiaries $\qquad$ S1 Ltd $\quad$ S2 Ltd

$\qquad$ S3 Ltd

Some very complicated relationships can arise. Given the aim of this chapter, which is to provide an *appreciation* of group accounts, it will be restricted to direct groups. The principles remain the same in more complex groups. Implementation just becomes rather more laborious.

7.7   Group accounts: the legal framework

No matter what the strict legal position of a subsidiary may be, the practical, economic reality is that it is wholly under the control of the parent company. This is just as true irrespective of whether the parent owns just 50% of the shares or all of them. A group can quite logically be seen as one single business which is all under the control of the shareholders, acting through the directors, of the holding or parent company. In effect, the holding company controls the entire group. Accounting tends to try to reflect economic reality, rather than the strict legal position. This explains why all of the subsidiary's assets and external claims are incorporated in the group balance sheet, even where the subsidiary is less than 100% owned by the parent.

The existence of a group of companies typically requires the presentation of a set of group accounts. The main objective of a set of group accounts is to disclose the results and state of affairs of the group as if it were a single company. The 1989 Companies Act provides the most recent update on the preparation of group accounts and effectively implements the European Community (EC) Seventh Directive on the subject.

In effect, UK company law requires that the holding company prepares and publishes a balance sheet and a profit and loss account for the entire group, in each case showing a true and fair view and viewed from the perspective of the shareholders of the holding company. These accounts are known as *group* or *consolidated accounts*.

7.8   Preparation of a set of group accounts

The aim of a set of group accounts is to disclose the state of affairs and the results of the group in such a way as would be appropriate if the assets and liabilities, revenues and expenses of the group were those of a single legal entity. In order to achieve this the assets and claims of the subsidiaries are effectively added to those in the holding company's balance sheet, and the revenues and expenses of the subsidiaries are effectively added to those in the holding company's profit and loss account, subject to certain adjustments.

Before going on to consider group accounts in more detail there are several points which you should be clear about. These are:

(a)   The holding company and the subsidiaries need to produce their own final accounts (profit and loss account and balance sheet). From these the group accounts will be prepared. The group accounts do not form part of the formal accounting system of the holding company or any of its subsidiaries.

(b) The only mention of the group relationship in the final accounts of the holding company is an asset *investment in subsidiary*, which will appear on its balance sheet, typically valued at cost to the holding company.

(c) In the final accounts of the subsidiary company, there is no explicit reference to the fact that it is a subsidiary of another company. Company balance sheets do not show who own each of the shares issued; the share capital is simply shown as one total, or at least, one total for each class of shares (ordinary, preference, etc.).

(d) The fact that companies may be members of a group may well affect their behaviour to one another. For example, trading may take place between them to an extent which might not be the case, were they not related. Indeed the very reason for the existence of many groups is to promote, or perhaps to force, closer trading links. Where one member of a group has some commercial relationship with another (e.g. buying from, selling to, borrowing from, lending to), these relationships are reflected in the final accounts of the individual companies in very much the same way as if the other company concerned is not a member of that group. As will be seen later in this chapter, when group accounts are prepared, the effect of some of these relationships may well cancel each other out.

7.9 The group balance sheet

This explanation of the preparation of a group balance sheet will restrict itself to consideration of a group containing the holding company and just one subsidiary. In fact, the principles involved are essentially the same in more complex groups. The explanation will start with the most straightforward group situation. After that, consideration will be given to the factors which make things a bit more complicated.

Example

The following balance sheets relate to H Ltd, and S Ltd as at 1 January 19X0, immediately after H Ltd had acquired all of the share capital of S Ltd for £3 million.

	H Ltd	S Ltd
	£000	*£000*
Fixed assets	4,500	2,500
Investments in S Ltd	3,000	—
Working capital	1,000	500
	8,500	3,000
Ordinary share capital (£1 shares fully paid)	6,000	2,000
Reserves	2,500	1,000
	8,500	3,000

To prepare a group balance sheet simply involves adding like items in the two balance sheets, except for the investment in S Ltd in the balance sheet of H Ltd and the shares and reserves at the date of acquisition of S Ltd. Since these two are equal in amount and one is an asset while the other is a claim, they completely cancel one another.

The group balance sheet would appear as follows:

Balance sheet as at 1 January 19X0

	£000	*Workings*
Fixed assets	7,000	(4,500 + 2,500)
Working capital	1,500	(1,000 + 500)
	8,500	
Ordinary share capital	6,000	(H Ltd share capital)
Reserves	2,500	(H Ltd share capital)
	8,500	

This example shows the logic of the group balance sheet, bearing in mind that it is meant to show the situation from the viewpoint of the holding company shareholders. The balance sheet shows that these shareholders have a total claim against the group of £8.5 million and that this is presently deployed in financing £7 million of fixed assets and £1.5 million of working capital.

The reason why the investment in S Ltd cancels exactly with the shares and reserves of S Ltd is because H Ltd acquired *all* of the shares of S Ltd for the *balance sheet value* of that company's net assets (£3 million in total, or £3 per share). As we shall see later, this is a relatively unusual situation. In practice, for one reason and/or another, the two items will not exactly cancel each other.

This example relates to the particular situation which arises at the time of acquisition. In subsequent years, the position is slightly different.

Example

The following balance sheets relate to H Ltd and S Ltd, as at 31 December 19X1.

	H Ltd	**S Ltd**
	£000	*£000*
Fixed assets	5,500	3,000
Investments in S Ltd	3,000	—
Working capital	2,000	1,000
	10,500	4,000
Ordinary share capital	6,000	2,000
(£1 shares fully paid)		
Reserves	4,500	2,000
	10,500	4,000

H Ltd acquired all of S Ltd's capital on 1 January 19X0 for £3 million when S Ltd's reserves stood at £1 million.

The group balance sheet would appear as follows:

Balance sheet as at 31 December 19X1

	£000
Fixed assets	8,500
Working capital	3,000
	11,500
Share capital	6,000
Reserves	5,500
	11,500

In this case it is necessary to distinguish between pre- and post-acquisition reserves of the subsidiary. As was seen in the first example, the cost of the investment in S Ltd cancels out with the share capital and reserves at the time of acquisition, and these represent the net assets obtained at the acquisition. Since that time the net assets of the subsidiary have increased, since profits have been made and (some at least) retained in the reserves. Any profits made and retained by a subsidiary since it became a member of the group will be profits of that group, and as such will be added to group reserves. As we have seen, where pre-acquisition reserves exist they will be cancelled out (together with the share capital) with the investment in the subsidiary.

Activity 3

The following balance sheets relate to H Ltd, and S Ltd, as at 31 December 19X2:

	H Ltd	S Ltd
	£000	£000
Net assets	5,000	4,500
Investments in S Ltd	3,500	—
	8,500	4,500
Ordinary share capital	6,000	3,000
(£1 shares fully paid)		
Reserves	2,500	1,500
	8,500	4,500

H Ltd acquired all of S Ltd's capital on 1 January 19X1, for £3.5 million, when reserves in S Ltd were £500,000.

Have a go at preparing a group balance sheet as at 31 December 19X2.

Your balance sheet should look something like this:

Balance sheet as at 31 December 19X2

	£000	
Net assets	9,500	
Ordinary share capital	6,000	
Reserves	3,500	£2.5 million in H Ltd and £1 million
	9,500	post-acquisition reserves in S Ltd

Goodwill (or capital reserve) arising on consolidation

In practice, there will be very few cases where the cost of the holding company's investments in a subsidiary will be the same as the book value of net assets acquired. Typically, the amount paid for the investments in the subsidiary will exceed the balance sheet value of the net assets obtained.

Activity 4

Why will the cost of the investment in the subsidiary likely be greater than the balance sheet value of that investment?

The reasons which occurred to us were:

- The various conventions of accounting, particularly the prudence convention, tend to lead to the balance sheet value of assets being understated relative to their market value.
- Certain assets, like goodwill, tend not to appear on the balance sheet at all. Again, this is caused by the effect of the accounting conventions, particularly the historic cost convention.

Under such circumstances, the investment in the subsidiary in the balance sheet of the holding company will not cancel with the shares and reserves of the subsidiary at the date of the acquisition.

Example

The following balance sheets relate to H Ltd and S Ltd as at 31 December 19X2:

	H Ltd	S Ltd
	£000	£000
Fixed assets	3,500	3,800
Investments in S Ltd	4,000	—
Working capital	1,000	700
	8,500	4,500

Ordinary share capital	6,000	3,000
(£1 shares fully paid)		
Reserves	2,500	1,500
	8,500	4,500

H Ltd acquired all of S Ltd's capital on 1 January 19X1, for £4 million in cash, when the reserves in S Ltd were £500,000.

Clearly the investment in S Ltd (£4 million) does not cancel out with the share capital and reserves at the time of acquisition (£3.5 million). There must be an amount of £500,000 which will need to be incorporated in some way into the group balance sheet. This is entirely logical, since if £4 million was paid for net assets with a balance sheet value of £3.5 million, there must be some undisclosed or undervalued asset involved. This asset is usually known as *goodwill on consolidation* or sometimes *cost of control*. The principle underlying goodwill on consolidation is the same as that underlying goodwill (in an accounting sense) generally, namely the amount paid for a complete business in excess of the total value placed on the individual assets (net of the liabilities).

Goodwill on consolidation can be calculated by comparing:

- what has been paid for the subsidiary (or part of it), with
- what has been obtained for it, i.e. the net assets at the time of acquisition (or part of them). The balance sheet value of the net assets at any point in time can be calculated, either by adding the balance sheet values of the individual assets of the subsidiary and deducting the sum of the liabilities or by adding the capital and reserves of the subsidiary. (The *balance sheet equation* ensures that you should get the same answer by either method.)

The reserves of S Ltd can be split £500,000 pre-acquisition and £1,000,000 post-acquisition. Thus, what the parent bought for its £4 million was £3,500,000 of balance sheet assets plus £500,000 of goodwill.

The group balance sheet would thus appear as follows:

Balance sheet as at 31 December 19X2

	£000
Fixed assets	7,300
Goodwill on consolidation	500
Working capital	1,700
	9,500
Share capital	6,000
Reserves	3,500
	9,500

Sometimes, the amount paid for the investments in the subsidiary is less than the net assets associated with the investment. Under such circumstances the difference will appear as a *capital reserve on consolidation* on the claims side of the balance sheet.

Activity 5

The following balance sheets relate to H Ltd and S Ltd as at 31 December 19X2:

	H Ltd	S Ltd
	£000	£000
Net assets	5,100	4,500
Investments in S Ltd	3,400	—
	8,500	4,500
Ordinary share capital	6,000	3,000
(£1 shares fully paid)		
Reserves	2,500	1,500
	8,500	4,500

H Ltd acquired all of S Ltd's capital on 1 January 19X1, for £3.4 million, when reserves of S Ltd stood at £500,000.

See if you can prepare a group balance sheet as at 31 December 19X2.

Your answer should be along the following lines:

Capital reserve on consolidation arrived at as follows:
Pay £3.4 million
Get £3.5 million
Therefore £0.1 million capital reserve

Balance sheet as at 31 December 19X2

	£000	
Net assets	9,600	
Ordinary share capital	6,000	
Capital reserve on consolidation	100	
Reserves	3,500	£2.5 million in H Ltd and
	9,600	£1 million in S Ltd

In practice, the calculation of goodwill is slightly more complicated than implied above, since the amount to be attributed to any purchased goodwill should be the difference between the *fair value* of the consideration given and the aggregate of the *fair value* of the net assets (valued separately). This means that the net assets are frequently revalued *in the group accounts*, at market value (but not necessarily in the accounts of the subsidiary). The effect will usually be to increase the net assets figures and decrease the amount of goodwill on consolidation.

This still leaves the question as to what should be done with goodwill when it is calculated. It has been shown above as an intangible asset, on the balance sheet. In practice, however, it is generally felt that purchased goodwill should be written off immediately to reserves. The 1989 Companies Act specifically precludes, for the first time, the use of a revaluation reserve to write off goodwill on consolidation. The normal treatment of goodwill is to write it off immediately against either accumulated revenue reserves or any capital reserves arising on consolidation. It is also possible to carry forward goodwill as an asset and write it off through the profit and loss account over its useful life.

Minority interests

So far it has been assumed that the holding company acquired 100% of the share capital of the subsidiary. From what was said earlier about effective control it is clear that this need not be the case. Other people or organizations may also own some shares in the subsidiary. This means that when group accounts are prepared these *minority interests* must be recognized. Minority interests in a group represent the claims of shareholders, other than members of the holding company, in the subsidiary. They represent the claim of these outside shareholders on the net assets appearing in the group balance sheet.

It must be remembered that the object of group accounts is to show the financial position of the group as a whole, as nearly as possible, in the way in which it would be shown if the holding company itself undertook all the activities of the members of the group, and all assets and liabilities of the group were attributable to a single company. This concept dismisses any suggestion that only the group's attributable proportion of assets and liabilities should be included in the group balance sheet. Conceptually, it is clear that all assets and liabilities of all group members should be included. It should be borne in mind that the parent company controls *all* aspects of its subsidiaries, not just the proportion of each of them which it owns, to the extent that shareholders other than shareholders of the holding company have a claim against these group net assets.

As we shall see later in the chapter, a similar approach is taken to minority interests in the group balance sheet.

Example

The following balance sheets relate to H Ltd and S Ltd as at 1 January 19X0;

	H Ltd	**S Ltd**
	£000	*£000*
Net assets	20,000	5,000
Investment in S Ltd	3,000	—
	23,000	5,000
Share capital (£1 shares fully paid)	23,000	5,000

H Ltd acquired 60% of the shares of S Ltd, on formation of both companies on 1 January 19X0.

When preparing the group balance sheet, it should be remembered that the parent company effectively controls all of the net assets. There is thus little point in including only 60% of the net assets of the subsidiary. It is more logical to include all of the assets controlled by the group and show the proportion funded by minorities, as follows:

Group balance sheet as at 1 January 19X0

	£000	
Net assets	25,000	
Share capital	23,000	
Minority interests	2,000	(i.e. 40% of net assets of subsidiary)
	25,000	

Where the subsidiary has traded either before or since the takeover, the calculation of minority interests is slightly more complex than this, since the minority share of net assets is arrived at by taking an appropriate proportion of the share capital and reserves (both pre- and post-acquisition) of the subsidiary.

The logic of the group balance sheet, where there are minority shareholders in the subsidiary, is fairly easy to follow. The group in the example has net assets of £25 million, all of which are under the control of the holding company's shareholders. This is financed mainly by those shareholders (£23 million), but partly by the minority shareholders of the subsidiary company.

Example

The following balance sheets relate to H Ltd and S Ltd at 31 December 19X4:

	H Ltd	S Ltd
	£000	£000
Net assets	5,500	4,500
Investments in S Ltd	3,000	—
	8,500	4,500
Ordinary share capital	6,000	3,000
(£1 shares fully paid)		
Reserves	2,500	1,500
	8,500	4,500

The investments in S Ltd had cost £3 million, for 2 million £1 shares, at a time when S Ltd's reserves stood at £900,000.

The *goodwill on consolidation* can be calculated as follows:

What was paid	£3.0 million
What was obtained	£2.6 million
(Net assets = capital + reserves at the time of	
acquisition, i.e. £3.9 million; H Ltd is entitled to two-thirds of this)	
Goodwill on consolidation	£0.4 million

The minority interests will be one-third of the net assets (capital + reserves) at the balance sheet date, namely £1.5 million. It should be noted that any distinction between pre- and post-acquisition profits is irrelevant as far as the minority shareholders are concerned.

The post-acquisition reserves in S Ltd are £600,000, two-thirds of which can be added to group reserves.

The **group balance sheet as at 31 December 19X4** is as follows:

	£000	
Net assets	10,000	
Goodwill on consolidation	400	
	10,400	
Ordinary share capital	6,000	
Reserves	2,900	(£2.5 million from H Ltd + £0.4 million from S Ltd)
Minority interests	1,500	
	10,400	

As was discussed above, the goodwill would not normally be retained on the balance sheet but written off in one way or another.

Activity 6

The following balance sheets relate to H Ltd and S Ltd at 31 December 19X4:

	H Ltd	S Ltd
	£000	£000
Net assets	5,100	3,700
Investments in S Ltd	2,200	—
	7,300	3,700
Ordinary share capital (£1 shares fully paid)	5,000	2,500
Reserves	2,300	1,200
	7,300	3,700

The investments in S Ltd had cost £2.2 million, for 2 million £1 shares, at a time when S Ltd's reserves stood at £500,000.

Try preparing a group balance sheet as at 31 December 19X4.

You should have written something like the following:

Capital reserve on consolidation
Pay   £2.2 million
Get   £2.4 million
Therefore £0.2 million capital reserve

Reserves   £
H Ltd   2,300,000
S Ltd   560,000   80% of post-acquisition reserves of £700,000
          2,860,000

Minority interests
20% of the capital and reserves (2.5 m + 1.2 m) = £740,000

Balance sheet as at 31 December 19X4

	£000
Net assets	8,800
Ordinary share capital	5,000
Capital reserve on consolidation	200
Reserves	2,860
Minority interests	740
	8,800

Self-assessment question 7.1

The summarized balance sheets of Matt Ltd and James Ltd as at 31 December 19X3 are as follows:

	Matt Ltd	James Ltd
	£000	*£000*
Fixed assets	800	24,000
Investments in James Ltd		29,000
(12,000 shares at cost)	400	2,000
Current assets	30,200	26,000
Current liabilities	(200)	(1,000)
	30,000	25,000
Ordinary share capital	20,000	15,000
Reserves	10,000	10,000
	30,000	25,000

The following information is also available:

1 Matt Ltd acquired the shares in James Ltd on 31 December 19X2 when the reserves of James Ltd were £5 million.
2 At 31 December 19X3 James Ltd owed Matt Ltd £100,000. This amount had been included in the current assets and current liabilities of Matt Ltd and James Ltd respectively.

Prepare a group balance sheet for the group as at 31 December 19X3.
   A suggested solution to this question appears at the end of the book.

7.10 The group profit and loss account

The objective of the group profit and loss account is to show a true and fair view of the earnings of the entire group for the particular period, distinguishing between that which is attributable to the shareholders of the holding company and that attributable to the minority shareholders of the subsidiary.

The procedure is to incorporate the whole of the subsidiaries' profit and loss accounts into that of the holding company, adding like items to one another. The portion of the resultant after-tax profit of the group which relates to any minority shareholders of subsidiaries is then deducted to arrive at the group profit attributable to the holding company's shareholders. This approach is consistent with the approach used in preparing a group balance sheet, of showing all of the subsidiaries' net assets and the minority interest in them. It has the advantage of showing the totals for revenues, expenses and profit, of all of the activities under the control of the group. This is necessary if meaningful conclusions are to be drawn about the group's success in trading operations.

The formats for published profit and loss accounts set out in the last chapter need some modification for a group. Given below is an example of format 1, modified for a group.

Group profit and loss account for the year ended ——

	£	Notes
Turnover	x	1
Cost of sales	(x)	1
Gross profit	x	1
Administration expenses	(x)	1
Distribution expenses	(x)	1
Other income	(x)	
Profit before tax	x	
Taxation	x	1
Profit after tax	x	1
Minority interest	x	2
Group profit for year	x	3
Appropriations		
Dividends	(x)	4
Reserves	(x)	4
Group retained profits for the year	x	
Retained profit brought forward	x	5
Retained profit carried forward	x	

Notes

1 Normally the group profit and loss account will reflect the total of the equivalent figures in the holding and subsidiary company profit and loss accounts.

2 The minority interest is calculated as the share of after-tax profits in the subsidiary.
3 The group profit will be that of the holding company plus the share of *after-tax profits* of the subsidiary, less any unrealized profits.
4 Dividends will be those of the holding company only. Other appropriations, such as transfers to reserves, will be the holding company figures plus the appropriate share of any transfers to reserves made in the accounts of the subsidiaries.
5 The retained profits brought forward will be those relating to the group, which will be the sum of the retained profits brought forward in the holding company accounts plus the appropriate shares of post-acquisition profits in the subsidiary at the beginning of the period.

Example

The following profit and loss accounts relate to H Ltd and S Ltd for the year ended 31 December 19X1:

	H Ltd	**S Ltd**
	£000	*£000*
Turnover	10,000	5,000
Cost of sales	(5,000)	(2,500)
Gross profit	5,000	2,500
Administration	(1,000)	(500)
Distribution	(1,000)	(500)
Profit before tax	3,000	1,500
Taxation	(1,000)	(500)
Profit after tax	2,000	1,000

H Ltd owns 80% of the share capital of S Ltd. No dividends were paid or proposed by either company.

The *group profit and loss account* would appear as follows:

	£000	*Workings*
Turnover	15,000	(10,000 + 5,000)
Cost of sales	(7,500)	(5,000 + 2,500)
Gross profit	7,500	
Administration	(1,500)	(1,000 + 500)
Distribution	(1,500)	(1,000 + 500)
Profit before tax	4,500	
Taxxation	(1,500)	(1,000 + 500)
Profit after tax	3,000	
Minority interests	(200)	(20% × 1,000)
Profit after tax attributable to the group	2,800	

Dividends

When the subsidiary pays a dividend, most of it will go to the parent company, because the parent company is the majority shareholder. From the point of view of the subsidiary company, such a dividend represents an appropriation of profit and must be recorded in the profit and loss account as such. From the parent company's point of view, the dividend from the subsidiary is a revenue and must be recorded as such. From a group point of view, however, a dividend paid by one member to another is simply a transfer of cash within the group. There is neither an appropriation of profit, nor a revenue. In the group profit and loss account the two aspects of these intragroup dividends must be cancelled.

Example

The following profit and loss accounts relate to H Ltd and S Ltd for the year ended 31 December 19X1:

	H Ltd	**S Ltd**
	£000	*£000*
Turnover	10,000	5,000
Cost of sales	(5,000)	(2,500)
Gross profit	5,000	2,500
Administration	(1,000)	(500)
Distribution	(1,000)	(500)
Income – dividends receivable	400	—
Profit before tax	3,400	1,500
Taxation	(1,000)	(500)
Profit after tax	2,400	1,000
Dividend paid	(1,000)	(500)
Profit and loss account balance c/f	1,400	900

H Ltd owns 80% of the share capital of S Ltd.

It should be clear that the dividends paid by S Ltd came *from* profits made by S Ltd. A total of 80% of these dividends are received by H Ltd and recorded in its accounts, reflecting the proportion of the shares owned. If the profits are included as shown in the preceding example, *and* the dividends receivable by H Ltd are added to them, a double counting would occur. The group profit and loss account would thus appear as follows:

	£000	*Workings*
Turnover	15,000	(10,000 + 5,000)
Cost of sales	(7,500)	(5,000 + 2,5000)
Gross profit	7,500	

Administration	(1,500)	(1,000 + 500)
Distribution	(1,500)	(1,000 + 500)
Profit before tax	4,500	
Taxation	(1,500)	(1,000 + 500)
Profit after tax	3,000	
Minority interests	(200)	(20% × 1,000)
Profit after tax attributable to the	2,800	
group less dividends	(1,000)	
Group retained profit for the year	1,800	

Only dividends of the holding company will appear in the group profit and loss account. In effect, the dividend due to H Ltd from S Ltd is cancelled. The dividend due from S Ltd to the minority shareholders is included in minority interests.

Activity 7

The following profit and loss accounts relate to H Ltd and S Ltd for the year ended 31 December 19X1:

	H Ltd	S Ltd
	£000	*£000*
Turnover	10,000	5,000
Cost of sales	(5,000)	(2,500)
Gross profit	5,000	2,500
Administration	(1,000)	(500)
Distribution	(1,000)	(500)
Income – dividends receivable	400	—
Profit before tax	3,400	1,500
Taxation	(1,000)	(500)
Profit after tax	2,400	1,000
Dividends paid		
Preference	—	(400)
Ordinary	(1,000)	(500)
Profit and loss account balance c/f	1,400	100

H Ltd owns 80% of the ordinary share capital of S Ltd and none of the preference shares.

  Have a try at preparing a group profit and loss account for the year ended 31 December 19X1.

Your profit and loss account should look something like this:

Group profit and loss account for the year ended 31 December 19X1

	£000	Workings
Turnover	15,000	(10m + 5m)
Cost of sales	(7,500)	(5m + 2.5m)
Gross profit	7,500	
Administration	(1,500)	(1m + 0.5m)
Distribution	(1,500)	(1m + 0.5m)
Profit before tax	4,500	
Taxation	(1,500)	(1m + 0.5m)
Profit after tax	3,000	
Minority interests	520	((20% × 0.6m) + 0.4m
Profit after tax attributable	2,480	preference dividend)
to the group		
Dividends	1,000	
Added to group reserves	1,480	

Reserves

Following on from the treatment of reserves in the group balance sheet, it should be clear that any balances brought forward on the group profit and loss account should include only those of the holding company and the post-acquisition element of those of the subsidiary.

Example

H Ltd acquired 80% of the ordinary share capital of S Ltd on 31 December 19X6. The companies' outline profit and loss accounts for the year ended 31 December 19X7 were as follows:

	H Ltd	S Ltd
	£000	£000
Profit after tax	2,000	1,000
Profit and loss balance b/f	1,000	1,000
	3,000	2,000
Dividends	(1,000)	(500)
Profit and loss balance c/f	2,000	1,500

This would result in a **group profit and loss account** for the year as follows:

	£000	
Profit after tax	3,000	
Minority interests	(200)	(20% × £1m)
Profit attributable to the group	2,800	

Dividends	(1,000)	(H Ltd only)
Profit retained for the year	1,800	
Profit and loss account balance b/f	1,000	(see below)
Profit and loss account balance of group c/f	2,800	

The profit and loss balance brought forward is made up of the balance brought forward in H Ltd (£1m), plus the post-acquisition share of the profit and loss account balance in S Ltd. Since the profit and loss account balance brought forward in S Ltd must represent the balance as at 31 December 19X6, it must all be pre-acquisition. None of it is included in the balance brought forward in the group profit and loss account.

Activity 8

The following information is available for the year ended 31 December 19X8:

	H Ltd	S Ltd	T Ltd
	£000	*£000*	*£000*
Profit after tax	20,000	4,000	5,000
Profit and loss account balance b/f	15,000	3,000	8,000
Profit and loss account balance c/f	35,000	7,000	13,000

H Ltd acquired 75% of the ordinary share capital of S Ltd on 31 December 19X6, when the balance on the profit and loss account of S Ltd was £1m.

H Ltd acquired 80% of the ordinary share capital of T Ltd on 31 December 19X7.

Show how this information would be reflected in the group profit and loss account for the year ended 31 December 19X8.

Your profit and loss account should look something like this:

Group profit and loss account for the year ended 31 December 19X8

	£000	*Workings*
Profit after tax	29,000	(20m + 4m + 5m)
Minority interests	2,000	(25% × 4m) + (20% × 5m)
	27,000	
Profit and loss balance b/f	16,500	(15m + {75% × [3m − 1m]})
	43,500	

7.11 Disclosure in group accounts

The requirement to publish group accounts does not relieve each individual company in the group from its statutory obligation to keep its own records, and to disclose its trading results and position. This means that, in practice, when accounts are published in the form of an annual report, they include not just a group profit and loss account and balance sheet, but a holding company profit and loss account and balance sheet, as well. Exemptions to the requirement to publish group accounts are obtainable for small and medium-sized groups and by parent companies which are subsidiaries of EC parents.

7.12 Associated companies

At the beginning of this chapter the point was made that companies sometimes invest in the shares of another company without necessarily obtaining control of that company. Under such circumstances no group accounts are legally required. Nor would the preparation of a set of group accounts be logical. Basically the effect on the final accounts of the investor company is that the investment in the other company would be shown, typically at cost, and any dividends received would be included as income in the investor company's profit and loss account, with a consequent increase in cash.

This is the normal treatment for an investment which constitutes a relatively small part of the share capital of the company whose shares are being purchased. Such a treatment can be quite misleading, however.

Example

Suppose that H Ltd acquired 10% of the shares of Y Ltd on formation of Y Ltd for £1 million. During the first year of its trading, Y Ltd made a profit after tax of £2 million, and paid out a dividend of £500,000. H Ltd would show in its balance sheet:

Investment in Y Ltd   £1 million

and in its profit and loss account:

Investment income: dividends from Y Ltd   £50,000

In fact, H Ltd's *share earnings* in Y Ltd is £200,000 (10% × £2 million). The recording of the dividends only, while following both the realization convention and the convention of prudence, does not adequately reflect the earnings of the investment in Y Ltd. This point needs to be recognized when dealing with investments of this type.

Where enough shares of a company are held for the investing company to exert a significant influence over the other company, the accounting treatment is modified to reflect the investing company's share of *earnings*, as opposed to its share of dividends. A company which is not controlled, but where the ownership is sufficient to exert a significant influence, is known as an *associated company* of the investor company. An associated company is one in which there is an investment which is long-term and substantial, but not controlling, or where the investing company interest in the shares makes it effectively a partner in a joint venture or consortium, or where the investing company actively participates in the commercial or policy decisions. Typically, associates are those where the investment covers 20–50% of the voting capital.

Where an associate company exists there will be amendments made to the consolidated accounts of the investing group (but not to the individual accounts of the investing company). In the group profit and loss account there will be lines relating to:

- the share of profits or losses before tax of the associate company;
- the share of tax attributable to the associate company;
- the share of retained profit in the associate company.

The *consolidated profit and loss account* is thus likely to appear, broadly, as follows:

		£
Net profit before tax (holding company plus subsidiaries)		x
Share of profit before tax of associates		$\underline{x}$
Less: Corporation tax		x
Holding company and subsidiaries	x	
Associates	$\underline{x}$	
		$\underline{x}$
Profit after tax		x
Minority interests		$\underline{x}$
Profit attributable to the group		x
Less dividends		$\underline{x}$
Net profit of year retained in group		$\underline{\underline{x}}$

Normally the amounts retained in the various companies (holding company, subsidiaries and associates) are also shown. In some formats the profit and loss balance brought forward from previous years will be added to give a profit and loss balance carried forward.

In the *consolidated balance sheet*, the investment in the associate company will need to be increased to reflect the inclusion of the share of net assets of the associate, together with any goodwill on acquisition.

If the investing company has no subsidiaries the share of associated company profits and retentions should be shown by way of a series of supplementary notes.

You should note that the treatment of associate companies is different to a conventional consolidation. The individual items in the profit and loss account are not consolidated. Only the group share of the associate's net profit before tax is brought in, together with the share of tax and retained profit for the year. Similarly, in the balance sheet the assets and liabilities are not consolidated. Effectively the investment in the subsidiary is enhanced to reflect the increase attributable to post-acquisition earnings which are retained in the associate. This may be increased by any goodwill on the acquisition of the associate. Reserves are increased to match this.

Example

X Ltd acquired 25% of the ordinary shares of Y Ltd on the formation of Y Ltd. During Y Ltd's first year of trading the company generated pre-tax profits of £1.4 million. Tax was estimated at £600,000 leaving an after-tax profit of £800,000. A dividend totalling £500,000 was paid by Y Ltd, leaving £600,000 in reserves.

If Y Ltd were not to be treated as an associated company of X Ltd, all that would appear in the profit and loss account of X Ltd in respect of its investment would be its dividend of £50,000 (i.e. 25% of £200,000).

When treated as an associate company, the adjustments to the group profit and loss account are:

- Eliminate the dividend as income in the profit and loss account (take out the £50,000 dividend in the example);
- Add to the pre-tax profit of the investor company, its share (£350,000) of the pre-tax profit of the associated company (i.e. 25% of £1.4 million);
- Add to the tax charge of the investor company its share (£150,000) of the associated company's tax charge (i.e. 25% of £600,000).

In practice, it will normally be necessary to add to the retained profits brought forward of the investor company, its share of those of the associated company. In this example there were no associated company-retained profits brought forward because it was the first year of trading.

In the group balance sheet X Ltd's investment in Y Ltd will need to be increased to reflect its share of retained profits in Y Ltd. Basically, the retained profit of Y Ltd will have increased by £150,000 (£200,000 less the £50,000 dividend previously included). The value of the investment in the shares of Y Ltd in the group balance sheet will thus need to be increased by the same amount. This is to reflect the fact that the investment has grown over the year as a result of undistributed profits.

Activity 9

The summarized profit and loss accounts of X Ltd and of Y Ltd for the year ended 31 December 19X2 are as follows:

	X Ltd £000	Y Ltd £000
Turnover	55,000	23,000
Cost of sales	32,000	12,000
Gross profit	23,000	11,000
Distribution costs	(9,000)	(5,000)
Administrative costs	(9,000)	(4,000)
	5,000	2,000
Dividends receivable from Y Ltd	100	—
Net profit	5,100	2,000
Corporation tax	2,000	800
Profit after tax for the year	3,100	1,200
Retained profit from last year	8,300	800
	11,400	2,000
Dividend paid	1,500	400
Retained profit carried to next year	9,900	1,600

X Ltd had paid £1.2 million for 25% of the ordinary share capital of Y Ltd on 1 January 19X1, on formation of Y Ltd. Y Ltd had £4 million of ordinary share capital.

Have a try at revising the profit and loss account of X Ltd to incorporate the results of its associated company, Y Ltd.

Also show the amounts which would be shown in the revised balance sheet of X Ltd for:

- Retained profit (reserve); and
- Investment in Y Ltd.

Your profit and loss account should look something like this:

Profit and loss account for the year ended 31 December 19X2

	£000	*Workings*
Turnover	55,000	
Cost of sales	(32,000)	
Gross profit	23,000	
Administration	(9,000)	
Distribution	(9,000)	
Profit before tax	5,000	
Share of profits in associate	500	25% × 2m
	5,500	

	£000	£000	Workings
Taxation: X Ltd	2,000		
A Ltd	200		25% ×0.8m
		(2,200)	
Profit after tax		3,300	
Dividends		1,500	
Added to reserves		1,800	
Profit and loss account			
Balance b/f X Ltd	8,300		
Y Ltd	200		25% ×0.8m
		8,500	
		10,300	

The balance sheet would thus show £10.3 million under reserves.

The investment would increase by £0.4 million, to reflect the share of profits retained in Y Ltd, namely £0.2m from 19X1 and £0.3m from 19X2 (share of profits less tax as shown above) less the dividend paid to X Ltd.

Self-assessment question 7.2

The following are the profit and loss accounts for A Ltd and B Ltd for the year ended 31 December 19X9:

	A Ltd	B Ltd
	£000	£000
Turnover	6,000	3,000
Cost of sales	(3,000)	(1,000)
Gross profit	3,000	2,000
Administration	(800)	(400)
Distribution	(1,000)	(400)
Investment income	1,000	—
Profit before tax	2,200	1,200
Taxation	(700)	(300)
Profit after tax	1,500	900
Appropriated as follows		
Dividends paid		
Preference	(300)	(100)
Ordinary	(600)	(500)
General reserve transfer	(400)	(200)
Retained profits for year	200	100
Profit and loss account balance b/f	500	500
Profit and loss account balance c/f	700	600

A Ltd purchased 80% of the ordinary share capital of B Ltd when the profit and loss account balance of B Ltd was £100,000. A Ltd owns none of B Ltd's preference shares.

A Ltd's investment income includes the dividend from B Ltd.

Prepare a group profit and loss account for the year ended 31 December 19X9.

7.13   Summary

In this chapter you have been introduced to the nature and special accounting requirements of groups of companies. The chapter also considered other aspects of one company investing in the shares of another.

A group of companies is formed when one company has control, usually through owning a majority of the shares, of another company or companies. Groups can take various forms, some of them quite complex.

Groups of companies are formed for a variety of reasons, of which a desire for expansion through acquisition is an important one. There are other ways for one company to acquire another than by buying sufficient shares to control it, but the formation of groups is a popular approach in practice. Groups of companies are required to prepare a balance sheet and a profit and loss account for the group as a whole, as well as for the individual companies which it comprises.

In essence, the preparation of the group accounts is simply a process of incorporating most of the assets, claims, revenues and expenses of the group members into the balance sheet of the parent company, adding like items together. The remaining items which will be related to the owners' claim of the subsidiary and the amount of the investment in subsidiaries of the parent will be set off against one another. If these two do not exactly cancel one another, it will be for one or both of two reasons:

* The amount paid by the parent for its investment in the subsidiary is greater than or less than the value of the net assets acquired, in which case the difference will appear on the group balance sheet either as 'goodwill on consolidation' or as 'capital reserve on consolidation'.
* The parent does not acquire all of the shares of the subsidiary. In this case the claim of the minority shareholders against the net assets of the group and the entitlement of those shareholders to share in the profits of the group must be recognized in the group balance sheet and profit and loss account respectively.

The overall objective of group accounts is to show the position and effectiveness of the entire group as if the assets, claims, revenues and expenses of all group members were actually those of the parent company.

Where a company owns shares in another company, though not enough to control it, yet despite this is able to exercise significant influence over it, the latter company is known as an associated company. In these circumstances the investor company's share of the trading results of the associated company are incorporated in the investor company's final accounts, albeit in summarized form.

Exercises

1   The balance sheets of H Ltd and S Ltd as at 31 December 19X1 are as follows:

	H Ltd £000	S Ltd £000
Net assets	80,000	25,000
Investments in S Ltd	20,000	–
	100,000	25,000
Ordinary share capital (£1 shares fully paid)	50,000	15,000
Reserves	50,000	10,000
	100,000	25,000

H Ltd acquired all the shares of S Ltd when reserves of S Ltd were £5 million.
   Prepare a group balance sheet as at 31 December 19X1.

2   Take the same balance sheets as in question 1, but assume that H Ltd acquired all of the shares of S Ltd when reserves of S Ltd were £3 million.
   Prepare a group balance sheet as at 31 December 19X1.

3   Take the same balance sheets as in question 1, but assume that H Ltd acquired all of the shares of S Ltd when reserves of S Ltd were £7 million.
   Prepare a group balance sheet as at 31 December 19X1.

4   The balance sheets of H Ltd and S Ltd as at 31 December 19X1 are as follows:

	H Ltd £000	S Ltd £000
Net assets	80,000	25,000
Investments in S Ltd	20,000	–
	100,000	25,000
Ordinary share capital (£1 shares fully paid)	50,000	25,000
Reserves	50,000	–
	100,000	25,000

H Ltd acquired 20 million of the shares of S Ltd when reserves of S Ltd were nil.
   Prepare a group balance sheet as at 31 December 19X1.

5   The balance sheets of H Ltd and S Ltd as at 31 December 19X1 are as follows:

	H Ltd	S Ltd
	£000	£000
Net assets	80,000	35,000
Investments in S Ltd	20,000	
	100,000	35,000
Ordinary share capital	50,000	25,000
(£1 shares fully paid)		
Reserves	50,000	10,000
	100,000	35,000

H Ltd acquired 15 million of the shares of S Ltd when reserves of S Ltd were £5 million.
   Prepare a group balance sheet as at 31 December 19X1.

6   The balance sheets of Great Ltd and its subsidiary Small Ltd at 31 December 19X5 are as follows:

	Great Ltd	Small Ltd
	£000	£000
Fixed assets		
Freehold land	2,000	1,500
Plant and equipment	1,500	1,200
Shares in Small Ltd (at cost)	3,300	
Current assets		
Stock	1,200	500
Debtors: Great Ltd		850
Others	600	300
Cash	1,000	150
	9,600	4,500
Current liabilities		
Creditors: Great Ltd	(850)	
Others	(400)	(100)
Debentures		(500)
	8,350	3,900
Ordinary share capital	6,000	3,000
(£1 shares fully paid)		
Share premium	250	
General reserve	1,100	400
Profit and loss account	1,000	500
	8,350	3,900

The following information is available:

(a) Great Ltd acquired its holding of 2.25 million shares in Small Ltd when the latter had balances of £300,000 on its general reserve and of £200,000 on its profit and loss account.
(b) In calculating the price payable by Great Ltd for its shares in Small Ltd the land owned by Small Ltd was professionally valued at £2 million.

Prepare a group balance sheet as at 31 December 19X5.

Part Four

The Analysis and Interpretation of Accounts

This section comprises five chapters, and provides a framework for using accounting information to help assess performance, and to make decisions about the future.

The first chapter in the section deals with the cash flow statement. This statement reveals the flow of liquid funds through the business, and provides a valuable insight to the financing and investing activities for a particular period. The chapter shows how the cash flow statement is prepared and how the contents can be interpreted.

The next chapter in this section is concerned with accounting for the future. It aims to change your perspective on accounting from one concerned with historic events to one concerned with future, albeit less certain, events. The chapter shows how the basic financial accounting framework, comprising the three statements (balance sheet, profit and loss account and cash flow statement) can be used either to assess future plans or as the basis of a corporate financial model of the future. Nowadays, computers play a key role in the preparation and alteration of the financial plans. Financial planning requires a clear understanding of the interrelationships between the three accounting statements and this chapter should reinforce your understanding of accounting principles.

The following two chapters deal with various techniques which can be used to analyse the position and performance of a business as revealed in the financial statements. The techniques are used to evaluate the strengths and weaknesses of the business and to provide a basis for future decisions.

The final chapter in this section is concerned with the quality of information revealed in the financial statements. It is important to bear in mind that the quality of analysis and interpretation will depend on the quality of the underlying information. In this chapter, the accounting conventions underpinning the financial statements are reviewed and their advantages, problems and limitations are identified. The chapter also considers the problems of accounting which are caused by changing prices, and the possible ways of dealing with them. Clearly such factors are also important in assessing performance. Finally, the chapter considers how the quality of financial reports might be improved if a more systematic and logical framework for accounting can be developed.

8

The cash flow statement

8.1 Introduction

The chapter explains the nature and purpose of the cash flow statement and how it is prepared. The chapter also discusses how the cash flow statement may be used as a basis for decision-making.

8.2 Objectives

On completion of this chapter you should be able:

- to discuss the purpose of the cash flow statement;
- to identify the main sources and uses of liquid funds;
- to prepare a cash flow statement;
- to interpret the significance of the information revealed in this statement.

8.3 Nature and purpose of the cash flow statement

The cash flow statement sets out the sources and uses of cash (and near cash) over a period. It is important to recognize that, while profitability is an essential ingredient of success, it is by no means sufficient. Even though profits may be high, a business must still retain enough liquid assets to meet its obligations as and when they arise. A lack of liquidity can lead to major problems for a business. Indeed, many business failures stem from an inability to manage liquidity. Liquidity is also an important consideration when funding new projects.

The cash flow statement provides a useful tool for analysing management decisions and strategy. It can reveal such things as:

- the amount of liquid funds generated from operating activities;
- the ways in which financing occurred; and
- investment (and disinvestment) activities during a period.

This kind of information can help users assess whether liquid funds generated are sufficient and whether they have been raised and applied in an appropriate way.

The importance of liquidity to a business is difficult to overstate. It is not uncommon for a profitable business to be forced to cease trading because it does not have enough liquid funds to meet its maturing liabilities.

Activity 1

How do you think this situation can occur? Consider the case of a young, expanding business and the problems it could face.

A young, expanding business is particularly prone to liquidity problems. A business may start with little capital and borrow heavily in order to finance fixed assets and stock. Any profits made may be ploughed back in order to finance more fixed assets and stock, with insufficient consideration being given to the liquid assets necessary to continue operations. The result may be that, when the liabilities mature, there are insufficient liquid funds to pay the amounts due. The creditors may, therefore, seek to wind up the business in order that assets may be sold to pay the amounts owing. This may occur despite the fact that the business is making good profits. Thus, the business must be concerned with liquidity as well as profitability.

Activity 2

It has been stated above that making profits will not necessarily ensure that there will be sufficient liquid funds to meet maturing obligations. Profits made over a period will not usually equate with liquid funds generated during that period. To demonstrate this point consider the effect (i.e. increase/decrease/no effect) of the following transactions on both profitability and liquidity (i.e. cash).

Transaction	Effect on profit	Effect on cash
(a) Issue of shares		
(b) Sale of goods on credit		
(c) Purchase of fixed assets for cash		
(d) Depreciation of fixed assets		
(e) Repayment of a loan		
(f) Payment of a dividend		
(g) The payment of a corporation tax liability		
(h) The sale of a fixed asset for cash		

The solutions are as follows:

Transaction	Effect on profits	Effect on cash
Issue of share	no effect	increase
Sale of goods on credit	increase	no effect
Purchases of fixed assets for cash	no effect	decrease
Depreciation of fixed assets	decrease	no effect
Repayment of a loan	no effect	decrease
Payment of a dividend	no effect	decrease
Settlement of a tax provision	no effect	decrease
The sale of a fixed asset for cash	increase/decrease by amount of profit or loss	increase by amount of sale proceeds

8.4 Relationship with other financial statements

The cash flow statement is an integral part of the annual financial report of limited companies. Its importance, therefore, as a financial statement is clearly recognized. However, the statement does not normally provide additional information to that already provided to users. Rather, it normally provides a selection, reclassification and summarization of information already shown on the profit and loss account and balance sheet. The statement is, nevertheless, very useful as it clearly identifies the changes in assets, capital and liabilities that occurred during the period and the effect of such changes on liquidity. Hence, the statement helps provide a more complete picture of the business and the changes that have occurred.

8.5 What is meant by 'cash'?

Before we look at the preparation of the cash flow statement in detail, it is necessary to be clear as to what is meant by the term 'cash' in this context. In order to adhere to the relevant accounting standard on this topic, cash is defined in rather broader terms than simply cash in hand and in the bank. The term also embraces 'cash equivalents', i.e. liquid investments which may be converted into cash immediately and which are within 3 months of maturing. Any short-term borrowings which are repayable within 3 months are deducted from the cash and cash equivalents held to achieve a net figure.

Activity 3

Why might this broader definition of 'cash' prove to be more useful to users? Can you think of any counterarguments for using this broader definition?

A broader definition may help users gain a better insight into the management of cash and a clearer picture of the liquidity of the business. A business which has a low cash balance in the bank may, nevertheless, be highly liquid if it has invested its surplus cash in short-term investments in order to generate a return for the business. Conversely, a business which has a high cash balance in the bank may be illiquid if it also has high short-term borrowings.

The problem with taking the broader definition, however, is that the term 'cash' becomes less certain. The period of 3 months used in defining short-term investments is an arbitrary one. In practice, short-term investments in shares etc. may be difficult to value and may fluctuate over time. This may create difficulties for users when assessing liquidity.

8.6 The main elements of the cash flow statement

In order to adhere to the relevant accounting standard, the cash flow statement must be presented in a format which contains five major elements. Each element represents a particular source of cash inflow or outflow for the business during a period. The five elements are as follows:

- *Operating activities*. This shows the cash flows arising from business operations.
- *Returns on investments and servicing of finance*. This sets out the interest and dividends both received and paid during the period.
- *Taxation*. This element sets out the taxation paid and any tax rebates that have been received.
- *Investing activities*. This sets out the payments made for the purchase of fixed assets and the proceeds from the sale of any fixed assets.
- *Financing*. This shows the amounts received from the issue of shares and loans and the amounts paid to purchase or redeem shares and to repay loans.

You may have noted that the first three elements deal with profit and loss account items and the last two elements deal with balance sheet items.

The relevant accounting standard requires that each element be separately identified and that the sequence shown above must be adhered to when preparing the cash flow statement.

8.7 The cash flow statement format

An example of the format for a cash flow statement is shown below. This format reveals the net cash inflow (outflow) figure for each of the five elements of cash flow. By adding together the net figures for each of the various elements, we derive a total of the net cash flows for the period.

Angles Ltd
Cash flow statement for the year ended 31 March 19X5

	£	£
Net cash inflow from operating activities		18,000
Returns on investments and servicing of finance		
Interest received	2,000	
Interest paid	(3,000)	
Dividends paid	(5,000)	
Net cash inflow (outflow) from returns on investments		
and servicing of finance		(6,000)
Taxation		
Corporation tax paid	(4,000)	
Tax paid		(4,000)
Investing activities		
Payments to acquire fixed assets	(8,000)	
Receipts from sales of fixed assets	3,000	
Net cash inflow (outflow) from investing activities		(5,000)
Net cash inflow before financing		3,000
Financing activities		
Issue of ordinary shares	10,000	
Repayment of loan capital	(12,000)	
Net cash outflow from financing		(2,000)
Increase in cash and cash equivalents		1,000

8.8 Preparing the cash flow statement – a worked example

In order to understand the way in which a cash flow statement is prepared, it is probably a good idea to work through an example. Consider the balance sheet and profit and loss account of Pentagon Ltd below:

Pentagon Ltd

Balance sheet as at 31 December		19X6			19X7	
	£	£	£	£	£	£
Fixed assets						
Cost		86,000			92,000	
Less: Accumulated depreciation		22,000			31,000	
		64,000			61,000	
Current assets						
Stock		25,000			30,000	
Debtors		28,000			36,000	
Short-term investments		—			2,000	
Cash		4,000			6,000	
		57,000			74,000	
Less: *Creditors falling due*						
within 1 year						

	£	£	£	£	£	£
Trade creditors	14,000			12,000		
Dividends proposed	4,000			3,000		
Corporation tax due	5,000	(23,000)	34,000	4,000	(19,000)	55,000
			98,000			116,000

		£			£
Less: *Creditors not due*					
within 1 year					
10% Debentures		20,000			10,000
Net assets		78,000			106,000
Financed by:					
Share capital and reserves					
£1 Ordinary shares		40,000			60,000
Share premium account		1,000			3,000
Profit and loss account		37,000			43,000
		78,000			106,000

Profit and loss account for the year ended 31 December 19X7

	£	£
Sales		96,000
Less: Cost of sales		64,000
Gross profit		32,000
Wages	7,000	
Administration expenses	1,000	
Depreciation	9,000	
		17,000
Net profit before interest and taxation		15,000
Interest payments		2,000
Net profit before taxation		13,000
Corporation tax		4,000
Net profit after tax		9,000
Appropriated as follows:		
Dividends proposed		3,000
Retained profit for the year profit		6,000
Add: Retained profit brought forward		37,000
Retained profit carried forward		43,000

Note
1   There was no sale of fixed assets during the year.

In order to prepare a cash flow statement for the year, we must identify the cash flows from each of the five elements discussed earlier. Let us now see how the cash flows from each element are calculated.

Net cash flows from operating activities

There are two ways in which the net cash flow from operating activities may be calculated:

- the direct method
- the indirect method

The *direct method* uses information which is gleaned from the underlying accounting records maintained by the business. These records should provide information concerning cash sales and cash received from trade debtors and cash paid out for goods and services for the period. The net cash flows from operating activities can be derived from this information as follows:

	£	£
Cash sales and amounts received from trade debtors		x
		x
Less: Cash purchases and amounts paid to trade creditors	(x)	
Cash expenses and amounts paid to suppliers		
of other goods and services	(x)	(x)
Net cash inflow (outflow) from operating activities		$x/(x)$

We can see that the calculations required only use cash-based figures and should, therefore, be verifiable and free from any bias.

The *indirect method* uses the information contained in the profit and loss account and balance sheet of the business to derive the net cash flow from operating activities. The starting point is the net profit before taxation. This accrual-based figure, however, requires a number of adjustments in order to derive the net cash flow from operating activities.

The net cash flow from operating activities can be derived from the accrual-based information as follows:

	£	£
Net profit from operating activities		x
Add: Interest payable	x	
Depreciation for the year	x	
Loss on sale of fixed assets	x	x
		x
Less interest receivable	(x)	
Profit on sale of fixed assets	(x)	(x)
		x
(Increase)/decrease in stock held	(x)	
(Increase)/decrease in debtors	x	
Increase/(decrease) in creditors	(x)	(x)
Net cash flow from operating activities		x

Activity 4

Can you explain the reason for each adjustment shown above?

These adjustments are necessary to convert the accrual-based figure of profit into an operating cash flow figure.

Depreciation and any profits or losses on the sale of fixed assets will appear in the profit and loss account of a business. However, they do not involve cash movements and are simply book entries. Thus, depreciation and any losses on sale should be added back to arrive at the cash flow from operations and any profits on sale of fixed assets should be deducted. (Although cash may be generated on the sale of a fixed asset, this will be dealt with in another part of the cash flow statement.)

An increase in *stocks and debtors* will involve a reduction in cash and a decrease in these current assets will mean an increase in cash. Similarly, a decrease in *creditors* will mean a reduction in cash and an increase will increase the cash available.

To illustrate this point let us take a simple example. We know that, where sales are on credit, the sales figure for an accounting period is unlikely to represent the cash received from sales for the period. The cash received from sales can be calculated from information contained in the profit and loss account and balance sheet as follows:

	£
Debtors at beginning of period	x
Plus sales during the period	x
Minus debtors at the end of the period	(x)
Equals cash received from sales during the period	x

If sales during a period were £100,000, debtors at the beginning of the period were £10,000 and debtors at the end of the period were £20,000, the cash received from sales for the period would be £10,000 + £100,000 − £20,000 = £90,000. Thus, the increase in debtors (from £10,000 to £20,000) over the period has led to a lower figure of cash generated. If the debtors had stayed constant over the period, the cash generated would have been £100,000. By a similar logic, we can show that increasing stocks will result in a decrease in cash and increasing creditors will result in an increase in cash.

Interest payable and receivable is likely to involve cash movements during the period − although the timing of interest payments and receipts must be identified. However, these are dealt with in another part of the cash flow statement and so interest payable must be added back and interest receivable must be deducted in arriving at the net cash flow from operations.

Whether the direct or indirect method is used, you should arrive at the same figure for net cash flow from operating activities.

Activity 5

Calculate the net cash flow from operations for Pentagon Ltd for the year ended 31 December 19X7 using the indirect method.

Your answer should be as follows:

	£	£
Net profit before tax		13,000
Add: Interest charges	2,000	
Depreciation	9,000	11,000
		24,000
Less: Increase in stocks held (30,000–25,000)	(5,000)	
Increase in debtors (36,000 – 28,000)	(8,000)	
Decrease in creditors (12,000 – 14,000)	(2,000)	(15,000)
Net cash flow from operating activities		9,000

The *indirect method* has the advantage that it focuses attention on the implications for liquidity of four different factors:

- the cash flow from profits
- the implications for liquidity of the management of stock
- the implications for liquidity of the management of debtors
- the implications for liquidity of the management of creditors

For example, it is perfectly possible for a profit to be acceptable, with the implication that liquid funds should increase by the amount of the profit plus any non-cash expenses. However, if this is accompanied by substantial increases in stock or debtors, it is not necessarily the case that the net cash flow will be positive. The contribution to liquid funds from substantial improvements in profitability may be completely cancelled out by the inefficient management of stock, debtors or creditors. The approach used above enables the separate components to be analysed. By way of illustration, consider the fact that in the above example not only have stock and debtors increased over the period (a factor which might be reasonable if sales are higher than they were in previous periods), but creditors have decreased. Such a situation is unusual. In practice, it is more usual for increases in stock and debtors to be partly financed by increases in creditors. A decrease in creditors at the same time as increases in stock and debtors should normally be investigated by management.

Returns on investments and servicing of finance

We saw above that this element of the cash flow statement identifies interest and dividends paid and received during the period. It is common for final dividends to be announced (and shown in the appropriation account) in one accounting period and paid in the following one. The dividend figure for the cash flow statement will be the dividend actually *paid* during the period rather than the dividend announced in that period.

   In the case of an interim dividend, it is likely that it will be both announced and paid within the same period. It will, therefore, be shown in the cash flow statement for that period.

Activity 6
Calculate the net cash inflow (outflow) on returns on investments and servicing of finance for the year ended 31 December 19X7 for Pentagon Ltd.

Your answer should be as follows:

	£	£
Interest paid	(2,000)	
Dividend paid	(4,000)	
Net cash outflow from returns on investments and servicing of finance		(6,000)

Taxation

This element of the cash flow statement will show the corporation tax which has been actually paid during the year. In the UK, corporation tax is often paid 9 months after the relevant year end. So, the corporation tax provision appearing in the profit and loss account for the year will normally be paid in the following year.

Activity 7
What is the taxation paid for the year ended 31 December 19X7 for Pentagon Ltd?

The figure is the corporation tax owing at the end of the year ended 31 December 19X6, which is £5,000.

Investing activities

This element reveals the acquisition and disposal of fixed assets during the period.

Activity 8
Calculate the net cash inflow (outflow) from investing activities for the year ended 31 December 19X7 for Pentagon Ltd.

We are told in the question that there are no sales of fixed assets during the period and so any change in the cost of fixed assets held must be due to acquisitions.

From the balance sheets we can see that the fixed assets at cost at the beginning of the period was £86,000 and the balance at cost at the end of the period was £92,000, so the acquisitions during the period must have cost £6,000 (£92,000 – £86,000). Where there are also disposals of fixed assets during the period things can be more complex. However, we will deal with this situation later.

Financing

This element shows the receipts and payments arising from share and loan transactions. The amounts received or paid during the year can often be deduced by simply comparing the balances on the share account or loan account at the beginning and end of the relevant period. However, where shares are issued at a premium, the total cash generated from the issue will be represented by the increase in both the share account and the share premium account.

Activity 9

Calculate the net cash inflow (outflow) from financing for the year ended 31 December 19X7 for Pentagon Ltd.

The answer to this activity is as follows:

	£	£
Issue of ordinary shares [(60,000 – 40,000) + (3,000 – 1,000)]	22,000	
Repayment of debenture loan (10,000 – 20,000)	(10,000)	
Net cash inflow from financing		12,000

We have now calculated all of the elements of cash flow for the period and are in a position to prepare the cash flow statement.

Activity 10

Prepare a cash flow statement for the year ended 31 December 19X7 for Pentagon Ltd.

Your answer should be as follows:

Pentagon Ltd
Cash flow statement for the year ended 31 December 19X7

	£	£
Net cash inflow from operating activities		9,000
Returns on investments and servicing of finance		
Interest paid	(2,000)	
Dividends paid	(4,000)	
Net cash inflow (outflow) from returns on investments and servicing of finance		(6,000)
Taxation		
Corporation tax paid	(5,000)	
Tax paid		(5,000)
Investing activities		
Payments to acquire fixed assets	(6,000)	
Net cash inflow (outflow) from investing activities		(6,000)
Net cash outflow before financing		(8,000)
Financing activities		
Issue of ordinary shares	22,000	
Repayment of debenture loan	(10,000)	
Net cash outflow from financing		12,000
Increase in cash and cash equivalents		4,000

8.9   Analysis of changes in cash and cash equivalents during the year

The £4,000 increase in cash and cash equivalents which is revealed in the above statement can be reconciled with the changes in the balance sheet as follows:

Analysis of changes in cash and cash equivalents for the year

	£
Balance as at 1 January 19X6	4,000
Net cash inflow during the year	4,000
Balance as at 31 December 19X7 (2,000 + 6,000)	8,000

This reconciliation, of course, provides us with a useful check on the accuracy of our workings. It is also a requirement of the relevant accounting standard that this reconciliation be shown as a note to the cash flow statement prepared by companies.

8.10 Some further issues about preparing a cash flow statement

The above example involved the preparation of a fairly simple cash flow statement. There are, however, a few points concerning the preparation of cash flow statements which can cause difficulties. When preparing such statements, therefore, it is important to bear in mind the following:

- When using the indirect method, the profit figure to be used in calculating the net cash flows from operations is the net profit before tax and other appropriations. Increases in reserves arising from appropriations during the period should be ignored. Since the net profit before tax and appropriations is regarded as a source of cash flows, any increases in reserves arising from appropriations should not be included as it would represent double counting.
- Share issues represent a source of cash with one exception, the bonus or scrip issue. A bonus issue represents a capitalization of reserves, i.e. a book entry, and does not result in an inflow of funds. As a result, bonus issues should be ignored when preparing the cash flow statement. However, all other share issues will result in additional cash being generated.
- Movements in fixed assets may involve both the disposal of existing assets, and the acquisition of new assets. Where depreciation provisions are kept for each type of fixed asset, it may be useful to tabulate fixed asset movements as follows:

	Cost	**Depreciation provision**	**Net**	**Notes**
	£	£	£	
Opening balance	x	x	x	
Less: disposals	$-x$	$-x$	$-x$	(a)
	x	x	x	
Plus: new acquisitions at cost	x	—	x	
	x	x	x	
Less: depreciation for the year	—	$+x$	$-x$	(b)
closing balance	x	x	x	

(a) Deduct the cost of any asset disposed of from the cost figure, deduct the depreciation figure on the asset being disposed of from the overall depreciation provision, and deduct the net book value of the asset from the net figure.

(b) The amount of depreciation taken in the year will increase the depreciation provision, which will, in turn, reduce the net book value of the asset.

- It is the cash received on the sale of fixed assets that must be included in the cash flow statement as an inflow of cash and not the profit arising on sale. Any profit (or loss) on sale is simply a book entry and usually represents over (or under) depreciation of the asset. Hence, it does not represent an inflow of funds and must not be included as such. Profits (or losses) on the sale of fixed assets which appear in the profit and loss account should be deducted (or added) to net profit before tax in order to derive the net cash flow from operations.

Activity 11

From the following balance sheet information relating to Octagon Ltd, prepare a cash flow statement for the year ended 31 December 19X7, using the indirect method. Also show the changes on cash and cash equivalents for the year as a note to the cash flow statement.

Balance Sheet as at 31 December

	19X6		19X7	
	£000s	*£000s*	*£000s*	*£000s*
Fixed assets				
Cost		1,800		2,700
Depreciation provision		400		600
		1,400		2,100
Current assets				
Stock	500		400	
Debtors	400		600	
Cash	300		700	
	1,200		1,700	
Less: *Creditors due within a year*				
Creditors	300		200	
Dividends proposed	100		150	
Corporation tax	300		500	
	(700)		(850)	
Net current assets		500		850
		1,900		2,950
Capital and reserves				
Issued ordinary share capital		1,000		1,200
Preference share capital		500		600
Reserves		400		1,150
		1,900		2,950

Profit and loss account for the year ending 31 December 19X7

	£000s	*£000s*
Sales		4,000
Cost of sales		1,300
Gross profit		2,700
Interest received		100
		2,800

	£000s	£000s
Depreciation	500	
Loss on sale of fixed asset	100	
Other expenses	600	
		1,200
Net profit before tax		1,600
Tax		500
Net profit after tax		1,100
Less: dividends proposed		150
Added to reserves		950

Additional information

1 During the year fixed assets were sold for £100,000. These had cost £500,000 and had been depreciated by £300,000.
2 There was a bonus issue to ordinary shareholders during the year on a one-for-five basis.

The solution is given below, together with workings.

Cash flow statement for the year ended 31 December 19X7

	£000s	£000s	Note
Net cash inflow from operating activities		1,900	1
Returns on investments and servicing of finance			
Interest received	100		
Dividends paid	(100)		2
Net cash inflow (outflow) from returns on investments and servicing of finance		—	
Taxation			
Corporation tax paid	(300)		
Tax paid		(300)	
Investing activities			
Payments to acquire fixed assets	(1,400)		3
Receipts from sales of fixed assets	100		
Net cash inflow (outflow) from investing activities		(1,300)	
Net cash inflow (outflow) before financing		300	
Financing			
Issue of preference capital	100		4
Net cash inflow (outflow) from financing		100	
Increase (decrease) in cash and cash equivalents		400	

£000s

Analysis of changes in cash and cash equivalents during the year

Cash at beginning of period	300
Net cash inflow during the year	400
Cash at end of period	700

Notes

1 Net cash inflow (outflow) from operations

	£000	*£000*
Net profit before taxation		1,600
Add: Depreciation for the year	500	
Loss on sale of fixed assets	100	600
		2,200
Less: Interest receivable		100
		2,100
(Increase)/decrease in stock held	100	
(Increase)/decrease in debtors	(200)	
Increase/(decrease) in creditors	(100)	(200)
Net cash flow from operating activities		1,900

2 The 19X6 final dividends are assumed to have been paid in 19X7.

3 The fixed assets movements can be seen as follows:

	Cost	Depreciation provision	Net
	£000s	*£000s*	*£000s*
Opening balance	1,800	400	1,400
Less: Disposals	−500	−300	−200
	1,300	100	1,200
Plus: New acquisitions at cost	1,400*	—	x
	2,700	100	x
Less: Depreciation for the year	—	500	−500
Closing balance	2,700	600	2,100

*Missing figure.
The sale proceeds of £100,000 are shown as an inflow.

4 The increase in ordinary share capital over the year was £200,000. All of this was attributable to a bonus issue. The increase in preference share capital, £100,000, is the result of a cash issue.

Self-assessment question 8.1
From the information provided below you are required to prepare a cash flow statement (using the indirect method) for the year ending 28 February 19X8. Also prepare an analysis of changes in cash and cash and cash equivalents during the year.

Balance sheet as at 28 February	19X7		19X8	
	£	£	£	£
Fixed assets				
Plant and equipment – cost	60,000		81,000	
Less: Depreciation provision	30,000		42,000	
		30,000		39,000
Motor vans – cost	14,000		17,000	
Less: Depreciation provision	6,000		9,000	
		8,000		8,000
		38,000		47,000
Current assets				
Stock	12,000		15,000	
Debtors	10,000		12,000	
Bank	3,000		1,000	
	25,000		28,000	
Less: *Creditors due within 1 year*				
Trade creditors	18,000		15,000	
		7,000		13,000
		45,000		60,000
Less: *Creditors due* *in more than 1 year*				
12% Debentures		0		10,000
		45,000		50,000
Represented by:				
Capital and reserves				
Ordinary £1 shares		30,000		30,000
Reserves		15,000		20,000
		45,000		50,000

Profit and loss account for the year ending 28 February 19X8

	£	£
Sales		120,000
Cost of sales	70,000	
Depreciation	15,000	
Other expenses	30,000	
		115,000
Net profit before tax		5,000
Add retained profit b/f		15,000
Profit and loss account balance at 28 February 19X8		20,000

8.11   Interpreting the cash flow statement

The cash flow statement identifies the cash flow from operations and provides a useful insight into the financing and investing activities of management.

Using the information provided, investors and other interested parties can decide whether the funding mix was appropriate given the financial policy and structure of the business and whether the funds generated were applied in the best possible way. A cash flow statement helps focus attention on the resources which are available for capital expenditure, and may provide useful insights into the best ways of financing such expenditure. For example, a choice may exist between leasing a new asset, or buying it, possibly using borrowed funds. The implications of the different financing methods need to be carefully considered, and the cash flow framework is particularly useful in this regard. A cash flow statement, or series of statements built up over time, may provide a useful indicator of security for lenders and creditors, and to likely profit distributions to owners. Such a statement may well suggest ways in which the working capital position may be improved.

While the emphasis of this chapter is on the preparation of a historic cash flow statement, forecast statements can be extremely useful to managers, investors and lenders in assessing the implications of potential future activities. This idea will be dealt with in more detail in the next chapter.

Activity 12

Outline the most significant factors revealed by the cash flow statement prepared in the self-assessment question above.

Your answer may be along the following lines:

- The statement reveals that a significant proportion of the cash inflows were from operating activities. The remainder was generated through the issue of debentures. This shows that the business relied largely on the re-investment of profit to finance the expansion of the business. Shareholders were not called upon to provide additional funds during the period.
- The funds raised (and more) were used for the purchase of more fixed assets. Hence, over the period there has been a decline in cash, which may give rise to concern.
- Using the indirect method, the impact of inappropriate working capital management can be seen. Increases in stock and debtors have an unfavourable effect on liquid funds, as has a reduction in creditors. Under normal circumstances, we would not expect changes in all three of these to result in a reduction in cash. Increases in sales might reasonably be expected to lead to increases in stock and debtors, but some of the resulting expen-

diture can usually be funded from increases in creditors. While there may be good reasons for the pattern revealed, some questions need to be asked about the reason for, and the consequences of, the reduction in cash.

Self-assessment question 8.2

The following information relates to the activities of Hexagon Ltd:

Balance sheet as at 31 March	19X7		19X8	
	£	£	£	£
Fixed assets				
Freehold land at cost		700,000		780,000
Plant and equipment – cost	560,000		660,000	
Less: Depreciation provision	230,000		296,000	
		330,000		364,000
		1,030,000		1,144,000
Current assets				
Stock	356,000		498,000	
Debtors	330,000		344,000	
Bank	30,000		—	
		716,000		842,000
Total assets		1,746,000		1,986,000
Less: *Creditors due within 1 year*				
Trade creditors	240,000		280,000	
Corporation tax	120,000		150,000	
Proposed dividend	40,000		50,000	
Bank overdraft	—		56,000	
		400,000		536,000
		1,346,000		1,450,000
Represented by:				
Capital and reserves				
Ordinary £1 shares		400,000		600,000
Share premium		160,000		160,000
General reserve		450,000		250,000
Profit and loss account		336,000		440,000
		1,346,000		1,450,000

Summarized **Profit and loss account for the year ended 31 March 19X8**

	£	£
Sales		4,520,000
Cost of sales	3,420,000	
Depreciation of plant	124,000	
Loss on sale of plant	8,000	
Other expenses	634,000	
		4,186,000
Net profit before tax		334,000

	£	£
Corporation tax		150,000
Net profit after tax		184,000
Less: Interim dividend paid	30,000	
Final dividend proposed	50,000	
		80,000
Retained profit for the year		104,000
Profit and loss account balance at 31 March 19X7		336,000
Profit and loss account balance at 31 March 19X8		440,000

You are informed that:

(a) In September 19X7 a bonus issue of one share for every two held was made out of the general reserve.
(b) Plant which originally cost £80,000 was sold for cash. Accumulated depreciation relating to the plant sold amounted to £58,000.

Required
Prepare cash flow statement and an analysis of changes in cash and cash equivalents for the year ended 31 March 19X8. Comment on the information provided.

8.12 Summary and conclusions

The cash flow statement, the profit and loss account and the balance sheet represent the principal financial statements presented to external users. The cash flow statement is similar to the profit and loss account in that both are concerned with flows over a period. The cash flow statement is concerned with the flow of liquid funds in and out of the business over a period whilst the income statement is concerned with the flow of profits over a period. Both the cash flow statement and income statement are dynamic statements, i.e. they are concerned with changes occurring over time. This contrasts with the balance sheet which provides a static picture of financial position. The cash flow statement, however, provides a useful link between the balance sheets at the beginning and end of each year. By showing the changes in assets, liabilities and capital which occur during the year, the cash flow statement helps explain how the business arrived at its current financial position. It is therefore a very useful tool of analysis.

Exercises

1 Are the following items added to or subtracted from the net profit before tax when deriving the net cash flow from operations? Mark your response with a cross under the appropriate heading.

	Added	**Subtracted**
Increase in stock		
Increase in debtors		
Increase in creditors		
Depreciation for the year		
Interest received		
Loss on sale of fixed asset		

2 Calculate the net cash inflows (outflows) from operating activities for the year using the direct method from the following information relating to H&S Ltd:

	£
Cash sales	280,000
Cash payments to trade creditors	323,000
Payments made to acquire fixed assets	75,000
Cash received from debtors	197,000
Cash expenses	54,000
Interest paid	22,000
Cash at bank at beginning of year	12,000
Cash at bank at the end of year	13,000
Dividends paid during year	26,000
Loan repaid	120,000

3 From the following information prepare a cash flow statement for 19X5:

Balance sheet as at 31 December

	19X4		19X5	
	£	£	£	£
Fixed assets				
Cost		1,800		2,700
Less accumulated depreciation		400		600
		1,400		2,100
Current assets				
Stock	500		400	
Debtors	400		600	
Cash	300		700	
	1,200		1,700	

	£	£	£	£
Less: *Creditors falling due within 1 year*				
Creditors	(300)		(200)	
Dividends proposed	(100)		(150)	
Corporation tax	(300)		(500)	
	(700)		(850)	
Net current assets		500		850
Total assets less current liabilities		1,900		2,950
Capital				
Issued ordinary share capital		1,000		1,200
Preference share capital		500		600
Reserves		400		1,150
		1,900		2,950

Profit and loss account for 19X5

	£	
		£
Sales		4,000
Cost of sales		1,500
Gross profit		2,500
Expenses	500	
Depreciation	500	
Loss on disposal of fixed assets	100	
		1,100
Net profit		1,400
Less appropriations		
Corporation tax	500	
Dividends proposed	150	
		650
Added to reserves		750

During the fixed year assets were sold for £100. These had cost £500 and had been depreciated by £300.

4 The management of your company is perplexed as to why its bank balance has gone down in the last year, even though profits have been satisfactory. From the following information prepare a cash flow statement to show how the cash has decreased during the year.

Balance sheet as at ——

	1 January		31 December	
	£	£	£	£
Fixed assets				
Premises		60,000		70,000
Plant – cost	25,000		35,000	
Less: Accumulated depreciation	15,000		16,000	
		10,000		19,000
Vehicles – cost	15,000		18,000	
Less: Accumulated depreciation	8,000		6,000	
		7,000		12,000
		77,000		101,000
Investments at cost		40,000		50,000
Current assets				
Stock	30,000		50,000	
Debtors	40,000		70,000	
Cash	49,000		9,000	
	119,000		129,000	
Less: *Creditors falling due within 1 year*				
Creditors	50,000		30,000	
Dividends proposed	6,000		10,000	
Corporation tax	10,000		12,000	
	(66,000)		(42,000)	
Net current assets		53,000		77,000
Total assets less current liabilities		170,000		228,000
Less: *Creditors falling due in more than 1 year*				
Debentures		10,000		40,000
		160,000		188,000
Capital				
Issued ordinary share capital		100,000		120,000
Reserves		60,000		68,000
		160,000		188,000

During the year vehicles costing £6,000, which had been depreciated by £5,000, were sold for £2,000. Total depreciation charges for the year were £4,000, debenture interest was £3,000 and net profit before tax was £30,000.

5   From the following balance sheet information relating to Squares Ltd prepare a cash flow statement for the year ended 31 December 19X7. Also prepare an analysis of changes in cash and cash equivalents for the year.

Balance sheet as at 31 December	19X6 £	19X6 £	19X7 £	19X7 £
Fixed assets				
Freehold land at cost		80,000		95,000
Plant – cost	75,000		85,000	
Less depreciation provision	30,000		40,000	
		45,000		45,000
		125,000		140,000
Current assets				
Stock	21,000		24,000	
Debtors	18,000		22,000	
Cash	4,000		1,000	
	43,000		47,000	
Less: *Creditors due within 1 year*				
Creditors	(20,000)		(18,000)	
Dividends proposed	(8,000)		(10,000)	
Corporation tax	(6,000)		(9,000)	
	(34,000)		(37,000)	
Net current assets		9,000		10,000
		134,000		150,000
Capital and reserves				
Issued ordinary share capital		70,000		80,000
Profit and loss account		44,000		46,000
General reserve		20,000		24,000
		134,000		150,000

The profit before tax for 19X7 was £25,000.

(Hint: In this question a profit and loss account is not provided. It is therefore necessary to derive the figures you require from the balance sheets. To calculate the net cash flows from operations look at the changes between the balance sheets in order to derive the depreciation charge for the period.)

The use of financial statements for planning and decision-making

9.1   Introduction

This chapter aims to show how the three basic financial statements (balance sheet, profit and loss account and cash flow statement) can be used on a forecast basis, rather than on a historic basis, and to identify the contribution that such forecast statements can make to planning and decision-making. The potential of computerized spreadsheets in this area will be illustrated.

9.2   Objectives

On completion of this chapter you should be able:

- to appreciate the need to formulate forecasts and plan in financial terms;
- to recognize the integrated nature of the three financial statements, and appreciate their potential as the basis of a financial planning model;
- to prepare forecast profit and loss accounts, forecast balance sheets and forecast cash flow statements from basic planning data and appreciate how the use of those statements can aid planning;
- to explain the advantages of using spreadsheets to formulate a planning model.

9.3   Financial statements as a basis for forecasting

So far in this book we have considered three major financial statements (namely the balance sheet, the profit and loss account and the cash flow statement) which provide a completely integrated financial picture of an organization. In effect, these three statements are a financial model of the organization.

   In considering plans for the future, there is no reason why the same three statements (or models) should not be used to provide a financial framework for assessing the financial implications, including the financial viability, of such plans. Eventually, after the end of the period to which the plans relate, accounting statements will be prepared to cover that period. At that time, it would seem sensible to assess the success of the plans by comparing the actual outcome for the period with that which was planned.

Activity 1
What are the advantages of doing this?

If the forecast statements indicate that profits will not be satisfactory, or that the financial position will have weaknesses, the plans may need to be modified. In fact, the preparation of forecasts is likely to be particularly useful in deciding upon the best methods of financing the business, or of financing any new projects forming part of that business.

The major difference between forecast and historical financial statements is that historical accounting statements are based upon actual events and objective evidence, whereas forecasts are based on expected events and rather more subjective evidence or opinions. Of course, in preparing forecasts as much objective evidence as can be obtained should be used.

Financial statements for the current year generally represent a good starting point, and provide an objective base position for the development of an integrated financial planning model. In order to illustrate the principles of forecasting using the three financial statements, consider the following example.

Example

The directors of Green Ltd are reviewing the company's financial requirements for the year to 31 December 19X8. The summarized balance sheet of Green Ltd as at 31 December 19X7 was as follows:

Fixed assets	£	£	£
Freehold warehouse			32,000
Fittings and equipment – cost		20,000	
Depreciation provision		8,500	
			11,500
			43,500
Current assets			
Stock		23,000	
Debtors		32,500	
		55,500	
Creditors due within 1 year			
Creditors	19,800		
Bank overdraft	3,000		
		22,800	
			32,700
			76,200
Capital and reserves			
Ordinary share capital			40,000
Reserves			36,200
			76,200

The company's plans are based upon the following expectations for the year to 31 December 19X8:

(a) The issue for cash of 10,000 £1 ordinary shares at a premium of 50p per share.
(b) The purchase of new equipment for £7,000 cash on 1 January.
(c) No dividends.
(d) Stock at the year end will be £29,000.
(e) The following trading transactions will occur at an even rate throughout the year:
Sales   £240,000
Purchases   £186,000
General expenses   £35,000
Directors' salaries   £8,000
(f) The period of credit allowed to customers will be 2 calendar months and the period of credit taken from suppliers will be 1½ calendar months. All amounts (including debtors and creditors outstanding at 31 December 19X7) will be paid in full at the end of the credit periods. No amounts for general expenses or directors' salaries will be outstanding, i.e. there will be no accruals or prepayments at the end of the year.
(g) Depreciation on all equipment held at the end of the year will be provided for at the rate of 10% per annum on cost.

The forecast statements for 19X8 should appear as follows (workings as shown below):

Forecast profit and loss account for the year ending 31 December 19X8

	£	£
Sales		240,000
Opening stock	23,000	
Purchases	186,000	
	209,000	
Less closing stock	29,000	
Cost of sales		180,000
Gross profit		60,000
Less: General expenses	35,000	
Wages and salaries	8,000	
Depreciation	2,700	
		45,700
Net profit		14,300

Forecast balance sheet as at 31 December 19X8

Fixed assets	£	£
Freehold warehouse		32,000
Fittings and equipment – cost	27,000	
Depreciation provision	11,200	
		15,800
		47,800

	£	£
Current assets		
Stock	29,000	
Debtors	40,000	
Cash	11,950	
	80,950	
Creditors due within a year		
Creditors	(23,250)	
		57,700
		105,500
Capital and reserves		
Capital		50,000
Share premium		5,000
Reserves		50,500
		105,500

Cash flow statement for the year ending 31 December 19X7

	£	£
Operating activities		
Net profit before tax	14,300	
Depreciation/loss on cash	2,700	
Increase/decrease in stock	(6,000)	
Increase/decrease in debtors	(7,500)	
Increase in creditors	3,450	
Net cash inflow from operating activities		6,950
Investing activities		
Purchase of fixed assets	(7,000)	
Net cash outflow from investing activities		(7,000)
Net cash outflow before financing		(50)
Financing activities		
Shares issued	15,000	
Net cash inflow from financing activities		15,000
Increase in cash and cash equivalents		14,950

(The indirect method of preparing the cash flow statement is used in this case as it highlights the relationship between profit and cash, while also focusing on issues relating to working capital management.)

Workings

1   The items in the profit and loss account are provided by notes (e) and (g) in the example. The depreciation is taken as 10% on the cost of fittings and equipment owned at the end of the year.

2   With regard to the balance sheet, changes are arrived at as follows:

Fittings and equipment (at cost) increase by £7,000 (the amount purchased during the year) to £27,000, with annual depreciation being 10% of this (£2,700). This in turn increases the amount of the depreciation provision at the year end to £11,200.

The closing stock figure is a directors' estimate (note (d)).

The debtors figure represents 2 months' credit, i.e. one-sixth of sales.

The cash figure reflects the opening overdraft and the increase in liquid funds expected for the year, which is in turn the figure resulting from the funds flow statement.

The creditors figure represents 1½ months' credit on the purchases [(£186,000/12) × 1.5)].

The capital is increased by the new issue at its nominal value.

The premium reflects the premium of 50p per share on the new issue.

The reserves reflect the opening balance plus the profit for the year.

3 When preparing forecast cash flow statements, it is appropriate (and usually more convenient) to make assumptions or plans about levels of stock, debtors and creditors, and to see the impact of such plans on the liquid funds, in this case cash. The resulting change in liquid funds will clearly need to be incorporated into the balance sheet, as was shown above. The figures in the cash flow statement were arrived at as follows:

Operating activities – net profit (from the profit and loss account) adjusted for depreciation and changes in working capital – the difference between the balance sheet figure at the end of 19X7 and 19X8.

Financing activities (capital) – the new issue at a premium.

Investing activities – the new equipment purchased.

It is important to recognize the interrelationships between the three statements, and to be able to assess the impact of changes in certain variables on all three statements.

Activity 2

Show the effect of the following alternative assumptions on the three financial statements:

	Profit and loss	**Balance sheet**	**Cash flow**
(a) Dividends of £10,000 being proposed			
(b) The period of credit allowed to customers being reduced to 1½ months			
(c) The period of credit taken from suppliers being reduced to 1 month			

(d) The period of credit allowed
to customers being
increased to 3 months
(e) Depreciation being taken at
20% per annum on cost
(f) Closing stock being
valued at £35,000
(g) An increase in sales
of £20,000
(h) An increase in general
expenses of £5,000

The solutions are:

		Profit and loss	**Balance sheet**	**Cash flow**
(a)	Dividends of £10,000 being proposed	appropriation of £10,000	increase liability dividends proposed	none
(b)	The period of credit allowed to customers being reduced to 1½ months	none	reduction in debtors to £30,000	reduction in debtors £2,500 – effective source
(c)	The period of credit taken from suppliers being reduced to 1 month	none	reduction in creditors to £15,500	reduction in creditors £4,300 – effective outflow
(d)	The period of credit allowed to customers being increased to three months	none	increase in debtors to £60,000	increase in debtors £27,500 – effective outflow
(e)	Depreciation being taken at 20% per annum on cost	reduce by further £2,700	reduce net assets by £2,700	adjustment to profit increased by £2,700
(f)	Closing stock being valued at £35,000	increase profit by £6,000	increase stock £12,000	increase in stock £12,000 – effective outflow
(g)	An increase in sales of £20,000	increase	increase in associated debtors/cash/ reserves	increase in profit

(h) An increase in   reduce   reduce reserves   reduce profit
     general expenses
     of £5,000

9.4 Likely information needed for forecast statements

It is clear from the example given in the previous section that a substantial number of assumptions, estimates and decisions need to be made about the future direction of the business before a set of financial forecasts can be completed. In the example given above, decisions were made about the acquisition of new plant, the new share issue, and not to pay dividends. Explicit decisions may have been made about such things as the desired level of stock, debtors and creditors. On the other hand, the level of these items may have been viewed more as an assumption, based upon previous trends. This still reflects an *implicit* planning decision. Given the importance of sound working capital management, it is suggested that these variables should reflect positive thinking, rather than be taken as something over which the business has little control. Some kind of estimates were made of expected revenues and associated costs. In practice, such estimates are likely to be rather more difficult than may have been implied by the above example.

Clearly the example given above was very simple, and in reality many more assumptions, estimates and decisions need to be made before a set of financial plans can be drawn up. The purpose of this section is to identify the kind of factors which are likely to arise in most businesses, so as to provide a more detailed framework in which to operate.

Estimates/assumptions/decisions relating to the profit and loss account

Sales

Sales estimates will need to be made to cover the range of products or services supplied by the business. It will probably be useful to separate existing products from new products, since a range of historic (and therefore objective) information is likely to exist for the former, which may well provide a sound base for estimates of future sales. Estimates of sales of new products are more likely to be supported by such things as market research studies. In both cases it will usually be necessary to estimate both sales quantity and sales price, and to establish likely *changes in sales volume* (i.e. changes due to the sale of a different number of products) and *changes in selling price* for future periods. Important factors relating to changes in sales revenue include: the state of the economy; changes in demand due to fashion and other factors; levels of inflation; product quality; after-sales service; and advertising. Some of these are capable of being influenced by an individual business: others are not.

Cost of sales and associated expenses

It is important in making estimates of expenses to distinguish between fixed and variable elements of cost. *Variable costs*, which frequently include things such as materials, wages and certain kinds of other expenses, are costs which vary in proportion to the level of output. As sales double, so variable costs double. *Fixed costs*, on the other hand, are costs which remain constant, or fixed, irrespective of the level of production. Of course, in practice many costs do not fall precisely into either category, and it may be necessary to make estimates of likely variations in costs over a range of output, using some kind of statistical cost analysis. In making estimates of future expenses, the split between variable and fixed elements is important since changes may be attributable to changes in the volume of output, and to changes in individual costs. Changes in the former should relate to sales (or changes in productivity), while changes in the latter may be unaffected by changes in volume, but be caused by factors outside of the control of an individual business. (The converse may, of course, be true.)

Activity 3

A business has sales of existing products as follows:

Product	Price per unit	Quantity	Sales revenue
A	£10	1,000	£10,000
B	£20	2,000	£40,000

Associated costs are as follows:

Product	Variable cost per unit	Fixed costs	Total costs
A	£5	£3,000	£8,000
B	£12	£6,000	£30,000

In the following year sales volume is expected to increase by 20% for product A, and 10% for product B. Selling price per unit will be held steady for product A, but will increase by 5% for product B. Costs are expected to increase by the expected rate of inflation for the next year, which is 7%.

Show the expected sales revenues and associated costs for products A and B for the next year.

The figures are as follows:

Product A

Sales	Quantity	Price/cost	Total
A	1,200 (1,000 + 20%)	£10	£12,000
B	2,200 (2,000 + 10%)	£21 (£20 + 5%)	£46,200

Variable costs

A	1,200	£5.35 (£5 + 7%)	£6,420
B	2,200	£12.84 (£12 + 7%)	£28,248

Fixed costs

A		£3,210 (£3,000 + 7%)	£3,210
B		£6,420 (£6,000 + 7%)	£6,420

Activity 4

How realistic is the assumption in the previous activity that costs are expected to increase by the expected rate of inflation for the year?

The rate of inflation reflects a kind of average, and individual types of costs may well behave in a variety of ways. In practice, estimates will need to be made of changes for each major type. Some costs may be fixed in money terms, and will not rise at all.

In making forecasts of fixed costs for the future, it may also be necessary to distinguish clearly between those costs which involve a cash outflow, and those which do not (e.g. depreciation). Costs not involving a cash outflow will clearly not be subject to cost inflation as such. It will also be necessary to identify separately any costs which are specified in money terms, since these are also not subject to cost inflation. New ventures may well lead to increases in fixed costs over and above any incurred in previous years.

Activity 5

A business has total fixed costs in a particular year of £500,000, comprising £200,000 depreciation (based upon straight-line depreciation of fixed assets costing £1 million), £100,000 interest (based upon a fixed-interest-rate loan of £1 million), and cash costs (e.g. labour, materials, power costs etc.) of £200,000.

Estimate the total for fixed costs in the next year if cost inflation is expected to be 10%.

The fixed costs of £500,000 may be broken down as follows:

	£
Depreciation	200,000
Interest	100,000
Cash costs	200,000

If the total of fixed assets remains the same (£1m), as does the method of depreciation, there is no reason to suppose that the depreciation charge in the next year will change. Similarly, interest is not subject to an inflationary adjustment. Only the cash costs will be subject to the 10% inflation. Expected fixed costs for the next year are thus:

	£
Depreciation	200,000
Interest	100,000
Cash costs	220,000
Total fixed costs	£520,000

Depreciation and related costs

In order to make estimates of depreciation in future periods it is necessary to establish expected fixed asset movements, and to make the necessary calculations from these. Projected depreciation figures should be based upon current fixed assets plus any projected new purchases of fixed assets, less any projected disposals of fixed assets. Since accounting policies with regard to depreciation are likely to be well-established, it should be possible to ascertain the implications of all expected transactions related to fixed assets by reference to a table along the lines shown below.

	Cost	Depreciation provision	Net
	£	£	£
Balance at the beginning of the year	x	x	x
Less disposals	(x)	(x)	(x)
Plus new assets acquired	x	—	x
Depreciation	—	x	x
Balance at the end of the year	x	x	x

In fact this approach will enable all fixed asset movements to be calculated, and relevant figures can then be put into each financial statement. The balances at the year end reflect the figures needed for the balance sheet. The depreciation figure will form part of the profit and loss account. When the proceeds from the sale of fixed assets are compared with the net book value of disposals, any profit or loss on disposal can be calculated and be put into the profit and loss account. The sale proceeds will be reflected in the cash flow statement as a source, while the depreciation and profit/loss on disposal will be shown as adjustments to profit. The new assets acquired will show as an outflow in the investing activities section of the cash flow statement.

Activity 6

A business has equipment shown in its accounts at £500,000 cost, and £200,000 depreciation provision. It uses straight-line depreciation, based on 20% of cost per annum, with depreciation being calculated on all assets held at a year end. In the next year it expects to spend £200,000 and in the following year £100,000 on new equipment. Using the tables below show the expected movements in fixed assets, and the relevant figures in the three major financial statements.

Balance sheet
Year 1

Equipment	*Cost*	*Depreciation provision*	*Net*
	£	£	£
Balance at the beginning of the year			
Plus new assets acquired			
Depreciation	———	———	———
Balance at the end of the year	═══	═══	═══

Year 2

Balance at the beginning of the year			
Plus new assets acquired			
Depreciation	———	———	———
Balance at the end of the year	═══	═══	═══

Profit and loss account entries	**Year 1**	**Year 2**
	£	£
Depreciation		

Cash flow statement entries	**Year 1**	**Year 2**
	£	£
Operating flows		
Adjustment for depreciation		
Investing activities		
New equipment		

The solution is as follows:

Balance sheet
Year 1

Equipment	*Cost*	*Depreciation provision*	*Net*
	£	£	£
Balance at the beginning of the year	500,000	200,000	300,000
Plus new assets acquired	200,000		200,000
Depreciation	———	140,000	(140,000)
Balance at the end of the year	700,000	340,000	360,000

Equipment	Cost	Depreciation provision	Net
	£	£	£
Year 2			
Balance at the beginning of the year	700,000	340,000	360,000
Plus new assets acquired	100,000		100,000
Depreciation		160,000	(160,000)
Balance at the end of the year	800,000	500,000	300,000

Profit and loss account entries	Year 1	Year 2
	£	£
Depreciation	140,000	160,000

Cash flow statement entries	Year 1	Year 2
	£	£
Operating activities		
adjustment for depreciation	140,000	160,000
Investing activities		
New equipment	200,000	100,000

Appropriations of profit

In making forecasts it will be necessary to make assumptions about tax rates, decisions about taxation planning (i.e. planned decisions which help reduce the tax burden), and decisions about dividends and transfers to reserves. Decisions with regard to preference share dividends are likely to be straightforward, since companies rarely pay less than the maximum amount. Decisions about ordinary dividends in large public companies also appear to follow fairly well-defined patterns, with dividends seldom being reduced, even in periods of quite poor trading results. Patterns in smaller companies are more variable.

Estimates/assumptions/decisions relating to the balance sheet

Fixed assets

As has been made clear, decisions need to be made about the future acquisition and disposal of fixed asset, and associated depreciation policies. Some consideration will need to be given to methods of financing new fixed assets, a point which will be returned to later.

Working capital

It is not the purpose of this chapter to explore working capital management in detail. Nevertheless, it should be clear from the earlier example that decisions should be made about the level of stock, debtors and creditors. The potential for problems in this area is enormous, and the analysis of working capital and liquidity will form an important part of the next chapter. Slack working capital management may result in large amounts of funds being tied up unnecessarily, with no increase in profits resulting. The link between the balance sheet and the cash flow statement should be clear.

Loans

It would be foolish to embark on a set of plans without some ideas on how plans are to be financed. Some decisions or assumptions in this area are required.

Capital

New capital issues occur infrequently. Where they do occur, detailed planning is appropriate. Retained earnings represent an important source of funds, and assumptions/decisions about levels of retentions are an important part of the planning process.

Estimates/assumptions/decisions about the cash flow statement

In fact, the items identified to date will frequently impact on any projections with regard to cash flow. These are:

(a) profit
(b) adjustments for depreciation
(c) fixed asset acquisitions
(d) levels of working capital
(e) loans raised and repaid
(f) taxation and dividends
(g) capital raised or redeemed

Self-assessment question 9.1
The management of G O Ahead and Co. Ltd are planning a vigorous expansion policy for the forthcoming year (19X9), and have asked you to look at the financial implications of their plans to date. The following assumptions and estimates have been made in order to provide a basis for the planning.

Market position

(a) The total estimated market for 19X8 was £60 million.
(b) Sales during 19X8 were £3 million, a market share of 5%. However, the company expects to be able to achieve an increased market share in 19X9, due to more aggressive marketing, with a 20% increase in sales volume being anticipated. It is expected that selling price will have to be held at current levels in 19X9 since product demand tends to be elastic.

The economic environment

(a) The rate of inflation is expected to be 5% per annum during 19X9. This may be assumed to be an appropriate rate to inflate the costs of the company.
(b) The rate of corporation tax is assumed to be 25% during 19X9.

Dividend policy

(a) The dividend to be recommended in 19X8 is 10% (of the nominal value of the share capital).
(b) It is planned that dividends should grow to 12% per annum in 19X9 to cover inflation and to share in the hoped-for increased prosperity of the company. This will not be paid until 19X0.

Financial structure of the company

(a) Share capital consists of 1 million shares of £1 each, fully paid.
(b) Reserves at the end of 19X8 stood at £390,000.
(c) Working capital has been controlled at levels considered to be optimal, and at the end of 19X8 its proportions was as follows:

Stock   12% of sales for the year
Debtors   20% of sales for the year
Creditors   10% of sales for the year

Other current liabilities at the end of 19X8 were:

- a provision for taxation on the profits for 19X8 amounting to £120,000.
- the estimated dividend for the year (no dividend was actually paid during the year).

(d) It is intended to maintain the same policy on stock, debtors and creditors through 19X9 as exists at 31 December 19X8.

(e) Variable costs 19X8 were 50% of sales revenue.

(f) Fixed costs, including depreciation of £100,000 computed at 10% on a straight-line basis, were £1 million in 19X8. It is expected that a further £150,000 will have to be spent on advertising in 19X9 in order to capture the increased share of the market, in addition to increased costs due to inflation.

Capital expenditure/fixed assets

(a) The company currently has fixed assets which cost £1 million; an associated depreciation provision stands at £200,000 at the end of 19X8. Depreciation is 10% straight-line.

(b) To sustain the expansion programme, the company plans to spend £350,000 on new fixed assets which will be purchased and set in use at the beginning of 19X9. Depreciation will be on the same basis as existing assets.

Required

(a) Make the necessary computations to reflect these plans.

(b) Comment on the feasibility of the plans, particularly in the light of the desire of the management that cash at the end of 19X9 should equal 5% of sales for that year. Suggest any courses of action that management might take.

9.5 Using forecasts to help in decision-making

Self-assessment question 9.1 was concerned with setting out the financial implications of a set of specific plans and assumptions. In reality planning and decision-making is usually an iterative (trial and error) process, where modifications are constantly made to the plans until they reflect an acceptable outcome. Management would hope that such plans will be at or near an optimum, but frequently the process will cease once an acceptable outcome has been achieved. In self-assessment question 9.1 it would seem reasonable to suppose that the management would react to the forecasts prepared in one of several ways:

(a) it would accept that its assumptions and decisions would lead to the fall in liquidity forecast, and implement the plans;

(b) it would find alternative ways of financing the plans, to ensure that the projected decrease in liquidity could be overcome;

(c) it would re-examine its plans to see if any changes could be made which would improve performance, probably with particular emphasis on liquidity.

Financial planning of the type described above is particularly amenable to any of these approaches. It undoubtedly identifies the financial implications of a set of plans. Hence, using self-assessment question 9.1 as an illustration, *if actual events coincide with forecasts*, a measure of the cash shortage can be obtained, and the necessary arrangements made in good time. Without a forecast of funds flow the potential liquidity problem may not have been anticipated, since expected profits will enable the desired level of dividends to be paid.

However, where planning of the above type is most useful is with regard to modifications in plans. For example, suppose that the reaction of management to the figures shown in the solution to self-assessment question 9.1 was to consider various ways of financing the new capital expenditure, so as to eliminate the liquidity problem. Such modifications can be made relatively easily, since the interrelationships are fairly clear.

Activity 7

Indicate the likely impact on both profitability and liquidity of G O Ahead and Co. Ltd of the following alternative approaches to the new capital expenditure:

(a) The capital expenditure to be 60% financed from a bank loan carrying an interest rate of 15% per annum. The loan is to be repaid in equal annual instalments over the next 4 years, commencing on 31 December 19X9.

(b) The new fixed assets to be leased on a 6-year basis, at an annual charge of £90,000.

The solution is:

(a) 60% financing – £210,000, carrying an interest rate of 15%, would result in a decrease in profits before tax of £31,500. It would affect liquidity by reducing the source from profits by £31,500, but increase the inflow under financing activities – 'loans raised' – by £210,000, giving an overall increase in liquid funds of £178,500.

(b) Leasing at an annual charge of £90,000 would reduce profits by £55,000 (£90,000 less the depreciation which would have been charged on the new assets – £35,000). The impact on liquid funds would be to reduce the inflow from profits by £90,000, and to eliminate the application for fixed assets of £350,000.

Either approach would solve the liquidity problem. Both reduce profits. The final decision reflects a balancing of concerns with profitability and liquidity.

It is suggested that the three forecast financial statements should be seen as an integrated financial model of the business, where the variables (i.e. the assumptions/decisions/estimates) can be changed to assess the implications of changes in the different variables on the expected future financial statements.

Sensitivity analysis is a particularly useful technique in this context. Sensitivity analysis essentially takes one variable and examines the effect of changes in that variable on the overall performance. It is thus particularly useful in identifying those variables which are most critical to the success or failure of the plans. Sensitivity analysis does not make any assumptions about the probability of occurrence of change in any one variable, but merely identifies the impact of such a change. Management must make its own interpretation of the probability of occurrence in reaching a decision.

Where a number of variables are to be changed at once, *scenario analysis* may be a useful technique to use. Essentially, scenario analysis is the analysis of likely results under a range of different assumptions about future events. Again, little is said about the likelihood of occurrence of the various scenarios, but the implications of different scenarios are at least worked out, and hopefully recognized.

Activity 8

Some businesses work out financial plans on a *doomsday* scenario.

  What do you think this means?

  What possible lessons do you think might be gleaned from such an approach, even if its probability of occurrence is very low?

A doomsday scenario is one in which everything which can go wrong does go wrong. It is particularly useful in identifying all possible problem areas, so that their impact on results may be ascertained, and appropriate alternative approaches examined.

9.6   The use of spreadsheets in financial planning

An electronic spreadsheet is a computer package which is, in essence, nothing more than a grid on which various text, figures, equations and relationships can be inserted, under a specific set of assumptions.

As we have seen, the three basic accounting statements are a financial model of a business. Figures in one of the statements are linked to at least one other figure in the same statement, or in one of the other statements. Frequently this link is a particular policy of the management. For example, the debtors figure in the balance sheet is linked directly to the sales figure, in the profit and loss account, by the policy of the business on how long to allow debtors to pay their debts. The debtors figure is also linked to the cash flow statement by the same policy; the shorter the time allowed to debtors, the more cash will be in the bank.

A spreadsheet is ideal for developing forecast accounting statements, mainly because it will, if correctly specified, be able instantly to carry through all of the effects of changing some variable. So, for example, if management wishes to see the effect on cash of shortening the debtors' collection period by, say, a week, this variable can be altered and the effect instantaneously reflected in all three statements.

Interrelationships between the various boxes on the grid need to be clearly established, with equations being used for all variables, i.e. those factors which could change. Absolute figures should only be inserted in the spreadsheet model for factors which are constants, i.e. there is little or no chance of them changing.

Provided that relationships have been properly defined and established on the spreadsheet, when changes in the variables are to be analysed, to assess the robustness of the plans, only these variables will need to be changed. Plans may thus be modified very easily, simply by changing a small number of variables, with the result that a far better 'feel' can be obtained of the implications of changes in any of the constituent parts of the plan than could otherwise be obtained.

The following *example* might be helpful in developing an understanding of the use of spreadsheets.

Example

Mike, a friend of yours, is considering buying a small workshop in which to carry out a variety of work to do with the manufacture and repair of agricultural equipment. He knows that you are doing an accounting course as part of your studies, and asks you to help him develop some 'proper' figures to help him in his negotiations with his bank manager. In discussions with him you identify the following facts.

(a) The workshop will cost £25,000, including related legal fees, and equipment is expected to cost a further £5,000. The equipment is expected to last for 10 years.
(b) The initial stocks of materials needed for manufacture and repair of equipment are likely to cost approximately £2,000. It is expected that a regular holding of this amount would avoid any problems with regard to delivery times. Material costs are expected to amount to approximately 25% of total revenue for the year.
(c) Mike has £5,000 of his own money to put into the business. He is currently thinking of asking his bank manager if he can borrow a further £30,000 from the bank. If he is successful interest will be at 15% per annum, and the debt will be repaid over 10 years in equal annual instalments. Mike will also bring his van, valued at £2,000, into the business. The van is expected to last another 5 years.
(d) On average revenue will be received 1 month after the work has been carried out. This revenue will be the result of work carried out by Mike

and his assistant John, and is based upon an assumed 40-hour week, 48-week year, and an hourly charge rate of £10, for both of them.

(e) Mike expects to make cash drawings based upon an hourly rate of £5. John will be paid £3.50 an hour. Both will be paid for 52 weeks, to include 4 weeks' holiday pay.

(f) Other annual expenses are estimated as follows:

- rates   £1,000
- heat and light   £600
- telephone   £1,000
- vehicle expenses   £1,500
- insurance   £600
- other materials   £500

(g) Mike intends to operate the business as a sole trader, *not* as a limited company.

This example, which is based upon an actual business, encapsulates the essence of most planning and decision-making. The problem may be broken down into the following components and related questions.

1   What assumptions can be made about the business, in terms of assets needed, likely levels of activity, and associated revenues and expenses?
2   Will a satisfactory profit be made, and what are likely profit levels in future years?
3   If the business plans are viable in terms of profitability, what are the working capital/liquidity needs of the business, how should the business be financed, and are there any potential liquidity problems which might arise in the future?
4   What might go wrong? How soundly based is the business? Can the business survive unfavourable events?

In this case, Mike has already made most of the critical assumptions. He has a very good idea of what the workshop will cost. (Indeed, cost of fixed assets is likely to be known fairly accurately, since it is probably based on actual prices and an estimate of inflation.) He has made assumptions, albeit implicitly in some cases, about working capital levels, revenue, expenses and work load. He has implicitly assumed that there will be enough work to keep himself and John working full-time (i.e. 40 hours per week for 48 weeks per year). This may be a questionable assumption, and it is one that will be reviewed later, but it is Mike's starting point. Given these assumptions, it should be possible to make an initial assessment of the likely financial performance of the business in its first year of operation.

In approaching a problem using a spreadsheet it is important to do a number of things:

1   Clarify all assumptions, and identify those factors which are to be treated as variables. In this example the variables chosen are: number of weeks'

work for both Mike and John; the number of hours' work per week; the charge rate per hour; the rate of pay per hour; and the interest rate. Clearly other factors (e.g. the period of credit, the relationship between sales and variable costs, the period of repayment of the loan, the impact of inflation on revenues and expenses) could, in real life, also change. To try to keep matters simple, we shall treat these factors as constants, i.e. we shall assume that there will not be any changes in these. The distinction between variables and constants is important in building the spreadsheet model. This is because we need to build into the model the facility to alter variables and for the full effect of those alterations to be reflected in all three statements. For constants, we need not go to the trouble of stating formulae, we can just insert the figure in £s.

2   Set out the spreadsheet so that figures can be calculated using some kind of formula relating to the variables which are to be examined in detail. This is likely to be more time-consuming than preparing a single forecast manually, but tremendous advantages accrue in terms of the potential for using sensitivity and scenario analysis.

3   Change the variables to identify the impact of such changes on the financial statements.

4   Using the results of the sensitivity analysis, identify the critical variables in terms of success or failure, assess the likelihood of their occurrence, establish whether they are within the control or influence of the company, and examine possible alterations in the plans which may improve the performance or position.

Given in Table 9.1 is a spreadsheet for Mike, setting out the forecast results for the first 3 years of business, under his initial assumptions. The assumptions are clearly identified in rows 1–10. Some of the figures in the financial statements have been inserted as actual figures, because they are constants. The variables have been put in using formulae. For example, the figure for revenue generated by John (C42) of £19,200 is calculated by multiplying the number of weeks worked by the number of hours per week worked, by the charge rate per hour. In effect, the instruction given to fill the box C4 is: insert in this box the result of multiplying the figure in C2 by the figure in C3, by the figure in C4. Any changes in any of the figures in rows 2–4, column C will thus *automatically* be reflected in changes in the figures in the profit and loss account. A similar approach is used to cover rows 43 (revenue generated by Mike), 48 (cost of sales; a function of sales), 49 (John's wages; a function of his hours worked) and 63 (Mike's wages; a function of his hours worked). All totals are based on formulae. Other links which are built in relate to the net profit and depreciation in the cash flow statement, both of which are picked up as formulae from the profit and loss account. Changes in working capital in the funds statement are also automatically calculated from the balance sheets, with closing figures for debtors reflecting sales for the year. The end result is, therefore, an integrated model which will respond correctly to changes in the underlying assumptions/variables.

Table 9.1

	A	B	C	D	E
1	**Assumptions**		**Year 1**	**Year 2**	**Year 3**
2	John – weeks		48	48	48
3	John – hours per week		40	40	40
4	John – charge rate per hour		10	10	10
5	Mike – weeks		48	48	48
6	Mike – hours per week		40	40	40
7	Mike – charge rate per hour		10	10	10
8	John – rate of pay per hour		3.5	3.5	3.5
9	Mike – rate of pay per hour		5	5	5
10	Interest rate		0.15	0.15	0.15
11					
12					
13	**Balance sheet**	**Start**	**End year 1**	**End year 2**	**End year 3**
14					
15	*Fixed assets*				
16	Buildings	25,000	25,000	25,000	25,000
17	Equipment	5,000	4,500	4,000	3,500
18	Van	2,000	1,600	1,200	800
19					
20	*Current assets*				
21	Stock	2,000	2,000	2,000	2,000
22	Debtors	0	3,200	3,200	3,200
23	Cash	3,000	–1,780	–2,910	–3,590
24					
25	Total assets	37,000	34,520	32,490	30,910
26					
27					
28	*Capital*	7,000	7,000	7,520	8,490
29	Net profit	0	10,920	11,370	11,820
30	Drawings	0	–10,400	–10,400	–10,400
31					
32	*Debt outstanding*	30,000	27,000	24,000	21,000
33					
34	*Current liabilities*				
35	Creditors	0	0	0	0
36					
37	Total liabilities	37,000	34,520	32,490	30,910
38					
39					

Table 9.1 *continued*

	A	B	C	D	E
40	**Profit and loss account**		**Year 1**	**Year 2**	**Year 3**
41	*Revenues*				
42	John		19,200	19,200	19,200
43	Mike		19,200	19,200	19,200
44					
45	Total revenues		38,400	38,400	38,400
46					
47	*Expenses*				
48	Cost of sales		9,600	9,600	9,600
49	John – wages		7,280	7,280	7,280
50	Rates		1,000	1,000	1,000
51	Heat and light		600	600	600
52	Telephone		1,000	1,000	1,000
53	Vehicle expenses		1,500	1,500	1,500
54	Insurance		600	600	600
55	Other materials		500	500	500
56	Depreciation – equipment		500	500	500
57	Depreciation – truck		400	400	400
58	Interest		4,500	4,050	3,600
59					
60	Total expenses		27,480	27,030	26,580
61					
62	*Net profit*		10,920	11,370	11,820
63	*Drawings*		10,400	10,400	10,400
64					
65					
66	**Cash flow statement**				
67					
68	*Operating activities*				
69	Net profit		10,920	11,370	11,820
70	Adjusted for depreciation		900	900	900
71	Changes in stock		0	0	0
72	Changes in debtors		–3,200	0	0
73	Changes in creditors		0	0	0
74					
75	*Investing activities*				
76	Sale of fixed assets		0	0	0
77	New assets		0	0	0
78					
79	*Financing activities*				
80	Loans repaid		–3,000	–3,000	–3,000
81	Drawings		–10,400	–10,400	–10,400

	A	B	C	D	E
82	Loans raised		0	0	0
83	New capital		0	0	0
84					
85	Net increase/decrease in cash		–4,780	–1,130	–680
86	Opening balance		3,000	–1,780	–2,910
87	*Closing balance*		–1,780	–2,910	–3,590

The plans reveal that, on the assumptions set out, Mike can make sufficient profits to pay himself the intended wage (drawings). However, the plans do also reveal a problem of cash flow, with an overdraft being likely at the end of the year. This suggests that further thought needs to be given to the amount of loan, and the period over which it is to be repaid. Further thought should also be given to the validity of the assumptions made, and the impact of changes therein.

It is clear from the solution that if the plans succeed, and the assumptions are correct, enough profit (£10,920) will be generated to enable Mike to cover his drawings (£10,400) for his own wages. However, the forecast cash flow statement shows a decrease in cash of £4,780 over the first year, with the result that the business would have an overdraft at the year end. Such a position might be somewhat disconcerting for both Mike and his bank manager. Given the assumptions about the work rates of both Mike and John, it would seem appropriate to have a rather larger cushion of cash. It might be possible to arrange further funding from the bank (probably with extra security being needed, e.g. a second mortgage on Mike's house) to cover working capital needs, or to arrange a different repayment profile for the loan, which would require lower repayments of principal (as compared with interest) in the early years of the business.

In practice, it is likely that both Mike and his bank manager are likely to want to probe further with regard to the business. The bank manager is, after all, being asked to provide in excess of £30,000 funding. He will presumably want to know what the chances of repayment are, without having to resort to such drastic actions as foreclosing on a mortgage. The bank manager is, thus, likely to want to see forecasts for more than 1 year. Mike is likely to want to do the same, to ascertain how his wealth may be affected through trading at a profit or a loss. Both Mike and the bank manager are likely to ask what happens if the work rate is not as assumed, either because demand is lower than expected, or because of such things as illness. The impact of such changes on profit levels and liquidity need to be ascertained, as does the potential impact of changes in the interest rate on the loan.

On the basis of the results shown in Table 9.1, the business appears to be capable of achieving results which are acceptable to Mike, subject to the earlier (significant) reservations on funding, and the possibility of taking out a slightly larger loan, provided that the assumptions made are correct. In order to assess the impact of unfavourable events, it is necessary to change the assumptions/variables

on which the figures are based. By way of illustration, assume that the charge rate
per hour proves to be unrealistic, and that only £8 per hour can be achieved. For
a new business, this is not an unrealistic assumption. If the new charge rate is now
put into column C of rows 4 and 7 new results can be obtained immediately. These
are shown in Table 9.2. The result is that the profit (£5,160) is insufficient to pay
Mike's wages, and that the cash flow pattern is disastrous. If a low charge rate is
reasonably likely the business looks to be a shaky venture.

Table 9.2

	A	B	C	D	E
1	**Assumptions**		**Year 1**	**Year 2**	**Year 3**
2	John – weeks		48	48	48
3	John – hours per week		40	40	40
4	John – charge rate per hour		8	8	8
5	Mike – weeks		48	48	48
6	Mike – hours per week		40	40	40
7	Mike – charge rate per hour		8	8	8
8	John – rate of pay per hour		3.5	3.5	3.5
9	Mike – rate of pay per hour		5	5	5
10	Interest rate		0.15	0.15	0.15
11					
12					
13	**Balance sheet**	**Start**	**End year 1**	**End year 2**	**End year 3**
14					
15	*Fixed assets*				
16	Buildings	25,000	25,000	25,000	25,000
17	Equipment	5,000	4,500	4,000	3,500
18	Van	2,000	1,600	1,200	800
19					
20	*Current assets*				
21	Stock	2,000	2,000	2,000	2,000
22	Debtors	0	2,560	2,560	2,560
23	Cash	3,000	–6,900	–13,790	–20,230
24					
25	Total assets	37,000	28,760	20,970	13,630
26					
27					
28	*Capital*	7,000	7,000	1,760	–3,030
29	Net profit	0	5,160	5,610	6,060
30	Drawings	0	–10,400	–10,400	–10,400
31					
32	*Debt outstanding*	30,000	27,000	24,000	21,000
33					

	A	B	C	D	E
34	*Current liabilities*				
35	Creditors	0	0	0	0
36					
37	Total liabilities	37,000	28,760	20,970	13,630
38					
39					
40	**Profit and loss account**		Year 1	Year 2	Year 3
41	*Revenues*				
42	John		15,360	15,360	15,360
43	Mike		15,360	15,360	15,360
44					
45	Total revenues		30,720	30,720	30,720
46					
47	*Expenses*				
48	Cost of sales		7,680	7,680	7,680
49	John – wages		7,280	7,280	7,280
50	Rates		1,000	1,000	1,000
51	Heat and light		600	600	600
52	Telephone		1,000	1,000	1,000
53	Vehicles expenses		1,500	1,500	1,500
54	Insurance		600	600	600
55	Other materials		500	500	500
56	Depreciation – equipment		500	500	500
57	Depreciation – truck		400	400	400
58	Interest		4,500	4,050	3,600
59					
60	Total expenses		25,560	25,110	24,660
61					
62	*Net profit*		5,160	5,610	6,060
63	*Drawings*		10,400	10,400	10,400
64					
65					
66	**Cash flow statement**				
67					
68	*Operating activities*				
69	Net profit		5,160	5,610	6,060
70	Adjusted for depreciation		900	900	900
71	Changes in stock		0	0	0
72	Changes in debtors		–2,560	0	0
73	Changes in creditors		0	0	0
74					
75	*Investing activities*				
76	Sale of fixed assets		0	0	0

Table 9.2 *continued*

	A	B	C	D	E
77	New assets		0	0	0
78					
79	*Financing activities*				
80	Loans repaid		−3,000	−3,000	−3,000
81	Drawings		−10,400	−10,400	−10,400
82	Loans raised		0	0	0
83	New capital		0	0	0
84					
85	Net increase/decrease in cash		−9,900	−6,890	−6,440
86	Opening balance		3,000	−6,900	−13,790
87	*Closing balance*		−6,900	−13,790	−20,230

Suppose now that Mike, knowing that John has been somewhat unwell recently, also wishes to know what would happen if John were ill for a reasonable time. A change in the expected number of weeks worked could be inserted into the assumptions section of the spreadsheet, and the impact examined.

Clearly the spreadsheet offers opportunities for the analysis of the sensitivity of a range of variables, with changes being made in individual variables or a collection of variables. Care is needed, however, in setting up a spreadsheet in such a way that all important variables can be changed easily and conveniently.

9.7 Other uses of spreadsheets/relationship with other methods of appraisal

The kind of approach to spreadsheets which has been used above may be used in a variety of other areas of appraisal and analysis. Later chapters cover the analysis and interpretation of accounts, with a variety of ratios being calculated and relationships examined. Spreadsheets can be used fairly easily to identify such relationships. There is no reason, for example, why the spreadsheet for Mike should not include the automatic calculation of various ratios relating to the forecasts. Considerable opportunities exist elsewhere.

It is important to recognize that the kind of planning and forecasting dealt with in this chapter typically represent only part of the overall process. Plans of this type are particularly effective in assessing future performance for a company as a whole. They will not provide an effective analysis for an individual project. Individual project appraisal, using techniques such as discounted cash flow, are likely to be dealt with in other parts of your studies. However, there is no reason why individual project appraisal and the kind of analysis carried out in this chapter should not both be carried out, and inter-related.

It is also important to note that the emphasis of the above plans is on a year by year basis. However, cyclical and seasonal variations may mean that more planning needs to be carried out on a shorter-term basis, say weekly or monthly. Exactly the same methodology could be used to deal with shorter periods. In practice, however, it is common to find that cash forecasting or cash budgeting on a short-term basis takes a slightly different form, identifying cash receipts and cash payments in rather more detail. Hence, instead of showing operating sources as net profit adjusted for depreciation, it is more common to identify cash received from sales, from debtors, from other revenues, and cash paid to creditors, paid for other expenses, etc. Such an approach should enable a much clearer picture to emerge of short-term cash fluctuations. Cash budgets are also likely to be dealt with in other parts of your studies.

9.8   Summary

This chapter has attempted to illustrate that the basic financial accounting statements can be used for planning and decision-making purposes. This is particularly important for business people, since the perspective on accounting is changed from one which is broadly historic to one which is rather more decision-oriented. The financial accounting framework can be used very effectively as the basis of a financial model of the business, and is thus at the heart of most systems of corporate planning or corporate strategy development. An understanding of the interrelationship of the main financial statements is necessary if full benefit is to be obtained from such a system. When coupled with the use of a computerized spreadsheet or other modelling package, the advantages of this approach become even more apparent, because of the facility to use techniques such as sensitivity analysis and scenario analysis.

Exercises

1   The balance sheet of Corplans Plc as at 31 December 19X6 is as follows:

	Cost	**Depreciation**	**Net**
	£	£	£
Fixed assets			
Land and buildings			540,000
Plant and machinery	500,000	100,000	400,000
Vehicles	<u>100,000</u>	<u>40,000</u>	<u>60,000</u>
			1,000,000

	£	£
Current assets		
Stock	100,000	
Debtors	150,000	
Cash	105,000	
	355,000	
Creditors: amounts falling due within 1 year		
Trade creditors	(120,000)	
Net current assets		235,000
Total assets less current liabilities		1,235,000
Creditors: amounts falling due after more than 1 year		
Loan capital: 10% debentures		200,000
		1,035,000
Capital and reserves		
Ordinary share capital		800,000
Revenue reserves		235,000
		1,035,000

The directors are now considering their plans for the next financial year, and have asked you to assist in converting their ideas and assumptions into a financial forecast. In discussions with them you ascertain the following:

(i)   During 19X6, sales totalled £1,200,000 (200,000 units at £6 each), variable costs per unit were £3.50, and total fixed costs (including depreciation and interest) were £350,000. Depreciation was on the basis of 20% per annum on cost for both plant and machinery and vehicles. No depreciation was taken on land and buildings.

(ii) In 19X7 the directors expect the volume of sales to increase by 20%. Selling price will probably need to fall to £5.70 per unit. Variable costs per unit are expected to increase by 5%, while fixed costs are expected to be subject to a 10% inflationary increase.

(iii) Working capital is expected to be maintained at similar levels to those existing at 31 December 19X6, namely:
- stocks will be 1/7 of variable costs;
- debtors will be given 1½ months' credit, on average;
- creditors will be 1/10 of sales.

Required

(a)   Prepare forecast profit and loss account for the year ending 31 December 19X7.

(b)   Prepare forecast balance sheet as at 31 December 19X7.

(c)   Prepare forecast cash flow statement for the year ending 31 December 19X7.

2   The balance sheet of AFC Plans Plc as at 31 May 19X9 is as follows:

	Cost	Depreciation	Net
	£	£	£
Fixed assets			
Land and buildings			1,000,000
Plant and machinery	800,000	400,000	400,000
Vehicles	200,000	60,000	140,000
			1,540,000
Current assets			
Stock		400,000	
Debtors		800,000	
Cash		400,000	
		1,600,000	
Creditors: amounts falling due within 1 year			
Trade creditors		(800,000)	
Net current assets			800,000
Total assets less current liabilities			2,340,000
Creditors: amounts falling due after more than 1 year			
Loan capital: 10% debentures			200,000
			2,140,000
Capital and reserves			
Ordinary share capital (£1 shares – fully paid)			1,000,000
Revenue reserves			1,140,000
			2,140,000

The directors are now considering their plans for the next financial year, and have asked you to assist in converting their ideas and assumptions into a financial forecast. In discussions with them you ascertain the following:

(a) The profit for the year ended 31 May 19X9 was £800,000, made up as follows:

	£
Sales revenue (800,000 at £10)	8,000,000
Variable costs (800,000 at £7)	5,600,000
	2,400,000
Fixed costs (including depreciation and debenture interest)	1,600,000
Net profit (added to reserves)	800,000

(b) In the year to 31 May 19X0 the directors expect sales to increase in volume by 15%. Selling price per unit is expected to remain the same. It is anticipated that additional advertising costing £150,000 will be needed to generate the volume increase identified above.

(c) The variable cost per unit of existing products is expected to rise by 5%, while the rate of change in fixed costs is expected to be 10%.

(d) The fixed costs shown in (a) above include depreciation of plant and machinery and vehicles. Depreciation is calculated at the rate of 20% on cost of all fixed assets (other than land and buildings) held at the year-end.

(e) Working capital levels at 31 May 19X0 are expected to be:
- Stock   5% of sales
- Debtors   10% of sales
- Creditors   10% of sales

Required

(a) Prepare profit and loss, balance sheet and cash flow forecasts for the year ending 31 May 19X0 to reflect the financial aspects of the plans.

(b) Discuss how the use of a spreadsheet could assist in this kind of exercise.

(c) Set up this exercise on a spreadsheet, with a facility to change a number of variables.

What happens to the results if:

(i) the advertising campaign only results in an increase in sales volume of 5%;

(ii) variable costs increase by 10% per annum (not 5%, as expected);

(iii) both (i) and (ii) occur?

(d) Comment on the plans. Are they satisfactory? Would you change any aspects of the plans? Why/why not?

Note: This question is fairly complicated, in terms of the number of variables which are subject to forecast. The question contains nothing, however, which should cause you any serious difficulties.

3 The balance sheet for Planning Ltd as at 31 May 19X6, and the profit and loss account for the year ended 31 May 19X6, are as shown below:

Balance sheet as at 31 May 19X6

	Cost	Depreciation provision	Net
	£	£	£
Fixed assets			
Land and buildings	500,000	—	500,000
Plant and machinery	300,000	100,000	200,000
Vehicles	50,000	20,000	30,000
	850,000	120,000	730,000

	£	£	£
Current assets			
Stock		50,000	
Debtors		40,000	
Cash		<u>40,000</u>	
		130,000	
Current liabilities			
Corporation tax (due 1/3/X7)	28,000		
Creditors	35,000		
Ordinary dividends	<u>25,000</u>		
		(88,000)	
			<u>42,000</u>
			772,000
Loans			<u>200,000</u>
			572,000
Capital and reserves			
Ordinary share capital			300,000
Reserves			<u>272,000</u>
			572,000

Profit and loss account for the year ending 31 May 19X6

	£	£
Sales		500,000
Less expenses		
Cost of goods sold	250,000	
Wages	50,000	
Depreciation		
Plant and machinery	50,000	
Vehicles	10,000	
Loan interest	24,000	
Administration	20,000	
Marketing	<u>16,000</u>	
		<u>420,000</u>
Net profit		80,000
Appropriated as follows:		
Corporation tax	28,000	
Ordinary share dividend	<u>25,000</u>	
		<u>53,000</u>
Unappropriated profit added to reserves		<u>27,000</u>

Additional notes

1 Sales were made up of 50,000 units at £10 each.
2 Cost of goods sold, and wages, vary in direct proportion to the volume of output and sales (i.e. the cost of goods sold figure is made up of 50,000 units at £5 each, while the wages figure represents 50,000 units at £1 each).

3   Annual depreciation charges are based upon the following:
     Land and buildings   – none;
     Plant and machinery   – 1/6 of cost;
     Vehicles   – 1/5 of cost.

4   The current loans carry interest at 10% per annum, and are repayable in
     equal instalments over the next 5 years.

The directors of the company are now considering their plans for the next
few years, and have asked you to assist in converting their ideas into formal-
ized financial plans. During discussions with them you ascertain the following facts:

1   A 10% increase in the sales volume of existing goods is expected for the
     next year. In passing, the directors indicate that the volume is expected to
     be stable for a further 2 years after this, with a decline being expected
     thereafter. A price rise of 5% is considered to be realistic for the next year.
2   The price indices for cost of goods sold and wages were 110 and 180
     respectively, as at 30 November 19X5. The forecast indices for 30
     November 19X6 are 120 and 190 respectively. It can be presumed that
     expenses for these two areas are incurred evenly throughout the year, so
     the use of averages is acceptable.
3   A new product is to be launched on 1 June 19X6. It is expected that
     20,000 units of this product will be sold in its first year, at a price of £15
     each. Cost of sales and wages are £3 per unit and £2 per unit respectively
     (i.e. both vary directly in proportion to output). The new product will
     require the purchase of new plant and machinery, expected to cost
     £150,000. Since it is expected to last 6 years, this new machinery will also
     be depreciated at 1/6 of cost each year. Old equipment which had origi-
     nally cost £50,000, on which depreciation had been taken to date totalling
     £30,000, is to be sold for £25,000. (Assume that the purchase of the new
     asset, and the disposal of the old, will occur on 1 June 19X6.) The new
     product is likely to require *additional* marketing expenditure in the next
     year amounting to approximately £20,000, and will lead to increased
     administration expenses of £15,000. Existing administration and market-
     ing expenses are expected to rise by 10% in the next year.
4   Dividends are expected to be *at least* maintained over the foreseeable
     future.
5   Corporation tax for the next accounting year can be assumed to be
     payable at the rate of 35% on profits for the year.
6   Working capital is expected to be maintained at the following levels:
     • stock   10% of sales
     • debtors   8% of sales
     • creditors   7% of sales
     • cash   4% of sales

Required
You are specifically asked to do the following:

(a) Prepare:
   (i)   forecast profit and loss account for the year ending 31 May 19X7;
   (ii) forecast balance sheet as at 31 May 19X7;
   (iii) forecast cash flow statement for the year ending 31 May 19X7;
   so as to show the directors the results of their plans in financial terms.
(b) Make comments on the forecasts prepared; in particular, consider whether the decision to introduce the new product and to acquire new machinery is sensible. What advice would you give the directors in this area?
(c) *Briefly* indicate to the directors how the use of a computerized spread-sheet could assist in a planning exercise of this type.

10

The analysis of financial statements: I

10.1 Introduction

This chapter is concerned with the analysis of financial statements. The chapter explains how financial ratios may be used to help assess the position and performance of a business.

10.2 Objectives

On completion of this chapter you should be able:

- to identify the key areas in which financial ratios are employed;
- to calculate the major financial ratios;
- to discuss the significance of each ratio in assessing the financial position and performance of a business;
- to discuss the strengths and weaknesses of ratios as tools of financial analysis.

10.3 Financial ratios

The purpose of calculating financial ratios is to help assess the position and performance of a business. An assessment of current or past position and performance is useful in determining whether or not the managers of the business have used the resources available in an efficient and effective manner. It can also help in formulating views about the future, which should be extremely valuable when making decisions. Ratios are an important and widely used tool of financial analysis. They are referred to frequently in newspapers, business journals and other literature. You should, therefore, be able to understand their uses and interpret their significance.

A ratio simply expresses the relationship of one figure with another figure and, provided the information is available, ratios can usually be calculated with little difficulty. In the case of financial ratios both figures used are often taken from the financial statements; however, a financial ratio can relate an item contained in the financial statements with some business resource (e.g. profit per employee, sales per square metre of floor space, etc.) or some output of the business (e.g. profit per passenger mile, etc.).

Ratios sketch out the financial profile of a business and are frequently employed by those who analyse accounting reports. Whilst the *calculation* of financial ratios is a fairly straightforward process, the *interpretation* of ratios is often more complex. The analyst must exercise skill and judgement in deciding whether or not the changes in a financial ratio are significant and what the underlying cause of any change might be.

By calculating ratios which reflect key relationships (e.g. the relationship between profit and sales) it is possible to reduce the complexity of the profit and loss account and balance sheet to a small number of key indicators. These key indicators provide the analyst with valuable clues concerning the financial health of the business. However, ratios alone do *not* provide a comprehensive analysis of financial condition. Rather, they provide a useful starting point for further analysis by highlighting areas which warrant investigation.

10.4 Standards of performance

A ratio by itself has no real significance. For example, if it was found that ordinary shareholders were receiving a 10% return on their investment in the business, it would not be possible (based on this information alone) to say whether such a return was good, bad or indifferent. It is only when this ratio is compared with some standard of performance that it can be properly evaluated.

There are three *standards of performance* by which ratios can be judged:

1   *Past periods*. This will indicate whether current ratios are better or worse than ratios of past periods. By employing past periods as a standard of performance it may be possible to detect trends which will be useful in predicting future performance. The major problem, however, is that economic conditions may differ significantly between periods and this will hinder a proper evaluation of current performance and position. There is also a potential problem that the results of past periods will reflect operating inefficiencies which have not been recognized.
2   *Planned performance*. This will indicate whether ratios for the current period meet with earlier, planned performance. The usefulness of this standard of comparison will, of course, depend on the validity of the assumptions employed in formulating earlier plans.
3   *Similar businesses within the same industry*. The advantage of this particular standard is that it offers an external basis for comparison. However, there may be problems in finding businesses providing similar services or products. No two businesses are identical. Furthermore, differences in accounting policies between businesses concerning stock valuation, depreciation, etc. may hinder comparisons. This problem, however, may be lessened

where there is an interfirm comparison scheme operating for the industry. Such a scheme involves a central body adjusting the financial statements of each participating business to conform with particular income and asset measurement procedures. The central body will then calculate ratios based on the adjusted figures.

There is a counter argument, however, for not standardizing accounting procedures between businesses in this way. The counter argument is that a business may have chosen particular policies which best reflect their economic characteristics and so standardization will hinder rather than help comparison.

It is clear from the above that there is no ideal standard of comparison. Nevertheless, some standard must be used and the skill and judgement of the analyst will be required to ensure that comparisons are properly interpreted.

10.5   Ratio classification

Ratios can be classified according to the particular aspect of a business's financial health it seeks to examine. There are four major classifications:

1   *Liquidity*. Liquidity ratios examine the ability of the business to meet its short-term commitments. It is vital that a business has the capacity to pay debts when they fall due. Even a profitable business may be forced to cease trading if it has insufficient liquid resources. Poor liquidity can lead to delays in paying debts which may, in turn, result in a loss of confidence amongst lenders and creditors.
2   *Gearing (leverage)*. Gearing is important in the assessment of financial risk. Gearing ratios examine the financial structure and financial capacity of the business. These ratios examine the relative contributions of investors and lenders towards financing the business. In addition, they examine the capacity of the business to service and repay loans.
3   *Activity (efficiency)*. Activity ratios measure the efficiency with which the business utilizes its assets. These ratios provide useful insights into management policy and operational efficiency.
4   *Profitability ratios*. Profitability ratios relate profit to other key figures in the financial statements. Profit represents the central measure of operating achievement and by relating this to other key figures a clearer view of performance can be gained.

The level of importance attached to each class of ratio will depend on the type of user and the purpose of the analysis. A trade creditor, for example, is likely to be interested in the short-term credit-worthiness of the business and may concentrate attention on the liquidity ratios. An investor, on the other hand, is likely to be interested in the risks and returns associated with the business. Hence, the investor may have a particular interest in gearing and profitability ratios. It is therefore important to be clear when calculating ratios, *for whom and for what purpose* the analysis is being undertaken.

Activity 1
Which classes of ratio are each of the following user groups most likely to be interested in and why?

User group	*Class of ratio*	*Reason*
Long-term lenders		
Government		
Employees		
Customers		
Management		

Your answer to this activity should be along the following lines:

User group	*Class of ratio*	*Reason*
Long-term lenders	Gearing profitability	Long-term lenders will be concerned with the extent to which they are financing the business and long-term viability
Government	Profitability	Government may use profit as a basis for taxation, grants and subsidies
Employees	Profitability Liquidity Activity	Employees will be concerned with job security and wage bargaining
Customers	Liquidity	Customers will seek reassurance that the business can survive in the short term and continue to supply
Management	Profitability Liquidity Activity Gearing	Management is interested in all aspects of the financial health of the business

Details of the main ratios, under each of the above headings, are given in the sections which follow. In order to provide worked examples for each ratio, appropriate calculations are made, based on a set of accounts (for Abacus Ltd) as set out in Appendix 1 to this chapter. This appendix also provides details of the industry average for comparison purposes. Please refer to this appendix to make sure you are clear about the source of the figures used in each of the ratios.

10.6   Liquidity ratios

To assess the liquidity of a business two ratios are commonly used. These are current ratio and acid-test (quick) ratio.

Current ratio

This ratio is calculated as follows:

$$\textbf{Current ratio} = \frac{\textbf{current assets}}{\textbf{current liabilities}} \quad \text{(i.e. amounts due within 1 year)}$$

Current assets include cash or assets intended to be converted into cash, such as stock and debtors. In dividing current assets by the current liabilities, an attempt is made to measure the amount of coverage available for short-term obligations.

The current ratio for Abacus is:

$$\frac{950}{450} = 2.11 \text{ (sometimes expressed as 2.11:1)}$$

This means that Abacus Ltd has £2.11 worth of current assets for every £1 worth of current liabilities. This ratio compares with a ratio of 2.2 for the industry average. Thus, the current ratio of Abacus Ltd is near the average for the industry as a whole. In that sense, the ratio may be considered satisfactory.

Acid-test (quick) ratio

The current ratio discussed above has been criticized for not being a particularly stringent test of liquidity. This is because certain current assets such as stock and prepayments may not be easily converted into cash. Hence, it is argued that such assets should be excluded when assessing the ability of the business to meet its short-term obligations. The acid-test ratio is based on this line of reasoning and is calculated as follows:

$$\text{Acid-test ratio} = \frac{\textbf{current assets – stock and prepayments}}{\textbf{current liabilities}}$$

For Abacus Ltd the acid-test ratio is:

$$\frac{570}{450} = 1.27 \text{ (sometimes expressed as 1.27:1)}$$

This means that Abacus Ltd has £1.27 worth of liquid current assets for every £1 worth of short-term obligations. The above ratio of 1.27 compares with an industry average of 0.90. Hence, Abacus Ltd has a satisfactory acid-test ratio which is higher than the industry average.

In evaluating these liquidity ratios it is worth noting that the relevant figures are taken from the balance sheet. This means the ratios only reflect the liquidity position at the point in time for which the balance sheet was prepared. A more detailed analysis of the business's liquidity position would involve monitoring cash flows over a period in time.

The lower the current and acid-test ratios, the lower the liquidity of the business. Clearly, liquidity ratios may be too low, thereby suggesting an inability to pay short-term obligations. However, it is also possible for liquidity ratios to be too high. A very high ratio may suggest that the business has excessive amounts tied up in current assets which could be used to more profitable ends. When examining liquidity ratios it is therefore useful to have in mind an acceptable range within which the ratios might occur.

Activity 2
From the information provided in Appendix 2 to this chapter, calculate the liquidity ratios of Vortex Ltd. What do you deduce from an analysis of these ratios over the 3-year period?

Liquidity ratios

	19X7	*19X8*	*19X9*
Current ratio	24,000	27,000	31,000
	12,000	14,000	19,000
	2.0	1.93	1.63
Acid-test ratio	16,000	15,000	14,000
	12,000	14,000	19,000
	1.33	1.07	0.74

Both ratios reveal a declining trend in liquidity over the 3-year period. The acid-test ratio has declined more sharply than the current ratio and this should be of particular concern. The acid-test ratio reveals that by 19X9 there are insufficient liquid current assets to meet short-term obligations. The business should seek to reverse the declining trend in liquidity in order to maintain the confidence of creditors.

10.7   Gearing (leverage) ratios

The relationship between the amount of fixed-return capital (preference shares and loan stocks) and ordinary shares in the capital structure is usually referred to as capital gearing or leverage. The term gearing or leverage is used because employing fixed-return capital can have the effect of accentuating the returns to ordinary shareholders, as we shall see below.

Example

Power Plc, which always pays its entire net profit to its ordinary shareholders as a dividend, has the following long-term capital structure:

	£m
5m ordinary shares of £1 each	5
£5m loan stock (10%)	5
	£10

Over 3 consecutive years, the net profits before loan stock interest were:

Year 1	£1.0m
Year 2	£2.0m
Year 3	£0.5m

The returns to the shareholders over the 3 years would be as follows:

Year	1	2	3
	£m	£m	£m
Net profit (before interest)	1.0	2.0	0.5
Loan interest (£5m × 10%)	0.5	0.5	0.5
Net earnings	0.5	1.5	0.0
Earnings per share (EPS)	£0.10	£0.30	£0.00

(EPS = net earnings available to ordinary shareholders ÷ number of ordinary shares.)

Note that the doubling of the profit from Year 1 to Year 2 has the effect of *trebling* the return to shareholders. Also, the halving of the profit from year 1 to year 3 has the effect of eliminating any return to shareholders.

Activity 3
Contrast the above returns to shareholders with the position which would arise in each year if there were no fixed-return capital and all of the finance was provided by 10m ordinary shares.

The position would be as follows for each year:

Year	1	2	3
	£m	£m	£m
Net profit	1.0	2.0	0.5
Earnings per share	£0.10	£0.20	£0.05

Here the return to shareholders fluctuates exactly in line with profit fluctuations.

We can see that the existence of a fixed-return element has the effect of accentuating fluctuations in the returns to ordinary shareholders. This is analogous to the effect of two meshing cog wheels of different sizes or of the movement of, and force exerted by, either end of a lever whose fulcrum is not at the centre of its length.

It is clear from the above example that a certain minimum profit before interest must be made before there is any return to the shareholders. This is because the use of debt carries with it an automatic and contractual expense (interest). In the above example, the profit before interest *must* be £0.5m for the company to cover the interest payable, otherwise the shareholders will suffer a loss. Only if the profit before interest is in excess of this figure will the shareholders make a positive return. Clearly, while the use of gearing provides the opportunity for far greater returns to shareholders when profits are good, it also brings with it much lower returns to shareholders when profits are not so good. In sustained periods of recession, the use of debt is likely to lead to far greater pressures than the use of shareholder funds, since dividends can be stopped as conditions worsen, whereas interest payments cannot.

The introduction of gearing into a business should therefore be seen as introducing a further dimension to risk, as far as the shareholders are concerned. Any business is faced with risks inherent in the type of business in which it is engaged. Such risk is referred to as *business risk*, and will not change irrespective of how a business is financed. The introduction of gearing introduces an additional facet of risk for the shareholders, as has been illustrated above. This risk is referred to as *financial risk*. This means that the returns to equity for a business with financial gearing will fluctuate more sharply than the fluctuating profits arising from business risk. This is depicted in Figure 10.1.

Shareholders must recognize there is a *risk–return trade-off* to be made. The higher the level of gearing, the higher the prospective returns to equity shareholders, but the higher the level of financial risk incurred.

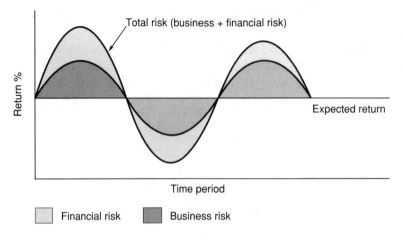

Figure 10.1

Activity 4
In the context of the above example, what relationship is there between the loan stock, interest rate and the fact that, at some levels of profit, gearing is beneficial to ordinary shareholders but at other levels it is not?

In the example given, the dividend per share is only the same in Year 1, when the net profit before interest is 10% of the net assets, which is the same as the interest payable on the loan. If the rate of return on assets exceeds the interest rate payable on the loan, the dividends per share will be higher the higher the level of debt used. Year 2 provides an illustration of this. Where the rate of return on assets is less than the rate of interest on the loan, the opposite is true. In practice, taxation complicates this relationship, but the general principle remains valid.

Activity 5
In what type of business would you expect to find high levels of capital gearing and why?

High levels of gearing tend to be found where some of the following conditions exist:

- earnings are stable over time or show an increasing trend
- there is adequate security available for the debt
- there is a risk of a dilution of control with respect to existing shareholders if new ordinary shares are issued

- the market value of ordinary shares is low and would prove to be an unattractive investment

Debt to equity ratio

This ratio is concerned with the relative contribution of debt and equity (ordinary shareholders) in financing the business. The ratio is calculated as follows:

Debt/equity ratio = $\dfrac{\textbf{total debt (i.e. long- and short-term liabilities)}}{\textbf{total equity (ordinary share capital plus reserves)}}$

For Abacus Ltd the debt to equity ratio is:

$$\frac{1,050}{1,800} = 0.58$$

This means that for every £1 contributed by equity shareholders to finance the business, lenders and creditors have contributed £0.58. The above ratio of 0.58 compares with a ratio of 0.85 for the industry average. Abacus Ltd is, therefore, well below the industry average.

Generally speaking, the higher the ratio (i.e. the higher the level of gearing), the less protection is being offered to lenders. However, this may not always be the case. Where lenders have been offered security for a loan by way of a charge on certain assets, they may feel well protected despite a high debt to equity ratio.

Debt to total assets ratio

This ratio measures the extent to which lenders and creditors are financing the assets of the business. It is calculated as follows:

Debt/total assets = $\dfrac{\textbf{total debt (i.e. long- and short-term liabilities)} \times \textbf{100}}{\textbf{total assets (i.e. fixed and current assets)}}$

In the case of Abacus Ltd the ratio is

$$\frac{1,050 \times 100}{2,850} = 36.84\%$$

The ratio indicates that lenders and creditors are providing over 36% of the total funds required to finance the assets of the business. This compares with an industry average of 38%.

Where a company has lower gearing ratios than the industry average it may suggest there is unused debt capacity. This means the company may be able to borrow more, if it so wished, without incurring any adverse reaction from lenders and creditors. However, we have seen that other factors such as the availability of security for borrowings will also be important in determining debt capacity.

Interest coverage (times interest earned) ratio

This ratio examines the ability of the business to meet its regular financial commitments. The ratio is calculated as follows:

$$\textbf{Interest coverage} = \frac{\textbf{net profit before interest and taxation}}{\textbf{interest charges}}$$

For Abacus Ltd the ratio is:

$$\frac{340}{60} = 5.67$$

This means that the business is generating £5.67 worth of profit to cover each £1 of interest charges. The above ratio of 5.67 compares with an industry average of 3.95. Thus, Abacus Ltd has a ratio well above the industry average.

This ratio is a *coverage* ratio similar to the liquidity ratios discussed earlier. It attempts to measure the amount of protection available to lenders. The higher the ratio, so it is argued, the greater the ability of the business to cover its interest payments. The lower the ratio, the greater the risk the business will default on its interest payments. This line of argument, however, is something of an oversimplification as the ability of a business to meet interest charges is related to cash flows rather than profit flows. A rough measure of cash flows for the year can be derived from the income statement by adding back to net profit items, such as depreciation, which do not involve any cash outlay. The cash flow coverage ratio is based on the above idea and is calculated as follows:

$$\textbf{Cash flow coverage ratio} = \frac{\textbf{net profit before depreciation, interest and taxation}}{\textbf{interest charges}}$$

For Abacus Ltd this ratio is:

$$\frac{400}{60} = 6.67$$

This compares with an industry average of 4.90. Thus, Abacus Ltd has a ratio well above the industry average and, in one sense, it is satisfactory. However, it also suggests the business may have the capacity to take on additional debt.

Failure to do so may indicate the business is not availing itself of a relatively cheap form of finance.

Activity 6
From the information provided in Appendix 2 to this chapter, calculate three gearing ratios for Vortex Ltd. What do you deduce from an analysis of these ratios over the 3-year period?

Gearing ratios

Debt to equity ratio	$\dfrac{12,000}{22,000}$	$\dfrac{15,000}{22,100}$	$\dfrac{21,000}{22,150}$
	0.55	0.68	0.95
Interest coverage ratio	—	$\dfrac{2800}{100}$	$\dfrac{1700}{200}$
		28 times	8.5 times
Cash flow coverage ratio	—	$\dfrac{4000}{100}$	$\dfrac{3200}{200}$
		40 times	16 times

All three ratios reveal a trend towards higher levels of gearing. This is partly due to the issue of debentures in 19X8 and 19X9 and partly to a considerable increase in creditors in 19X9. The coverage ratios (i.e. interest and cash flow coverage) have declined sharply between 19X8 and 19X9 because of the sharp fall in profits and the increase in interest charges which have occurred. This sharp decline will do little to inspire confidence amongst existing lenders. However, the coverage ratios have not yet declined to a point where lenders should be alarmed.

10.8 Activity (efficiency) ratios

Activity ratios are concerned with how efficiently the resources of the business are being managed. The most important activity ratios are as follows:

Ratios related to stock

The stock turnover ratio expresses the relationship between the average stock held and the cost of sales. The ratio is as follows:

Stock turnover ratio = $\dfrac{\text{cost of sales}}{\text{average stock held}}$

The average stock figure is usually calculated by taking the average of the opening and closing stock figures. However, where the business is seasonal in nature and closing stocks are not representative of average stock held, information concerning stockholdings throughout the year should be used (wherever possible) to calculate an average figure.

For Abacus Ltd the stock turnover ratio is:

$\dfrac{2{,}500}{300} = 8.3$

If required, the above ratio can be inverted to arrive at an *average period of stockholding*:

Average period of stockholding = $\dfrac{\text{average stock held}}{\text{cost of sales}} \times 12$

Multiplying by 12 will give the period in months for which the stock is held. If the period is to be expressed in days, the number will need to be 365.

For Abacus Ltd the period of stockholding is:

$\dfrac{300}{2{,}500} \times 12 = 1.44 \text{ months}$

This compares with 1.1 months for the industry average. Thus, Abacus Ltd has a ratio above the average, which may not be satisfactory. (Comparing the stock turnover rate of 8.3 with an industry figure of 10.9, should lead to an identical conclusion.)

Activity 7

What possible interpretations (positive or negative) may be placed on the following:
(a)   a higher-than-average stockholding period?
(b)   a lower-than-average stockholding period?

A high stockholding period may suggest the existence of slow-moving or obsolete stocks, or poor utilization of resources. However, other interpretations of this ratio may be possible. For example, management may acquire large amounts of stock, and thereby lengthen the stockholding period, if a shortage of supplies or a significant rise in the price of stocks is predicted. Management may also accumulate stocks in anticipation of higher sales in the following period as a result, for example, of a price-cutting campaign to be launched.

Further investigation into stockholding policies and practice would, therefore, be required.

A low stockholding period may also suggest poor stock management. Where the level of stock is low in relation to sales this may indicate the company is understocked and this, in turn, can lead to lost sales and lost customer goodwill. On the other hand, it may indicate a very efficient management of stocks. If stock movements are carefully recorded and checked frequently and it is possible to obtain new stocks from suppliers quickly, it may be possible to reduce the amount of stocks held and, thereby, reduce the stockholding period.

Like the liquidity ratios discussed earlier, it is probably a good idea to establish an acceptable range within which this ratio might fluctuate.

Ratios related to debtors

Similar ratios can be calculated for debtors as for stock. In order to calculate debtors' turnover the following ratio is used:

$$\textbf{Debtors' turnover} = \frac{\textbf{credit sales}}{\textbf{trade debtors}}$$

For Abacus Ltd debtors' turnover would be:

$$\frac{3{,}200}{520} = 6.15$$

Inversion of the ratio will give a figure for the average credit period allowed. This ratio measures the average length of time it takes trade debtors to pay. It is calculated as follows:

$$\textbf{Average credit period allowed} = \frac{\textbf{trade debtors}}{\textbf{credit sales}} \times \textbf{12}$$

Once again, the ratio is multiplied by 12 to derive the average period in months. In calculating the ratio, the year end trade debtors figure is usually employed as the appropriate figure. However, where demand is seasonal, or where there has been considerable sales growth during the year, some calculation of average debtors using monthly data is preferable.

For Abacus Ltd the average credit period allowed (based on year end debtors) is:

$$\frac{520}{3{,}200} \times 12 = 1.95 \text{ months}$$

This compares with 1.90 months for the industry average. Hence, Abacus is very near the average for the industry and, in that sense, the ratio is satisfactory.

Activity 8

What possible interpretations (positive or negative) might be placed on:

(a) a higher-than-average credit period allowed?
(b) a lower-than-average credit period allowed?

If the debtors' turnover was much lower, or (using the inverse ratio) the period of credit much higher, than the industry average, this might suggest the business adopts a more liberal credit policy than its competitors, or that the business has weak credit control procedures. Conversely, a higher debtors' turnover period or lower credit period allowed may indicate tighter credit control standards and/or procedures. The decision concerning the appropriate credit control policy to adopt will involve weighing the expected benefits of a particular policy against expected costs. For example, a liberal credit policy may result in higher sales but may also result in higher credit administration costs and high levels of bad debts. A tight credit control, on the other hand, may reduce the level of bad debts but may also reduce the level of sales.

It is important to recognize that it is the *average* credit period allowed which is being calculated. This ratio may be influenced by a few large debtors who are slow to pay and, therefore, care must be taken in interpreting the results.

Ratios related to creditors

In addition to calculating ratios relating to debtors, it may also be useful to calculate ratios relating to creditors. The ratios calculated are similar to those calculated for debtors.

In order to calculate creditors' turnover the following ratio is used:

$$\text{Creditors' turnover} = \frac{\text{credit purchases}}{\text{trade creditors}}$$

For Abacus Ltd the creditors' turnover ratio is:

$$\frac{2{,}600}{380} = 6.84$$

In calculating this ratio, it is assumed that all purchases during the year have been made on credit.

Inversion of the ratio will give a figure for the average credit period taken. Thus:

$$\text{Average credit period allowed} = \frac{\text{trade creditors} \times 12}{\text{credit purchases}}$$

For Abacus Ltd the average credit period taken (in months) is:

$$\frac{380}{2,600} \times 12 = 1.75 \text{ months}$$

This compares with the industry average of 1.8 months and may therefore be regarded as satisfactory.

Activity 9
'A business should have a high average credit period for creditors as the amounts owed represent a free source of finance to a business.'
  Do you agree with this statement?

It is often true that trade creditors provide a free source of finance for a business. However, there may be costs involved if a business takes an excessive time to pay. Such a policy may result in lost supplier goodwill which may, in turn, lead to withdrawal of credit, delays in processing orders, lower priority in the future and perhaps interest charged on overdue amounts. Where a supplier offers a cash discount for prompt payment, the benefits of delaying payment must be weighed against the discounts foregone.

A high average credit period taken may indicate the business has liquidity problems, i.e. creditors are not being paid because there is no cash available. It may therefore be a symptom of financial distress.

Fixed asset turnover ratio

This ratio measures how effectively the business is using its fixed assets to generate sales. The ratio is calculated as follows:

$$\textbf{Fixed asset turnover ratio} = \frac{\textbf{sales}}{\textbf{fixed assets}}$$

The year end fixed asset figure is often taken as the appropriate figure for this ratio. However, an average of the opening and closing fixed assets may also be used. This would be particularly relevant if the business were rapidly expanding.

For Abacus Ltd, the ratio (employing the year end fixed asset figure) is

$$\frac{3,200}{1,900} = 1.68 \text{ times}$$

This means that for every £1 invested in fixed assets, the business is generating £1.68 in sales. The above ratio of 1.68 companies with an industry average of

1.60. Thus, Abacus Ltd is slightly above the industry average and, therefore, the ratio may be seen as satisfactory. It is important, however, to recognize that differences in the age and condition of fixed assets between businesses will complicate interpretation of this ratio. Given the same level of sales, a business with old, highly depreciated fixed assets will have a higher fixed asset turnover ratio than one with new, barely depreciated fixed assets.

Total asset turnover ratio

This ratio measures how effectively the business is using its assets to generate sales. The ratio is calculated as follows:

$$\textbf{Total asset turnover ratio} = \frac{\textbf{sales}}{\textbf{total assets}}$$

For Abacus Ltd, the ratio (employing year end asset figures, although an average figure can also be used) is:

$$\frac{3,200}{2,850} = 1.12 \text{ times}$$

This means that for every £1 invested in assets the business is generating £1.12 in sales each year. The above ratio of 1.12 compared with a ratio of 1.2 for the industry average. Abacus Ltd is, therefore, not performing as well as the industry average.

Too low a ratio may suggest the business is not using its assets productively. A very high turnover ratio, on the other hand, may suggest the business is overtrading on its assets, i.e. it has an inadequate amount of assets in relation to the sales generated. Overtrading will often arise when a new business attempts to expand too quickly. Sales may increase but the finance may not be available to invest in fixed assets and working capital. As a consequence, the business will suffer from liquidity problems and will be unable to supply customers as the funds will not be available to purchase the necessary stocks. These liquidity problems may ultimately force the business to cease trading if it is unable to meet its maturing debts.

Activity 10
From the information given in Appendix 2 to this chapter, calculate the activity ratios for Vortex Ltd. What do you deduce from an analysis of these ratios over the 3-year period?

Activity (efficiency) ratios

Stock turnover period	$\dfrac{7,500}{15,000} \times 12$	$\dfrac{10,000}{22,000} \times 12$	$\dfrac{14,500}{30,000} \times 12$
	6 months	5.45 months	5.8 months
Average credit period allowed	$\dfrac{6,000}{24,000} \times 12$	$\dfrac{9,000}{30,000} \times 12$	$\dfrac{14,000}{38,000} \times 12$
	3 months	3.6 months	4.42 months
Fixed asset turnover ratio	$\dfrac{24,000}{10,000}$	$\dfrac{30,000}{10,100}$	$\dfrac{38,000}{12,150}$
	2.4 times	2.97 times	3.13 times
Total asset turnover ratio	$\dfrac{24,000}{34,000}$	$\dfrac{30,000}{37,100}$	$\dfrac{38,000}{43,150}$
	0.71 times	0.81 times	0.88 times

The stock turnover period has remained fairly stable over the 3-year period. However, the ratio does seem very high and further investigation of stock-holding policy is required. The average credit period allowed has sharply increased over the 3-year period. By 19X9 trade debtors were taking, on average, almost 4½ months to pay. This ratio again seems very high and further investigation of credit policy is required. Notice that over the 3-year period sales have increased by nearly 60%. This increase may have arisen, at least in part, as a result of a more liberal credit policy. Asset turnover ratios have increased over the period as a result of the increase in sales.

10.9   Profitability ratios

Profitability ratios help assess the operating performance of the business. The major profitability ratios are as follows:

Gross profit margin

This ratio expresses the gross profit as a percentage of sales. The ratio is, therefore:

Gross profit margin = $\dfrac{\textbf{gross profit} \times \textbf{100}}{\textbf{sales}}$

The gross profit margin can be used to assess trading performance and pricing policy. For Abacus Ltd the gross profit margin is:

$$\frac{700 \times 100}{3,200} = 21.87\%$$

This means for every £1 of sales generated the business earns £0.22 (approx.) gross profit. The above ratio of 21.87% compares with an industry average of 21% and may, therefore, be regarded as satisfactory.

Net profit margin

This ratio expresses the net profit as a percentage of sales. It therefore measures the percentage return from sales after taking account of all expenses (including tax). The ratio is:

$$\textbf{Net profit margin} = \frac{\textbf{net profit after tax}}{\textbf{sales}} \times \textbf{100}$$

For Abacus Ltd the ratio is:

$$\frac{210}{3,200} \times 100 = 6.56\%$$

This ratio is below the industry average of 8.2%. In view of the fact that the gross profit margin of Abacus Ltd is in line with the industry average, it would appear that the lower net profit margin can be attributed to higher than average overheads for the level of sales generated. It may be useful to express each overhead as a percentage of sales to see how much each absorbs of gross revenue. The percentages calculated can then be compared with those of similar businesses to assess relative efficiency.

Some businesses are prepared to work on very low profit margins in order to stimulate sales and thereby increase total profits. The early success of Tesco Plc, for example, was founded on the philosophy 'stack it high and sell it cheap'.

Return to equity

This ratio expresses the profit available to equity (ordinary) shareholders as a percentage of the equity shareholders stake in the business. The ratio is as follows:

$$\textbf{Return to equity} = \frac{\textbf{net profit (after tax and preference dividends)}}{\textbf{ordinary share capital plus reserves}} \times \textbf{100}$$

This ratio measures the return the equity shareholders are receiving from their investment in the business. The ordinary share capital plus reserves figure used in the ratio is usually based on the year end figures. However, an average of opening and closing balances can be used.

For Abacus Ltd, the return to equity (based on year-end figures) is:

$$\frac{210}{1,800} \times 100 = 11.67\%$$

This ratio is below the industry average of 13.11% and may be regarded as unsatisfactory.

Return on capital employed (ROCE)

This ratio expresses the profit available to suppliers of long-term capital as a percentage of the long-term capital employed. The profit available to long-term suppliers of capital is the net profit before interest (and taxation). It is an important and useful measure of performance as it measures *input* in the form of capital employed against *output* in the form of profit. The return to equity ratio discussed above is, of course, another example of an input/output ratio.

Return on capital employed is calculated as follows:

$$\textbf{ROCE} = \frac{\textbf{net profit before interest and taxation}}{\textbf{share capital + reserves + long-term loans}} \times \textbf{100}$$

For Abacus Ltd, the ratio is:

$$\frac{340}{2,400} \times 100 = 14.17\%$$

This ratio is below the industry average of 16.59% and, therefore, may be regarded as unsatisfactory.

Return on investment (ROI)

This ratio expresses the net profit (after tax) as a percentage of total assets. The ratio is therefore:

$$\textbf{ROI} = \frac{\textbf{net profit (after tax)}}{\textbf{total assets}} \times \textbf{100}$$

This ratio is also considered to be very important as it measures the profit available after all obligatory charges have been deducted in relation to the assets held by the business. The total assets figure used in the ratio is often the year end figure but again, an average of opening and closing figures may be used.

For Abacus the ratio (based on year end figures) is:

$$\frac{210}{2,850} \times 100 = 7.36\%$$

This compares with an industry average of 9.84%. Abacus Ltd's ratio is therefore below the industry average.

Differences between businesses in the age and condition of their fixed assets will complicate interpretation of this ratio. Given the same net profit after tax, a business with highly depreciated fixed assets will have a higher ROI than a business with newer, less depreciated, fixed assets.

Activity 11

From the information in Appendix 2 to this chapter, calculate the profitability ratios of Vortex Ltd. What do you deduce from an analysis of these ratios over the 3-year period?

Profitability ratios

Gross profit margin	$\dfrac{9{,}000}{24{,}000} \times 100$	$\dfrac{8{,}000}{30{,}000} \times 100$	$\dfrac{8{,}000}{38{,}000} \times 100$
	37.5%	26.67%	21.05%
Net profit margin	$\dfrac{3{,}600}{24{,}000} \times 100$	$\dfrac{1{,}900}{30{,}000} \times 100$	$\dfrac{1{,}050}{38{,}000} \times 100$
	15%	6.33%	2.76%
Return to equity	$\dfrac{3{,}600}{22{,}000} \times 100$	$\dfrac{1{,}900}{22{,}100} \times 100$	$\dfrac{1{,}050}{22{,}150} \times 100$
	16.36%	8.6%	4.74%
ROCE	$\dfrac{5{,}200}{22{,}000} \times 100$	$\dfrac{2{,}800}{23{,}100} \times 100$	$\dfrac{1{,}700}{24{,}150} \times 100$
	23.64%	12.12%	7.04%
ROI	$\dfrac{3{,}600}{34{,}000} \times 100$	$\dfrac{1{,}900}{37{,}100} \times 100$	$\dfrac{1{,}050}{43{,}150} \times 100$
	10.59%	5.12%	2.43%

There has been a sharp decline in all profitability ratios over the 3-year period. The sharp decrease in the gross profit margin and the corresponding sharp increase in sales may suggest the business has lowered prices in order to stimulate sales. The fall in the net profit margin reflects, to a large extent, the fall in the gross profit margin. However, the net profit margin has not fallen by quite the amount of the gross profit margin as certain overhead expenses have not increased proportionately with sales. The fall in profit margins has not been adequately compensated for by increases in sales. Hence, the return to equity, ROCE and ROI ratios have declined. The sharp decline in these ratios is likely to cause concern amongst investors and lenders. Efforts to reverse the trends should therefore be made. The starting point may be to reconsider pricing policy over recent years.

10.10 Trend analysis

Ratios may be computed for a business over time and the results plotted on a graph. This can be useful when seeking to identify trends over time. An example of this form of trend analysis is shown in Figure 10.2.

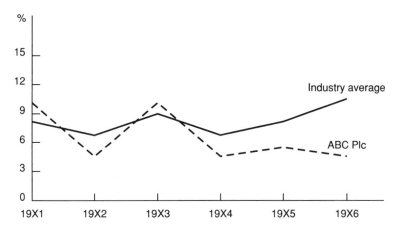

Figure 10.2 *Return on investment*

Self-assessment question 10.1

Bradbury Ltd is a family-owned clothes manufacturer based in the southwest of England. For a number of years the chairman and managing director of the company was David Bradbury. During his period of office the company's sales turnover had grown steadily at a rate of 2–3% each year. David Bradbury retired on 30 November 19X8 and was succeeded by his son, Simon. Soon after taking office Simon decided to expand the business. Within weeks he had successfully negotiated a 5-year contract with a large clothes retailer to make a range of sports and leisurewear items. The contract will result in an additional £2 million sales during each year of the contract. In order to fulfil the contract new equipment and premises were acquired by Bradbury Ltd.

Financial information concerning the company is given below:

Profit and loss account for the year ended 30 November

	19X8	19X9
	£000	*£000*
Turnover	9,482	11,365
Profit before interest and tax	914	1,042

	£000	£000
Interest charges	22	81
Profit before tax	892	961
Taxation	358	385
Profit after tax	534	576
Dividend	120	120
Retained profit	414	456

Balance sheet as at 30 November

	19X8		19X9	
	£000	£000	£000	£000
Fixed assets				
Freehold premises at cost		5,240		7,360
Plant and equipment (net)		2,375		4,057
		7,615		11,417
Current assets				
Stock	2,386		3,420	
Trade debtors	2,540		4,280	
Cash	127		—	
	5,053		7,700	
Creditors: amounts falling due within 1 year				
Trade creditors	1,157		2,245	
Taxation	358		385	
Dividends payable	120		120	
Bank overdraft	—		2,424	
	1,635		5,174	
Net current assets		3,418		2,526
		11,033		13,943
Creditors: amounts falling due in more than 1 year				
Loans		1,220		3,674
Total net assets		9,813		10,269
Capital and reserves				
Share capital		2,000		2,000
Reserves		7,813		8,269
Net worth		9,813		10,269

Required:

(a) Calculate for each year the following ratios:
   (i) Net profit margin.
   (ii) Return on capital employed.
   (iii) Current ratio.
   (iv) Debt ratio.

> (v) Days' debtors (collection period).
> (vi) Net asset turnover.
> (b) Using the above ratios, and any other ratios or information you consider relevant, comment on the results of the expansion programme. The solution to this question will be found at the end of the book.

10.11 The usefulness of financial ratios

The usefulness of ratio analysis will largely depend upon:

- the quality of the underlying financial statements, and
- the validity of the standards of comparison employed.

Where the underlying statements upon which the ratios are based are unreliable, the quality of the analysis will be undermined. Sometimes managers may wish to undermine the quality of financial statements prepared for users. For example, managers may seek to provide a healthier picture of the performance and position of the business than is really the case in order to be viewed in a favourable light, or they may seek ways of hiding contractual or financial obligations which are burdensome to the business in order to obscure the true level of financial risk taken by lenders and shareholders. It is therefore important for users not to rely exclusively on the annual financial statements in order to assess performance and position. Other sources of information available should be used to confirm the reliability of the financial statements and to provide a fuller picture of the business.

> **Activity 12**
> What other sources of information might be used to confirm or supplement the information contained in the annual financial statements? (A similar question was posed in Chapter 1; however, at this stage in your studies you should be able to answer this question more fully.)

The following sources of information may prove useful:

- interim (i.e. half-yearly or quarterly) financial reports prepared by the company
- the financial statements of similar businesses in the same industry
- newspaper and journal articles relating to the business
- newspaper and journal articles relating to the industry and the economy as a whole

- industry reports
- announcements made by the directors of the company
- share price movements
- stockbrokers' reports
- rumours
- prospectuses/offers for sale
- discussions with directors/managers

This is not an exhaustive list. You may have thought of others.

The standards used for comparison purposes must be valid for a proper interpretation of results. We saw earlier that there are three major standards which may be used, and considered some of their drawbacks. Information relating to similar businesses in the same industry provides an external source of data which many find useful. This information is becoming increasingly available through computerized databases produced by commercial companies and represents an easy and relatively cheap form of information. However, there may be problems with using such a database. Not all businesses may be included in the database. For example, businesses considered to be less important to database customers such as small businesses or businesses whose shares are not traded on the Stock Exchange may be excluded. In addition, the classification methods used by the database may exclude or obscure valuable items of information relating to a company. There is also a risk that the database may not include up-to-date information or may include recording errors. Users must be aware of these potential problems when employing this source of information.

Ratios have the advantage of controlling for differences in size. For example, two businesses may be quite different in size but can be compared in terms of profitability, liquidity, etc. by the use of ratios. Thus, Business A may have sales of £1m and a net profit of £100,000 and Business B may have sales of £10m and a net profit of £1m. The net profit margin ratio will reveal that the profitability of each business is identical. Whilst this ability to control for size differences can be useful, it can also have its drawbacks. It may be, for example, that the size of a business is an important factor in identifying profitable businesses within a particular industry or in identifying businesses which are likely to fail. If we rely only on ratios, these kinds of relationships will not be picked up.

10.12 Summary

Financial ratios offer a useful means of highlighting the strengths and weaknesses of a business. As a result they provide useful signposts for further analysis. Although the calculation of financial ratios is fairly straightforward, skill and judgement are required in interpreting the results. A ratio has a numerator and denominator and changes in the ratio can occur from changes in either or both. It is therefore important to be clear why a ratio has changed.

It must be emphasized that ratios alone do not provide a sufficient basis for arriving at firm conclusions concerning the position and performance of a business. If an increase in stocks results in a higher stock turnover period we cannot say for sure that this reflects poor stock control. In certain circumstances an increase in stockholdings may be both desirable and deliberate, e.g. where future supplies will cost significantly more or are likely to be disrupted. Ratios provide a starting point for further investigation and conclusions based on ratios alone must be regarded as extremely tentative.

In this chapter only the more widely used ratios have been considered. Many more ratios may be computed to determine the financial health of a business. Some of these ratios relate figures on the financial statements to particular resources held by the business or particular outputs in order to measure efficiency. It has been mentioned above that measures of output such as sales and profit can be related to employee or floor space, passenger miles to devise ratios such as sales (profit) per employee, sales (profit) per square metre of floor space, profit per passenger mile, etc.

Exercises

1 White and Black are sole traders. Both are wholesalers dealing in a similar range of goods. Summaries of the profit calculations and balance sheets for the same year have been made available to you, as follows:

Profit and loss accounts for the year

	White £000	White £000	Black £000	Black £000
Sales		600		800
Cost of goods sold		450		624
		150		176
Administration expenses	64		63	
Selling and distribution expenses	28		40	
Depreciation – equipment and vehicles	10		20	
Depreciation – buildings	—	102	5	128
Net profit		48		48

Balance sheets as at end of the year

	White £000	White £000	Black £000	Black £000
Buildings		29		47
Equipment and vehicles		62		76
Stock		56		52
Debtors		75		67

	£000	£000	£000	£000
Bank balance		8		—
		230		242
Creditors	38		78	
Bank balance	—	38	4	82
Capital		192		160

Required

Compare the performance and position of the two businesses on the basis of the above figures, supporting your comments where appropriate with ratios and noting what further information you would need before reaching firmer conclusions.

2 Joseph Brown Ltd is a medium-sized enginering company based in the north-east of England, an area of high unemployment. It has been owned by the Brown family for the last 120 years and has recently appointed James Barratt as its new managing director. Barratt, who previously worked very successfully as general manager of a similar company owned by a large group, has been hired to rationalize the company's activities. His first task is to tackle the company's high manning levels, and he has negotiated a redundancy deal with the unions which is expected to cost £400,000, payable over the next 6 months. This will, however, result in savings in labour costs of £300,000 per year.

Financial information relating to the company is as follows:

Profit and loss account – year ending 31 December

	19X4	19X5	19X6
	£000	£000	£000
Turnover	12,430	10,874	11,450
Profit before interest and taxation	1,183	476	1,243
Term loan interest	(420)	(350)	(280)
Bank overdraft interest	(481)	(540)	(500)
Profit before taxation	282	(414)	463
Taxation	(132)	—	(15)
Profit after taxation	150	(414)	448
Dividend payable	(100)	—	—
Retained	50	(414)	448

Balance sheets at 31 December

	19X4	19X5	19X6
	£000	£000	£000
Fixed assets			
Freehold premises	4,025	4,025	4,025
Plant and equipment	3,047	3,167	3,750
	7,072	7,192	7,775
Less depreciation	3,045	3,825	4,680
	4,027	3,367	3,095

	£000	£000	£000
Current assets			
Stock	2,590	3,625	2,863
Debtors	3,065	3,277	2,980
Cash	75	—	—
	5,730	6,902	5,843
Creditors: amounts falling due in under 1 year			
Trade creditors	(1,295)	(2,175)	(1,432)
Bank overdraft	(3,700)	(4,246)	(3,710)
	(4,995)	(6,421)	(5,142)
Total assets less current liabilities	4,762	3,848	3,796
Less creditors: amounts falling due in more than 1 year – loans	3,000	2,500	2,000
	1,762	1,348	1,796
Capital and reserves			
Share capital	1,000	1,000	1,000
Reserves	762	348	796
	1,762	1,348	1,796

To meet the costs of the redundancy scheme, and to allow for reasonable fluctuations in working capital requirements, the company has decided to approach its clearing bankers with a request to extend its overdraft limit from £4 million to £4.5 million.

Notes
1   The term loan is repayable to Venture Capital Ltd in instalments of £500,000 per year. It is secured on factory premises, which have a market value of £6,000,000.
2   The overdraft, which has been obtained from the Barland National Bank, is secured by a floating charge on the company's assets.
3   The net book value of plant and equipment is £1,875,000.

Required
(a)   Calculate the following ratios from the accounts, using 19X6 figures:
    (i)   Times interest earned.
    (ii)   Debt/equity ratio.
    (iii) Acid-test ratio.
    (iv) Return on investment.
    (v)   Return on equity.
    (vi) Days' debtors.
(b)   Discuss the request for the extension to the overdraft from a banker's viewpoint. If the banker granted the request, what terms and conditions do you think he might impose?

3   Business A and Business B are both engaged in retailing, but seem to take a different approach to this trade according to the information available. This information consists of a table of ratios, shown below:

Ratio	Business A	BusinessB
Current ratio	2:1	1:5:1
Quick assets (acid–test) ratio	1.7:1	0.7:1
Return on capital employed	20%	17%
Return on owner's equity	30%	18%
Debtors' turnover	63 days	21 days
Creditors' turnover	50 days	45 days
Gross profit percentage	40%	15%
Net profit percentage	10%	10%
Stock turnover	52 days	25 days

Required

(a) Explain briefly how each ratio is calculated.

(b) Describe what this information indicates about the differences in approach between the two businesses. If one of them prides itself on personal service and one of them on competitive prices, which do you think is which and why?

4   You are given summarized results of an electrical engineering business, as follows. All figures are in £000.

Profit and loss account

	Year ended 31.12.X1	31.12.X0
Turnover	60,000	50,000
Cost of sales	42,000	34,000
Gross profit	18,000	16,000
Operating expenses	15,500	13,000
	2,500	3,000
Interest payable	2,200	1,300
Profit before taxation	300	1,700
Taxation	350	600
(Loss) profit after taxation	(50)	1,100
Dividends	600	600
Transfer (from) to reserves	(650)	500

Balance sheet

Fixed assets

Intangible	500	—
Tangible	12,000	11,000
	12,500	11,000

Current assets

Stocks	14,000	13,000
Debtors	16,000	15,000
Bank and cash	500	500
	30,500	28,500
Creditors due within 1 year	(24,000)	(20,000)
Net current assets	6,500	8,500

Total assets less current liabilities	19,000	19,500
Creditors due after 1 year	6,000	5,500
	13,000	14,000
Capital and reserves		
Share capital	1,300	1,300
Share premium	3,300	3,300
Revaluation reserve	2,000	2,000
Profit and loss	6,400	7,400
	13,000	14,000

Required

(a) Prepare a table of the following ratios, calculated for both years, clearly showing the figures used in the calculations.

  (i) current ratio
  (ii) quick assets ratio
  (iii) stock turnover in days
  (iv) debtors' turnover in days
  (v) creditors' turnover in days
  (vi) gross profit (%)
  (vii) net profit (%; before taxation)
  (viii) interest cover
  (ix) return on owner's equity
  (x) return on capital employed
  (xi) gearing

(b) Making full use of the information given in the question, of your table of ratios, and your common sense, comment on the apparent position of the business and on the actions of the management.

5 Extracts from the accounts for the year ended 30 June 19X8 of two companies appear below:

	Dover Printers Ltd	Folkestone Engineers Ltd
	£000	*£000*
Fixed assets	468	330
Current assets	580	870
	1,048	1,200
Less: Amounts due in under 1 year		
Creditors	(230)	(150)
Overdraft	(160)	(50)
Total assets less current liabilities	658	1,000
Less: Amounts due in over 1 year		
Loans	460	200
	198	800

	£000	£000
Share capital and reserves		
Ordinary share capital	80	300
Reserves (note 1)	118	500
	198	800
Profit before interest and taxation	95	165
Interest (note 2)	62	45
Profit before taxation	33	120
Taxation	12	42
Profit after taxation	21	78
Less: Ordinary dividends	10	10
Retained	11	68
Note 1: Includes revaluation reserve	—	300
Note 2: Includes overdraft interest	16	15

Required

(a) For each company, calculate the two ratios listed below. You should describe the purpose of each ratio and state to whom they are of most interest. You should include brief notes explaining your calculations.
  (i) Return on capital employed.
  (ii) Return on equity.

(b) Explain the difficulties that may be encountered when attempting to compare the performance of each company on the basis of the ratios above.

(c) Explain the term gearing and demonstrate its impact on profitability using some illustrative numbers.

6 Threads Ltd is a company which manufactures nuts and bolts which are sold to industrial users. The abbreviated accounts for 19X8 and 19X7 are given below.

Threads Ltd
Profit and loss account for the years ended 30 June

	19X8		19X7	
	£000	£000	£000	£000
Sales		1,200		1,180
Cost of sales		(750)		(680)
Gross profit		450		500
Operating expenses	(208)		(200)	
Depreciation	(75)		(66)	
Interest	(8)		(—)	
		(291)		(266)
Profit before tax		159		234
Tax		(48)		(80)
Profit after tax		111		154
Dividend – proposed		(72)		(70)
Retained profit for year		39		84

Balance sheets as at 30 June

	19X8		19X7	
	£000	*£000*	*£000*	*£000*
Fixed assets (note 1)		687		702
Current assets				
Stocks	236		148	
Debtors	156		102	
Cash	4		32	
	396		282	
Creditors (amounts due within 1 year)				
Trade creditors	(76)		(60)	
Other creditors and accruals	(16)		(18)	
Dividend	(72)		(70)	
Tax	(48)		(80)	
Bank overdraft	(26)		(—)	
	(238)		(228)	
Net current assets		158		54
Creditors (amounts due after more than 1 year)				
Bank loan (note 2)		(50)		—
		795		756
Ordinary share capital of £1 (fully paid		500		500
Retained profits		295		256
		795		756

Note 1: Fixed assets

	Buildings	Fixtures and fittings	Vehicles	Total
	£000	*£000*	*£000*	*£000*
Cost 1.7.X7	900	100	80	1,080
Purchases	—	40	20	60
Cost 30.6.X8	900	140	100	1,140
Depreciation 1.7.X7	288	50	40	378
Charge for year	36	14	25	75
Depreciation 30.6.X8	324	64	65	453
Net book value 30.6.X8	576	76	35	687

Note 2

The bank loan was taken up on 1 July 19X7 and is repayable on 1 January 19X3. It carries a fixed rate of interest of 12% per annum and is secured by a fixed and floating charge on the assets of the company.

Required

(a) Calculate the following financial statistics for *both* 19X8 and 19X7, using end of year figures where appropriate:

(i)   Return on capital employed
(ii)   Net profit margin
(iii)   Gross profit margin
(iv)   Current ratio
(v)   Liquid ratio
(vi)   Days' debtors
(vii)   Days' creditors
(viii) Stock turnover ratio

(b) Comment on the performance of Threads Ltd from the viewpoint of a company considering supplying a substantial amount of goods to Threads Ltd on usual credit terms.

(c) What action could a supplier take to lessen the risk of not being paid should Threads Ltd be in financial difficulty?

Case study: Housewarm Central Heating Supplies Plc

Housewarm Central Heating Supplies Plc (HCHS) is a business which specializes in manufacturing and marketing oil-fired domestic central heating systems. All the company's sales are made to housebuilders and plumbers. The company was established on 1 August 19X6 when three managers of United Industrial Trust Plc (UIT) negotiated a management buyout of Petersen Ltd, one of its subsidiaries. Most of the £2.5 million finance needed to fund the buyout had come from the Enterprise Finance Fund (EFF), though the managers themselves had raised between them about £500,000, mainly by second-mortgaging their homes. EFF is a consortium of City institutions which had been formed at the instigation of the government to provide finance for smaller businesses, particularly management buyouts.

Petersen Ltd had been long-established family-run heating engineers. When the last of the Petersen family died in 1973, UIT had bought the company but had not really taken very much interest in it subsequently. Throughout the period of UIT's ownership Petersen had lacked focus in its production and marketing, being a general provider of commissioned heating systems, both industrial and domestic. Petersen's high-quality workmanship had enabled the company to produce enough profit to satisfy UIT and to prevent interference from the parent company in its affairs.

The three managers involved with the buyout were James Atkinson, the production manager, Mike Wimborne, the sales manager, and Terry Pike, the chief accountant. Following the buyout, they had become the production, marketing and finance directors, respectively, with Wimborne also acting as chief executive and chairman. The membership of the board of directors was completed by the inclusion of a nominee of EFF, Arthur Peters, as a non-executive director. Peters had made it plain from the outset that neither he nor EFF was keen to interfere, provided that he was confident that EFF's investment was prospering. Generally the strategic decisions had been easy to take, since there had been little disagreement between the three executive directors as to the direction which the company should take, partly because Wimborne's strong personality and leadership qualities had influenced his more passive colleagues. Peters had been true to his word and had not sought to influence them.

Almost the first decision taken after the buyout was to focus more clearly the company's target market. In the future the company was to produce a limited range of domestic central-heating systems to be sold only to the trade, i.e. to builders and plumbers. It was also decided to have a change of company name which would reflect more the nature of the work they were to undertake.

The board recognized that competition in the supply of central heating systems had grown in recent years and were anxious to ensure that the company established a competitive edge in terms of both price and quality.

During the 3 years since the management buyout the company had succeeded in increasing its market share each year. This had been achieved through a combination of aggressive marketing and the development of a very competitive range of products. The quality of workmanship and adherence to delivery dates had created goodwill amongst customers and the order book for the forthcoming year suggested that sales turnover would reach new peaks. Although this news was pleasing, the board also recognized that the company was experiencing a number of difficulties.

The financial position and performance for each of the first 3 years following the management buyout were as follows:

Abridged accounts for the 3 years ending 31 July 19X9

Trading and profit and loss account	**19X7**	**19X8**	**19X9**
	£000	*£000*	*£000*
Sales	4,940.5	6,175.2	7,412.3
Less cost of sales	3,458.0	4,693.7	6,298.5
Gross profit	1,482.5	1,481.5	1,113.8
Less overheads	1,037.4	1,160.9	1,171.2
	445.1	320.6	(57.4)
Add income from investments	49.4	49.4	—
Net profit (loss)	494.5	370.0	(57.4)
Profit and loss appropriation account			
Net profit (loss) for the year	494.5	370.0	(57.4)
Less: Dividend	(250.0)	(150.0)	—
Corporation tax	(167.5)	(136.1)	—
Retained profit (loss)	77.0	83.9	(57.4)
Add retained profit brought forward	—	77.0	160.9
Retained profit carried forward	77.0	160.9	103.5

	19X7		19X8		19X9	
	£000	£000	£000	£000	£000	£000
Balance sheet						
Fixed assets						
Freehold land and buildings		494.5		494.5		494.5
Machinery and plant,						
net of depreciation		617.5		543.4		774.3
		1,112.0		1,037.9		1,268.8
Trade investments		294.0		294.0		—
		1,406.0		1,331.9		1,268.8
Current assets						
Stock-in-trade	637.3		938.6		1,468.6	
Sundry debtors	823.3		1,235.1		1,675.5	
Cash	451.4		336.2		—	
	1,912.0		2,509.9		3,144.1	
Less: *current liabilities*						
Sundry creditors	(741.0)		(1,180.9)		(1,729.1)	
Bank overdraft	—		—		80.3	
	(741.0)		(1,180.9)		(1,809.4)	
		1,171.0		1,329.0		1,334.7
Net assets		2,577.0		2,660.9		2,603.5
Capital and reserves						
Ordinary £1 shares		2,500.0		2,500.0		2,500.0
Retained profit		77.0		160.9		103.5
		2,577.0		2,660.9		2,603.5

The non-executive director, Arthur Peters, was becoming increasingly concerned about the dividend policy of the board. He recognized that, whilst EFF saw the company as a long-term investment, the failure to pay any dividend for the year ended 31 July 19X9 would cause EFF to take a closer interest in the company's affairs. Soon after publication of the accounts for the year ended 31 July 19X9, representatives of EFF sought a meeting with the board. The board was concerned that EFF might begin to influence strategic decisions unless confidence in the company and its future direction could be restored.

In addition, the company recently had a loan application turned down. The board had hoped to borrow £1.0 million over a 15-year period in order to finance an expansion to its existing production facilities. The company was currently utilizing its production facilities almost to the full and the board was aware that this situation could constrain future growth. The prospective lender, however, felt that the programme was too ambitious and rejected the loan application. The board was now considering whether or not to approach another lender with its expansion plans.

During the past year the company had been relying on a bank overdraft to finance its working capital requirements. The overdraft limit had been raised on three separate occasions to accommodate the company's financing needs. However, the bank was becoming increasingly uneasy about the current level of the overdraft (now standing at £92,700) and the company had been asked to reduce the overdraft over the next 6 months to a maximum of £40,000.

A meeting of the board was scheduled in order to review the current strategy of the company and to deal with what appeared to be a crisis of confidence amongst investors and lenders.

Required

(a)   Analyse the performance of Housewarm Central Heating Supplies Plc over the 3 years ended 31 July 19X9.

(b)   How might the board deal with the crisis of confidence amongst investors and lenders?

Abacus Ltd

Profit and loss account for the year ended 31 October 19X9

	£000	£000
Sales		3,200
Less cost of sales		
Opening stock	250	
Purchases	2,600	
	2,850	
Closing stock	350	
		2,500
Gross profit		700
Less operating expenses		
Selling expenses	210	
Administrative expenses	90	
Interest payable	60	
Depreciation	60	
		420
Net profit before taxation		280
Less corporation tax		70
Net profit after taxation		210

Balance sheet as at 31 October 19X9

	£000	£000	£000
Fixed assets			
Freehold land at cost			1,000
Plant and machinery at cost		1,500	
Less accumulated depreciation		600	
			900
			1,900
Current assets			
Stock		350	
Trade debtors		520	
Prepayments		30	
Cash at bank		50	
		950	

	£000	£000	£000
Creditors: amounts falling due within 1 year			
Trade creditors	380		
Corporation tax	70		
		450	
			500
Total assets less current liabilities			2,400
Creditors: amounts falling due after more than 1 year			
10% Debentures			600
			1,800
Capital and reserves			
£1 ordinary shares			600
Share premium account		200	
General reserve		680	
Profit and loss account		320	
			1,200
			1,800

Comparative ratios based on the industry average

	Abacus Ltd	Industry average
Liquidity		
Current ratio	2.11	2.2
Acid-test ratio	1.27	0.9
Gearing		
Debt/equity ratio	0.58	0.85
Debt/total assets	36.84%	38.00%
Interest coverage ratio	5.67	3.95
Cash flow coverage ratio	6.67	4.90
Activity		
Stock turnover	8.3	10.9
Period of stockholding	1.44m	1.1m
Debtors' turnover	6.15	6.3
Period of credit to debtors	1.95m	1.9m
Period of credit from suppliers	1.75m	1.8m
Fixed asset turnover ratio	1.68	1.6
Total asset turnover ratio	1.12	1.2
Profitability		
Gross profit margin	21.87%	21.0%
Net profit margin	6.56%	8.2%
Return to equity	11.67%	13.11%
Return on capital employed	14.17%	16.59%
Return on investment	7.36%	9.84%

Appendix 2

The abridged accounts for Vortex Ltd for the past 3 years are as follows:

Profit and loss accounts

	19X7		19X8		19X9	
	£000	£000	£000	£000	£000	£000
Sales		24,000		30,000		38,000
Less *Cost of sales*		15,000		22,000		30,000
Gross profit		9,000		8,000		8,000
Less Selling expenses	2,000		2,500		3,000	
Admin. expenses	1,000		1,500		1,800	
Interest payable	—		100		200	
Depreciation	800		1,200		1,500	
		3,800		5,300		6,500
Net profit before tax		5,200		2,700		1,500
Less: *corporation tax*		1,600		800		450
Net profit after tax		3,600		1,900		1,050
Less: *Dividends*		1,800		1,800		1,000
Retained profit for year		1,800		100		50

Balance sheets

	19X7		19X8		19X9	
	£000	£000	£000	£000	£000	£000
Fixed assets						
Freehold land		2,000		2,000		2,000
Plant and machinery	12,000		13,300		16,850	
Less: depreciation	4,000		5,200		6,700	
		8,000		8,100		10,150
		10,000		10,100		12,150
Current assets						
Stock	8,000		12,000		17,000	
Debtors	6,000		9,000		14,000	
Cash at bank	10,000		6,000		—	
	24,000		27,000		31,000	
Creditors: due within 1 year						
Sundry creditors	12,000		14,000		19,000	
		12,000		13,000		12,000
		22,000		23,100		24,150

Creditors: due after 1 year			
10% Debentures	—	1,000	2,000
	22,000	22,100	22,150
Capital			
Ordinary £1 shares	10,000	10,000	10,000
Reserves			
Profit and loss account	12,000	12,100	12,150
	22,000	22,100	22,150

Stock at beginning of 19X7 – £7,000

The analysis of financial statements – II

11.1 Introduction

This chapter is concerned with further aspects of financial analysis. It examines ratios which are of particular value to investors and explains how techniques such as common-size financial statements can be used in the evaluation of performance. The chapter also considers the way in which ratios may be used to predict financial distress and vulnerability to takeover.

11.2 Objectives

On completion of this chapter you should be able:

- to analyse the return on investment ratio into its component ratios and explain the significance of this form of analysis;
- to prepare common-size financial statements and explain their usefulness;
- to measure the variability of earnings;
- to calculate the major investment ratios and explain their significance.
- to explain how ratios may be used to predict financial distress and vulnerability to takeover.

11.3 Return on investment

In the last chapter the return on investment (ROI) ratio was examined. This is a primary ratio which measures the ability of the business to use its assets in a profitable way. It will be recalled that the ratio is calculated as follows:

$$\text{ROI} = \frac{\text{net profit after tax}}{\text{total assets}} \times 100$$

This ratio can be separated into two component ratios, the net profit margin and sales to total assets. Hence:

$$\frac{\text{Net profit after tax}}{\text{total assets}} = \frac{\text{net profit after tax}}{\text{sales}} \times \frac{\text{sales}}{\text{total assets}}$$

The breakdown of ROI in this way reveals that the profitable employment of assets will be determined by both the net profit margin and the efficient use of assets. This may be useful in understanding trends in ROI. To illustrate this point, consider the financial data of Alpha Plc set out below:

	19X7	**19X8**	**19X9**
Sales	£10m	£20m	£30m
Net profit after tax	£2m	£3m	£4m
Total assets	£16m	£18m	£20m
ROI	12.5%	16.6%	20%
Net profit margin	20%	15%	13.3%
Sales/total assets	0.625	1.11	1.5

These data reveal that, over the 3-year period, the net profit margin has declined. However, over the same period sales have increased at a faster rate than the increase in assets and, therefore, the sales/total assets ratio has increased. Because the increase in the sales/total assets ratio has been greater than the decrease in the net profit margin, the net effect has been that ROI over the period has increased. Thus, a decrease in net profit margins has been more than offset by more efficient use of assets.

The two component ratios can also be broken down to reveal, in detail, the factors influencing ROI. Table 11.1 shows that ROI can be influenced by changes in sales, expenses and assets.

Table 11.1 Factors influencing return on investment

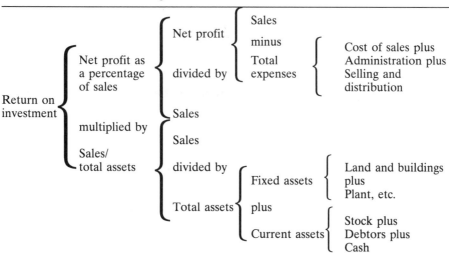

Activity 1
Beta Plc and Gamma Plc are similar businesses operating in the same industry. Extracts from their most recent accounts are set out below:

	Beta Plc	**Gamma Plc**
Sales turnover	£42m	£74m
Net profit after tax	£4m	£6m
Total assets	£28m	£30m

Do the following:

(a) Calculate ROI for each business.
(b) Analyse the ROI of each ratio into its component ratios.
(c) Discuss whether you feel ROI is sufficient for an equity shareholder to assess the profitability of the business.

Your answer to this activity should be as follows:

		Beta Plc	**Gamma Plc**
(a)	$ROI = \dfrac{\text{net profit after tax}}{\text{total assets}} \times 100$	14.29%	20.0%
(b) (i)	Net profit/sales	9.52%	8.11%
(ii)	Sales/total assets	1.5	2.47

(c) Equity shareholders will be interested in the rate of return on equity as well as return on total assets. Maximizing return on assets is not necessarily the same as maximizing returns to equity shareholders. The latter will be affected by the level of gearing the business adopts.

Activity 2
Indicate whether you would expect the component ratios of ROI to be high or low for each of the following businesses:

		Net profit margins (High/Low)	**Sales/total assets** (High/Low)
(a)	A supermarket chain		
(b)	A car manufacturer		
(c)	A petrol station		
(d)	A heavy engineering business		
(e)	A professional firm of accountants		

Your answer should be as follows:

	Net profit margins	Sales/total assets
(a) A supermarket chain	Low	High
(b) A car manufacturer	High	Low
(c) A petrol station	Low	High
(d) A heavy engineering business	High	Low
(e) A professional firm of accountants	High	High

A professional firm of accountants is likely to be different from the other types of business mentioned. The professional rules for accountants demand that they must practise as either a sole proprietor business or a partnership. In both cases, any amounts payable to the owners (who usually work in the business) will not be shown as wages in the profit and loss account but as withdrawals of capital. This, in turn, means that a higher net profit margin will be shown than if the firm operated as a limited company and the owners were drawing salaries as directors of the company. A firm of accountants is likely to have few fixed assets and no stock-in-trade. So the return on investment may well be high, particularly given that the net profit margin is likely to be high.

Activity 3

How would each of the following affect ROI?

(a) An increase in administration expenses
(b) An increase in sales (and the net profit margin remains the same)
(c) A decrease in stock levels
(d) An upward revaluation of land and buildings

Your answer should be as follows:

	Effect on ROI Increase	Decrease
(a) An increase in administration expenses		Yes
(b) An increase in sales	Yes	
(c) A decrease in stock levels	Yes	
(d) An upward revaluation of land and buildings		Yes

11.4　Common-size financial statements

Common-size financial statements relate individual figures appearing on the conventional statements to some base figure. By relating all figures to a common base it may be possible to detect trends occurring within a business over time or to make useful comparisons between similar enterprises in the same industry for a particular period of time.

One form of common size statement compares figures appearing on a conventional financial statement with a base figure taken from the same statement. This is referred to as *vertical analysis*. To illustrate this form of analysis, consider the financial data relating to Delta Plc set out below. The conventional and common-size profit and loss accounts for a 4-year period are displayed. To prepare the common-size profit and loss accounts the sales figure for each year has been set at 100 and all other figures are expressed as a percentage of the sales for the relevant year.

Delta Plc
Conventional profit and loss account for the year ending 30 June

	19X6		19X7		19X8		19X9	
	£m	£m	£m	£m	£m	£m	£m	£m
Sales		130.0		150.0		170.0		200.0
Less cost of sales		78.0		93.0		108.0		130.0
Gross profit		52.0		57.0		62.0		70.0
Wages and salaries	13.0		18.0		22.5		28.0	
Rent and rates	6.5		7.5		8.5		8.0	
Heat and light	5.2		4.5		6.8		10.0	
Depreciation	2.6		3.0		3.4		4.0	
		27.3		33.0		41.2		50.0
Net profit before tax		24.7		24.0		20.8		20.0
Taxation		13.2		6.0		6.8		8.0
Net profit after tax		11.5		18.0		14.0		12.0
Dividends		9.0		3.0		12.0		6.0
Retained profit		2.5		15.0		2.0		6.0

Common-size profit and loss account for the year ending 30 June

	19X6	19X7	19X8	19X9
	%	%	%	%
Sales	100.0	100.0	100.0	100.0
Less cost of sales	60.0	62.0	63.5	65.0
Gross profit	40.0	38.0	36.5	35.0
Wages and salaries	10.0	12.0	13.2	14.0
Rent and rates	5.0	5.0	5.0	4.0
Heat and light	4.0	3.0	4.0	5.0
Depreciation	2.0	2.0	2.0	2.0
Net profit before tax	19.0	16.0	12.3	10.0
Taxation	10.2	4.0	4.0	4.0

	%	%	%	%
Net profit after tax	8.8	12.0	8.3	6.0
Dividends	6.9	2.0	7.1	3.0
Retained profit	1.9	10.0	1.2	3.0

The common-size profit and loss accounts reveal that cost of sales, as a percentage of sales turnover, has risen steadily over the 4-year period. This has resulted in a decline in both the gross profit margins and the net profit margin. Wages as a percentage of sales turnover have also increased steadily over the 4-year period and this has contributed further to the decline in net profit margins. As can be seen, this form of analysis highlights why changes in profit margins have occurred and provides a starting point for further investigation.

Common-size balance sheets provide another useful form of analysis. By preparing such statements it is possible to see more clearly the distribution of assets held and the ways in which the enterprise is funded. The conventional and common-size balance sheets for Delta Plc for a 4-year period are set out below. To prepare the common-size balance sheets the total assets and total liabilities figures are set at 100 and individual assets and liabilities are then expressed as a percentage of the base figure.

Delta Plc
Conventional balance sheet as at 30 June

	19X6		19X7		19X8		19X9	
	£m	£m	£m	£m	£m	£m	£m	£m
Fixed assets								
Freehold land and property		25.0		25.0		25.0		25.0
Plant and equipment		40.0		44.0		48.0		60.0
Motor vehicles		20.0		21.0		22.0		22.0
		85.0		90.0		95.0		107.0
Current assets								
Stock	52.2		59.0		64.8		51.0	
Debtors	20.0		27.0		23.0		25.0	
Cash	15.0		10.0		10.0		8.0	
		87.2		96.0		97.8		84.0
		172.2		186.0		192.8		191.0
Financed by								
Share capital		70.0		70.0		70.0		70.0
Retained profit		5.0		20.0		22.0		28.0
		75.0		90.0		92.0		98.0
Creditors: due beyond 1 year								
Debentures		60.0		60.0		60.0		60.0
Creditors: due within 1 year								
Trade creditors	15.0		27.0		20.0		19.0	
Tax and dividends	22.2		9.0		20.8		14.0	
		37.2		36.0		40.8		33.0
		172.2		186.0		192.8		191.0

Common-size balance sheets as at 30 June

	19X6 %	19X7 %	19X8 %	19X9 %
Fixed assets				
Freehold land	14.5	13.4	13.0	13.1
Plant and equipment	23.2	23.7	24.9	31.4
Motor vehicles	11.6	11.3	11.4	11.5
Current assets				
Stock	30.3	31.7	33.6	26.7
Debtors	11.6	14.5	11.9	13.1
Cash	8.8	5.4	5.2	4.2
	100.0	100.0	100.0	100.0
Financed by:				
Share capital	40.7	37.6	36.3	36.6
Retained profit	2.9	10.8	11.4	14.7
Creditors: due beyond 1 year				
Debentures	34.8	32.3	31.1	31.4
Creditors: due within 1 year				
Trade creditors	8.7	14.5	10.4	10.0
Tax and dividends	12.9	4.8	10.8	7.3
	100.0	100.0	100.0	100.0

The common-size balance sheets above highlight the increasing investment in plant and equipment and the steady decline in cash over the 4-year period. These statements also reveal the growing importance of retained profit in financing the business.

It is important to recognize that a change in the percentage figure for a particular item may be due to either a change in the absolute size of the figure or a change in the size of the group of which it forms part. It is therefore important when examining common-size statements to examine also the conventional statements in order to ensure percentage changes are properly interpreted.

In the above examples, common-size statements were prepared for a single business over a 4-year period. However, common-size statements can also be prepared using data from similar businesses within the same industry. Such statements may prove useful for comparing cost structures, profit margins, sources of finance and the distribution of assets between enterprises.

The common-size statements illustrated above were based on a *vertical analysis* of the conventional financial statements, i.e. figures appearing on a particular statement were compared to a base figure taken from the same statement. However, it is also possible to prepare common-size statements based on a *horizontal analysis* of the conventional statements. This involves selecting a base year and setting all the figures appearing within the financial statements for that year at 100. Figures appearing in the financial statements of subsequent periods are then compared to the relevant figures relating to the base year. Horizontal analysis can help reveal how a business has arrived at its current position.

To illustrate this form of analysis, the conventional profit and loss accounts of Delta Plc set out above have been used as a basis to perform horizontal analysis. The appropriate common-size statements are shown below. These statements reveal that the increase in sales for the period has been less than the increase in cost of sales and therefore gross profit has not risen in line with sales. The statement also reveals the particularly high increase in wages over the 4-year period. Common-size balance sheets may also be prepared using horizontal analysis. These statements will help highlight the relative changes in assets and sources of finance over time.

Delta Plc
Common-size profit and loss accounts for the year ending 30 June

	19X6	19X7	19X8	19X9
	%	%	%	%
Sales	100	115.4	130.8	153.8
Less cost of sales	100	119.2	138.5	116.7
Gross profit	100	109.6	119.2	134.6
Wages and salaries	100	138.5	173.1	215.4
Rent and rates	100	115.4	127.8	123.1
Heat and light	100	86.5	130.8	192.3
Depreciation	100	115.4	130.8	153.8
Net profit before tax	100	97.2	84.2	81.0
Taxation	100	45.5	51.5	60.6
Net profit after tax	100	156.5	121.7	104.3
Dividends	100	33.3	133.3	66.7
Retained profit	100	600.0	80.0	240.0

Activity 4

Below are the conventional profit and loss accounts of Omega Plc for a 4-year period:

Profit and loss account for the year ended 30 September

	19X6		19X7		19X8		19X9	
	£m	£m	£m	£m	£m	£m	£m	£m
Sales		140		160		190		240
Less cost of sales		90		96		105		122
Gross profit		50		64		85		118
Administration expenses	20		28		34		43	
Selling and distribution	22		31		46		68	

Finance charges	3		3		3		3	
		45		62		83		114
Net profit		5		2		2		4

Do the following:

(a) Produce common-size profit and loss accounts for each year based on a vertical analysis of the above statements.
(b) Discuss the main points arising from an examination of these statements.

Your answer should be as follows:

(a) Common-size profit and loss accounts – vertical analysis

	19X6 %	19X7 %	19X8 %	19X9 %
Sales	100.0	100.0	100.0	100.0
Cost of sales	(64.3)	(60.0)	(55.3)	(50.8)
Gross profit	35.7	40.0	44.7	49.2
Admin. expenses	(14.3)	(17.5)	(17.9)	(17.9)
Selling expenses	(15.7)	(19.4)	(24.2)	(28.3)
Finance charges	(2.1)	(1.9)	(1.6)	(1.3)
Net profit	3.6	1.2	1.0	1.7

(b) Although the enterprise has managed to increase the gross margin substantially over the period, the benefits have not filtered through to the net profit margin. This is largely due to the fact that selling expenses as a percentage of sales have almost doubled over the 4-year period. There has also been some increase in administration expenses as a percentage of sales. Although finance charges as a percentage of sales have decreased over the period, this has not been sufficient to prevent a fall in net profit margins.

Activity 5
Refer to the conventional profit and loss accounts set out in Activity 4 above.
  Using this information:

(a) Produce common-size profit and loss accounts for each year based on a horizontal analysis of the conventional statements.
(b) Explain what additional insights these statements provide to those mentioned in Activity 4(b).

Your answer should be as folows:

(a) Common-size profit and loss accounts – horizontal analysis

	19X6	19X7	19X8	19X9
	%	%	%	%
Sales	100.0	114.3	135.7	171.4
Cost of sales	100.0	106.7	116.7	135.6
Gross profit	100.0	128.0	170.0	236.0
Admin. expenses	100.0	140.0	170.0	215.0
Selling expenses	100.0	140.9	209.1	309.1
Finance expenses	100.0	100.0	100.0	100.0
Net profit	100.0	40.0	40.0	80.0

(b) Common-size statements, based on horizontal analysis, provide information concerning changes in items over time. For Omega Plc, these statements reveal that sales have increased by more than 70% over the 4-year period whereas cost of sales have only increased by half this amount. Although finance charges have remained constant over the period, administration expenses have more than doubled and selling expenses have more than trebled.

11.5 Variability of earnings

In order to obtain some sort of 'feel' for the quality of earnings generated by a business it is useful to measure variability of earnings over time. A simple measure of earnings variability is as follows:

$$\text{Earnings variability} = \frac{\begin{array}{c}\textbf{range of earnings ratio over recent years}\\ \textbf{(i.e. highest-lowest earnings ratio)}\end{array}}{\textbf{average (mean) earnings ratio}}$$

The higher the measure of variability obtained, the greater the level of risk and, therefore, the lower the quality of earnings.

In order to illustrate the application of this measure let us look at an example. Consider the net profit to sales ratios (expressed below as decimals rather than percentages as the variability ratio is not usually expressed in percentage form) of three companies over a 5-year period:

Year	Red Ltd	Amber Ltd	Green Ltd
19X2	0.03	0.08	0.04
19X3	0.10	0.11	0.12
19X4	0.09	0.09	0.14
19X5	0.07	0.14	0.16
19X6	0.11	0.13	0.04

The earnings variability of Red Ltd can be calculated as follows:

$$\text{Earnings variability} = \frac{0.11 - 0.03}{0.08}$$

$$= \underline{\underline{1.0}}$$

This measure must be compared with the results of other companies in order to derive relative variability.

The net profit-to-sales ratio is used for illustration purposes; however, other earnings ratios could also be used.

Activity 6

Calculate the earnings variability of Amber Ltd and Green Ltd. Which of the three companies has the highest variability and which has the lowest variability of earnings? Can you think of any weaknesses of this measure?

The earnings variability of the other two companies is as follows:

	Amber Ltd	**Green Ltd**
Earnings variability =	$\dfrac{0.14 - 0.08}{0.11}$	$\dfrac{0.16 - 0.04}{1.0}$
=	$\underline{\underline{0.55}}$	$\underline{\underline{1.2}}$

From the measures derived, it can be seen that Green Ltd has the highest level of variability and Amber Ltd has the lowest variability of earnings.

Whilst this measure may be useful, it suffers from the major weakness that an extreme figure for just one period may seriously affect the measure of earnings variability even though earnings may vary little in other periods. Thus, the measure may not provide a truly representative picture.

11.6   Investment ratios

In addition to the ratios discussed in the preceding chapter, there are certain ratios designed specifically for the investor. These ratios provide measures of return and coverage which may help in deciding whether to buy, hold or sell shares in a particular business. To show how these ratios are calculated, the financial data of Phi Plc, set out below, will be used. It will be seen that some of the ratios discussed employ the market value of equity shares in their calculation. This means that the application of these ratios is normally confined to businesses whose shares are traded on a stock market.

Phi Plc
Abridged profit and loss account for the year ended 31 October 19X9

	£m
Sales	<u>200</u>
Net profit before taxation	100
Less corporation tax	<u>35</u>
Net profit after taxation	65
Dividends paid	<u>30</u>
Retained profit for the year	<u>35</u>

Abridged balance sheet as at 31 October 19X9

	£m
Net assets	<u>122</u>
Financed by:	
Share capital and reserves	
200 million ordinary shares of 25p	50
Retained profit	<u>57</u>
	107
Creditors due beyond 1 year	
10% Debentures	<u>15</u>
	122

At 31 October 19X9 the ordinary shares of Phi Plc were quoted at £2.50 each on the Stock Exchange.

Dividends per share

This ratio relates the dividends announced each year to the number of shares issued, to obtain a figure of the dividends which relate to each share. The ratio is calculated as follows:

$$\textbf{Dividends per share} = \frac{\textbf{Ordinary share dividends}}{\textbf{Number of ordinary shares issued}}$$

For Phi Plc the dividends per share are calculated as follows:

$$\frac{£30m}{200m} = 15p \text{ per share}$$

Dividend yield

This ratio relates the dividends announced during the year to the market value of the shares. In effect, the ratio measures the cash return the investor will receive on his/her investment. The ratio is calculated as follows:

$$\textbf{Dividend yield} = \frac{\textbf{dividends per share}}{\textbf{market price per share}} \times \textbf{100}$$

As was shown above, the dividends per share for Phi Plc are 15p. The dividend yield is therefore:

$$\frac{15p}{£2.50} \times 100 = \underline{6\%}$$

This yield can be compared with the yields obtained from alternative investment opportunities.

It is important to bear in mind that the total returns from an investment in shares is made up of two elements: the cash dividend and the increase (decrease) in share price. A company may have a low dividend yield because it ploughs back profit to strengthen its financial position further. However, this, in turn, should result in high future share price growth.

Dividends from UK businesses are distributed net of taxation. However, returns from other forms of investment are often shown on a pre-tax basis. To compare the returns from dividends with other forms of investment it is therefore useful to calculate the gross value of the dividend. Assuming a standard rate of taxation of 25%, the net dividend will represent 75% (i.e. 100% − 25%) of the gross dividend.

To 'gross up' the net dividend of Phi Plc the following calculation is required.

$$6\% \times \frac{100}{75} = \underline{8\%}$$

Dividend cover

This ratio relates the dividends announced during the year to the profit available for dividend in that year. The ratio may be useful in assessing the ability of the business to maintain its existing level of dividends. The dividend cover ratio is calculated as follows:

$$\textbf{Dividend cover} = \frac{\textbf{profits for year available for dividends}}{\textbf{dividends announced for the year}}$$

For Phi Plc the profit available for dividend to ordinary shareholders is the net profit after taxation. (If Phi had issued preference shares, the preference share dividend would also have to be deduced in arriving at the profit available for dividend to ordinary shareholders.) The ratio is therefore:

$$\frac{£65m}{£30m} = \underline{£2.17}$$

This means that for every £1 of dividend, Phi has generated £2.17 in profits to cover it. Thus, profits would have to fall substantially before the current level of dividend would not be covered.

Earnings per share

The earnings per share (EPS) ratio is a widely used measure of performance. This ratio relates the profits available for dividend to ordinary shareholders to the number of ordinary shares issued. It is calculated as follows:

$$\text{EPS} = \frac{\textbf{profits for year available for dividend to ordinary shareholders}}{\textbf{number of ordinary shares issued}}$$

EPS represents the profits attributable to each share. In some cases, a business may report an increase in profits as a result of an injection of fresh capital in the form of ordinary shares. If, however, the growth in profits is less than the growth in ordinary shares the effect will be to decrease EPS. Hence, equity shareholders are unlikely to be pleased, even though profits have risen. For Phi Plc the EPS ratio is:

$$\frac{£65m}{200m} = \underline{32.5p}$$

Earnings yield ratio

This ratio relates the earnings per share to the market price per share. It is calculated as follows:

$$\text{Earnings yield} = \frac{\textbf{EPS}}{\textbf{market price per share}} \times \textbf{100}$$

For Phi Plc the earnings yield is:

$$\frac{32.5p}{£2.50} \times 100 = \underline{13\%}$$

The earnings yield represents an alternative measure of return to the dividend yield discussed earlier. The dividend yield focuses on the cash return to investors and will be influenced by the dividend policies of the particular business. The earnings yield, on the other hand, compares the total profits attributable to each share to the market price per share and is unaffected by the dividend policies of the particular business.

Price earnings ratio

The price earnings (P/E) ratio also relates the earnings per share to the market price per share. The ratio is calculated as follows:

$$\text{P/E ratio} = \frac{\text{market price of ordinary shares}}{\text{EPS}}$$

For Phi Plc the P/E ratio is:

$$\frac{£2.50}{32.5\text{p}} = \underline{7.69}$$

The significance of this ratio lies in the fact that share prices normally reflect investors' expectations concerning future earnings. Thus, by comparing share price (which reflects expected future earnings) to current earnings a measure of future growth prospects is obtained. The higher the P/E ratio, the greater will be investors' expectations concerning future growth (other things being equal). Thus, differences in P/E ratios between businesses will reflect differences in investor perceptions concerning the growth prospects of each enterprise.

Activity 7
Below are extracts from the *Financial Times* share information service.

Financial Times Tuesday 17 March 19X7
19X6/7 Hotels and caterers

High	Low	Stock	Price	+/–	Div. net	Cover	Y'ld Gr's	P/E
229	81	Friendly Hotels 10p	224	–2	0.7	3.1	0.4	10.2
608	332	Grand Metrop 50p	485	–4	10.25	2.7	3.0	14.4
810	440	Lond. Park Hotels	809	+10	10.0	2.8	1.7	24.6
79¼	48	Queens Moat 5p	79	—	1.33	2.3	2.4	20.8
405	348	Savoy 'A' 10p	400	+1	3.5	6.9	1.2	15.7
88	57	Stakis 10p	84	+4	1.4	3.0	2.3	18.5
226½	140	Trusthouse Forte	217	–2	6.0	1.8	3.9	17.5

Answer each of the following:

(a) Explain what you think each column represents
(b) Identify which company has:
    (i) the highest cover for its dividends
    (ii) the best cash return on investment
    (iii) the best growth prospects

Your answer to this activity should be as follows:

(a) High   The highest share price achieved during the year (in pence – unless otherwise indicated)

     Low   The lowest share price achieved during the year (in pence – unless otherwise indicated)

     Stock   The name of the listed company and the par value of the share

     Price   The price at which shares are currently being traded at the close of business

     +/–   The change in share price from the previous price at which shares were traded at the previous day's close of business

     Div. net The net dividend per share (in pence – unless otherwise indicated)

     Cover   The dividend cover

     Y'ld Gr's The gross dividend yield

     P/E   The price/earnings ratio

(b) (i)   Savoy A

     (ii) Trusthouse Forte

     (iii) Lon. Park Hotels

Self-assessment question 11.1

Conday and Co. Ltd have been in operation for 3 years and produce antique reproduction furniture for the export market. The most recent set of accounts for the company are set out below:

Balance sheet as at 30 November 19X0

	£000	£000	£000
Fixed assets			
Freehold land and buildings at cost			228
Plant and machinery at cost		942	
Less: Accumulated depreciation		180	762
			990
Current assets			
Stocks		600	
Trade debtors		820	
		1420	
Less: Creditors: amounts falling due within 1 year			
Trade creditors	665		
Taxation	95		
Bank overdraft	385	1145	275
			1265

	£000
Less: Creditors: amounts falling due in more than 1 year	
12% Debentures (see Note 1)	200
	1065
Capital and reserves	
Ordinary shares of £1 each	700
Retained profits	365
	1065

Profit and loss account for the year ended 30 November 19X0

	£000	£000
Sales		2600
Less: Cost of sales		1620
Gross profit		980
Less: Selling and distribution expenses		
(see Note 2)	408	
Administration expenses	174	
Finance expenses	78	660
Net profit before taxation		320
Corporation tax		95
Net profit after taxation		225
Proposed dividend		160
Retained profit for the year		65

Notes
1 The debentures are secured on the freehold land and buildings.
2 Selling and distribution expenses include £170,000 in respect of bad debts.

An investor has been approached by the company to invest £200,000 by purchasing ordinary shares in the company at £6.40 each. The company wishes to use the funds to finance a programme of further expansion.

Required:
(a) Analyse the financial position and performance of the company and comment on any features you consider to be significant.
(b) State, with reasons, whether or not the investor should invest in the company on the terms outlined.

The answer to this question can be found at the end of the book.

11.7 Financial distress prediction

Increasing attention has been paid in recent years to testing the usefulness of financial ratios for decision-making. As decision-making involves predicting the future, it can be argued that the usefulness of ratios rests on their predictive ability. One area in which the usefulness of ratios has been tested is in predicting financial distress. This is an extremely important area to all those connected with the business. When a business is in financial difficulties investors, lenders, employees, suppliers and customers may all suffer loss.

In order to see whether financial ratios could help predict financial distress, Beaver (1966) matched 79 US businesses which failed during the period 1954–64 with similar businesses in the same industry which did not fail during that period. For each business he calculated 30 separate ratios for each of the 5 years *prior* to failure and then computed the means (averages) of each ratio for the failed group of businesses and the non-failed group. He found that there was a substantial difference, generally, in the behaviour of the mean ratios of each group. He summarized his findings thus:

> *The ratio distributions of non-failed firms are quite stable throughout the 5 years before failure. The ratio distributions of the failed firms exhibit a marked deterioration as failure approaches. The result is a widening gap between the failed and non-failed firms. The gap produces persistent differences in the mean ratios of failed and non-failed firms, and the difference increases as failure approaches (p. 101).*

Beaver recognized that differences in the mean ratios may be caused by a few extreme observations within either of the groups. He, therefore, ranked each ratio according to size to see whether it could successfully discriminate between failed and non-failed businesses. (When ranking liquidity ratios, for example, it may be expected that failed businesses would be ranked lower than non-failed businesses.) Beaver found that some ratios predicted failure better than others. A ratio of cash flow to total debt appeared to discriminate extremely successfully between failed and non-failed enterprises throughout the 5 years prior to failure, whereas liquidity ratios (somewhat surprisingly) did not perform well.

One problem with the approach adopted by Beaver is that it examines each ratio individually. Thus, one ratio might predict failure whereas another might not. In order to avoid possible conflicts of this nature attempts have been made to combine ratios in such a way that a single index or score is produced which will point to either failure or non-failure. However, in the absence of any theory of financial distress it is difficult to determine which ratios should be combined or how they might be combined. Thus, researchers have had to rely largely on trial and error.

In the UK Taffler (1983) has shown how a *z-score model* may be used to predict financial distress. (The work of Taffler has been based on the earlier work of Altman (1968) in the US.) The z-score of a business is derived by calculating four key ratios, attaching weights to each ratio, and then adding together the weighted ratios. If the z-score is greater than 0 this means the enterprise is solvent and will not fail in the forthcoming year. If, on the other hand, the z-score is less than 0 the business is considered 'at risk' which, according to Taffler, means a more than 50/50 chance of failure at some future time.

Taffler states that separate z-score models are required for quoted manufacturing, quoted distribution and privately owned companies because of their differing financial structures. The z-score model for quoted manufacturing businesses, which is broadly similar to the other models, is as follows:

$$Z = C_0 + C_1 \frac{PBT}{CL} + C_2 \frac{CA}{TL} + C_3 \frac{CL}{TA} + C_4 NCI$$

where:

Z	= the Z score
C_0	= a constant
$C_1 - C_4$	= the ratio weights
PBT	= profit before tax
CL	= current liabilities
TL	= total liabilities
TA	= total assets
NCI	= no-credit interval, i.e. $\dfrac{\text{liquid current assets}}{\text{daily operating expenses}}$

The no-credit internal ratio reveals how long, in days, the enterprise can finance its operations in the event of a complete cessation of revenues. It is, therefore, a liquidity ratio for extreme circumstances.

Although a negative z-score indicates a business is at risk, it does not necessarily mean the business will fail. According to Taffler, failure will depend on how bad the z-score is, how many years the z-score has persisted, and the trend in the z-score. Taffler claims the z-score model works extremely well and provides z-score information to clients on a commercial basis. The ratio weights for the model are not made publicly available by Taffler and must usually be purchased in order to make the model operational.

Activity 8
How might each of the following groups use the z-score of a particular business?

(a)   Shareholders
(b)   Trade creditors
(c)   Management
(d)   Customers
(e)   Auditors of the business

Shareholders may use z-scores to provide an early-warning signal of failure. (If shares are traded on the stock market, however, it is likely that share prices will reflect any financial difficulties a business is experiencing.) The z-scores will be useful in assessing the degree of risk attached to the investment.

Trade creditors will be interested in using z-scores to assess the credit-worthiness of a business. It may be useful in establishing the degree of risk associated with the credit allowed and in establishing the terms and conditions of trade credit.

Management have a general interest in the position and performance of the business relative to similar enterprises in the same industry. A poor z-score may prompt management into taking corrective action. This may involve restricting the business or seeking a suitable business with which to merge.

Customers may be interested in the continuity of future supplies. A poor z-score may prompt customers to seek alternative sources of supplies. Where the customer is another business, it may be prepared to offer financial help or to take over the supplier business, particularly if it is the sole supplier of important items.

Auditors must satisfy themselves that the accounts of the enterprise show a true and fair view. Usually accounts are prepared on the basis that the business is a going concern. If, however, the z-scores suggest the impending failure of the business, the auditors may feel the accounts should not be prepared according to the going concern convention. As a result assets may be valued at realizable values rather than acquisition values (less any amounts written off).

Activity 9
Should z-scores be publicly available? What are the advantages and disadvantages of publishing z-scores for enterprises with negative z-scores?

Z-scores are based on ratios which, in turn, are based on publicly available accounting information. Hence, it is difficult to argue that z-scores should not be published. It has been shown above that various groups may find z-scores useful for decision-making purposes. However, there is a danger that poor z-scores will become a self-fulfilling prophecy, i.e. because z-scores are poor, lines of credit and investment will be withdrawn from the business which will result in its financial collapse.

11.8   Financial ratios and vulnerability to takeover

Another area in which financial ratios have been widely used has been in explaining or predicting vulnerability to takeover by a predator company. One such study has been carried out in the UK by Barnes (1990). This study matched 92 companies taken over during the period 1986–87 with companies in the same industry and of similar size which were not taken over. Barnes found that, using the following five ratios, it was possible to obtain a 68.48% level of accuracy in classifying companies between takeover target and non-takeover target companies:

- Return on equity
- Gross profit margin before tax
- Net profit margin after tax
- Current ratio
- Acid-test ratio

As you can see, the study suggests profitability and liquidity ratios provide the key to explaining vulnerability to takeover.

Activity 10

Why do you think each of the five ratios identified above may be useful in identifying a takeover target?

In answering this activity you may have thought of the following:

- *Return on equity*. A poor return on equity may attract the interest of another company because the managers of the predator company may feel the target company is not fully exploiting profitable opportunities and that they could do a better job. A high return, on the other hand, would make a company a more difficult target as shareholders of that company may not feel a predator company could match or improve profitability.
- *Gross profit margin before tax*. Profit may indicate an ability to generate cash and to meet maturing obligations as they arise. Thus, a relatively low margin may be a sign of financial weakness whereas a high margin may suggest a strong independent company which can survive as a separate entity. However, this need not always be the case. Some companies may deliberately adopt a lower profit margin in order to increase sales demand.
- *Net profit margin after tax*. As we saw earlier, a company with high profitability will mean it is more difficult for a predator company to convince shareholders of the target company that a takeover is in their interests. Moreover, if profits after tax are high, the company will also have profits available to distribution. A predator company may find it difficult to match a high dividend policy adopted by the target company. However, there is a counterargument which states that high profit margins can actually attract predators, thereby making the company more vulnerable to takeover. Thus, the reliability of this measure in predicting takeovers may be affected by these conflicting forces.
- *Current ratio*. The liquidity of a business, as mentioned earlier, provides a measure of ability to meet short-term obligations. A company with liquid-

ity problems may require outside funding and thereby be more vulnerable to takeover. The current ratio, however, may not be a very reliable measure of liquidity as stocks are regarded as liquid assets, which is not always the case. A high level of stocks may simply indicate a high number of slow-moving and obsolete items being held.

- *Acid-test ratio*. This is a more stringent test of liquidity as stocks are excluded from the calculation. However, there can be problems in interpreting this ratio in so far that a high debtors figure (resulting in a high acid-test ratio) may indicate poor credit control and a low creditors figure (also resulting in a high acid-test ratio) may indicate that suppliers are unwilling to provide credit on normal industry terms.

In the USA, Wansley, Roenfelt and Cooley (1983) developed a multivariate model to explain and predict vulnerability to takeover. The sample was based on 44 companies that were taken over during the period 1975–76 and a further 44 companies randomly selected from the population of companies which had the same year end dates as the companies acquired. The variables used in the model were:

- P/E ratio
- Market value of equity to total assets
- Compound growth in net sales
- Long-term debt to total assets
- Natural log of net sales (in millions)

Using these variables it was possible to obtain a 75% level of accuracy overall in classifying companies between takeover and non-takeover targets. It is interesting to note that the size of the companies was seen as an important variable in this particular study.

Perhaps the most interesting part of the study was the second stage, which used the multivariate model developed to predict from a sample of 754 companies which were most likely to be taken over. Although, during the time period under review (1977–78), none of those identified by the models as having a high likelihood of being taken over were actually taken over, the researchers found that it was possible to make higher than normal returns by investing in those companies which were identified as acquisition targets.

11.9 Summary

This chapter has dealt with various aspects of financial analysis. It began by analysing the ROI ratio in rather more detail, and identifying the factors which can influence ROI. We have seen how profitability and productivity ratios interact to produce a measure of ROI for a business. We have examined common-size financial statements, using both vertical and horizontal methods, and seen how they can assist in analysing and interpreting results.

In order to try to assess the quality of earnings generated, a measure of earnings variability can be calculated. We have examined one such measure and the weakness of this measure has been discussed. Ratios have been discussed which relate specifically to the investor and which are widely quoted in financial journals and newspapers. Most of these ratios have particular relevance to those companies whose shares are traded on a Stock Exchange. All of the techniques examined in this chapter should provide further insights into the performance of a business, and can be used in conjunction with the ratios discussed in Chapter 12.

The chapter concludes with an examination of the use of ratios in predicting financial distress and company takeovers.

References

Altman E.I. Financial ratios, discriminant analysis and the prediction of corporate bankruptcy. *Journal of Finance* September 1968 pp 589–609.

Barnes P. The prediction of takeover targets in the UK by means of multiple discriminant analysis. *Journal of Business Finance and Accounting* Spring 1990.

Beaver W.H. Financial ratios as predictors of failure. *Empirical Research in Accounting: Selected Studies* 1966 pp 71–111.

Taffler R.J. The z-score approach to measuring company solvency. *The Accountants Magazine* March 1983 pp 91–96.

Wansley J., Roenfelt R. and Cooley P. Abnormal returns from merger profiles. *Journal of Financial and Quantitative Analysis* June 1983 pp 149–162.

Exercises

1 Rose Ltd operates a small chain of retail shops which sell high-quality teas and coffees. Approximately half of sales are on credit. Abbreviated and unaudited accounts are given below.

Rose Ltd
Profit and loss accounts for the years ended 31 March

	19X0		19X9	
	£000	£000	£000	£000
Sales		12,080		7,800
Cost of sales		6,282		4,370
Gross profit		5,798		3,430
Labour costs	2,658		2,106	
Depreciation	625		450	
Other operating costs (note 1)	1,003		92	
		4,286		2,648
Net profit before interest		1,512		782
Interest payable		66		—

	£000	£000
Net profit before tax	1,446	782
Tax payable	259	158
Net profit after tax	1,187	624
Dividend payable	300	250
Retained profit for year	887	374
Retained profit brought forward	872	498
Retained profit carried forward	1,759	872

Balance sheets as at 31 March

	19X0		19X9	
	£000	£000	£000	£000
Fixed assets (note 2)		2,728		1,536
Current assets				
Stocks	1,583		925	
Debtors	996		488	
Cash	26		312	
	2,605		1,725	
Creditors: amounts due within 1 year				
Trade creditors	(1,118)		(660)	
Other creditors	(417)		(321)	
Tax	(259)		(158)	
Dividends	(300)		(250)	
Overdraft	(180)		—	
Net current assets		331		336
Creditors: amounts due after more than 1 year				
Secured loan (1995)		(300)		—
		2,759		1,872
Share capital (50p shares, fully paid)		750		750
Share premium		250		250
Retained profit		1,759		872
		2,759		1,872

Note 1

The other operating costs include profit on sale of fixed assets of £20,000.

Note 2: Schedule of fixed assets

	Short leasehold	**Fixtures and fittings**	**Motor vehicles**	**Total**
	£000	£000	£000	£000
Cost				
At 1.4.X9	1,198	1,155	560	2,913
Disposals	—	—	(210)	(210)
Additions	947	780	120	1,847
	2,145	1,935	470	4,550

	£000	£000	£000	£000
Depreciation				
At 1.4.X9	547	558	272	1,377
Disposals	—	—	(180)	(180)
Charge for year	329	178	118	625
At 31.3.X0	876	736	210	1,822
Net book value				
at 31.3.X0	1,269	1,199	260	2,728

Required

(a) Calculate the following financial statistics for Rose Ltd for both 19X0 and 19X9, using end of year figures where possible.

    (i)   Return on capital employed.

    (ii)   Return on shareholders' funds.

    (iii)   Dividend per share.

    (iv)   Earnings per share.

    (v)   Net profit margin.

    (vi)   Gross profit margin.

    (vii)   Current ratio.

    (viii) Liquid ratio.

    (ix)   Days' debtors.

    (x)   Days' creditors.

    (xi)   Stock turnover.

(b) Comment on the performance of Rose Ltd from the viewpoint of:

    (i)   a shareholder with a 5% holding who believes that Rose Ltd will announce a rights issue in the near future.

    (ii)   the bank which has given Rose Ltd its current overdraft facility.

2   The following financial statements for Blackstone Plc are a slightly simplified set of published accounts. Blackstone Plc is an engineering firm, which developed a new range of products in 19X9; these now account for 60% of turnover.

Blackstone Plc
Profit and loss account for the year ended 31 March 19X1

	Notes	19X1 £000	19X0 £000
Turnover		11,205	7,003
Cost of sales		(5,809)	(3,748)
Gross profit		5,396	3,255
Operating expenses	1	(3,087)	(2,205)
Operating profit		2,309	1,050
Interest payable		(456)	(216)
Profit before taxation		1,853	834
Taxation		(390)	(210)
Profit after taxation		1,463	624
Dividends		(400)	(300)

	£000	£000
Retained profit for the year	1,063	324
Retained profit brought forward	685	361
Retained profit carried forward	1,748	685

Balance sheet as at 31 March 19X1

	Notes	19X1 £000	19X1 £000	19X0 £000	19X0 £000
Fixed assets					
Intangible assets	2	700		—	
Tangible assets	3	7,535		4,300	
			8,235		4,300
Current assets					
Stocks		2,410		1,209	
Trade debtors		1,372		807	
Other debtors		201		134	
Cash		4		28	
		3,987		2,178	
Creditors: Amounts falling due within 1 year					
Trade creditors		1,306		607	
Other creditors		201		124	
Taxation		390		210	
Dividends		400		300	
Overdraft		1,625		—	
		(3,922)		(1,241)	
Net current assets			65		937
Creditors: Amounts falling due after more than 1 year					
Bank loan (repayable 19X5)			(3,800)		(1,800)
			4,500		3,437
Share capital	4		1,800		1,800
Share premium			600		600
Capital reserve			352		352
Retained profits			1,748		685
			4,500		3,437

Notes to the accounts

1   Operating costs include the following items:

	£000
Exceptional items	503
Depreciation	1,251
Administrative expenses	527
Marketing expenses	785

2   Intangible assets represents the amounts paid for the goodwill of another engineering business acquired during the year.

3   The movements in tangible fixed assets during the year are set out below.

	Land and buildings £000	Plant and machinery £000	Fixtures and fittings £000	Total £000
Cost				
At 1 April 19X0	4,500	3,850	2,120	10,470
Additions	—	2,970	1,608	4,578
Disposals	—	(365)	(216)	(581)
At 31 March 19X1	4,500	6,455	3,512	14,467
Depreciation				
At 1 April 19X0	1,275	3,080	1,815	6,170
Charge for year	225	745	281	1,251
Disposals	—	(305)	(184)	(489)
At 31 March 19X1	1,500	3,520	1,912	6,932
Net book value at				
31 March 19X1	3,000	2,935	1,600	7,535

Proceeds from the sale of fixed assets in the year ended 31 March 19X1 amounted to £54,000.

4   Share capital comprises 3,600,000 fully paid ordinary shares of 50p each.

Required:
1   Calculate the following financial statistics for Blackstone Plc, using year end figures where possible, for both 19X0 and 19X1.

   (a)   Return on capital employed;
   (b)   Return on shareholders' funds;
   (c)   Gross profit margin;
   (d)   Net profit margin;
   (e)   Gearing ratio (total debt/total equity);
   (f)   Current ratio;
   (g)   Liquid ratio (acid-test ratio);
   (h)   Days' debtors;
   (i)   Days' creditors;
   (j)   Stock turnover.

2   Comment on the performance of Blackstone Plc, using the published financial statements and the information prepared in 1 above, from the viewpoint of:

   (a)   an individual who owns 10% of the issued share capital;
   (b)   the bank which has granted Blackstone Plc its overdraft facility.

3 The financial statements for Harridges Ltd. are given below for the 2 years ended 30 June 19X6 and 19X7. Harridges Ltd. operates a department store in the centre of a small town.

Profit and loss account for the year ending 30 June

	19X7 £000	19X7 £000	19X6 £000	19X6 £000
Sales		3,500		2,600
Cost of sales		2,350		1,560
Gross profit		1,150		1,040
Expenses: Wages and salaries	350		320	
Overheads	200		260	
Depreciation	250		150	
		800		730
Operating profit		350		310
Interest payable		50		50
Profit before taxation		300		260
Taxation		125		105
Profit after taxation		175		155
Dividend proposed		75		65
Profit retained for the year		100		90

Balance sheet as at 30 June

	19X7 £000	19X7 £000	19X6 £000	19X6 £000
Fixed assets (note 1)		1,525		1,265
Current assets				
Stock	400		250	
Debtors	145		105	
Bank	115		380	
	660		735	
Creditors: amounts falling due within 1 year				
Trade creditors	(300)		(235)	
Dividend	(75)		(65)	
Other	(110)		(100)	
Net current assets		175		335
Total assets less current liabilities		1,700		1,600
Creditors: amounts falling due after more than 1 year				
10% loan stock (19X8)		(500)		(500)
		1,200		1,100

Capital and reserves	£000	£000
Share capital: £1 shares fully paid	490	490
Share premium	260	260
Profit and loss account	450	350
	1,200	1,100

Note 1: Fixed assets schedule

	Freehold property* £000	Fixtures and fittings £000	Motor vehicles £000	Total £000
Cost or valuation				
At 1.7.X6	905	620	80	1,605
Additions	—	480	30	510
Disposals	—	—	(20)	(20)
At 30.6.X7	905	1,100	90	2,095
Depreciation				
At 1.7.X6	—	300	40	340
Disposals	—	—	(20)	(20)
Charge for year	—	220	30	250
At 30.6.X7	—	520	50	570
Net book value	905	580	40	1,525

*The freehold property is the department store operated by Harridges Ltd which was valued at £905,000 in June 19X2. The directors consider the property to be worth at least this amount at June 19X7.

Required:

(a) Choose and calculate eight ratios which would be helpful in assessing the performance of Harridges Ltd. Use end-year values and calculate for 19X6 and 19X7.

(b) Using the ratios calculated in (a) above and any others you consider helpful, comment on the performance of Harridges Ltd from the viewpoint of a prospective purchaser of a majority of the shares of Harridges.

4   The following financial statements for Xenith Plc are based upon the financial statements of a UK company in the form in which they were published. The main activity of Xenith Plc is home retailing whereby customers can order, from a series of catalogues, goods which are delivered to their homes. Customers usually pay for the goods over a period of 3 or 6 months.

Xenith Plc
Group profit and loss account for the year ended 31 March 19X2

Note		19X2	19X1
		£000	£000
	Turnover	140,166	126,568
	Cost of sales	68,277	62,965
	Gross profit	71,889	63,603
	Distribution costs	(14,320)	(12,239)
	Sales and administration expenses	(38,109)	(33,897)
	Operating profit	19,460	17,467
	Interest payable	(5,651)	(5,250)
	Income from listed investments	205	301
	Profit on ordinary activities before taxation	14,014	12,518
1	Taxation on ordinary activities	(4,414)	(4,184)
	Profit on ordinary activities after taxation	9,600	8,334
	Extraordinary items	—	70
	Profit for the year	9,600	8,264
	Dividends	(3,572)	(3,261)
	Retained profit	6,028	5,003

Group balance sheet at 31 March 19X2

Note		19X2	19X1
		£000	£000
	Fixed assets		
2	Tangible assets	25,314	10,591
	Investments	1,797	1,907
	Current assets		
	Stocks	23,948	20,249
	Trade debtors	63,078	54,632
3	Other debtors	5,697	4,559
	Cash at bank and in hand	2,445	472
		95,168	79,912
4	Creditors: amounts falling due within 1 year	33,219	30,517
	Net current assets	61,949	49,395
	Total assets less current liabilities	89,060	61,893
5	Creditors: amounts falling due after more than 1 year	48,028	35,065
6	Provisions for liabilities and charges	894	—
		40,138	26,828
	Capital and reserves		
	Called-up share capital (10p shares)	6,446	6,021
	Share premium account	7,881	867
7	Revaluation reserve	3,168	3,278

	£000	£000
8 Other reserves	1,884	1,931
Profit and loss account	20,759	14,731
	40,138	26,828

Notes to the accounts

1 The amount of tax actually paid in the year ended 31 March 19X2 was £4,031.

2 Schedule of tangible fixed assets

	Freehold property	Long leasehold property	Equipment and motor vehicles	Total
	£000	£000	£000	£000
At cost or valuation				
At 1.4.X1	6,337	143	7,846	14,326
Additions	3,619	48	13,710	17,377
Disposals	—	—	(2,167)	(2,167)
At 31.3.X2	9,956	191	19,389	29,536
Accumulated depreciation				
At 1.4.X1	98	27	3,610	3,735
Charge for the year	32	5	890	927
Disposals	—	—	(440)	(440)
At 31.3.X2	130	32	4,060	4,222
Net book value at 31.3.X2	9,826	159	15,329	25,314

During the year ended 31 March 19X2 the proceeds from fixed assets disposals amounted to £1,957,000.

3 Other debtors at 31 March 19X1 included an amount for recoverable advance corporation tax of £263,000. During the year ended 31 March 19X2 this amount has been written off against the deferred taxation provision.

4 Creditors falling due within 1 year include:

	19X2	19X1
	£000	£000
Bank loans and overdrafts	1,732	3,872
Trade creditors	17,072	13,836
Current taxation	3,474	4,248
Other creditors	8,362	6,348
Proposed dividend	2,579	2,213
	33,219	30,517

5 Creditors falling due after more than 1 year comprise bank loans which are repayable between 2 and 5 years.

6 Provisions for liabilities and charges comprise the provision for deferred taxation only.

7 Reserves

	Revaluation reserve £000	**Other reserves** £000
Balance at 1.X.91	3,278	1,931
Deficit on revaluation of listed investments	(110)	
Goodwill purchased and written off		(47)
Balance at 31.3.X2	3,168	1,884

8 Five-year review

	Turnover £m	**Pre-tax profit** £m	**Earnings per share** p
19X8	73.4	9.2	11.5
19X9	100.5	13.5	15.8
19X0	107.7	6.1	7.1
19X1	126.6	12.5	To be
19X2	140.2	14.0	calculated

Required:

1 Calculate the following financial statistics for Xenith Plc for both 19X2 and 19X1, using year end figures where possible.
   (a) Return on capital employed
   (b) Earnings per share
   (c) Gross profit margin
   (d) Net profit margin
   (e) Gearing ratio
   (f) Current ratio
   (g) Liquid ratio
   (h) Days' debtors
   (i) Days' creditors
   (j) Stock turnover

2 Using the financial statements and the data that you have prepared in answer to question 1 above, comment on the performance of Xenith Plc from the viewpoint of:
   (a) a shareholder who owns 0.1% of the issued share capital (you should be aware that the board of directors of Xenith Plc have recently announced their intention of raising £16m by a rights issue);
   (b) a bank which has made a substantial medium-term loan to Xenith Plc.

12

The accounting framework and value measurement

12.1 Introduction

The accounting conventions suffer from a number of weaknesses which undermine their usefulness. This has led to attempts to develop a conceptual framework in order to place accounting on a sounder footing. The nature of a conceptual framework is examined in this chapter and its potential usefulness assessed. In addition, this chapter examines the major proposals to deal with the effect of changing prices in financial reports.

This chapter should be seen in the context of the last of five chapters on analysis and interpretation. Its aim is to review the framework on which accounting statements are built and to identify both the strengths and weaknesses of accounting information. This should make you more able to interpret accounting information and to search out additional information where appropriate.

12.2 Objectives

At the end of this chapter you should be able to:

- discuss the problems associated with the major conventions of accounting;
- explain the purpose of a conceptual framework and discuss the problems in deriving a workable conceptual framework for accounting;
- explain the major approaches to dealing with the price-level problem in accounting and identify the strengths and weaknesses of each price-level accounting method.

12.3 Derivation of the traditional framework

The conventions of accounting which provide the framework in which accounting is practised, virtually throughout the world, have evolved as they have in order to satisfy a need. An analogy is language. Living languages have developed, new words have been introduced and redundant words fallen into disuse as the need has arisen or receded. For example, the word 'television' has been introduced to meet a need to refer to a phenomenon which only started to exist relatively recently. Language provides a good analogy for accounting since accounting can itself be seen as a kind of language. This is because it is a means of collecting, storing, analysing and communicating information, albeit information of a particular type.

Accounting, as it is currently practised, is undoubtedly found to be useful by most users. However, the fact that it has emerged from practice, rather than being the result of a thoroughgoing assessment of what framework would be most useful, may have led to the fact that in some aspects it is less useful than it might otherwise be.

12.4   A review of the conventions of accounting

The principal conventions which provide the framework on which modern accounting in the UK is based will now be reviewed. Although you will have encountered these conventions in earlier chapters, the problems associated with these conventions have not yet been discussed.

Money measurement

Items in accounting statements are described in terms of money. Items or factors which are incapable of being described in this way, perhaps because they are qualitative, rather than quantitative, must therefore be excluded from accounting statements. Thus the money measurement convention can lead to somewhat limited information. It is like a primitive language which has not developed a word for certain phenomena. In such a language reference to those phenomena would be impossible, or at least, difficult.

It is perhaps easy to overstate the deficiency of adherence to the money measurement convention. Accounting seeks to deal with information of an economic nature. Most information of this type can be expressed in monetary terms. Money is also a useful common denominator of much economic activity. Describing and assessing economic activities and phenomena in a quantitative manner does, it has been argued, give accounting a rigour of analysis which it might otherwise lack. In any case, there are other means of communicating information besides the use of accounting statements. Such means, which include narrative statements, are available to those who need to communicate information which cannot be communicated through accounting statements.

Self-assessment question 12.1
A narrative statement to supplement the accounts produced may be extremely valuable to users. It could help in analysing the performance and position of a business and in assessing its future prospects. Some large companies now produce a mainly narrative statement (known as an operating and financial review) as a supplement to the accounts.

What kind of information do you think such a statement might usefully include?

The answer to this question can be found at the end of the book.

Business entity

This convention simply says that, from an accounting point of view, the business is to be treated as a self-contained entity, separate from all who are connected with it. The most striking effect of this is that the owner(s) of the business and the business itself are viewed as being separate for accounting purposes. One way in which this separateness manifests itself is that in the balance sheet of the business, the capital of the owner(s) is dealt with essentially in the same way as the claim of all other claimants.

Note that the business entity convention says nothing about the legal relationship between the business and its owner(s). In unincorporated business forms (e.g. sole proprietorships and partnerships) there is no legal distinction between the business and its owner(s). With companies there is a legal distinction between the company and its shareholders. Both unincorporated businesses and companies follow the business entity convention.

The business entity convention is seen by most people as necessary and useful. It would be impossible to look at the position and performance of the business without including matters relating to the owner(s), which are irrele-

---

Activity 1
During a period of trading, the owner of a small business did the following:

(a) Paid for her private house to be decorated using a cheque drawn on the business bank account;
(b) Bought a photocopying machine for the business using her personal bank account cheque to pay for it.

How would each of these transactions be dealt with in the accounts of the business?

What effect does the business entity convention have on the treatment of these transactions?

---

vant to those two aspects. This is because the convention sets boundaries to what is being accounted for.

Your answer to Activity 1 should be as follows:

(a) The business cash would be reduced and this would be treated as drawing of the owner and so deducted from capital.
(b) This would be treated as an injection of capital into the business. Capital would be increased and the acquisition of the photocopier would be shown as an asset.

In effect, the business entity convention causes the capital to reflect, in each of these transactions, the fact that private assets of the owner had been affected by a transaction which also affected the business.

Duality

This convention requires that each transaction concerning the business has two effects on the accounts (double entry). It rather emphasizes the self-contained nature of the business, from an accounting point of view. Without the convention of duality, the business entity convention could not really function. This is because the full effect on the business of each transaction would not be recorded.

The duality convention is linked to the existence of the balance sheet equation:

Assets = capital plus liabilities

Historic cost

This convention holds that assets should be shown in accounts at their outlay cost to the business. This approach has the advantage that what a business actually paid out to acquire the asset is typically a matter of demonstrable fact. Any other value placed on the asset is likely to involve some expression of opinion. Defenders of the historic cost approach to accounting argue that this approach is very suitable as a basis of managers reporting to owners on their stewardship of the owners' assets. The traditional balance sheet, in essence, shows from where the business obtained its resources (the claims portion of the balance sheet) and how those resources have been deployed (the assets). Using historic cost to describe the assets, it is argued, is entirely logical since that value represents the amount of resources which were actually deployed. This is much the same as the way in which an individual might explain how a sum of money was spent. Reporting in this way leads to a much greater level of objectivity since the managers' opinions are reduced to a minimum. Any other approach than one based on historic cost inevitably increases the level of subjectivity involved.

Though the use of the historic cost convention may lead to objectivity, it is questionable if it always promotes the provision of useful, relevant information, as can be seen from the following examples:

Example

Jenkins Garage occupies a fairly large site in the centre of an attractive market town. The business was acquired by George Jenkins in 1961 when he bought an existing garage business. The garage sells petrol, undertakes repairs and buys and sells second-hand cars. The premises appear in the accounts of the business at what George paid for them – £30,000.

Following the advice of a friend, George recently applied to his District Council for outline planning permission to demolish the garage buildings and erect a block of luxury flats. The application was successful and as soon as it became public knowledge George was approached by Property Developments Plc who offered him £250,000 for the site as it stands. George has decided not to sell the site but to continue to operate the business for a few more years while he considers his future.

Clearly, to continue to show the premises in the accounts at £30,000 is potentially misleading. The original cost may have been £30,000 but that figure has become useless and irrelevant. For example, if George wishes to assess his return on capital employed, to base the capital employed on the £30,000 would be thoroughly misleading.

Example

Precision Engineering Plc has just paid £2 million to buy, and have installed, a highly specialized piece of equipment. The equipment is expected to help generate buoyant profits for the business for a number of years. The equipment is very highly specialized to the company's work. It would also be very expensive to move the equipment to other premises. Consequently, the equipment has virtually no realizable value.

At what value should the equipment be shown in the accounts?

It would obviously be misleading to show the asset at its realizable value. To Precision Engineering Plc the equipment is very valuable. It would probably be more appropriate to show it at historic cost, less an allowance for depreciation. It could be argued that better still would be to show the equipment at its value to the company, which could easily be above cost.

Example

Telesales retails television sets and other electrical equipment. It has just sold a popular model of television set for £300. This had cost £210 from the manufacturer a month earlier. The manufacturer has announced a price increase on the model. All future purchases of the model by Telesales will cost £250 each.

The traditional (historic cost) approach to income measurement would calculate the gross profit on the television sold at £90 (i.e. £300 – 210). This could be misleading because at the time of making the sale the effective cost of the television was £250, implying a gross profit of £50. The reason why the £250 cost is more appropriate is that leading directly from the sale of this set will be the need to replace it (it is a popular model). Thus the effective cost of making the sale is £250. Had the set not been sold, the need to replace it would not have arisen.

To view this from a slightly different angle, ask yourself what Telesales would feel itself deprived of if the particular television was stolen just before it was due to be delivered to the customer. The answer is £250, since this is what it will cost to replace the set and make the sale.

These three examples serve to show that the historical cost convention is not always effective in providing the most useful information. In none of the three examples does historic cost provide a particularly meaningful result. In none of these cases would historic cost be the most useful basis to help a user to make a rational decision.

Activity 2
Can you think of any advantages in applying the historic cost convention when preparing accounts?

The advantage that this convention has is that it leads to the use of figures which are, generally speaking, objective (capable of independent verification). Use of the convention can lead to readers having confidence that the figures have not been manipulated to give one impression rather than another. For this reason it is often seen as relevant to the *stewardship function* in accounting. The use of any other basis than historical cost does raise questions about the choice of the alternative. There is no consensus concerning a method of valuation which should replace historic cost.

Stable monetary unit

Closely related to the historic cost convention is the assumption that the measurement unit in accounting, the unit of currency, retains a stable value relative to other assets over time. However, in recent times this has not usually been the case.

Example

Apex Property Company owns two identical buildings on the same site in central London. The first was bought 10 years ago for £1 million; the second was bought last year for £3 million. They are each let as office space for the current commercial rent of £0.5 million, with the tenant responsible for all costs in both cases.

The stable monetary unit convention holds that it is assumed that the value of each £ sterling was the same when each of the buildings was bought. This would lead to the balance sheet of the business including an amount of £4 million for the sum of the two buildings. In fact, it is known that the value of the £ sterling has fallen in every year since the Second World War, not necessarily relative to other currencies but relative to the amount of goods and services which each £ will buy. In recent years, particularly during the 1970s and 1980s, the effect of inflation has been very dramatic. Obviously, the aggregation of assets expressed in pounds of different purchasing power leads to meaningless figures appearing in the accounts.

Following the stable monetary unit convention can lead to more than merely the presentation of anomalous figures; it can give misleading figures. If a user of the accounts wanted to assess the relative effectiveness of the two investments the conclusion might be reached that the first building yields a return of 50% p.a. (i.e. £0.5m/1.0 × 100%), whereas the second one only generates a return of 16.7% p.a. (i.e. £0.5m/3 × 100%). Since the value of money, the yardstick of measurement, has altered, these return figures are each misleading and they are not comparable. It is illogical to seek to relate the rent from either building (an amount measured in £s of one value), with the cost of the buildings (amounts measured in £s of another value). Even worse, perhaps, is to try to compare the two rates of return.

Later in this chapter we shall consider some suggestions which have been made to try to overcome the misleading effects of both the historic cost and stable monetary unit conventions.

Going concern convention

This convention holds that, unless there is reason to take a different view, the business should be treated as if it will continue for the foreseeable future. The relevance of the convention tends to be in the area of asset valuation for inclusion in the balance sheet. Broadly, where an asset is expected to be realized (turned into cash) in the near future it should be valued at its net realizable value, or at cost if relevant and if cost gives a lower figure. So, for example, stock in trade is typically valued at the lower of cost and net realizable value. Similarly, trade debtors are usually valued at net realizable value (i.e. the amount of the unpaid debts less any debts written off as uncollectable, also less a provision for doubtful debts). By contrast, fixed assets are typically valued at cost, less an allowance for depreciation. No attempt is made to value fixed assets on a current market value basis except just before their planned disposal date. The reason for this contrast is the fact that fixed assets, by definition, are not bought with the intention of disposing of them. If the going concern status of the business is in question, the possibility that fixed assets may need to be sold to meet creditors' claims becomes a real possibility. At that point any excess of book value over current market value will have to be treated as an expense so as to reduce the fixed asset value to its net realizable value.

In effect, the going concern convention supports the use of historic cost as the valuation base for fixed assets. It is argued that, since realizable value is only important when the asset is to be realized in the relatively near future, the assumption that the business will continue beyond that time horizon means that the fixed assets can be reasonably valued on the basis of historic cost rather than realizable values.

Activity 3

Is this last argument concerning support for the historic cost convention valid? Can you think of a counterargument?

It can be argued that a business will adapt to a changing environment by selling assets in the normal course of business and buying new ones. So, even if the business is expected to continue operations for the foreseeable future, information concerning the current realizable values of assets held may still be useful. Some argue that the realizable value of assets held can provide users with an indication of the financial adaptability of a business which can be extremely useful.

Realization

The convention of realization maintains that revenues should be recognized when they are actually realized. This tends to be interpreted as:

- when the amount of the revenue is capable of objective measurement; and
- when the work necessary to earn the revenue is substantially completed; and
- the receipt of cash (or other asset) in consideration is fairly certain.

Thus revenues tend to be recognized when the goods or services pass to, and are accepted by, the customer. However, there are certain industries where a different point in the production/selling cycle is taken.

Activity 4

Can you think of a type of business where revenue could be recognized:

- when the goods are produced?
- after goods have been passed to the customer but before payment is made?
- after payment is made?

- *When the goods are produced.* A gold mining business may recognize the revenue as soon as they have extracted the metal from the earth. This is presumably because at that point the sale is virtually certain and there is a known current market price. There may also be no selling and marketing costs to be incurred. Civil engineering businesses tend to recognize part of the revenue from protracted contracts as the contract progresses rather than at the end.
- *After the goods have been passed to the customer.* A business which operates on a mail order basis such as a book or record club, a language tuition centre, etc. may offer customers a certain period (e.g. 7 days) of free trial before they have to make an irrevocable commitment to buy. If the goods are returned within the stated period no payment is required. Recognition of revenue may then take place at the end of the trial period.
- *After payment is made.* Some businesses which operate on a mail order basis, such as those identified above, may ask for payment before the goods are despatched. However, return of the goods within a specified period will require repayment of monies received. Once again, revenue will be recognized after the trial period.

While the realization convention is generally seen as being sensible and prudent, there are circumstances in which it can give misleading results. These circumstances arise because the convention prevents the reporting of changes in wealth which are not verified by a market transaction.

Example

A building firm recently bought a small plot on which it erected two identical houses. Though the property market was very buoyant, the firm was short of cash and had to sell one of the houses immediately for £100,000. The firm decided that it would retain the second house because it was felt that property prices were likely to increase. The total cost of both houses, including the cost of the land, was £120,000. Following the realization convention, as it would typically be applied, the profit on the sold house (£100,000 – 60,000 = £40,000) would be recognized, but the other house would be shown as an asset at its cost (£60,000). If these two houses represented the only work undertaken by the firm in a particular accounting period, the gross profit would be £40,000. This is despite a buoyant market in which the second house could be sold easily.

This example not only illustrates the point that the realization convention can have a misleading effect. It also shows that the realization convention is closely related to the historic cost convention, since the fact that no profit is typically recognized until the goods pass to the customer means that assets tend to be shown at historic cost rather than at historic cost, plus expected profit.

Matching

This convention holds that expenses should be matched to the revenues which they helped to generate such that the revenue and its associated expenses are set against one another in deducing the income of a business for a particular accounting period. Clearly this is a logical approach to take. Without the matching convention there would be no rule which, for example, advocated that in deducing the income for a period the cost of the stock sold must be deducted from the sales revenue to which it gave rise. With direct expenses (i.e. expenses linked directly to sales) like cost of sales, matching is a fairly easy process. The problems with the matching convention start to show when it is expenses like depreciation which must be matched. In most cases, the depreciation of a fixed asset does not relate directly to a particular revenue or set of revenues. This means that the accountant is forced to use some fairly arbitrary basis of matching. Several bases of deducing the depreciation expense for particular accounting periods are found in practice. All of them rely very substantially on judgements of expected useful life of the asset and potential residual value as well as the choice of the actual method used.

In practice, the allocation of expenses to accounting periods is a major problem of accounting.

Activity 5
What is the effect of the matching convention on the portrayal of fixed assets on the balance sheet? Does this undermine the usefulness of the balance sheet?

Some argue that the matching convention can undermine the usefulness of the balance sheet as a statement of financial position. This is because the effect of the matching convention is to show the fixed assets at their unexpired cost (i.e. cost less accumulated depreciation). In other words, the balance sheet portrays to users what is left of the fixed assets after matching (i.e. the depreciation of these assets in past periods) has occurred, which may not be particularly useful for decision-making purposes. The amounts remaining which are shown on the balance sheet will be matched against revenues generated in future periods.

Accruals

This convention maintains that profit (or loss) for a period is the difference between revenues earned and expenses incurred during the period, *not* the difference between cash receipts and payments for the period. It really adds support to the matching convention by stating that expenses should be matched to revenues within a time period on the basis of the wealth consumed in generating revenues, not on the basis of cash (if any) relating to an expense paid during the period.

Prudence

This convention maintains that preparers of accounting statements should take a pessimistic rather than an optimistic view of future events to the extent that it is necessary to view future events in the preparation of those statements. Put another way, losses should be anticipated and included, but profits should not be taken into account until they are realized. Prudence is, perhaps, the important valuation principle in accounting. Where there is a conflict between prudence and another valuation convention (such as historic cost or realization) it is the former which will always prevail. However, the role of prudence in financial reporting has been questioned increasingly over the years. This convention was considered important in financial reporting in the past when the emphasis was on the protection of lenders and creditors. However, in more recent times the emphasis in financial reporting has shifted towards providing information for investors.

Activity 6
What is the problem with adopting this convention? Could this convention work to the disadvantage of an investor?

The problem with the convention is that it encourages the production of accounting statements which show a systematic bias towards understatement of profit (or overstatement of loss) and understatement of asset values. Moreover, it is not always clear how much bias has been applied in measuring profit or loss. This understatement of profit and asset values may work to the advantage of an investor purchasing shares (who may pay less than if more realistic figures were used in the accounts) and to the disadvantage of investors who are selling shares in the company (as they may sell the shares too cheaply).

There may be some logic for this approach, in that it may be beneficial to exercise caution in business life. It is probably better, however, to produce unbiased information and let the decision-maker exercise caution to the extent required in making any decisions based on the information. It has been argued that, if the future events which bear on accounting statements are uncertain, it might be more appropriate to give users statements based on a range of possible outcomes and let the users make their own judgements.

Consistency

Where a particular transaction or event could legitimately be treated in more than one way, the convention of consistency says that the same treatment should be applied from one accounting period to the next. Comparison of that which is shown by accounting statements will be easier where the same accounting policies are consistently applied over time.

Depreciation provides an example of following the convention. When a business acquires a depreciating fixed asset it should, in order to follow the convntion, use the same method (e.g. straight-line or reducing balance) as is applied to other similar assets owned by that business. The method should then be applied throughout the life of the asset. This is not to say that it is never acceptable to alter an accounting policy, such as the depreciation method. If, in the light of other conventions, there seems good reason for a change, then a change should be made and the new policy regarded as standard for the foreseeable future. It should be noted that the convention does not seek to establish comparability between the accounting reports of *different* businesses, though many would argue that such comparability is very useful.

The consistency convention probably leads to the provision of more useful information, but it can encourage adherence to accounting policies which may be difficult to support on grounds other than consistency.

Materiality

Where strictly following a particular convention involves only immaterial amounts, then the convention concerned need not be followed. A problem lies in assessing what is meant by 'immaterial'. This would normally be interpreted as an amount so trivial as not to be capable of having an effect on the judgements of a reader of the accounts.

An area where the materiality convention is often involved is in the strict interpretation of the matching convention.

Example

A business bought a box of paperclips costing £1 during a particular financial year. At the end of the year most of the paperclips had been used. Strictly following the matching convention requires that the remaining paperclips should be counted and valued to deduce the part of the £1 cost which is an expense for the year and the part which should be treated as an asset. Clearly, to follow the matching convention will involve use of staff time in counting paperclips and other similarly insignificant items. The effect that strictly following the matching convention would have on the usefulness of the accounts is almost certainly zero. Thus ignoring the matching convention and treating the cost of the paperclips as an expense of the year in which they were bought seems much more practical.

Activity 7

To what extent is the convention of materiality related to the idea of relevance which we considered in Chapter 1?

It can be argued that the convention of materiality is closely related to the idea of relevance. You may recall that relevance is concerned with providing information which has the ability to influence the decisions of users. The convention of materiality is concerned with what *should* be disclosed for decision-making purposes. It also involves deciding between what is likely to have an influence on decisions and what is not. Too much information may be as difficult for users to deal with as too little information. There is often a danger that important items in the financial statements may be submerged by less important items. By applying the convention of materiality, less important items may be aggregated in order to allow the key items to be highlighted and to make the financial statements more relevant for decision-making purposes.

Objectivity

This convention maintains that accounting statements should be based on unbiased, verifiable facts, rather than on matters of judgement.

Adherence to this convention has obvious appeal. Surely we should all regard the provision of unbiased verifiable facts as preferable to expressions of opinion? However, the preparation of accounting statements does inevitably rely to some extent – sometimes to a great extent – on opinions. For example, it is necessary to take account of depreciation of fixed assets to achieve some sensible assessment of the trading success or efficiency of a business. Calculation of the depreciation expense for an accounting period in respect of a particular fixed asset relies on four factors:

1   The cost of the asset
2   The economic life of the asset
3   The residual value of the asset at the end of that economic life
4   The method (e.g. straight-line, reducing balance, etc.) of apportioning the cost less the residual value over the economic life of the asset

At the time that it is necessary to deduce the depreciation expense for the period, only the cost of the asset is typically a verifiable fact. The other three factors are matters of judgement.

The discussion of the deficiencies of both the historic cost and stable monetary unit conventions, earlier in this chapter, includes examples of circumstances where, using verifiable facts, the historic cost of an asset could seriously mislead a user of an accounting statement. Substitution of a figure based on

---

Activity 8
Can you think of three accounting conventions which emphasize the use of subjective judgement rather than objective facts in preparing financial reports?

judgement and opinion, e.g. current market value, could make the statement much more useful. Clearly, there can be a conflict between verifiability and objectivity on the one hand, and usefulness on the other.

Three particular conventions which seem to promote subjectivity are matching, prudence and materiality. All of these require making judgements rather than reliance on unbiased, verifiable facts. This emphasis on subjective judgement provides an example of conflict between conventions.

12.5   Towards a conceptual framework

The conventions of accounting discussed above were developed by accountants in order to deal with the practical problems which are encountered in the preparation of financial reports. To date, these conventions have provided the only agreed framework available to deal with accounting issues and problems. The conventions offer the accountant some practical guidance concerning *what to record* and *how to record* financial transactions. The conventions are rather broad in nature and do not provide detailed guidelines. Moreover, they do, at times, conflict with each other. However, the fact that they represent a distillation of practical experience in preparing financial reports is viewed by some as a major strength.

There has been an increasing recognition, however, of the limitations of conventions in providing an adequate foundation for the development of accounting. Although it is true that the conventions offer guidance concerning *what* and *how* to record, they do not provide guidance concerning *why* we should record transactions in certain ways or, indeed, why we should record at all. What is required, it is argued, is a clear rationale for accounting, i.e. we need to have a framework which clearly defines the purpose of accounting and the nature and content of financial reports. Such a framework would address fundamental questions such as:

- What are the objectives of accounting?
- For whom are accounting reports prepared?
- What kind of accounting reports are required?
- What should these accounting reports contain?

By answering such questions it is believed that a more logical and systematic approach to the development of accounting practice can be achieved.

In recent years there have been attempts to develop a framework for accounting which deals with the fundamental questions identified above. Perhaps the most notable attempt has been by the Financial Accounting Standards Board (FASB) in the USA. Work on this project began in the early 1970s. The impetus for the FASB effort can be traced to the dissatisfaction of the business community with the quality of accounting reports produced. This dissatisfaction was due to a number of reasons which included:

- the fact that more than one method of accounting could be applied to the same basic data, with each method producing quite different results;
- that less conservative accounting methods were being used in preparing financial reports compared with earlier periods;
- that too much emphasis was being placed on the form of financial statements rather than the underlying economic substance.

As a result of this dissatisfaction, the FASB felt that it was necessary to identify more clearly the aims of accounting in order to provide a basis for developing more consistent accounting policies. The FASB hopes that its efforts will help restore the credibility of accounting in the eyes of users of accounting information and will help ensure that standard-setting in the USA remains free of government intervention.

The FASB has attempted to develop what it has referred to as 'a conceptual framework'. This has been defined as

> a constitution, a coherent system of interrelated objectives and fundamentals that can lead to consistent standards and that prescribes the nature, function, and limits of financial accounting and financial statements (FASB, 1977).

The conceptual framework developed consists of a number of elements which are as follows:

- *Objectives of financial reporting.* This element identifies for whom and for what purpose financial reports are prepared. It also sets out in broad terms what financial statements should contain in order to be of value to users. This provides the logical starting point for a fundamental examination of the nature and content of financial reports.
- *Qualitative characteristics of financial information.* This element establishes criteria by which financial policies and reports can be judged and sets out such qualities as relevance, reliability, comparability, etc. The development of such criteria helps to distinguish between 'good' and 'bad' accounting.
- *Elements of financial statements.* This examines the nature of capital, assets and liabilities and the nature of revenue and expenses. These items form the basic building blocks of financial statements.
- *Recognition criteria.* This examines the process by which an item should be incorporated into the financial statements as an asset, liability, revenue, expense, etc.
- *Measurement.* This element examines the methods of measuring assets and liabilities such as historic cost, constant purchasing power, current cost, net realizable value, etc.
- *Form and content of financial statements and reports.* This element considers the form and content of the statements and reports that should be published and whether it is necessary for all organizations, irrespective of size, to publish the same information.

- *Income reporting*. This examines the nature of 'comprehensive income' and identifies its components (revenue, expense, gains and losses). This element also examines which capital maintenance concept should be adopted, i.e. whether financial or physical capital should be maintained.
- *Funds flow and liquidity*. This element examines how information concerning liquidity should be presented to users.

Activity 9
Explain how a conceptual framework may be of value to:

- a standard-setting body such as the Accounting Standards Board (ASB)
- the auditors of a company
- preparers of financial statements
- users of financial statements

In answering this activity you may have thought of the following:

- *Standard-setting body*. A body, such as the ASB, should find a conceptual framework useful in developing a more consistent approach to the development of accounting standards as it will provide a clearer basis for deciding between alternative accounting methods. It should also help in reviewing existing standards.
- *The auditors of a company* should find a conceptual framework useful in forming an opinion as to whether financial statements conform with accounting standards. The underlying principles should also provide a guide to the application of particular standards.
- *Preparers of financial statements* should find it useful in deciding how to apply financial standards. A conceptual framework, which sets out broad principles, may also be helpful in dealing with issues not falling within the scope of particular standards.
- *Users of financial statements* should find a conceptual framework useful in interpreting financial reports which are prepared in accordance with accounting standards. The adherence to underlying principles should help eliminate or reduce any uncertainty concerning the treatment of particular items appearing in the accounts.

The FASB is not alone in attempting to develop a conceptual framework for accounting. There have also been attempts by accounting bodies in other countries such as those in Canada and Australia. In addition, the International Accounting Standards Committee (IASC) has also produced a conceptual framework. The development of this framework follows a similar pattern to that of the FASB framework above.

In the UK, the ASB has produced a statement on the principles that underpin accounting and the preparation of financial reports for external users. This statement recognizes, and draws heavily on, the work produced by the other accounting bodies referred to above. In developing a statement of principles, the ASB identified the following areas as being relevant:

- the objectives of financial statements
- the attributes or qualities of financial statements that enable them to fulfil their purpose
- the elements that make up financial statements
- when items are to be recognized in financial statements
- how resources and performance are to be measured
- how items can best be presented in the financial statements
- the principles underlying the consolidation of groups of companies

The first stage of the work of the ASB was to set out their views on the first two of the areas mentioned, i.e. the objectives of financial statements and the qualitative characteristics of financial statements. The objective of financial reports according to the ASB is:

> to provide information about the financial position, performance and adaptability of an enterprise that is useful to a wide range of users in making economic decisions.

In addition, the financial statements should also show:

> the results of the stewardship of management, that is, the accountability of management for the resources entrusted to it.

These objectives have not provoked a great deal of debate. They are broad in nature, they emphasize the user-orientation of accounting which has gained increasing acceptance over the years and are similar to objectives proposed by various leading bodies in the past. However, they can be criticized for making a distinction between economic decisions and the stewardship function. A wider view of stewardship, based on whether management was acting in the best interests of the owners, would mean that the distinction between economic decision-making and stewardship is really an artificial one.

The ASB statement identified relevance and reliability as the two key qualities of financial statements. The main qualities of financial statements were considered in Chapter 1 and so will not be discussed here. However, a diagram produced by the ASB showing the factors which influence relevance and reliability is shown below (Fig. 12.1). The figure also identifies secondary characteristics of accounting which, if lacking, would limit the usefulness of the information.

12.6 Problems in developing a conceptual framework

Whilst many may agree that, in principle, the development of an agreed conceptual framework would be extremely valuable, they remain sceptical that such a

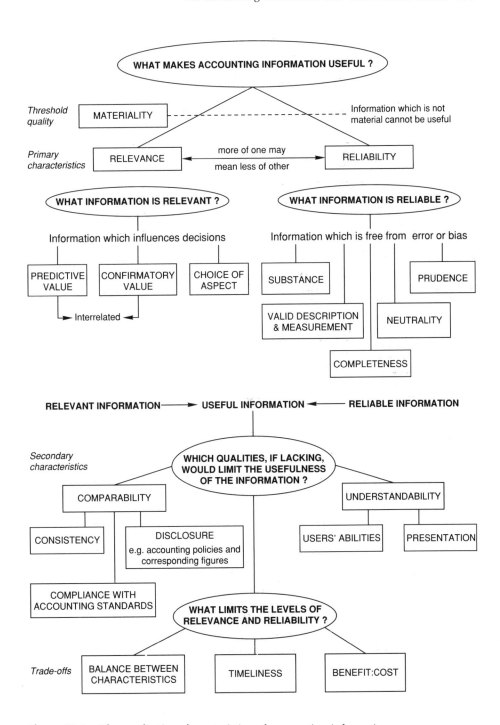

Figure 12.1 *The qualitative characteristics of accounting information*

framework can actually be developed. Others believe that, in order to secure widespread agreement, a conceptual framework would have to be couched in such broad terms that it would prove meaningless as a guide to action. Certainly there is a number of difficulties to be encountered when seeking a framework which would command broad support. For example, in recent years there has been a number of studies which have attempted to define the objectives of financial reports and/or to identify the users of these reports and their information needs. These studies have, at times, reached similar conclusions but at other times have displayed marked differences in the conclusions reached.

There are also problems of resolving conflicts involving the exercise of judgement. The preparation of financial statements will always involve a need to exercise judgement due to such problems as the allocation of items over time and the existence of uncertainty concerning future outcomes which, nevertheless, have to be taken into account in the current period. As a result, disputes are likely to continue concerning the most appropriate way of dealing with these problems.

Activity 10
Can you think of four areas where judgement is required in the preparation of financial statements and which may have a significant effect on the calculation of profit and financial position?

Four areas which require the exercise of subjective judgement are as follows:

1   *Depreciation.* The calculation of depreciation requires making estimates concerning the useful life of the asset, the residual value of the asset, and judgement is required as to the most appropriate depreciation method to employ.
2   *Stocks.* The calculation of stock requires that an appropriate stock flow assumption is made (i.e. FIFO, LIFO, etc.). It also requires that a judgement be made as to the net realizable value of stocks. If this is lower than cost then the net realizable value becomes the reported figure.
3   *Goodwill.* Goodwill paid for on the acquisition of a going concern should be written off. It can either be written off immediately or over a number of years. Judgement is required on the appropriate write-off policy.
4   *Bad and doubtful debts.* Judgement is required in determining the debts which are bad and which are doubtful.

Some find it is difficult to believe that a conceptual framework, if adopted by the accounting profession, would eliminate fundamental debates concerning the nature and purpose of accounting. It has been suggested that, in one sense, a conceptual framework can be compared to the Bible. The Bible, as you probably know, sets out the basic tenets of Christian faith and provides guidelines on how Christians should live. However, the contents of the Bible are interpreted by different Christian sects in different ways and this can sometimes lead to quite profound differences in viewpoints.

This tendency for us to interpret the same things differently has been highlighted by Horngren who states:

> most of us have an incredible talent for processing new facts in such a way that our prior conclusions remain intact. Therefore, no matter what conceptual framework is developed, its success will be heavily affected by individual interpretations.

A conceptual framework, once developed, would have to adapt to economic, social and political changes. It cannot become a static framework with an indefinite life. However, the nature of possible changes to the framework and the pace of any change are likely to provoke further debate. What some may regard as progress, others are likely to regard as a backward step.

In view of the problems discussed, we should perhaps not expect too much from a conceptual framework, even though such a framework would be desirable. The major benefit so far derived from recent efforts in developing a conceptual framework is that it has helped to identify the important issues in accounting. It has stimulated an investigation into the purpose of accounting reports, the users of accounting information and their likely needs. Thus, it can be argued that we are now, at least, beginning to ask the right sort of questions. However, it seems unlikely that an agreed conceptual framework for accounting will emerge in the foreseeable future.

12.7 Measurement of profit and the maintenance of capital

It has been seen earlier in this chapter that following the historic cost and stable monetary conventions can lead to the production of accounting reports which could seriously mislead a user. The misleading effects tend to be particularly concerned with questions of profit measurement (see, for example, the Telesales example which was considered in the context of the historic cost convention, earlier in this chapter). There are also distortions in asset valuation and assessment of performance (see the Apex Property Company example which was discussed earlier in this chapter in the context of the stable monetary unit convention).

We shall now look at some other approaches which have been advocated which, it is claimed, might lead to more useful and more relevant information.

It was established in the early chapters of this book that revenues are trading events which increase capital and that expenses are trading events which reduce it. The net effect of revenues and expenses over a period is a profit or a loss and this has the effect of increasing capital or of decreasing it, respectively. This leads to an alternative version of the definition of profit. This version says that profit is the *net amount of assets which the owner(s) of the business can withdraw (as dividend, etc.) during the period and leave the business, or the owners, as well-off at the end of the period as at the beginning.* This is an important version of the definition of profit in that it relates to the general desire of the owners of the business not to let the business, or their investment in it, decline in size as a result of capital withdrawals by the owners.

When there is an environment of changing price levels, either general or specific to a particular asset, profit measurement becomes difficult. This may lead to the problem that more capital is withdrawn than the amount which would leave the business, or the owners' investment in it, as much in real terms as it was at the beginning of the period.

There are two major approaches proposed to try to deal with the problem of changing prices, though other methods have been put forward as well. Which of the two major methods is preferred is essentially concerned with whether it is the 'well-offness' or wealth of the *owners* which the definition of profit seeks to save from decline, or whether it is the ability of the *business* to continue at existing levels of activity which the definition of profit seeks to protect. This point and the two methods will now be explained.

Preserving owners' wealth – current (constant) purchasing power (CPP) accounting

If the wealth of the owners which is invested in the business is to be as much at the end of the accounting period as at the start, then the owners should be able to buy as much with their wealth at the end of the accounting period as they could at the beginning.

If all of the prices of goods and services which the owners may wish to buy remain constant over the accounting period, then profit is fairly easy to measure.

Example

Jackie Jones runs a small business during her spare time, buying crockery and selling it at a local street market. She started it a year ago when she cashed in an insurance policy for £1,200 which she used to open a bank account for the business. Jackie had decided not to take any of her capital out of the business as drawings during the first year.

The balance sheet, which her accountant drew up as at the end of Jackie's first year of trading, included the following, under the heading of 'Capital':

Capital introduced	£1,200
Net profit for the year	3,574
Capital at the end of the year	£4,774

This implies that if Jackie were now to withdraw her £3,574 of profit, that part of her wealth remaining invested in the business (£1,200) would be equal to that which she started with. If general prices of goods and services had remained constant over the year, the £1,200 which she invested to start the business would have the same value to her as £1,200 at the end of the year.

Suppose, however, that during the year the price of goods and services within the economy had increased in price by a factor of 10% of the start of the year prices. This would mean that, to obtain the same amount of goods and services at the end of the year that £1,200 would have bought at the start would cost £1,200 plus 10%, i.e. £1,320. In this case, would it still be true to say that Jackie could take £3,574 out of the business and still be as well-off in terms of her investment in the business as at the start of the year? Of course she would not be as well off in these circumstances. Given the definition of profit which is being adopted here, the profit is £3,454 [£3,574 – (£1,320 – 1,200)].

Preserving the ability of the business to trade at existing levels – current cost accounting (CCA)

The second approach defines profit as the amount which the owners of the business can withdraw and leave the business as well-off, in terms of its ability to continue to trade, at the end of the period as it was at the beginning.

Example

Suppose that Jackie Jones (the street market crockery trader from the last example) needed her original capital of £1,200 because that was how much she felt it necessary to spend on crockery stocks each week. Out of her takings she felt would pay her rent to the local authority and the hire of the stall to the person from whom she rented it. Although the general level of consumer prices may have moved up by 10% over the year, suppose that the type of crockery in which Jackie trades has increased in price by 20% over that period.

In these circumstances, for the business to be as well-off at the end of the year as it was at the start, in terms of its ability to continue to trade at the same level, at least £1,440 (£1,200 × 120/100) must be left after Jackie has withdrawn her profit. This means that according to the CCA version of the definition of profit, the profit is £3,334 (£3,574 – £240). Any more than this will not enable the business to trade at the original level, should all of the profit be withdrawn.

You should note that CPP and CCA are based upon *different* definitions of profit. Both have advantages and disadvantages. However, it is important to recognize that one is not right and the other wrong. They both provide useful, but different, insights into profit measurement. Indeed, it is possible to obtain more information by using both methods, or at least certain aspects of them. For example, Jackie Jones' profit on a CPP basis was measured as £3,454, whereas on a CCA basis it was £3,334. This means that if Jackie wishes to continue in business at the same level of activity as at the start of the year, she can only withdraw £3,334. She must retain capital in the business of £1,440.

However, this investment is £120 more than is needed to preserve her own *personal* purchasing power. This £120 therefore represents an increase in her purchasing power which cannot be distributed without impairing the ability of the business to continue at the same level of activity.

Activity 11

You run a garage business. You start your year with 10,000 gallons of fuel which cost you £1.50 per gallon. Your capital is £17,000. Immediately following the start of the year the buying price of petrol increases to £2.00 per gallon, as a result of which you increase the price to your customers. At the end of your first month of trading you re-fill the tanks with 10,000 gallons at £2.00 per gallon. Your profit and loss account for the first month of the year, on a historical cost basis, is as follows:

		£
Sales	10,000 gallons @ £2.50	25,000
Cost of sales	10,000 gallons @ £1.50	15,000
Gross profit		10,000
Overheads (including rent of premises and tank,		
paid at the start of the month)		2,000
Net profit		£8,000

(a) What would be the profit on a CCA basis?

(b) How much would you feel able to take out as drawings for the first month?

(c) By how much would you as the owner feel better off if the cost of goods and services which you regularly buy increased by 1% on the month?

(a) On a CCA basis, the profit and loss account would be:

		£
Sales	10,000 gallons @ £2.50	25,000
Cost of sales	10,000 gallons @ £2.00	20,000
Gross profit		5,000
Overheads		2,000
Net profit		£3,000

(b)   If you wish to continue to hold stocks at the level of the start of the month so that your ability to trade is not reduced, the maximum which can be withdrawn is the £3,000 CCA profit.

(c)   Under CPP, assuming a rate of inflation of 1% over the month, the profit and loss account would be as follows:

		£
Sales	10,000 gallons @ £2.50	25,000
Cost of sales	10,000 gallons @ £1.50 × 101/100	15,150
Gross profit		9,850
Overheads	(£2,000 × 101/100)	2,020
Net profit		£7,830

The £170 difference between the historical cost and the CPP profit arises because it will cost £17,170 (£17,000 × 101/100) to buy goods and services at the end of the month which would have cost £17,000 at the start. Thus to preserve the purchasing power of your capital, the maximum withdrawal is £7,830.

CPP – a more detailed consideration

A closer look will now be taken at CPP accounting. When this approach is used in the preparation of final accounts, all of the figures in the accounts are usually expressed in pounds of purchasing power as at the balance sheet date (end of the profit and loss account period). This operation, which can be a little laborious (but not typically too difficult), is effected through the use of a general price index. This is simply a statistical device which relates the cost (in pounds) of a set of goods and services at various points in time. The one whose use is usually advocated in the context of CPP is the retail price index (RPI) which is compiled and published by the UK government and updated monthly.

Under CPP each expense and revenue is revised from the original historical cost figures. The revision is based on the price index used. In practice, it is not usually considered necessary to identify each sale on an individual basis. Usually, the view is taken that to adjust the sales figure as if all of the sales took place at the mid-point in the financial year is acceptable, provided that the sales were spread fairly evenly over the year. Where this is not the case or the sales are in large discrete units, as they might be, say to a small housebuilder, each revenue should be dealt with on an individual basis.

The balance sheet figures are also revised so that they are all expressed in terms of pounds at the year end value. This includes the fixed assets, so that the depreciation charge for the year, in the profit and loss account, will be calculated with reference to the revised values. Some of the items in the historical cost account balance sheet will not need adjustment since they are already expressed in terms of pounds of year end value. These are those assets and claims whose amount is fixed in money terms. These include all forms of debtor and creditor, both long- and short-term, and cash itself. Such items are usually referred to as *monetary items*.

There is one more adjustment necessary, to reflect the fact that a business with assets whose value is fixed in money terms loses during a period of inflation, while one with such liabilities gains. This is because a debtor of £100 (or £100 in cash) held for a period is worth less in terms of purchasing power at the end of the period than it was at the beginning. Similarly, a liability loses value in terms of purchasing power, which is to the benefit of the business, since it will have to give up less in real terms to settle the obligation, if inflation has been present during the period that the liability was outstanding. Thus the profit will be reduced where the business has an excess of monetary assets over monetary liabilities and the profit will be increased where the opposite is the case.

It should be emphasized that the final profit and loss account and balance sheet prepared under CPP simply take the original, historic cost versions of these statements and translates them into £s of balance sheet date value. In principle, this is much the same as would be necessary to convert final accounts prepared in one currency, say French francs, into another, say pounds sterling.

Activity 12

Honest John deals in a fairly small way in second-hand cars. John started the year with no cars in stock and during the year the following transactions took place:

	RPI at date of transaction	**Bought**	**Sold**
1 January	317	Ford (£800)	—
1 February	321	Rover (£,000)	—
1 April	325	Jaguar (£2,500	Rover (£,300)
			Ford (£1,000)
1 May	327	Renault (£1,500)	—
1 June	331	Nissan (£2,000)	—
1 August	340	BMW (£5,000)	Nissan (£2,100)
1 September	344	Citroen (£2,000)	Renault (£1,400)
1 October	347	Fiat (£900)	Jaguar (£2,000)
			BMW (£5,200)
1 December	353	Skoda (£1,000)	Fiat (£1,100)
			Citroen (£2,400)
31 December	357	—	—

You are required in respect of the year to 31 December:

(a) to deduce the total CPP sales figure
(b) to deduce the total CPP cost of sales figure
(c) to deduce the CPP closing stock figure

Your answer should be as follows:

CPP cost of sales		**CPP sales**	
	£		£
£800 × 357/317	901	£4,300 × 357/325	4,723
£3,000 × 357/321	3,336	£2,100 × 357/340	2,205
£2,500 × 357/325	2,746	£1,400 × 357/344	1,453
£1,500 × 357/327	1,638	£7,200 × 357/347	7,407
£2,000 × 357/331	2,157	£3,500 × 357/353	3,540
£5,000 × 357/340	5,250		
£2,000 × 357/344	2,076		
£900 × 357/347	926		
	£19,030		£19,328
Closing stock			
£1,000 × 357/353	£1,011		

Advantages and disadvantages of CPP

The advocates of using the CPP approach argue that:

- It is relatively objective. It is based on historic costs which are adjusted by using a statistical index derived outside the business.
- Using a general index to make the adjustments makes those adjustments standard across businesses.
- It emphasizes the cost and benefits of holding monetary items during inflationary periods.
- It attempts to deal with the distortions caused by general inflation.
- As it is based on historic accounts, it is more evolutionary than other methods proposed.

Its detractors point out that:

- It is of dubious value for managerial decision-making purposes since decisions are likely to involve replacement of the specific assets of the business, rather than with goods and services generally.
- Using a general price index to make adjustments is considered irrelevant since this is likely to reflect price changes in a way which is quite different from those experienced by various users of the accounts.
- It is regarded by many as conceptually difficult to understand and to interpret the results from CPP.
- As the CPP accounts represent an adjustment to the historic cost accounts, they can only be regarded as *supplementary* statements. They cannot replace the historic cost accounts.
- The assets are shown in the CPP balance sheet at their adjusted historic cost. However, this is not the same (or as useful) as the current value of the assets.

CCA – a more detailed consideration

In practice, not all businesses are as simple as that of Jackie Jones, which was used earlier to illustrate the principles of CCA. They are much more likely to have fixed assets and other current assets, as well as stock. When the CCA approach is used to prepare the final accounts the general principle is that the expenses which are charged against the revenues, in the profit and loss account, should represent the current cost of the assets used to achieve those revenues. With stock sold this amounts to identifying, strictly in respect of each sale, the current cost of the stock sold. With most other expenses it is simply the actual amount spent on them. Depreciation is typically based on the current cost of the asset to the business at the mid-point in the year, this being regarded as a reasonable approximation. Current cost is typically (though not always) the amount that it would cost the business to replace the asset *at the time of its sale or use.*

The balance sheet shows the assets at their value to the business at balance sheet date. Their value to the business would typically be their replacement cost since, if the business were deprived in some way of any of its assets, it would typically replace them.

In the basic CCA accounts, gains and losses on monetary asets and liabilities are ignored.

There is no attempt made with CCA to reflect year end values in the profit and loss account. Revenues are left unadjusted and the expenses reflect the cost of replacing the asset consumed at the date of the expense, hence the tendency is towards the profit and loss account to reflect the average revenues and expenses for the year.

Advantages and disadvantages of CCA

Those who favour CCA point out that:

- Since it relates to specific costs as they affect the business concerned, it is more relevant and helpful as an aid to management decision-making.
- It gives a more valid measure of how much capital can be withdrawn so that the business is as well-off at the end of the period as it was at the beginning. Thus, it helps to ensure the productive capacity of the business is maintained.
- The balance sheet gives a realistic measure of the assets employed in the business on which to assess returns.

The critics of CCA argue that:

- The profit measure does not necessarily reflect the efficiency of management.

- Gains and losses on monetary items are ignored and so some useful information is omitted.
- Determining value to the business (typically replacement cost) can be difficult and inevitably strays into areas of subjectivity.
- CCA does not really deal with the distortions caused by general inflation.

12.8   Accounting for changing price levels in the UK

The history of the last 20 years of the UK accounting profession is littered with unsuccessful attempts to establish a means of accounting for inflation, which could command sufficient general support for it to be regarded as the standard approach.

CPP, CCA and hybrid versions of the two have been proposed by standard setters but none of these has gained general acceptance. This is seen by many as particularly unfortunate since the last 20 years have also seen rates of price inflation in the UK which are historically unprecedented. The objections to proposals can probably be classified broadly as:

- genuine objections to a particular proposal on the grounds that it was not appropriate to user needs;
- a belief that the benefits of producing adjusted accounts, in terms of making the information more useful as a basis for decision-making, do not justify the cost of producing the adjusted accounts;
- reluctance from some commercial and industrial directors to publish final accounts adjusted for inflation since almost inevitably such adjustments have the effect of showing lower profit numbers.

Whether a generally agreed approach to accounting for changing price levels will ever emerge is doubtful and this is probably unfortunate. Despite this many progressive companies publish inflation-adjusted accounts of one sort or another, or use such accounts for internal management purposes.

It is important to recognize the implications of the two major approaches, and the associated problems of historic cost accounting. Shareholders should certainly be aware of the impact of general inflation on their investments, and associated returns. Specific changes in costs and revenues associated with a particular business may also provide investors with both opportunities and threats. Managers must consider the implications of current cost accounting as regards the amount of profit which is distributable, without reducing the ability of a business to continue, in the same line of business, without further recourse to new funds. The two alternative systems provide useful but different viewpoints of profit.

> **Self-assessment question 12.2**
> In this chapter we have dealt with two important issues: the development of a conceptual framework and accounting during a period of changing prices. We have seen that both of these issues provoke considerable controversy and many believe that progress in each area is only likely to be made if broad agreement can be reached on how we should proceed. This raises an issue about how accounting *should* develop in the future.
>
> On the one hand, it can be argued that accounting is a *political process* where the interests of different groups (users, preparers, government, etc.) have to be reconciled in order to make progress. On the other hand, it can be argued that the role of accounting is to report objective reality. Thus, we should consider what is *technically correct* and not be concerned with the views of particular interest groups.
>
> Which of these two views (if either) do you support and why? Are these two views reconcilable?

12.9 Summary

In this chapter the major conventions of accounting have been examined. It has been seen that they suffer from a number of serious weaknesses which undermine their usefulness. They tend to be rather broad in nature and may conflict with one another. As a result there have been a number of attempts to develop a conceptual framework which would provide a more logical and systematic guide to why we record and how we record items. However, the development of a conceptual framework is not without its problems and no agreement on this issue is likely in the near future. The chapter also examined the problem of accounting for changing price-levels. It was seen that there are two main schools of thought on this issue but as yet neither school has achieved widespread acceptance.

References

Financial Accounting Standards Board *Objectives of Financial Reporting and Elements of Financial Statements of Business Enterprises*. FASB 1977.
Accounting Standards Board. *Exposure Draft – Statement of Principles* 1991
Horngren C.T. Uses and limitations of a conceptual framework. *Journal of Accountancy* 1981 pp 86–95.

Exercises

1   Three men, H, M, and A, each invest £10,000 in securities (shares) on 1 January. Their transactions, and those for the rest of the year, as as follows:

H   1 January   Buys equity shares costing £10,000
    30 June   Receives £1,100 in dividends, which is reinvested in
                    further shares
M   1 January   Buys government loan stock for £10,000
    30June   Receives £1,100 interest, which he puts on current
                    account in his bank
A   1 January   Borrows £7,500 at 10%
                    Buys equity shares costing £10,000 (i.e. puts in £2,500
                    of his own funds)
    30 June   Receives £1,100 in dividends, which is reinvested in
                    more equities
    31 December   Pays (from his overdraft) £1,200 interest

The retail price index stood at 100 on 1 January, 110 on 30 June, and 121 on 31 December. Assume that equity prices keep pace with inflation, as measured by this index.
Required
Compare the three ventures by setting out profit and loss accounts and balance sheets for each, based on:

(a) historic cost accounting conventions
(b) CPP accounting conventions (in £s stabilized at 31 December)

Ignore accrued revenue.

2   A company has the following purchases and sales in a period:

    1 January   Purchases 150 units at £10 each
    31 January   Sells 50 units at £12 each
    1 February   Receives notification of an increase in the purchase price
                    of goods to £11 per unit, to take effect immediately
    28 February   Sells 50 units at £13 each
    1 March   Purchases 100 units at £11 each
    31 March   Sells 50 units at £14 each
    1 April   Buys 100 units at a new price of £12 per unit
    30 April   Sells 50 units at £15 each

Prepare a profit and loss account using:

(a) conventional accounts, assuming that stock is sold in the order in which it was bought.
(b) costs current at the time of sale.

Appendix

Practical accounting

A1 Introduction

The aim of the book is to provide you with an understanding of the basic principles of accounting, particularly with regard to the balance sheet and the profit and loss account, and to enable you to prepare final accounts from a set of transactions. It will no doubt have become apparent, however, in working through activities and examples, that the system adopted becomes more of a problem as the number of transactions increases. In practice a business with a large number of transactions would need to use a system which is able to cope rather more effectively with increased amounts of data. The system of pluses and minuses, made on the face of a balance sheet and profit and loss account, will not do. In practice a business is likely to use one, or a combination, of the following:

(a) a system of *ledger accounts*, based upon the system of double-entry bookkeeping; and
(b) a *computerized system* – typically based upon the same principles used to date, but with a capability to handle large volumes of data.

This appendix aims to provide an introduction to these two systems. It does not aim to provide you with a detailed understanding of these systems, but rather to give an overview of systems found in practice, and to show that the *end-product* of these systems is the same as that achieved in the book, in Chapters 1 to 4, and that the underlying principles are identical. Clearly those wishing to specialize in accountancy will need to become more familiar with the systems outlined in this appendix.

The emphasis of this appendix is primarily on accounting systems as they relate to the preparation of final accounts. However, information of an accounting nature may well be useful in a variety of other ways, e.g. stock control, credit control, assistance with planning and decision-making, establishing how actual results compare with planned performance, etc. The design of accounting systems should clearly reflect these needs. As will be seen, the use of the database concept, and the idea of management information systems, means that the typical computer system has considerable advantages over a manual system, particularly as regards flexibility of use of the information contained within it.

A2   Objectives

On completion of this appendix you should be able:

- to explain the practical limitations of the system used so far in this book to record accounting transactions, and appreciate the need for a system able to cope rather better with a large volume of transactions;
- to explain the basic principles of double-entry book-keeping;
- to appreciate the role of the trial balance;
- to appreciate the relationship between ledger accounts and final accounts;
- to outline the main components of a computerized accounting system, and its relationship with the systems introduced to date.

A3   Ledger accounts – double-entry book-keeping

In preparing final accounts we use the following basic equation:

Assets   =   capital + liabilities

At the end of a period of trading this equation has been modified as follows:

Assets at   =   capital at the beginning of the period
the end   + injections of new capital
of a period   + net profit/ – net loss
**   – drawings**
**   + external liabilities**

Since Profit = revenue – expenses this can be modified as follows:

Assets   =   opening capital
**   + injections**
**   + revenue – expenses**
**   – drawings**
**   + external liabilities**

This can be rearranged as follows:

Assets   opening capital
+ drawings   =   + injections
+ expenses   + external liabilities
**   + revenues**

This is an equality which must exist, unless mistakes have been made.

Clearly, if a list can be prepared which sets out the above components, it would be fairly straightforward to convert it into a set of final accounts. The procedure would be broadly as described in Chapters 1 to 4. Revenues and expenses would be summarized in a profit and loss account, from which the net profit or loss could be calculated. This figure would then be added to (or subtracted from) the capital, with drawings being deducted from the resulting figure.

The system of *ledger accounts* is based upon the equality shown above, and permits a system whereby assets, drawings and expenses may be effectively recorded on one side of the equation, while capital, liabilities and revenues may be recorded on the other side.

The basic record used in a system of ledger accounts is called an account. An *account* is a record of one or more items, relating to some person or thing, kept under an appropriate heading. A separate account is opened for each category of asset, expense, claim and revenue which can be found on the balance sheet or on the profit and loss account. Individual accounts provide a location where all of the transactions relating to a particular asset, expense, claim or revenue can be collected and cumulated. The form of an account is:

Debit side		Title of the account			Credit side
Date	Detail	Amount	Date	Detail	Amount
		£			£

Each transaction is recorded in accounts for the particular person or thing it affects. All transactions are entered in date order. The words debit and credit are used to denote the side of an account on which an entry is made. The word debit means to make an entry on the left-hand side, while the word credit means to make an entry on the right-hand side.

By convention assets and expenses are recorded on the debit side, while capital, liabilities and revenues are recorded on the credit side. Reductions in assets or expenses are recorded on the credit side of these accounts, while reductions in capital, liabilities or revenues are recorded on the debit side. It is not surprising that increases in assets and expenses, on the one hand, and claims and revenues, on the other hand, are shown on opposite sides of their respective accounts. They do, after all, appear on opposite sides of the balance sheet.

When using a system of ledger accounts, the convention of duality results in a system whereby every entry has both a debit and a credit, hence the phrase 'double-entry book-keeping'. The 'detail' column in each ledger account provides a cross-reference facility, and shows the title of the account in which a corresponding double-entry is being made.

Example

Record the following in ledger accounts:

(a)   1 January   J. Jones invests £10,000 in a business.
(b)   5 January   The business buys stock for £5,000 cash.
(c)   8 January   It buys a further £1,000 of stock on credit.
(d) 15 January   It sells stock which had cost £1,000 for £1,500 cash.
(e) 21 January   It acquires a new machine for £4,000 cash.
(f) 28 January   It pays rent of £500 relating to January and February.

The double entry required is as follows:

(a) Debit cash   £10,000
     Credit capital   £10,000
(b) Debit stock   £5,000
     Credit cash   £5,000
(c) Debit stock   £1,000
     Credit creditors   £1,000
(d) Debit cash   £1,500
     Credit sales   £1,500
     Debit cost of sales   £1,000
     Credit stock   £1,000
(e) Debit machinery   £4,000
     Credit cash   £4,000
(f) Debit rent   £500
     Credit cash   £500

The ledger accounts are shown below:

Capital

		£			£
			Jan 1	Cash	10,000

Cash

		£			£
Jan 1	Capital	10,000	Jan 5	Stock	5,000
15	Sales	1,500	21	Machinery	4,000
			28	Rent	500
			31	Balance	2,000
		11,500			11,500
Feb 1	Balance	2,000			

Stock

		£				£
Jan 5	Cash	5,000	Jan 15	Cost of sales	1,000
8	Creditors	1,000	31	Balance	5,000
		6,000			6,000
Feb 1	Balance	5,000			

Creditors

		£				£
			Jan 8	Stock	1,000

Cost of sales

		£				£
Jan 15	Stock	1,000			

Sales

		£				£
			Jan 15	Cash	1,500

Machinery

		£				£
Jan 21	Cash	4,000			

Rent

		£				£
Jan 28	Cash	500			

At the end of a period each account can be *balanced off*. This is nothing more than comparing the sum of each of the two sides of the balance sheet and carrying the difference forward. The process of balancing off can be seen in the cash account and the stock account above, where debits exceed credits, with the excess being brought down as a debit balance.

At this point every transaction has been recorded in ledger accounts, and each account has been totalled, and balances carried forward. It should thus be possible to extract a list of balances which gives the identity referred to earlier, namely:

Assets		**capital**
+		**+**
drawings	**=**	**liabilities**
+		**+**
expenses		**revenues**

This list, when prepared from a set of ledger account balances, is known as a *trial balance*. The trial balance for the business of J. Jones would be as follows:

Trial balance as at 31 January

	Debit £	Credit £
Assets		
Cash	2,000	
Stock	5,000	
Machinery	4,000	
Expenses		
Cost of sales	1,000	
Rent	500	
Capital		10,000
Liabilities		
Creditors		1,000
Revenues		
Sales		1,500
	12,500	12,500

The figures which appear in a trial balance reflect the *cumulative effect* of the transactions recorded in the accounts. Following on from Chapters 1 to 4 it should be fairly easy to prepare a set of final accounts from such a list, subject to any adjustments which need to be made. All that is needed is for the items included in the trial balance to be put into the profit and loss account or balance sheet, as appropriate, with adjustments being made where necessary. Any adjustments needed will require a double entry to be made. That is not true of items in the trial balance, which reflect the results of double entry already made.

Self-assessment question A.1

From the following trial balance of W. Lamb, draw up a trading and profit and loss account for the year ended 31 December 19X7, and a balance sheet at that date.

Trial balance as at 31 December 19X7

	Debit £	Credit £
Stock	34,000	
Capital		120,000
Purchases	126,000	
Sales returns	1,200	
Salaries and wages	37,500	
Motor vehicles (cost)	15,000	
Motor vehicles (depreciation provision)		3,000

Furniture and fittings (cost)	4,000	
Furniture and fittings (depreciation provision)		800
Debtors	36,000	
Creditors		16,000
Doubtful debts provision		2,200
Sales		195,200
Purchases returns		2,000
Rent and rates	3,500	
Insurance	800	
Motor expenses	6,500	
Office expenses	2,200	
Heating and lighting	1,600	
General expenses	2,900	
Premises	50,000	
Cash	10,000	
Drawings	8,000	
	339,200	339,200

Notes to be taken into account at 31 December:
(a) Stock in hand at the year end is valued at £30,000.
(b) Rates of £500 are owing.
(c) Insurance prepaid amounts to £200.
(d) The bad debts provision is to be adjusted to 5% of debtors.
(e) Depreciation is to be provided at the rate of 20% on cost for vehicles and 10% on cost for furniture and fittings.

In a system of ledger accounts, the profit and loss account is a formal part of the ledger accounting system. Revenues and expenses are transferred to the profit and loss account. The net profit or loss is subsequently transferred to the capital account, along with drawings. The balance sheet is nothing more than a list of balances in the ledger accounts, at a particular time, which must represent assets or claims. Any prepayments, accruals and similar adjustments must therefore be shown as balances on an account. In the example used above (J. Jones), assuming that a profit and loss account was required for January, and a balance sheet as at 31 January, the only adjustment needed would be for rent, the payment for which relates to both January and February. Since £500 was paid covering these two months it is reasonable to suppose that £250 relates to January, and should be shown as an expense of January, while the remaining £250 represents a prepayment at the end of January, which should be carried forward as a balance, and thus be listed in the balance sheet.

A complete set of accounts for the business of J. Jones is given below, along with a balance sheet as at 31 January. The trading and profit and loss accounts could, of course, be presented in a variety of formats, but the underlying principles hold in all cases.

Capital

		£			£
			Jan 1	Cash	10,000
Jan 31	Balance	10,250	31	Net profit	250
		10,250			10,250
			Feb 1	Balance	10,250

Cash

		£			£
Jan 1	Capital	10,000	Jan 5	Stock	5,000
15	Sales	1,500	21	Machinery	4,000
			28	Rent	500
			31	Balance	2,000
		11,500			11,500
Feb 1	Balance	2,000			

Stock

		£			£
Jan 5	Cash	5,000	Jan 15	Cost of sales	1,000
8	Creditors	1,000	31	Balance	5,000
		6,000			6,000
Feb 1	Balance	5,000			

Creditors

		£			£
Jan 31	Balance	1,000	Jan 8	Stock	1,000
		1,000			1,000
			Feb 1	Balance	1,000

Cost of sales

		£			£
Jan 15	Stock	1,000	Jan 31	Trading	1,000

Sales

		£			£
Jan 31	Trading	1,500	Jan 15	Cash	1,500

Machinery

		£				£
Jan 21	Cash	4,000	Jan 31		Balance	4,000
		4,000				4,000
Feb 1	Balance	4,000				

Rent

		£				£
Jan 28	Cash	500	Jan 31		Profit and loss	250
			31		Balance	250
		500				500
Feb 1	Balance	250				

Trading

		£			£
Jan 31	Cost of sales	1,000	Jan 31	Sales	1,500
	Gross profit	500			
		1,500			1,500

Profit and loss

		£			£
Jan 31	Rent	250	Jan 31	Gross profit	500
	Net profit	250			
		500			500

In practice the trading and profit and loss account is likely to be presented in one of the ways shown earlier. The above represents the entries in the actual ledger accounts.

The balance sheet, which is simply a list of account balances appropriately set out, is as follows:

Balance sheet as at 31 January

	£		£
Machinery	4,000	Capital	10,250
Stock	5,000	Creditors	1,000
Prepaid rent	250		
Cash	2,000		
	11,250		11,250

As with the profit and loss account, this would typically be *presented* in one of the ways set out earlier.

Several points emerge from the above example.

1 Every transaction has a double entry, with a debit entry being matched by a corresponding credit entry.

- Increases in assets, expenses and drawings are debits
- Reductions in assets, expenses and drawings are credits
- Increases in capital, liabilities and revenues are credits
- Reductions in capital, liabilities and revenues are debits.

2   The question as to whether such things as rent are assets or expenses does not arise at the recording stage, since the entry is the same. The split into assets and expenses only needs to be made at the end of the period, when a profit and loss account is being prepared. Any prepayments or accruals (which appear as debit or credit balances b/d) will be dealt with automatically using a system of ledger accounts. The same is true of revenues, liabilities and related adjustments.
3   Ledger accounts can cope with quite large numbers of transactions neatly and effectively.
4   The end-product of a system of ledger accounts is identical to that of the system used in Chapters 1 to 4.

Self-assessment question A.2

The following items appear in the balance sheet of a business as at 31 December 19X6:

Current assets	£
Prepaid insurance	300
Prepaid heating	100

Current liabilities	
Accruals wages	1,000
Deferred revenue rent	500

During the year to 31 December 19X7 the following cash receipts and payments were recorded:

Cash receipts
Rent (relating to the period 1 April 19X7 to 30 September 19X7) £1,000

Cash payments	£
Wages	25,000
Insurance	1,200
Heating	1,000

At the year end (31 December 19X7) you ascertain that £500 of wages and £200 of heating bills remain outstanding, and that £400 of insurance has been prepaid.

Prepare ledger accounts showing the entries for rent receivable, insurance, heating, and wages, clearly showing the transfer that would be made to the profit and loss account.

> What figures, if any, relating to these transactions, would be included
> in the balance sheet as at 31 December 19X7, and under what heading
> would they appear?

A4   Computerized systems

Increasingly accounting records are maintained on a computer rather than on
paper, but following precisely the same principles and rules of double entry.
Systems vary considerably, but the end-product must still include the profit and
loss account and balance sheet. A computerized system is likely to be associated with larger numbers of transactions, particularly relating to such things as
sales, purchases, stock issues, receipts and payments of cash (or cheques),
wages, etc. It is also likely that a computerized system will offer other considerable advantages with regard to the printing of documents necessary to the
efficient running of the business, and in the opportunity it provides to use
information in a variety of ways. In designing a computerized system it is thus
important to ensure:

1   That the system will cope with these large amounts of data.
2   That the variety of documents necessary to the efficient running of the
    business can be produced by the system (e.g. sales invoices, delivery notes,
    stock records, cheques for payment, wages slips, etc.).
3   That the data kept on computer can be analysed and summarized in ways
    which will be of use to the decision-making process within the firm. Among
    other things this should include a set of final accounts.

The essence of a computerized system is that a computer record will need to
be maintained for each item to be found in a set of accounts. In many instances
these records will need to be broken down into more detail. For example,
records are likely to be kept for debtors, creditors, stock and wages, all of which
will almost certainly need to have more detailed records kept within them.
Individual records will need to be maintained for each debtor and creditor, for
each item of stock, and for each employee (for purposes of tax, national insurance, etc.). These records will be updated to reflect such things as sales and
purchases, returns, stock issues and returns, and weekly or monthly wages and
salaries. Only the totals of such records would be needed for a set of final
accounts, but the detailed records are a necessary part of day-to-day decision-
making and control. For example, the maintenance of detailed stock records
should help in establishing on the spot stock availability or expected delivery
time, as well as assisting with regard to decisions about such things as re-order-
ing, optimal stock levels, etc. Detailed debtors' records are needed for purposes
of cash collection and credit control. Detailed creditor records are necessary to
ensure payment is made at an appropriate time, and that available discounts

are taken. Individual wages records need to be maintained to ensure the correct deduction of such things as tax, national insurance and pension contributions, and the payment of any bonuses, overtime, holiday pay, etc.

In order to operate effectively a computerized system must be based on an adequate system of coding. This is nothing more than the identification of an appropriate code for each type of asset, liability, revenue or expense. The coding system must be sufficiently detailed to permit a range of analyses and printouts in as much detail as is considered necessary by the business. Information can then be fed into the computer, by keyboard, tape, scanning, mark sensing or other methods, to update the records and print out documents as required. The method used to update records is one of pluses and minuses, so the approach used in Chapters 1 to 4 is essentially the same as that used in a computerized system.

Accounting packages typically operate by the use of menu-driven screens, in which the user can select the part of the routine he or she wishes to operate. It is not uncommon to find that the various parts of the routine correspond reasonably closely to the components of a manual system described earlier.

In a properly designed computer system, while the concept of duality still applies, it is usual to find that the information which forms the basis of a double entry is only put into the computer once. The system, which should be properly integrated, should then be designed to ensure that this basic information is recorded and analysed as needed. This is not to say that all of the parts of the system need to be updated at the same time. Indeed, it is quite common to find that the two entries relating to a transaction take place at a different time. For example, one part of a system might be to print out sales invoices. The printing of the invoices is likely to be carried out in conjunction with a detailed updating of individual debtors' accounts. However, the updating of the sales account may occur at a somewhat later date, and be entered in total. As long as the system is designed to ensure that the second entry is made at some stage before the preparation of final accounts, this need cause no problems. What is important is that the system is designed in a way which can take a single input, and record and analyse it as needed.

In the final analysis a computerized system still follows the same basic principles as were set out earlier. However, it is likely to take the form of a series of sub-routines dealing with different aspects of the business, producing necessary documents and detailed accounts, which can then be integrated and analysed to produce a set of final accounts.

In practice a computerized accounting system is likely to be part of a *management information system* (MIS). An MIS is one in which a variety of information is collected, analysed and communicated through the organization so as to help in its efficient management and functioning. Typically an MIS uses the database concept, in which data is stored in an appropriate way, and then accessed and analysed as needed, both routinely and on an *ad hoc* basis. Routine transactions may relate to sales, payments of customers' accounts, wages, etc. Less routine analysis may relate to forecasting and financial modelling, which is introduced in Chapter 9.

A computerized accounting system is likely to have fewer errors than a manual system. Errors of addition, or errors which arise because the two aspects of a transaction are not both correctly recorded, should be eliminated. Nevertheless, computerized accounting systems can create additional security problems. For example, it is necessary to ensure that information is input correctly; it is necessary to ensure that both data and software are not corrupted by unauthorized users; and the amount of documentation is likely to be less, thus reducing the ability to check for errors/fraud, etc.

Overall, computerized systems have advantages over manual systems where there are many transactions, where documents need printing, and where flexibility and speed of analysis are important.

A5 Summary

This appendix has provided you with a brief review of systems of accounting in practice. The system of ledger accounts was outlined and illustrated. The principles of manual and computerized systems were outlined, with emphasis on the need to develop effective control mechanisms. In practice most systems of accounting are now computerized, at least in part.

Since this book aims to provide an introduction to accounting for the non-specialist (the *users* of accounting information), this appendix is deliberately restricted in scope. It provides only a very broad overview of accounting in practice. Should you wish to pursue this area further you will need to study a more specialist accounting text, where you will find a number of descriptions of more fully developed systems. You should not be too surprised if the accounting systems you encounter in practice are rather more sophisticated than the system of pluses and minuses used in this book. What should be clear, however, is that any system used in practice will follow the principles adopted in this book, and the end-product, in terms of final accounts, is identical.

Exercise

The following is the trial balance of a sole trading business at the end of its financial year:

Trial balance as at 30 June 19X9

	Debit £	Credit £
Stock-in-trade at 1 July 19X8	27,500	
Capital		80,380
Purchases	103,700	
Sales		179,800

Rent and rates	2,760	
Insurance	700	
Motor expenses	5,780	
Office expenses	2,540	
Heating and lighting	1,820	
General expenses	2,840	
Freehold premises	45,000	
Cash	3,200	
Salaries and wages	24,600	
Motor vehicles (cost)	17,500	
Motor vehicles (depreciation provision)		5,300
Furniture and fittings (cost)	12,800	
Furniture and fittings (depreciation provision)		3,960
Debtors	28,400	
Creditors		13,100
Doubtful debts provision		1,800
Drawings	5,200	
	£284,340	£284,340

The following information is also available:

(a) Stock-in-trade at 30 June 19X9 was physically counted and was valued at £26,300.
(b) Rates of £570 were owing at 30 June 19X9.
(c) A motor vehicle repair carried out in June 19X9 costing £220 was still unpaid at the end of the year.
(d) The doubtful debts provision is to be established at 5% of debtors at 30 June 19X9.
(e) Depreciation is to be provided at the rate of 25% p.a. on cost for vehicles and 15% p.a. on cost for furniture and fittings.

Prepare a trading and profit and loss account for the year ended 30 June 19X9 and a balance sheet as at that date for the business.

Answers to self-assessment questions

Chapter 1

Self-assessment question 1.1

Profit and loss account (income statement) for Day 1

	£	£
Sales of ice cream		120
Purchase of ice cream	100	
Less: closing stock of ice cream	20	
Cost of ice cream sold		80
Net profit (increase in wealth)		40

Cash flow statement for Day 1

	£
Receipts from sales	120
Less: payment for stock	100
Net increase in cash	20
Opening balance	100
Closing balance	120

Balance sheet (position statement) as at end of Day 1

	£
Stock of unsold ice cream	20
Cash (closing balance on Day 1)	120
	140
Therefore:	
Russell's business wealth is	140

Profit and loss account (income statement) for Day 2

	£	£
Sales of ice cream		165
Opening stock of ice cream	20	
Purchase of ice cream	100	
	120	
Less: closing stock of ice cream	10	
Cost of ice cream sold		110
Net profit (increase in wealth)		55

Cash flow statement for Day 2

	£
Receipts from sales	165
Less: payment for stock	<u>100</u>
Net increase in cash	65
Opening balance	<u>120</u>
Closing balance	<u>185</u>

Balance sheet (position statement) as at end of Day 2

	£
Stock of unsold ice cream	10
Cash (closing balance on Day 2)	<u>185</u>
	195
Therefore:	
Russell's business wealth is	<u>195</u>

Profit and loss account (income statement) for Day 3

	£	£
Sales of ice cream		60
Opening stock of ice cream	10	
Purchase of ice cream	<u>100</u>	
	110	
Less: closing stock of ice cream	<u>70</u>	
Cost of ice cream sold		<u>40</u>
Net profit (increase in wealth)		20

Cash flow statement for Day 3

	£
Receipts from sales	60
Less: payment for stock	<u>100</u>
Net decrease in cash	(40)
Opening balance	<u>185</u>
Closing balance	<u>145</u>

Balance sheet (position statement) as at end of Day 3

	£
Stock of unsold ice cream	70
Cash (closing balance on Day 3)	<u>145</u>
	215
Therefore:	
Russell's business wealth is	<u>215</u>

Profit and loss account (income statement) for Day 4

	£	£
Sales of ice cream		56
Opening stock of ice cream	70	
Purchase of ice cream	–	
	70	
Less: closing stock of ice cream	–	
Cost of ice cream sold		70
Net loss (decrease in wealth)		14

Cash flow statement for Day 4

	£
Receipts from sales	56
Less: payment for stock	–
Net increase in cash	56
Opening balance	145
Closing balance	201

Balance sheet (position statement) as at end of Day 4

	£
Stock of unsold ice cream	–
Cash (closing balance on Day 4)	201
	201
Therefore:	
Russell's business wealth is	201

We can see that, for the first 3 days, Russell managed to make a profit on each day of his venture and his business wealth rose steadily. However, on the fourth day he made a loss and there was also a corresponding decrease in his business wealth. Overall his wealth increased from £100 at the beginning of the venture to £201 after 4 days and so he may feel satisfied with the venture.

Chapter 2

Self-assessment question 2.1

	Assets	*Claims*
(a)	+ vehicle	
	– cash	
(b)	– cash	– creditor
(c)	+ equipment	+ creditor

(d)   + cash
      – debtor

(e)   + cash   + loan

(f)   + stock
      – cash

(g)   + stock   + creditors

(h)   – cash   – capital (drawings)

Self-assessment question 2.2

		Assets	*Claims*
(a)	Office equipment	*	
(b)	Fixtures and fittings	*	
(c)	Creditors		*
(d)	Debtors	*	
(e)	Loan from E. Mac		*
(f)	Outstanding bill for fuel		*
(g)	Bank balance	depends on whether cash in hand or overdrawn. If it is cash in hand it is an asset. If it is an overdraft it is a liability.	

Self-assessment question 2.3

(a)   Reference to conventions of business entity and duality.

(b)   Capital   £10,000
      Capital   £18,000
      Liabilities   £15,000
      Liabilities   £8,000
      Assets   £20,000
      Assets   £35,000

(c)   The answer depends on whether the car is for his personal use (in which case it will not appear in the business balance sheet), or for business use (in which case it will appear in the business balance sheet).

(d)   Refer to convention of business entity.

Self-assessment question 2.4

(a), (d), (f) and (h).
(b), (c) and (g) are fixed assets.
(e) is an intangible asset.

Self-assessment question 2.5

Balance sheet as at 31 January 19X1

	£	£		£
Fixed assets			*Capital*	25,000
Premises		20,000	+ Retained profits	9,250
Equipment		8,000		34,250
		28,000		
Current assets			*Long-term loan*	12,000
Stock	10,000		*Current liabilities*	
Debtors	15,000		Creditors	10,000
Bank	3,000			
Cash	250			
		28,250		
		56,250		56,250

Since Assets = capital + liabilities
Capital = assets − liabilities
Therefore Capital = 56,250 − 22,000 = 34,250
Since £25,000 was put into the business originally, a further £9,250 profit must have been retained in the business since that time.

Chapter 3

Self-assessment question 3.1

Wight Enterprises
Balance sheet as at 31 January

	+ £	− £	Net £		+ £	− £	Net £
Fixed assets				*Capital*			
Premises	3,000c		3,000	Opening balance	10,000a		10,000
				Injection		400k	400
				Net profit		340	340
							10,740
				Less drawings		500j	500
							10,240

Current assets

Stock	800d	600f	3,000					
	2,200e	200g						
	2,000n	600l		*Loans*		5,000b		5,000
		100m						
		500r						
Stationery	100p	20 adj	80					
Debtors	200g	200i	590					
	90m							
	500r			*Current liabilities*				
				Creditors		2,200e 800h		3,000
Cash	10,000a 3,000c	11,570				2,000n 400k		
	5,000b	800d						
	600f	800h						
	200i	500j						
	800l	30o						
	250r	100p						
		50q						
		18,240						18,240

Profit and loss account for the month of January

	+	−	Net		+	−	Net
	£	£	£		£	£	£
Expenses				*Revenues*			
Cost of	600f		2,000	Sales	600f		2,440
sales	200g				200g		
	600l				800l		
	100m				90m		
	500r				750r		
Rent	30o		30				
Miscellaneous	50q		50				
expenses							
Stationery	20adj		20				
			2,100				
Net profit			340				
			2,440				2,440

Self-assessment question 3.2

(a)   Revenue – sales – £1,500
      Current assets – debtors £1,500

(b)   Revenue – rent receivable £6,000
      Current assets – debtors (rent receivable) – £1,000

(c)   Revenue – rent receivable – £6,000
      Current liabilities – deferred revenue (rent) – £1,500

Self-assessment question 3.3

(a) Expense – £350
Asset – stationery under the heading current assets £150

(b) Expense – £550
Current liabilities – accrued expenses (accruals) £100
(This relates to the period November/December 19X6)
Note that although a bill has been received which relates to January, as well as November and December, an accrual is only set up for that part which relates to the period of account

(c) Expense – £100
Current liabilities – accrued expenses £100

Self-assessment question 3.4

Revenues/expenses for the year ending 31 December 19X7

Expenses
Rent   £2,000 (N.B. The first payment clears last year's accrual)

Electricity   £460   (i.e. £50 relating to January 19X7
                        +£120+£70+£120
                        + an estimate of £100 for November/December 19X7)

Rates   £875   (i.e. £200 prepaid in 19X6 + £450
                        +£225 relating to the period October to December 19X7)

Revenues
Interest   £800   (i.e. £200 deferred revenue in 19X6 + £400
                        +£200 owing at year end to cover October-December 19X7

Balance sheet extracts as at 31 December 19X7

Current assets		*Current liabilities*	
Prepayments – rent	£500	Accrued electricity	£100
(covering the quarter ending 31 March 19X8)			
Prepayments – rates	£225		
(covering the quarter ending 31 March 19X8)			
Debtors – interest receivable	£200		
(covering the quarter ending 31 December 19X7)			

Self-assessment question 3.5

Milly
Balance sheet as at 28 February 19X7

	+	–	Net		+	–	Net
Fixed assets				*Capital*			
Premises	55,000		55,000	Opening balance	60,000		60,000
Fittings	2,000		2,000	Net profit	1,742	–	1,742
Vehicles	3,000	100	2,900				61,742
Till	500		500	less drawings		1,000	–1,000
			60,400				60,742
Current assets							
Stock	2,000	2,900	1,900				
	4,200	1,250					
		150		*Loans*	20,000		20,000
Debtors	2,000	1,800	200	*Current liabilities*			
Prepayments	300adj1		400				
	100adj2			Creditors	2,000	150	2,450
Cash	60,000	55,000	20,415		4,200	3,600	
	20,000	3,000		Accruals	75adj3		123
	5,000	360			48adj4		
	1,800	500					
		2,000					
		500					
		150					
		3,500					
		300					
		75					
		1,000					
			83,315				83,315

Profit and loss account for the 2 months ended 28 February 19X7

	+	–	Net		+	–	Net
	£	£	£		£	£	£
Expenses				*Revenues*			
Cost of sales	2,900		4,150	Sales	5,000		7,000
	1,250				2,000		
Wages	500		500	Discount recd.		100	100
Vehicle	360	300adj1	210				
expenses	150						
Rates	300	100adj2	200				
Electricity	75		150				
	75adj3						
Telephone	48adj4		48				
Depreciation							
vehicles	100adj5		100				
			5,358				
Net profit			1,742				
			7,100				7,100

Notes

Adjustment 1 relates to the fact that the road tax and insurance relate to a full year, whereas the period of account is only 2 months.

Adjustment 2 relates to the fact that rates paid cover 3 months, with a resulting prepayment for 1 month.

Adjustment 3 relates to the fact that no electricity bill has been included for February. An estimate thus needs to be made, with a resulting accrual in the balance sheet.

Adjustment 4 relates to the need to incorporate an appropriate amount to cover telephone expenses to the end of February (estimate 8 of the 10 weeks for which a bill has been received – namely £48), and its related accrual.

Adjustment 5 relates to depreciation of vehicles – 20% on cost of £3,000 – for 2 months – £3,000 × 20/100 × 2/12 = £100.

Note that withdrawals by the owner are shown as drawings, whatever they are called (e.g. salary).

Self-assessment question 3.6

Trading and profit and loss account for the year ended 31 December

			Workings
Sales		59,700	
Less cost of sales		27,500	
Gross profit		32,200	
Less *other expenses*			
Wages	7,700		8,000 – 300
Rates	1,500		2,000 – 500
Carriage	300		
Rent	3,200		3,000 + 200
Stationery	100		250 – 150
General expenses	2,750		2,500 + 250
Fuel and electricity	1,150		1,000 + 150
Motor expenses	1,150		1,250 – 100
Depreciation – equipment	800		
Depreciation – vehicles	1,000		
Interest	1,000		
		20,650	
Net profit		11,550	

Balance sheet as at December 31

		Workings
Fixed assets		
Premises	25,000	
Equipment	5,200	6,000 – 800
Vehicles	2,500	3,500 – 1,000
	32,700	

Current assets			
Stock	4,000		3,000 + 30,000
			−27,500 − 1,500
Debtors	5,200		4,500 + 59,700
			−59,000
Prepayments	250		100 + 150 Stat.
Cash	9,700		2,000 − 300
	19,150		−3,000 − 8,000
			− 5,000 − 2,000
			− 250 − 2,500
			+59,000 −
			−28,000 − 1,000
			− 1,250
Less liabilities due within 1 year			
Creditors	4,000		2,000 + 30,000
			−28,000
Accruals	1,400		150 + 250
		5,400	+ 1,000
			loan interest
Net current assets		13,750	
		46,450	
Less liabilities due			
more than 1 year from now			
Loans		10,000	
Net assets		36,450	
Financed by:			
Capital – opening balance		31,400	
Net profit		11,550	
		42,950	
Less drawings		6,500	
		36,450	

Chapter 4

Self-assessment question 4.1

Cost £20,000, disposal value £4,000.
Total to be depreciated £16,000.
Using straight-line depreciation, a full year's depreciation would be £3,200.
(a) 19X5 entries
Since the lorry was acquired on 1 July, depreciation will be on a pro-rata basis,
i.e. £1600.

- Include depreciation expense in profit and loss account, £1,600.
- Increase depreciation provision by £1,600.

The balance sheet would show:

Vehicles (cost)	£20,000
Depreciation provision	£ 1,600
	£18,400

19X6 entries
- include depreciation expenses in profit and loss account, £3,200
- increase depreciation provision by £3,200

The balance sheet would show:

Vehicles (cost)	£20,000
Depreciation provision	£ 4,800
	£15,200

(b) **19X7 entries**
- increase cash by £11,000
- reduce asset (vehicles) by £20,000
- reduce depreciation provision (vehicles) by £4,800
- increase expense (loss on disposal) by £4,200

(c)   There is an almost infinite number of methods that could be used. Either the reducing balance or the sum-of-the-digits methods might be more appropriate in the case of an asset like a lorry. This is because such an asset is likely to require increasing amounts of maintenance and repairs as it becomes older. Use of one of these two methods would tend to lead to a more equal total lorry expense to be matched against revenues, each year. Assuming that the lorry is helping to generate equal amounts of revenues each year, this would probably lead to a fairer matching of expenses to revenues.

Self-assessment question 4.2

(a) See text
(b) **FIFO method**
   Trading and profit and loss account

	19X5	19X6	19X7
	£	£	£
Sales	16,000	25,000	36,000
Cost of sales	10,000	14,000	21,000
Gross profit	6,000	11,000	15,000
Overheads	4,000	5,000	6,000
Net profit	2,000	6,000	9,000

Stock account

	19X5			19X6			19X7		
	Qty	Price	£	Qty	Price	£	Qty	Price	£
Opening balance	–			100 @ £50	=5000		150 @ £60	=9000	
Purchases	300 @ £50	=1500		300 @ £60	=1800		250 @ £80	=20000	
Issues (cost of sales)	200 @ £50	=10000		100 @ £50	=5000		150 @ £60	=9000	
							150 @ £60	=9000	150 @ £80	=12000
Closing stock	100 @ £50	=5000		150 @ £60	=9000		100 @ £80	=8000	

LIFO method
Trading and profit and loss account

	19X5	19X6	19X7
	£	£	£
Sales	16,000	25,000	36,000
Cost of sales	10,000	15,000	23,000
Gross profit	6,000	10,000	13,000
Overheads	4,000	5,000	6,000
Net profit	2,000	5,000	7,000

Stock account

	19X5		19X6		19X7	
	Qty Price £		Qty Price £		Qty Price £	
Opening balance	–		100 @ £50=5000		100 @ £50=5000	
					50 @ £60=3000	
Purchases	300 @ £50=15000		300 @ £60=18000		250 @ £80=20000	
Issues (cost of sales)	200 @ £50=10000		250 @ £60=15000		250 @ £80=20000	
					50 @ £60=3000	
Closing stock	100 @ £50=5000		100 @ £50=5000		100 @ £50=5000	
			50 @ £60=3000			

AVCO method
Trading and profit and loss account

	19X5	19X6	19X7
	£	£	£
Sales	16,000	25,000	36,000
Cost of sales	10,000	14,375	21,468
Gross profit	6,000	10,675	14,532
Overheads	4,000	5,000	6,000
Net profit	2,000	5,675	8,532

Stock account

	19X5		19X6		19X7	
	Qty Price £		Qty Price £		Qty Price £	
Opening balance	–		100 @ £50=5000		150 @ £57.5=8625	
Purchases	300 @ £50=15000		300 @ £60=18000		250 @ £80=20000	
Therefore AVCO	15000/300=50		23000/400=57.5		28625/400=71.56	
Issues (cost of sales)	200 @ £50=10000		250×57.5=14375		300 @ 71.56=21468	
Closing stock	100 @ £50=5000		150 @ 57.5=8625		100 @ 71.56=7156	

Self-assessment question 4.3

Firstly deal with the doubtful debts. The amount of provision required is £1,455 [i.e. £300 + (£23,400 – 300) × 5%]. The entries are:

- increase an expense – creation of doubtful debts provision (£1,455)
- increase doubtful debts provision (£1,455)

The expense 'creation of doubtful debts provision' will be included in the profit and loss account. In the balance sheet debtors will appear as follows:

	£
Debtors	23,400
Less doubtful debts	
provision	1,455
	21,945

The net amount of £21,945 represents the expected future benefit associated with debtors, taking a prudent view.

When the sales were made the entries are:

- increase the revenues (sales) by £147,800*
- increase debtors by £147,800

When the cash was received the entries are:

- increase cash by £143,700*
- decrease debtors by £143,700

When the 19X6 debts go bad the entries are:

- decrease debtors by £910*
- decrease the provision for doubtful debts by £910

When the 19X7 debts go bad the entries are:

- decrease debtors by £890* (i.e. £1,800 – 910)
- increase the expense (bad debts written off) by £890

(*These will not all occur at one point, e.g. the sales total will be made up of lots of individual sales which will be recorded as they occur.)

At the end of the year the remaining provision against the 19X6 doubtful debts will no longer be required. The entries are:

- reduce doubtful debt provision by £545 (i.e. £1,455 – 910)
- increase revenues (doubtful debt provision no longer required) by £545.

Lastly, create a provision for doubtful debts as at 31 December 19X7. The balance of debtors at 31 December 19X7 is:

Debtors at 1 January 19X6	£23,400
add: Sales for the year	147,800
	171,200
less: Cash received during the year	143,700
	27,500
less: Bad debts written off	1,800
Debtors at 31 December 19X7	£25,700

The entries are:

- increase an expense (creation of doubtful debts provision) £1,285 (i.e. £25,700 × 5%)
- increase doubtful debts provision by £1,285.

In the balance sheet debtors will appear as follows:

	£
Debtors	25,700
Less doubtful debts provision	1,285
	24,415

Chapter 5

Self-assessment question 5.1

(a) £2.

(b)

Assets	£	Claims	£
Net assets	450,000	Ordinary share capital	200,000
		Reserves	100,000
		Share premiums account	150,000
	450,000		450,000

(c) £2.25.

(d) Book value per share reflects the share of net assets, which are shown at cost less depreciation. As such it is not a particularly meaningful figure. Market price per share reflects expected earnings, perceived risk, financial strength, market value of assets, etc. Since it results from the interaction of supply and demand it may be considered an efficient current price.

Self-assessment question 5.2

Corfu Ltd

Assets	£	Claims	£
Net assets	950,000	Ordinary share capital	
		(600,000 shares of £1 each	
		fully paid)	600,000
		Share premium account	50,000
		Revaluation reserve	200,000
		Revenue reserves	100,000
	950,000		950,000

The bonus issue results in a decrease in reserves and an increase in share capital of £100,000. Since the share premium has limited uses, and cannot be distributed as a dividend, it is sensible to convert this account first.

The rights issue results in an increase of £100,000 in share capital (the bonus issue had increased share capital to £500,000), making it £600,000; cash increases by £150,000, while the share premium account needs to be increased by £50,000.

Self-assessment question 5.3.

RAC Ltd
Trading profit and loss and appropriation account for the year ended 31 December 19X7

	£	£
Sales		530,000
Opening stock	30,000	
Purchases	300,000	
	330,000	
Less closing stock	35,000	
Cost of sales		295,000
Gross profit		235,000
Less *other expenses*		
Directors' remuneration	31,000	
Selling and distribution expenses	29,000	
Loan interest	4,000	
Administration	42,000	
Wages and salaries	50,000	
Bad debts	2,000	
Depreciation – equipment	5,000	

Depreciation – fittings	5,000		
		168,000	
Net profit		67,000	
Profit and loss balance brought forward		25,000	
Total available for appropriation		92,000	
Appropriated as follows:			
General reserve	25,000		
Preference dividends	5,000		
Ordinary dividends	40,000		
		70,000	
Unappropriated profit carried forward		22,000	

Balance sheet as at 31 December 19X7

	£	£	£
Fixed assets			
Premises			200,000
Equipment – cost		50,000	
– depreciation provision		25,000	
			25,000·
Fittings – cost		50,000	
– depreciation provision		30,000	
			20,000
			245,000
Current assets			
Stock	35,000		
Prepayments	1,000		
Debtors	50,000		
Cash	100,000		
		186,000	
Less *Creditors due within 1 year*			
Creditors	30,000		
Accruals	4,000		
Proposed pref. dividends	5,000		
Proposed ord. dividend	40,000		
		79,000	
Net current assets			107,000
			352,000
Creditors due in more than 1 year			
Loans			40,000
Net assets			312,000
Financed by:			
Capital			
Ordinary share capital			200,000
Preference share capital			50,000
			250,000

Reserves
General reserve   40,000
Profit and loss account   22,000
                                                                    62,000
                                                                   312,000

Chapter 6

Self-assessment question 6.1

(a) **Marina Plc**
     Profit and loss account for the year ended 31 December 19X7

	£000	£000	£000
Sales			5,000
Opening stock		250	
Purchases		3,000	
		3,250	
Less closing stock		300	
Cost of sales			2,950
Gross profit			2,050
Less expenses			
Wages and salaries			
– Production/warehousing		200	
– Administration		200	
– Selling and distribution		400	
Motor expenses			
– Administration		20	
– Distribution		80	
General distribution expenses		350	
General administration expenses		150	
Debenture interest		28	
Directors' remuneration		200	
Bad debts		120	
Depreciation			
– Plant and machinery		24	
– Motor vehicles		50	
			1,822
Net profit			228
Less corporation tax			58
			170
Plus profit and loss balance b/f			50
			220
Appropriated as follows:			
General reserve		20	
Preference share dividend		50	
Ordinary share dividend		60	
			130
Profit and loss balance c/f			90

(b) Profit and loss account for the year ended 31 December 19X7

	£000
Turnover	5,000
Cost of sales*	(3,150)
Gross profit	1,850
Distribution costs*	(894)
Administration costs*	(700)
Interest payable	(28)
Corporation tax	(58)
Profit for the year after tax	170
Transfer to general reserve	(20)
Dividends	(110)
Added to reserves	40

*Workings

Expense	Cost of sales £000	Distribution £000	Administration £000
Cost of sales	2,950		
Wages and salaries	200	400	200
Motor expenses	—	80	20
General expenses	—	350	150
Directors' remuneration	—	—	200
Bad debts	—	—	120
Depreciation			
– Plant and machinery	—	24	—
– Motor vehicles	—	40	10
Total	3,150	894	700

Balance sheet as at 31 December 19X7

Fixed assets	Note	£000	£000	£000
Land and buildings				1,800
Plant and machinery	1			66
Motor vehicles	2			100
				1,966
Current assets				
Stock			300	
Debtors			600	
			900	
Creditors: amounts falling due within 1 year				
Loans		100		
Overdraft		13		
Trade creditors		200		

Taxation		58	
Dividends	3	<u>85</u>	
		456	
Net current assets		444	
Less: *Creditors falling due*			
after more than 1 year			
Debenture loans	4	<u>400</u>	
			<u>44</u>
Net assets			2,010
Capital and reserves			
Ordinary share capital	5		1,000
Preference share capital	6		500
Share premium			200
General reserve	7		220
Profit and loss account			<u>40</u>
			1,960

Notes

1 The plant and machinery figure comprises:

Plant and machinery – cost	£120,000
Less depreciation provision	<u>£54,000</u>
	£66,000

2 The motor vehicles figure comprises:

Motor vehicles (at cost)	£200,000
Less depreciation provision	<u>£100,000</u>
	£100,000

3 The dividends relate to the final preference dividend of £25,000 and the ordinary dividend of £60,000.

4 Debenture loans carry a 7% interest rate.
They are redeemable in 1995.

5 The ordinary share capital consists of 2 million shares of £0.50 each, fully paid.

6 The preference share capital consists of 500,000 £1 preference shares, fully paid, which carry a dividend entitlement of 10%. The shares are cumulative.

7 £20,000 has been transferred to the general reserve, increasing it to £220,000.

Chapter 7

Self-assessment question 7.1

Goodwill on consolidation
Paid   £29m
Got   £16m   (£12m ordinary share capital + £4m reserves – 80%
                      at time of acquisition)
Goodwill   £13m

Reserves
Matt   £10m
James   £4m   (80% of post-acquisition reserves)
              £14m

Minority interests
Capital James   £15m
Reserves James   £10m
                 £25m × 20% = £5m

Balance sheet as at 31 December 19X3

	£000	*£000*
Fixed assets		24,800
Goodwill on consolidation		13,000
Current assets	2,300	
Current liabilities	1,100	
		1,200
		39,000
Ordinary share capital		20,000
Reserves		14,000
Minority interests		5,000
		39,000

Typically the goodwill will be written off against the reserves.

Self-assessment question 7.2

Group profit and loss account for the year ended 31 December 19X9

	£000	*£000*	
Turnover		9,000	(6,000 + 3,000)
Cost of sales		(4,000)	(3,000 + 1,000)
Gross profit		5,000	
Distribution	(1,400)		(1,000 + 400)

Administration	(1,200)	(800 + 400)
Investment income	600	(1,000 – 400)
	(2,000)	
Profit before tax	3,000	
Tax	(1,000)	(700 + 300)
After-tax profit	2,000	
Minority interests	(260)	[pref. divis. 100 + 20% (900 – 100)]
Profit attributable to the group	1,740	
Profit and loss balance b/f	820	[500 + 80% (500 – 100)]
	2,560	
Transfer to general reserve	(560)	[400 + 80%(200)]
Preference dividends	(300)	
Ordinary dividends	(600)	
	(1,460)	
Profit and loss account balance c/f	1,100	

Chapter 8

Self-assessment question 8.1

Cash flow statement for the year ending 28 February 19X8

	£	£
Net cash inflow from operating activities (note 1)		12,000
Investing activities		
Payments to acquire fixed assets – plant and equipment	(21,000)	
Motor vehicles	(3,000)	
Net cash inflow (outflow) from investing activities		(24,000)
Financing		
Issue of debentures	10,000	
Net cash inflow (outflow) from financing		10,000
Increase (decrease) in cash and cash equivalents		(2,000)

Analysis of changes in cash and cash equivalents during the year

	£
Cash at beginning of period	3,000
Net cash outflow during the year	(2,000)
Cash at end of period	1,000

Note

1   *Net cash flow from operations*

	£	£
Net profit before taxation		5,000
Add Depreciation for the year		15,000
		20,000
(Increase)/decrease in stock held	(3,000)	
(Increase)/decrease in debtors	(2,000)	
Increase/(decrease) in creditors	(3,000)	(8,000)
Net cash flow from operating activities		12,000

Self-assessment question 8.2

Cash flow statement for the year ending 28 February 19X8

	£	£
Net cash inflow from operating activities (note 1)		350,000
Returns on investment and servicing of finance		
Dividends paid (note 2)	(70,000)	
Net cash inflow (outflow) from returns on investments and servicing of finance		(70,000)
Taxation		
Corporation tax paid (note 3)	(120,000)	
Tax paid		(120,000)
Investing activities (note 4)		
Payments to acquire fixed assets – plant and equipment	(180,000)	
– land	(80,000)	
Sale of plant	14,000	
Net cash inflow (outflow) from investing activities		(246,000)
Net cash inflow (outflow) before financing		(86,000)
Financing		
Issue of shares (note 5)	—	
Net cash inflow (outflow) from financing		—
Increase (decrease) in cash and cash equivalents		(86,000)

Analysis of changes in cash and cash equivalents during the year		
Cash at beginning of period		30,000
Net cash outflow during the year		(86,000)
Overdraft at end of period		(56,000)

Note

1   *Net cash flow from operations*

	£	£
Net profit before taxation		334,000
Add Depreciation for the year/loss on sale		132,000
		466,000

	£	£
(Increase)/decrease in stock held	(142,000)	
(Increase)/decrease in debtors	(14,000)	
Increase/(decrease) in creditors	40,000	(116,000)
Net cash flow from operating activities		350,000

2   *Dividends* paid are assumed to be last year's proposed dividends and the current year's interim dividends.

3   *Tax* paid is assumed to be the amount owing at the beginning of the year, on the assumption of a 9-month lag between provision and payment.

4 *Plant and equipment*	Cost	Depreciation provision	Net
	£000s	£000s	£000s
Opening balance	560	230	330
Less disposals	−80	−58	−22**
	480	172	308
Plus new acquisitions at cost	180*	—	x
	660	172	x
Less depreciation for the year	—	124	−124
Closing balance	660	296	364

*Missing figure.
**Plant with a book value of £22,000 is sold at a loss of £8,000. Sale proceeds must therefore be £14,000.

Freehold land	£
Cost at beginning of year	700,000
Cost at end of year	780,000
Acquisitions	80,000

5   Movements in *share capital* are all the result of the bonus issue. None are attributable to a cash offer.

Chapter 9

Self-assessment question 9.1

GO Ahead and Co. Ltd.
Profit and loss account

	19X8	19X9	Notes
	£	£	
Sales	3,000,000	3,600,000	20% increase
Less variable costs	1,500,000	1,890,000	50% of sales
			+ 5% inflation
Contribution	1,500,000	1,710,000	
Less fixed costs (see below)	1,000,000	1,230,000	

	£	£	
Profit before tax	500,000	480,000	
Taxation	120,000	120,000	25% of profit
Profit after tax	380,000	360,000	
Dividends	100,000	120,000	12% of nominal capital
Added to reserves	280,000	240,000	

Workings

Fixed costs	£	
Current year's total	1,000,000	
Less depreciation	100,000	
Current year's cash costs	900,000	
Inflation adjustment	45,000	5%
	945,000	
Depreciation	135,000	10% of cost
Additional fixed costs in new year	150,000	
	1,230,000	

Forecast balance sheet as at 31 December

		19X8		19X9
	£	£	£	£
Fixed assets		1,000,000		1,350,000
Cost				
Depreciation provision		200,000		335,000
		800,000		1,015,000
Current assets				
Stock	360,000		432,000	
Debtors	600,000		720,000	
Cash	150,000		63,000	
	1,110,000		1,215,000	
Creditors due within 1 year				
Creditors	300,000		360,000	
Dividends proposed	100,000		120,000	
Corporation tax	120,000		120,000	
	520,000		600,000	
Net current assets		590,000		615,000
		1,390,000		1,630,000
Capital and reserves				
Ordinary share capital		1,000,000		1,000,000
Reserves		390,000		630,000
		1,390,000		1,630,000

Workings

Current assets	%	**19X8**	**19X9**	**Change**
Stock	12	360,000	432,000	+72,000
Debtors	20	600,000	720,000	+120,000
Current liabilities				
Creditors	10	300,000	360,000	+60,000

Forecast cash flow statement for 19X9

	£	£
Operating activities		
Net profit before tax	480,000	
Depreciation	135,000	
Increase in stock	(72,000)	
Increase in debtors	(120,000)	
Increase in creditors	60,000	
Net cash inflow from operating activities		483,000
Returns on investment and servicing of finance		
Dividends	(100,000)	
Net cash outflow from returns		
on investment and servicing of finance		(100,000)
Taxation		
UK corporation tax paid	(120,000)	
Tax paid		(120,000)
Investing activities		
Purchase of fixed assets	(350,000)	
Net cash outflow from investing activities		(350,000)
Net cash outflow before financing		(87,000)
Financing		—
Decrease in cash and cash equivalents		(87,000)

The plans are feasible, other than with regard to cash. The figures projected would lead to a decrease in cash of £82,000, as compared with the desired increase of £30,000. Some thought should be given to this problem, before the plans proceed. The profits, in spite of the expansion, are expected to fall, giving rise to some concern. Questions will need to be asked about this, although these results may well be much better than a 'do nothing new' policy.

Chapter 10

Self-assessment question 10.1

	19X8	*19X9*
Net profit margin	9.4%	8.5%
ROCE	8.3%	7.5%
Current ratio	3.1T	1.5T
Debt/total assets ratio	22.5%	46.3%
Days' debtors	98 days	138 days
Total asset turnover	0.75	0.59

Although the net profit has increased in absolute terms, there has been a decline in the net profit margin in 19X9. This, in turn, has led to a decline in the ROCE ratio in 19X9. The increase in sales for 19X9 is probably due to the new contract. However, to support this increased level of activity, the company has increased its asset base by a more than proportionate amount. As a result, the sales to total assets ratio of the business has shown a significant decline. The increase in assets has been financed mainly by borrowing and the debt/total assets ratio has more than doubled over the period. However, this ratio may still be within acceptable limits.

The current ratio has shown a substantial decline in 19X9 and this should be cause for concern. There has also been a corresponding fall in the acid-test ratio. This fall in liquidity has been accompanied by reliance on a large bank overdraft in order to finance the activities of the business. The continuing goodwill of the bank is now an important factor for the business to consider.

The increase in sales arising from the new contract has resulted in a large increase in the average days' debtors. The funding of this additional level of debtors is causing a strain on the company's liquidity and steps should be taken to reduce the days' debtors if possible. If this cannot be achieved for contractual or other reasons, the company must consider an injection of new long-term capital to ensure it can support the trading policies adopted.

Chapter 11

Self-assessment question 11.1

The following ratios may be calculated:

Profitability
Net profit margin	12.3%
Gross profit margin	37.7%
Return to equity	21.1%

Gearing
Debt to total assets	55.8%

Liquidity
Current ratio	1.2
Acid-test ratio	0.7

Efficiency
Stockholding period	135 days
Average credit period allowed	115 days

Investment ratios
Earnings per share	32.1p
Dividend cover	1.4T
Dividend yield	4.8%

The gross profit margin appears to be quite high and the return to equity seems to be reasonable. However, it is clear that a large amount of the gross profit is taken in overheads and this should cause some concern. The liquidity ratios reveal that the company liquidity is low and this, coupled with the fact that the bank overdraft seems very high, may be a problem for the company. The continuing support of the bank in the short term is of vital importance to the company. The efficiency ratios suggest room for improvement in the use of resources. The average credit period allowed seems high and this may be partly due to the fact that Conday and Co. Ltd. operates an export business. However, when this ratio is viewed along with the high level of bad debts, it suggests weak credit control or excessive concern for making sales. The stock turnover ratio also seems rather high and a question must arise over the level of stock control operated by the company. The earnings per share seems reasonable but the dividend cover is rather low. The high level of dividend payout is puzzling given the liquidity problems of the company. The level of gearing is not high and so it may be possible to borrow more; however, it is not clear whether or not the company has sufficient security to do this.

Whilst the company is profitable, it is difficult to recommend investment in the company on the terms mentioned. The company really needs to strengthen its financial base rather than expand at this point. Further expansion without improvements in liquidity and efficiency could prove fatal for the company. In addition, the dividend policy of the company should be reconsidered. If any money raised, however, was employed simply to reduce the bank overdraft there is unlikely to be a significant improvement in profits and so the returns to equity may actually reduce. A value per share of £6.40 suggests a P/E ratio for the company of nearly 20, which seems rather high. This suggests the company has overvalued the shares being offered.

Chapter 12

Self-assessment question 12.1

In answering this question you may have thought of the following matters which could be included in such a review:

- *Operating results*. This could include a discussion of the results of the business as a whole as well as individual segments. Any changes in the business or industry resulting from factors such as market conditions, new products, changes in exchange rates, changes in market share or profit margins would be useful.
- *Dynamics of the business*. Any factors which may affect future results such as scarcity of materials or skilled labour, new legislation, exchange rate fluctuations, dependence on major customers or suppliers, etc. could be discussed.
- *Investment in the future*. Steps taken to increase or maintain profits in the future such as capital investment expenditure, staff training programmes, marketing campaigns, research and development, and refurbishment programmes could be identified.

- *Accounting policies*. Any areas where subjective judgement has been used and where this may have a significant effect on the measurement of performance and position could be mentioned.
- *Dividends*. Some discussion on the dividends announced in relation to profits may be useful.
- *Capital structure*. A discussion of the type of debt raised, interest rate structure and maturity dates of debt could be included.
- *Treasury policy*. A discussion of such matters may include foreign currency borrowings and the ways in which foreign currency risk is dealt with, the extent to which fixed interest borrowing is used and the currencies in which cash or near cash is held.
- *Cash flows*. Any special circumstances affecting cash flows from operations or other sources could be discussed.
- *Liquidity*. Any factors affecting the liquidity of the business and any future commitments which will reduce liquidity could be identified.
- *Unquantified resources*. Any resources not shown on the balance sheet but which are of value to the business such as brands or other intangible items could be identified.

Self-assessment question 12.2

Three closely related arguments in favour of the political approach are:

- By introducing accounting policies and rules on how to do things, the rule-making bodies are placing restrictions on how individuals and businesses must behave. These restrictions should be introduced only after gaining the acceptance of those affected.
- In a democratic society, rule-making bodies such as the ASB should only gain their authority through general acceptance. Unless this is done, they really do not have the right to expect others to obey their rules.
- Rules will only work if they receive general acceptance by those affected. Hence, a process of negotiation and compromise should be undertaken in order to secure widespread acceptance.

The arguments for a technical approach (or against the political approach) are:

- The political approach is unlikely to produce the sort of radical shift in policies which may, at times, be required. The need for compromise suggests that any change in policy will be incremental.
- The rules developed using the political approach may have to be very broad in nature in order to secure agreement and this may result in a lack of rigour.
- Accounting should be neutral and should not bow to the requirements of particular interest groups. This would damage the confidence of users in the credibility of the information produced.

Some believe the two views can be reconciled. It can be argued that rule-making is a two-stage process. First, a solution to an accounting problem which is technically correct must be found. Having done this it is then necessary to secure broad agreement amongst interested parties for the solution proposed. Hence, accounting rules should be regarded as being determined by both a technical and a political process rather than simply one or the other.

Appendix

Self-assessment question A.1

This answer is based on a vertical format. A two-sided approach is also acceptable.

Trading and profit and loss account for the year ended 31 December 19X7	£	£	£	Workings
Sales			195,200	
Less returns			1,200	
			194,000	
Opening stock		34,000		
Purchases	126,000			
Less returns	2,000			
		124,000		
		158,000		
Less closing stock		30,000		
Cost of sales			128,000	
Gross profit			66,000	
Plus *other revenues*				
Decrease in DDP			400	
			66,400	
Less *other expenses*				
Salaries and wages		37,500		
Rent and rates		4,000		3,500 + 500
General expenses		2,900		
Heating and lighting		1,600		
Insurance		600		800 – 200
Motor expenses		6,500		
Office expenses		2,200		
Depreciation – fixtures and fittings		400		
Depreciation – vehicles		3,000		
			58,700	
Net profit			7,700	

Balance sheet as at 31 December 19X7

	£	£	£
Fixed assets			
Premises			50,000
Fixtures and fittings – cost		4,000	
Less depreciation provision		1,200	800 + 400
		2,800	
Vehicles – cost		15,000	
Less depreciation provision		6,000	3,000 + 3,000
			9,000
			61,800
Current assets			
Stock		30,000	
Debtors	36,000		
Less DDP	1,800		2,200 – 400
		34,200	
Prepayments		200	
Cash		10,000	
		74,400	
Less *liabilities due within 1 year*			
Creditors	16,000		
Accruals	500		
		16,500	
Net current assets			57,900
Net assets			119,700
Financed by:			
Capital			
Opening balance			120,000
Net profit			7,700
			127,700
Less drawings			8,000
			119,700

Self-assessment question A.2

Rent receivable

19X7		£	19X7		£
Dec 31	Profit and loss	2,000	Jan 1	Balance b/d	500
			Dec 31	Cash	1,000
				Balance c/d	500
		2,000			2,000
19X8					
Jan 1	Balance b/d	500			

Insurance

19X7		£	19X7		£
Jan 1	Balance b/d	300	Dec 31	Profit and loss	1,100
			Dec 31	Balance c/d	400
Dec 31	Cash	1,200			
		1,500			1,500
19X8					
Jan 1	Balance b/d	400			

Heating

19X7		£	19X7		£
Jan 1	Balance b/d	100	Dec 31	Profit and loss	1,300
	Cash	1,000			
Dec 31	Balance c/d	200			
		1,300			1,300
			19X8		
			January	Balance b/d	200

Wages

19X7		£	19X7		£
Dec 31	Cash	25,000	Jan 1	Balance b/d	1,000
	Balance c/d	500	Dec 31	Profit and loss	24,500
		25,500			25,500
			19X̌8		
			January 1	Balance b/d	500

Balance sheet extracts

Current assets	£	*Current liabilities*	£
Prepaid insurance	400	Accrued heating	200
Debtors (rent receivable)	500	Accrued wages	500

Index